ROGUE REGIMES

ROGUE REGIMES
Terrorism and Proliferation

Raymond Tanter

St. Martin's Press
New York

ISBN 0-312-17300-8

Library of Congress Cataloging-in-Publication Data
Tanter, Raymond.
    Rogue regimes : terrorism and proliferation / Raymond Tanter.
        p. cm.
    Includes bibliographical references (p.   ) and index.
    ISBN 0-312-17300-8
    1. Dictators—Biography. 2. Khomeini, Ruhollah. 3. Hashimi
Rafsanjani, 'Ali Akbar. 4. Hussein, Saddam, 1937- . 5. Qaddafi,
Muammar. 6. Assad, Hafez, 1928- . 7. Castro, Fidel, 1927- .
8. Kim, Chong-gil, 1926- 9. State-sponsored terrorism. 10. Nuclear
nonproliferation. 11. National security—United States. 12. United
States—Foreign relations—20th century. I. Title.
D412.7.T26 1997.
327.1'17—dc21   97-21494
                                             CIP

Design by Acme Art, Inc.
First edition: January, 1998
10 9 8 7 6 5 4 3 2

To Kirk and Shawn

CONTENTS

ACKNOWLEDGEMENTS

Thanks to those who provided insights for this book. These include Russell Bailey (North Korea); Joseph Gigliotti (politics and policies); Stephen Hessler (Syria); Chris Hodges (Serbia); Michael Janson (Libya); Chris LaRocco (Cuba); Jonathan Mallin (Libya); Aman McLeod (Libya); Kristin McLean (Iran); John Post (Iraq, Syria); Randall Roth (North Korea); Anna Vania Song (North Korea, prospect theory); Jonathan Strauss (Cuba); Charles Spies (American politics); and John Valentine (Libya). Thanks to the University of Michigan Faculty Assistance Fund, to Mishkenot Sha'ananim for a peaceful writing place in Jerusalem, to Maya Savarino for companionship, Jan DiRomualdo for assistance, as well as to Alice and John Tanter for inspiration.

PREFACE

CONTAIN OR EMBRACE

In deciding whether to contain or embrace foreign countries, Americans love to personalize conflicts between the United States and its enemies. The three leaders in the photographs on the dust jacket of this book are well known to the American people: Fidel Castro, Muammar Qadhafi, and Saddam Hussein. When *Time* magazine places such "rogue" leaders on its cover, the editors exploit a desire to demonize foreigners who dare to confront Washington. Americans see the rogue leaders of this book, the Ayatollah Khomeni and his colleagues, Saddam, Qadhafi, Hafez al-Assad, Castro, and Kim Jong-Il, as candidates for a gallery of adversaries. As the East-West conflict fades in intensity, a rogues' gallery imagery replaces photographs of Cold War notables such as Stalin, Brezhnev, and Mao. Fidel and Kim, however, represent two leftovers from the Cold War days. While the threat of global nuclear war and the prospect of a Soviet invasion of Germany were major dangers during the Cold War, the principal threats in the post–Cold War era stem from the rise of outlaw regimes led by members of our gallery.

As these men go about the unsavory business of terrorism and acquiring weapons of mass destruction, the world has a choice: to contain, embrace, or pursue a mixed policy toward these outlaw regimes. The new international villains are leaders of nations that have large conventional military forces and that condone international terrorism and/or seek weapons of mass destruction, including nuclear, biological, and chemical armaments.[1]

Iran, Iraq, Libya, Syria, and North Korea have large conventional military forces, sponsor or practice international terrorism, and are developing or acquiring weapons of mass destruction. Cuba, however, hardly fits these three criteria. Yet because of historical tensions, Washington considers Castro a rogue leader—thus Cuba itself is an outlaw regime.

While international terrorism alone is a menace to the world community, the joint occurrence of terrorism and weapons proliferation is a double threat. Accordingly, Congress acted in 1994 to expand the term "terrorism" to include efforts by any individual, group, or nonnuclear-weapon state to acquire unsafeguarded, special nuclear material or to use, develop, produce, stockpile, or otherwise acquire any nuclear explosive device.[2] If a state engages in either terrorism or proliferation of weapons of mass destruction, it enters the rogues' gallery; once there, they are candidates for this book.[3]

With the exception of Cuba, the remaining five rogue states in this volume have sought to acquire weapons of mass destruction. Regarding nuclear weapons development, Iran, Iraq, and North Korea are on the hunt, while chemical armaments are the main weapons of choice for Libya and Syria. Demonizing the leaders of another nation is one way to justify imposition of sanctions for their pursuit of weapons of mass destruction. In addressing this menace, there are three main approaches: (1) to contain these states with economic sanctions and deter or coerce them with threats of force; (2) to embrace them with promises of rewards; and (3) to embrace as well as contain them with these carrots and sticks. The best option to pursue depends upon whether a defender favors retribution or rehabilitation. If the goal is retribution, the policy is to contain. But if the goal is rehabilitation, the approach may be either to contain or embrace, or to do both.

RETRIBUTION OR REHABILITATION

In writing this book with the help of a group of research assistants, we formed a computer conference. A flurry of E-mail messages reflected heated debate among the participants. An assistant noticed that our research group of eight students, dubbed "the Rogues," was divided over a core concern. At issue was what to do about ineffective deterrent and coercive policies. This problem goes beyond our study and cuts across different societal domains. Should a parent punish a child who continues to misbehave? Should a state government drop a death penalty that fails to deter murder? Should international coercive policies continue in the face of evidence that they fail to change behavior? To the last of these questions, three of the students, Joseph Gigliotti, Jonathan Mallin, and Randall Roth, immediately answered with a booming "yes." Five others, Rachael Farber, Thekla Fischer, Jeffrey Binder, Danielle Frappier, and Erin Ross, promptly countered with a resounding "no."

The members of the first group would persist with "fruitless" punishment of children, continue "ineffective" death penalties, and retain "futile" international coercive policies. They were ideologues who would punish wrongdoing for retributive purposes, irrespective of rehabilitation. They believed in the intrinsic worth of symbolic action.

The members of the second group would cease "ineffective" child discipline, abolish "pointless" death penalties, and abrogate "unprofitable" international coercive diplomacy. They were pragmatists who could not justify actions that did not produce behavioral change. They were unwilling to inflict pain without the prospect of gain. The entire debate added fuel to the fire over whether nations should retain or abandon coercive policies that fail to rehabilitate.

Retribution involves punishment to right a wrong; rehabilitation consists of punishment to correct misbehavior. This theme is a central concern of the literature on political theory and is a constant in our daily lives. The students who supported retribution advocated unilateral or individual action to ward off international chaos; the rehabilitative students preferred multilateral or collective action because it had the legitimacy of international consensus. Therefore, the research students who advocated retribution suggested an ideologically based unconditional containment, while the students supporting rehabilitation suggested a pragmatically based policy of contain, embrace, or both, depending upon their expected effects.

In developing a rationale for the unilateral imposition of economic sanctions, I sided with the retributive group. We reasoned that it is possible to recognize rogue behavior—that is, unacceptable international conduct. And once you detect rogue deeds, there is an obligation to act against their perpetrators—with sanctions, for example. The rehabilitative students questioned whether the term "rogue" should be used to describe regimes. They agreed that unacceptable behavior did exist in international politics, but differed from the retributive students on how to explain this behavior. Retributive students underestimated present compliant behavior and focused on prior deeds and the nature of the regime. Rehabilitative students, however, overestimated present compliant behavior and discounted prior deeds and the regime's nature. In making a choice between punishment for retribution or rehabilitation, moreover, a distinction must be made between opportunity and fear.

"WINDOWS OF OPPORTUNITY" OR "BASEMENTS OF FEAR"

Those who favor retribution would punish regardless of challengers' motivations. But defenders who support rehabilitation want to know the motivations of the challengers before deciding to embrace, contain, or both. Those who would punish for retributive justice would do so irrespective of whether an actor's conduct derives from gain or fear. Those who would punish in order to rehabilitate would do so only if behavior stems from net gain; that is, the actor subtracts costs from benefits and is thereby approximately rational.[4]

But the rehabilitative approach assumes that sanctions are valid tools of coercion only if leaders are acting from a "window of opportunity" rather than from a "basement of fear." When people act out of opportunity, they weigh gains and losses about equally and are approximately rational in their behavior. Because opportunistic challengers have the capacity to understand the effects of their behavior, sanctions are appropriate. For supporters of rehabilitation, sanctions would not be considered for paranoids, who are fear-driven challengers and do not have the capacity to comprehend their actions. Fear allows biases to distort threat perception. As such, people motivated by fear are not likely to understand the consequences of sanctions.

When people act out of fear, they tend to be less rational. Opportunists, however, can be held accountable for their behavior, and for them, sanctions are a legitimate response to misbehavior. It is illegitimate to hold paranoids accountable for their irresponsible behavior; sanctions seem inappropriate responses to their desperate actions. Yet, it is legitimate to punish opportunistic individuals. In other words, it is comparatively difficult to penalize persons whose behavior derives from apprehension and easier to justify being tough on those whose misbehavior stems from opportunity.

The research group also debated whether economic sanctions should be imposed if they are instrumental failures but symbolic successes. An explicit purpose of sanctions generally is to change behavior, but an implicit aim may be to punish in order to right a wrong. We concluded that it was justifiable to use sanctions for symbolic aims. Our group discussed retribution as a tacit goal in the imposition of economic penalties and surmised that the persistence of ineffective sanctions was an indicator of their retributive nature.

One of the assistants suggested that when ineffective sanctions continue, it might be due to pressure for continuity by important domestic political constituencies. She explained that even when the original purpose of sanctions is solely for rehabilitation, its goal could shift later to retribution. For example, even if sanctions fail to bring about the desired change, they may nevertheless continue due to domestic pressure for reprisal. And even before succeeding, or failing to achieve, the end goal of rehabilitation, the process of adopting sanctions itself serves to send a retributive message. The group applauded this insight, with only a few low grumbles from dissenters.

In conclusion, decisions about containment and accommodation of rogue states take place in the context of an American tendency to personalize conflicts. Once "demonization" occurs, one is on the slippery slope of choosing sanctions. Depending upon whether challengers' motivations stem more from gain than fear, sanctions are legitimate. But sanctions for retribution are legitimate, irrespective of the challengers' purposes.

LAYOUT OF THE BOOK

Rogue Regimes divides six states along geopolitical and historical lines. The first two chapters pair cases linked by geography but separated by ideology and history—Iran and Iraq. This approach is consistent with the dual containment policy of the United States, which treats Iran and Iraq as twin pariahs. Although both reject being classified as a pair, American policy groups them together. The Clinton White House refrains from the traditional practice of supporting either Iran or Iraq in order to block expansion by the other. The administration tries to work with the world community and regional allies to isolate and contain both rogue states. It has had more success in isolating Iraq than Iran.

In contrast to the Clinton policy of dual containment toward Iran and Iraq, the Reagan and Bush Administrations followed the Nixon tradition of balance of power diplomacy in the Gulf—alternately supporting Iran or Iraq. At times, the rationale was to prevent either state from gaining the upper hand. On other occasions, the United States responded to Iranian pressure, in order to bargain for the release of American hostages, or to Iraqi offers to facilitate the Israeli-Palestinian peace process.

The next two chapters of the book include Libya and Syria. Libya entered the gallery based on its status as a rogue even within the Arab world. It has a tradition of confrontation with neighboring states like Egypt, Tunisia, and Chad, as well as with the West in general and the United States in particular. As an offspring of an era of Arab national-ism and anti-colonialism, Libya is also a rejectionist state that does not accept the American-led peace process with Israel. Syria, in addition to Libya, is in a confrontation with the United States over issues like chemical weapons, state-sponsored terrorism, and the Israeli-Palestinian peace process. Damascus aligns with Iran against Iraq, is in conflict with Turkey over terrorists based there, and is in a no-peace, no-war status with Israel.

The final chapters address two additional cases—Cuba and North Korea. As children of the Cold War, Havana and Pyongyang retain their communist systems and hence belong together. In the waning days of the regimes in Cuba and North Korea, these relics of a bygone era may be even more dangerous than in earlier times. Because their rulers feel insecure without the Cold War safety net, the danger of political implosion or military explosion has increased. By the middle of the 1990s, sanctions had not yet changed the behavior of either Cuba or North Korea. The question, however, is whether sanctions may have the unintended effect of destabilizing their governments in an undesirable fashion.

Personality, Politics, and Policies

IN THE COLD WAR ERA, the "stars" that dominated the world stage came from the superpowers. In the post–Cold War world, players from less powerful states have surfaced onto the international scene. One way to discuss these new celebrities is to organize their "infamy" by key dates that epitomize their rule. Absent the checks and balances of a democratic order and the bureaucracies of a large totalitarian state, rogue regimes are more subject to the politics of personality. In this respect, the policies of the new rulers are more a reflection of the whims of charismatic individuals than the outcome of bargaining among multiple centers of power.

TIMES TO RELIVE[1]

November 4, 1979. Americans held their collective breath as some 3,000 Iranian students raided the U.S. embassy in Tehran. Our eyes were glued to television sets, waiting to hear the fate of the seventy Americans held inside against their will. Government officials were sweating. Military minds were turning. The public was not only dazed and confused, but angry as well. Who would dare do this to the United States of America, and how was Washington to respond? Six months later, America got its answer.

Washington launched a secret special-operations rescue mission called Desert One, only to see it fly to a fiery crash, leaving eight soldiers dead. After 444 days, the supreme spiritual and political leader of Iran, the Ayatollah Khomeni, released the hostages to President Ronald Reagan. Americans focused hostility and fear on Khomeni, who appeared on television as the personification of evil. Khomeni and everything associated with him invaded the American conscience. Never again could the United States look toward Iran without thinking of Khomeni and the acts of terrorism he seemed to condone.

August 2, 1990. The self-described "Knight of the Arab Nation," Saddam Hussein, ordered Iraqi troops to invade the small neighboring country of Kuwait. In response, President Bush ordered a huge military deployment of American troops, created a coalition of Western and Arab states, and subsequently authorized air and ground combat operations against Iraq.

Again, Americans watched on television as Scud missiles flew over the western Iraqi desert over Jerusalem en route to Tel Aviv. Coalition aircraft launched waves of strikes against Iraq. We held our collective breath as the Iraqi military took its first prisoners of war. Television viewers watched in horror as U.S. soldiers and Israeli citizens donned gas masks in anticipation of chemical warfare. Pundits reminded us of Saddam's ruthless use of poison gas against the Iranian military, against innocent civilians, and against the Kurds of his own country. Americans quickly forgot that this man was once a distant ally of the United States, and only saw Saddam Hussein as "the Butcher of Baghdad."

February 1982. Saddam is not the only Middle Eastern dictator who tried to annihilate his own citizens. Hafez al-Assad is the calculating, seemingly rational leader of Syria.[2] He is known to be just as ruthless and cruel as his counterpart in Iraq and has frequently shocked the world with violent and bloody displays of cruelty.

Assad ordered an attack on Hama, a city of about 180,000 people: over 10,000 individuals died.[3] The city harbored an organization, the Muslim Brotherhood, that opposed him. After a failed assassination attempt on his life, Assad first retaliated by torturing and executing 600 to 1,000 imprisoned Muslim Brothers. Then, in an effort to extinguish further opposition, he unleashed his military upon Hama.[4]

December 21, 1988. Another day that remains seared into America's collective memory—the day of the Pan Am 103 disaster over Lockerbie, Scotland. According to the U.S. State Department, two Libyans planted a bomb set to explode one hour after the commercial flight's departure. After an investigation, the U.S. Department of Justice and Scottish officials uncovered a trail that led to senior Libyan intelligence officers. Evidence also pointed to involvement by the infamous Muammar Qadhafi. As the 1990s close, the two suspects remain at large in Libya. Colonel Qadhafi may be shielding them from the international demands for justice.[5]

Pan Am 103 was neither the first nor the last act of terrorism involving Qadhafi. On October 6, 1981, Egyptian dissenters whom Washington believed were backed by Colonel Qadhafi assassinated Egyptian President Anwar El-Sadat.[6] After that incident, Libya and the United States became locked in a spiral of escalation. The mutual hostility reached a height on April 15, 1986, when President Reagan ordered airstrikes on various Libyan sites. One of them was Qadhafi's personal residence on a military base. The attacks killed his infant daughter and wounded two of his sons. The assault was in immediate response to a bombing of the La Belle discotheque in Berlin, a place known to be frequented by U.S. service men and women. American analysts traced the Berlin disco bombing to the government of Libya.

Perhaps because of Washington's use of force, Qadhafi cut back his sponsorship of terrorist organizations that assault American citizens. Many Americans, nevertheless, retain a knee-jerk image of a Qadhafi-like character. This archetype would be blamed for acts of terrorism, such as the bombing of Centennial Park during the 1996 Summer Olympics in Atlanta.

Despite Qadhafi's trend toward moderate behavior, incidents like Pan Am 103 serve to strengthen stereotypes of Middle Eastern leaders. The image is of an evil, domineering man in a green military suit who masterminds terror targeting the United States. Because of the relative frequency of terrorist incidents that occur in the Middle East, there is a mental picture in American culture that the region is an incubator for terrorists. Witness the wild speculation that Middle Eastern terrorism was responsible for the 1995 bombing of the Federal Building in Oklahoma City and the loss in 1996 of TWA 800 off the coast of New York. Militiamen from the Middle West and "Good-Old Boys" from the South were not the images that came to mind when we learned about these explosions. However, there are other regimes outside the Middle East that have become painful thorns in Washington's side. Two cases stem from the Cold War era: Cuba and North Korea.

October 16, 1962. One of the most terrifying moments in American history—the Cuban Missile Crisis. Washington saw a charismatic Fidel Castro at the helm of a regime that tacked against the American-dominated winds in Latin America. A strong proponent of Marxism during the Cold War, Castro looked to Moscow for support and guidance. This challenge to American hegemony was unacceptable to Washington. Cuba is only 90 miles south of Florida. When American spy planes discovered Soviet missiles in Cuba, President Kennedy and Premier Khrushchev waged a war of coercive diplomacy to achieve their objectives while averting nuclear annihilation. All the while, Castro basked in the limelight afforded by superpower crisis diplomacy.

For Americans growing up at the time of the Cuban Missile Crisis, the memories are almost always the same: because they thought the world might come to an end, people can tell you what they were doing at the height of the crisis. Ever since the 1960s, a generation of Americans has viewed Castro and Cuba as twin threats. The demand for exported sugar and Havana cigars is irrelevant. Cuba is not the only country the United States has confronted over nuclear weapons. As the twentieth century closes, another small country remains as a relic from the Cold War—North Korea. American-North Korean relations have evolved from the days of the Korean War, through a crisis over nuclear weapons development, to crises regarding humanitarian issues.

October 17, 1994. Pyongyang and Washington reached an agreement on the text of a framework document on North Korea's nuclear program. Even though most of the international community had made a movement toward nonproliferation, the Democratic People's Republic of Korea pursued nuclear weapons until Pyongyang and

Washington struck a deal in 1994. At issue is whether that accord will be sufficient to steer North Korea away from the acquisition of weapons of mass destruction. Hence, a prudent assumption is that Pyongyang will continue its pursuit of nuclear weapons. Global pressures against proliferation are less effective against North Korea because Kim Jong-Il is not as concerned with international censure as other leaders.

As confrontation over nuclear weapons subsided, new crises arose over floods and famine. North Korea has suffered from floods and a devastating rice famine. But Kim Jong-Il has used his country's resources to build a monumental skyscraper. This misallocation of resources suggests that his concern with personal aggrandizement might be at the expense of the people of North Korea. While Pyongyang's long time rival, Seoul, was sending shipments of rice to alleviate the starvation in the North, Kim Jong-Il sent saboteurs to infiltrate the South. He has commented, "No one can figure me out, especially the Americans . . . but it is they who are confused."[7] He is correct. When you bite the hand that feeds you, it appears to be inexplicable.

Not since the Ethiopian famine of the 1980s, has the world seen such horrors as the scenes in North Korea during the 1990s. In a rare, and perhaps desperate move, the Stalinist-like North Korean regime allowed Western reporters to document the suffering and starvation that had rocked its population. Floods and famine have wiped out much of this small country's crops, leaving millions of faces hollow and blank. Photographers panned over live bodies that looked like corpses. Pictures of babies with swollen stomachs circulated around the world, tugging at hearts and consciences.[8] Though this image alone was horrifying, the civilized world suspected that Kim Jong-Il hid even more appalling and gruesome scenes.

In fact, this same man used his starving country to strong-arm the United States into negotiations with neighboring countries Japan and South Korea. Kim Jong-Il's regime pointed fingers at Tokyo and Seoul, which were reluctant to give rice, even though they had warehouses full of rotting crops. True, other countries hesitated to come to North Korea's aid. Their unwillingness may be due to North Korea's million-man army, which exercises along the demilitarized zone. Because

Pyongyang siphons off humanitarian assistance for the military before
rationing it out to the population, the international community
struggles with the following dilemma. Should we save the lives of
millions of North Koreans at the risk of strengthening the military
regime that threatens 37,000 American soldiers and millions of South
Koreans? To anticipate the conclusion of Chapter Seven, the regime
needs to be contained, but the North Korean population needs to be
saved. At issue is how to contain a puzzling leader like Kim Jong-Il and
embrace his starving population.

PERSONALITY AND POLITICS[9]

Because the actions of the rogue leaders appear puzzling, there is a
need to answer the question, "Why?" With every rogue act, all eyes
turn to the leaders of these international troublemakers. In an attempt
to answer this question, it is imperative to look to the stars on the stage
of the New World Order for their motives, fears, and beliefs.

Rogue Regimes analyzes the luminaries of the post–Cold War era:
the Ayatollahs Khomeni and Khameni, Presidents Rafsanjani and
Khatemi of Iran, Saddam Hussein of Iraq, Muammar Qadhafi of Libya,
Hafez al-Assad of Syria, Fidel Castro of Cuba, and Kim Jong-Il of the
Democratic People's Republic of Korea.

Personality, politics, and policies form a triangle that describes
rogue leaders. These three factors are manifest in an intricate framework of emotions and experiences, a drive for power, and a willingness
to use violence to accomplish their goals. Most of these leaders were
born around the same time period, and thus they can be considered in
the same generation. A pattern of violence is evident in their behavior.

IRAN'S LEADERS: KHOMENI,
KHAMENI, RAFSANJANI, AND KHATEMI

Like most of the rogue leaders and their nations, the Ayatollah
Khomeni was the heart and soul of postrevolutionary Iran. Before the
revolution, Iran was dominated by foreign powers that exploited the

resources of the nation. From the coup that toppled Mossadegh to the revolution that ousted the Shah, the period of 1953-1978 was a time of growing resentment and hostility against the United States.[10]

Khomeni had many reasons to be bitter toward the ruling secular elite of Iran and the West. Assassins sent by an absentee landlord supposedly murdered and hence martyred Khomeni's father in the winter of 1903.[11] Some Iranians believe that a baby brings good or bad luck to its family. In the case of the assassination of Khomeni's father, many took this event to be a sign of bad luck, especially because it was a violent death. Consequently, the villagers called Khomeni "bad-qadam" or "ill-omened." His mother then gradually decreased her visits with him until they stopped altogether. Not willing to withstand the harsh treatment from the villagers, the mother abandoned Khomeni, leaving him with his aunt. When both mother and aunt died, their deaths left Khomeni under the care of his brother. Essentially, Khomeni grew up without ever knowing the love of his parents.[12] He had honored the legacy of his father by giving his first-born son the father's name—Mostafa. But Khomeni suspected that agents of the ruler of Iran, Reza Shah, killed Khomeni's son, Mostafa.[13] And because of the strong ties between the Shah and the West, Khomeni's dislike of the United States grew.

During the Eisenhower years, the United States supported Mohammed Reza Shah, whose father's regime Khomeni thought was responsible for Mostafa's death. The Shah's regime lasted until 1978, when Khomeni began his bloody ascent to power. Khomeni had a deep-rooted hatred for the West that he used to fuel his climb to the top. Disgusted with the corruption capitalism had brought to the predominately Islamic Iran, Khomeni vowed to bring death to the "Great Satan."

At the time, Mohammed Reza Shah was under intense attack from Iran's Islamist factions. They criticized him for betraying the teachings of Islam. The Shah, more preoccupied with his international image than the threat of Khomeni and his growing group of Shiite Muslim followers, became increasingly dependent on Washington's advice and support. As increasing numbers of influential Iranians defected to Khomeni's camp, the Shah fled the country. Finally, taking advantage of the power vacuum in Iran after the Shah's flight, Khomeni seized the reins of the country. The overthrow signaled the beginning of a rapidly deteriorating relationship between Tehran and Washington.

Khomeni's eventually monopolized secular and sacred power in Iran. His supporters viewed him as the champion of the poor and the working class. His disdain for the monarchy and the capitalist West brought him strong political support, which was evident in the frequent sight on the nightly news of huge crowds screaming, "Death to the Great Satan!" The Ayatollah's reign, characterized by terrorism and war, was marked by three factors: an intense belief in Islam, a great hatred of the West, and aggressive reaction toward perceived threats.

During his reign, he maintained power through executions, expulsions, and torture. The walls of many buildings in Tehran were painted with pictures and messages of hatred aimed at the West, a visual representation of Khomeni's attitude. From 1978 to 1981, Khomeni dominated Iran's politics and religion. One of the most poignant examples of his monopoly of power is his portrait in the center of Tehran. Years after his death, Khomeni's face still broods over the city, watchfully inspecting the daily activities of his people.

Khomeni's facial demeanor was not the only feared aspect of the man. His actions gave the world good reason to fear him. The danger that Khomeni posed became obvious when Iranian "students" seized the United States embassy in Tehran and held its occupants as hostages. Though the Carter Administration made many attempts to persuade or coerce Khomeni into releasing the hostages, the government of Iran did not free them until President Carter left office.

Why did Khomeni continue to defy the United States in spite of the painful losses that were threatened? Evidence suggests that his tightening grip on power was chafing many disgruntled factions within his regime. As the economic situation in Iran began to deteriorate, two opposing views began to develop inside the country; one argued for continuing the fight against Western imperialism and corruption, but the second felt that Iran needed Western assistance to recover from years of war and internal conflict. During the remainder of the Ayatollah's reign, small voices of opposition began to emerge, and Khomeni felt he had to expend more energy in extinguishing them. Influenced by his traumatic upbringing and tapping into his country's collective hatred for the West, he began to lash out more strenuously. Most of Khomeni's rhetoric was laced with themes of overcoming Western decadence and resisting the Great Satan. He continued to rail against the "evils" of the West, for which he felt both hatred and fear.

Upon the death of Khomeni in 1989, two men assumed his role, the Ayatollah Khameni and President Ali Akbar Hashemi Rafsanjani. Although Khomeni would have frowned upon any separation of mosque and state, the sharing of power between the two men hints at such a division. As a result, ideology became less instrumental in governance under them than it was under a single charismatic ruler.

Ayatollah Khomeni's religious successor, Khameni, was a power beyond the mosque precisely because he was from the mosque. Yet, he lacked the one dominating characteristic of Khomeni—charisma. While Khomeni was worshiped and feared, politicians dared to maneuver around Khameni. Such coalition-building would have been unthinkable under Ayatollah Khomeni. Perhaps it should also be noted that not much has been said about Khameni as an individual. Writing about Ayatollah Khomeni was a tribute to him as a person. The fact that much less was written about Khameni is indicative of his status as one among many ayatollahs.

Toning down Khomeni's anti-Western rhetoric, President Rafsanjani appeared to be something of a moderate. Under him, Iran's focus was largely a secular one. He made efforts to distance himself from both the radical politics of the Ayatollah Khomeni and those who sought to reintroduce Khomeni's policies. His regime was a liberal one by Iranian standards. He paid attention to economic development and private property, calming ethnic minorities, and rebuilding Iran after years of bitter warfare. Under Rafsanjani, Iran legalized foreign loans, merged the religious Revolutionary Guards into the army, welcomed foreign investment in Iran's oil reserves, and moved to privatize industries that had been nationalized after the revolution in 1979.[14]

Within Iran, there was opposition to Rafsanjani's reforms. Some opposed him because they felt he betrayed the egalitarian nature of Islam. In addition, the failure of his economic plans to come to fruition lent support to his hard-line opponents. Both the mullahs and the bazaari merchant class opposed his reforms, and they formed a powerful coalition.[15] Indeed, opposition culminated in an assassination attempt on February 1, 1994. By placing secular goals ahead of religious objectives Rafsanjani exposed himself to criticism from the "Islamists."[16]

It is inaccurate, however, to view Rafsanjani as a true liberal by Western standards simply on the basis of his economic reforms. Though not as adamant about ridding the world of the Great Satan, he nevertheless contributed his share to the tension between Tehran and Washington. Under the rule of Rafsanjani and the influence of Khameni, Iran still supported terrorist groups. Many terrorist suspects had been trained in an Iranian camp that Rafsanjani created. His Iran supported the 1992 bombing of the Israeli embassy in Buenos Aires as well as the assassination of former Iranian Prime Minister Shapur Bakhtiar in Paris that same year.[17] But many Iranians saw Rafsanjani as sacrificing the revolution in favor of the state. He, unlike Khomeni and Khameni, was more preoccupied with the economic rejuvenation of Iran.

In the May 1997 elections, Mohammed Khatemi won the Iranian presidency with about 70 percent of the vote. He defeated Natiq Nouri, the speaker of the Iranian parliament, which has a majority of mullahs as deputies. Nouri was the handpicked successor of the mullahs, like Khameni. Although Khatemi is also a mullah, his colleagues did not favor him. But Khatemi may prove even more pragmatic than Rafsanjani (another mullah) and thus continue to stress economic growth.

Though the most popular description of Khatemi is "pragmatic," this portrayal ignores the social influences that hinder him. As of the late 1990s, Iran had been in dire economic straits for more than fifteen years. Nevertheless, the country's economic need was overshadowed by its strict adherence to Islam. There is a pull between economic growth, which calls for Western technology, and religious "Islamism." This gap could spell disaster for Khatemi. His Iran is one with which Europe, if not America, can strike deals. Yet even as the idea of globalization becomes more enticing to the Iranian population, Khameni, Rafsanjani and Nouri, remain ready to pounce on any misstep Khatemi makes. This intricate web of personalities, politics, and policies may make Tehran amenable to striking a grand bargain with Washington.

IRAQ'S SADDAM HUSSEIN: THE GODFATHER

While there is bargaining and collective leadership in Iran, Iraq is under the firm hand of Saddam Hussein. In this respect, it is no surprise to learn that his favorite movie is *The Godfather.*[18] What is astonishing in this choice is the many similarities between Saddam and the protagonist of the movie, Don Vito Corleone. Both men grew up without a father in a time of turbulence. Both sought respect and power, and they committed murder when necessary. They also share a sense of paranoia. But where Vito Corleone trusted a few in the extended Mafia family, Saddam only trusts those in his immediate family.

Circumstantial evidence of Saddam's paranoia comes from the wiretaps that have resulted in the execution of many Iraqi citizens. Some of these executions have stemmed from the whispered rumors about one of Saddam's family members. For example, Saddam married his second wife, Samara Shahbandar, after her first husband stepped aside so that Saddam could court her. For giving up his wife, the erstwhile husband not only saved his own life, but he also received a promotion! After the wedding, a member of the Shahbandar clan confided to his wife in the privacy of their bedroom that Samara was not a legitimate member of the family. Little did he know that Saddam had bugged their bedroom. Both the husband *and* the wife were given life sentences in prison.[19]

Another incident occurred when one of Saddam's generals insulted his mother, Subha. General Omar al-Hazzah made the fatal mistake of bragging about a love affair between himself and Subha. Like the Shahbandar clan member, Hazzah had no idea that Saddam had bugged his confidant's room. When Saddam heard this conversation, he first wept and then became enraged. He then ordered the execution of Hazzah and his son.[20]

Again, we see a connection between Saddam's life and *The Godfather.* In the movie, family honor was something that no one could demean. If anybody dared to offend the Corleone family, death was inevitable.[21] Think of Saddam as the Don of the Hussein family. Anyone who dares insult the family name, can be assured of an early end.

In his childhood, Saddam developed a sense of suspicion. He brought this distrust into the political arena.[22] This paranoia and his drive for power became evident when Saddam overthrew President Ahmed Hassan al-Bakr on July 16, 1979. The overthrow of a regime was not enough to satisfy Saddam. He used violence to attain power, and he used violence to maintain power.[23]

One explanation for Iraq's invasion of Kuwait is Saddam's paranoid personality. During the Iran-Iraq war of 1980-1988, he adopted the name "Knight of the Arab Nation" for defending Arab interests. After the war, Iraq was physically ravaged and financially devastated. Saddam was suspicious of the other Arab leaders. Kuwait contributed to Saddam's feeling of betrayal and Iraq's mounting economic difficulty. He felt betrayed because Kuwait refused to forgive Baghdad's debts that Iraq incurred in the Iran-Iraq war. Kuwait also deliberately exceeded the oil production quota of the Organization of Petroleum Exporting Countries. Accordingly, Saddam felt justified in teaching Kuwait, and the world, a lesson on August 2, 1990.[24]

The bottom line to this explanation is that Saddam's paranoid personality drives him to seek absolute power. This motivation constrains the type of policies that Iraq pursues. While multiple power centers in Iran created room for bargaining and thus moderation, a monopoly of power in Iraq limits bargaining space and promotes extremism. Another Middle Eastern nation, Libya, is more like Iraq than Iran. Ruled by Colonel Muammar Al-Qadhafi, Libya is a virtual unitary actor in the style of Saddam's Iraq.

LIBYA'S QADHAFI: A ROGUE ELEPHANT

Within the global village, the Islamic world, and the Arab nation, Qadhafi is like a rogue elephant. He wanders away from the mainstream norms of the herds to which he belongs. At issue is whether Qadhafi's actions are cool and calculated, fearful and desperate, or reasonable *and* reckless. His tendency to combine reason and recklessness goes back to his early childhood.

Qadhafi was born in 1942 to a nomadic Berber tribe in Italian-occupied Libya. Like Khomeni, Qadhafi's hatred for Western imperialism began at an early age. His grandfather had been brutally murdered by an Italian colonist in 1911, just as agents of an absentee landlord murdered Khomeni's father. Following the Second World War, the British victors took over Libya from the defeated Italians. One imperial ruler replaced another in the eyes of the Libyans who opposed foreign domination. Libyan tribes continued to resent imperial occupation and were finally granted a reprieve by the international community in 1947, when the UN General Assembly approved Libyan independence. The measure became effective in 1951. Nevertheless, the colonial powers still determined the course of events in Libya for some time. It was not until 1956 that the powers lifted the yoke of foreign occupation, and Libya became autonomous.

During those years of foreign control, Qadhafi became an adult. At the age of sixteen, Egypt's Gamal Abdel Nasser's pan-Arabism greatly influenced him. Young Qadhafi started a revolutionary cell that aspired to take over Libya. By the age of twenty-seven, he and his group of revolutionaries successfully overthrew the regime and took control of every government office and media outlet.[25]

Qadhafi's speeches exhibit a belief that violence is an effective tool for achieving his goals. One interpretation of Qadhafi's anti-American statements is that, "There will be blood in American streets." In pursuit of his goals, Qadhafi protects those accused of international terrorism, such as the suspects linked to the Lockerbie bombing. The international community has demanded that Tripoli deliver the suspects for a trial, yet Qadhafi refuses to release them to the criminal justice system in London and Washington. Failure to do so has increasingly isolated him not only from the international community but from most of the Arab world as well.

It is extremely difficult to understand Qadhafi's continued sponsorship of international terrorism. From a rational choice perspective, the balance of expected benefits and punishments would argue against the sponsorship of terror. But by attributing a degree of irrationality to his actions, we also lessen Qadhafi's responsibilities over such actions.[26]

One act of retaliation by the United States was the April 15, 1986, air raid on Qadhafi's military base, in which he and his family suffered intense emotional and physical trauma. As stated earlier, he lost a daughter and two sons in the attack. Since the airstrike, Qadhafi has constantly moved, rarely sleeping in the same place for two consecutive nights.

Qadhafi may be like a rogue elephant, but he is not demented. Another member of the rogue gallery is Hafez al-Assad. Like Qadhafi, he too is not deranged. And unlike Qadhafi, Assad seems closer to the mainstream of the global village and the Arab Nation. But in fact, this façade is just that—a mask that fronts the true identity of a brutal dictator.

SYRIA'S ASSAD: THE HAMA RULES

Like Qadhafi and Saddam, Assad uses rough tactics to bully his opponents, international and domestic. The "Hama rules" refer to the brutal slaying of 10,000 residents of the Syrian city of Hama. This massacre gave Assad the reputation of having a ruthless, calculating mind. Indeed, an anecdote about him reflects this rancor. "After a national 'election' in Syria, an aide comes to President Assad and says, 'Mr. President, you won the election with 99.7 percent majority. That means only three-tenths of 1 percent of the people did not vote for you. What more could you ask for?' Assad replies, 'Their names.'"[27]

If President Hafez al-Assad did seek those who would defy him, what would he do? Perhaps the Hama massacre can provide a possible scenario. Survivors of Assad's wrath reported horrific torture techniques involving the removal of fingernails and heated probes.[28]

But what makes Assad tick? Who is he? On the outside, he looks like a distinguished gentleman. With silver hair and a nice smile, he could be anybody's grandfather, or a high school teacher. But it is widely believed that Assad is responsible for the deaths of thousands of people in order to keep his political position.[29]

Like Qadhafi, Assad came from a stable family. His family was warm, large, and a respectable pillar of the community. Assad's father, Ali Sulayman, was one of the very few literate Syrians in the early 1900s, and was highly respected for it. His emphasis on education carried over to his sons. Liberal French teachers educated Assad because France controlled Syria after the First World War. But this liberal education went for naught in transmitting humanitarian values.

At the age of nine, Assad was sent to a school in Latakia, where he lived with his older sister. Tragically, his sister and her husband were forced to move, abandoning Assad in a city that hated him because of his Alawite faith. Though he was homesick, alone, in a place where people despised him, Assad refused to give up and excelled in school. His tough-mindedness may come from the disciplined training he received from his father and grandfather. His grandfather built a family reputation of being physically domineering and morally steadfast. Assad's grandfather supposedly came down from the mountains into a little village and physically challenged potential opponents. When he thoroughly defeated his first opponent, the townspeople cried, "He's a wild man!" From that point on, they viewed Assad's family as courageous and strong. From his father, Assad gained prominence and prestige. He acquired a love for learning and took up literature and art to become a well-rounded, educated man.[30]

Several of the same factors that drive Saddam Hussein also motivate Assad. Both men strive for power, demand respect, and resort to violence in order to sustain their dominance. Also, they insist on absolute power in their respective nations. And they have taken severe actions against opponents to demonstrate their resolve as the embodiment of their nation's identity.[31]

Another example of Assad's ruthlessness was the assassination of a rival Lebanese tribal chief, Kemal, for crossing him.[32] When Kemal's successor, his son Walid Jumblat, made a visit to Syria, Assad asked him to do a small task for him. Jumblat tactfully declined, so Assad answered, "You know, Walid, I look at you sitting there and you remind me exactly of your dear father. What a man he was. What a shame he is not with us."[33] Jumblat understood what Assad was telling him—the son could be killed just as easily as the father had been.

Personality, politics, and policies constitute a triad useful for analyzing the mullahs of Iran, as well as rulers of Iraq, Libya, and Syria. These three factors also apply to two rulers of nations left over from the Cold War—Fidel Castro and Kim Jong-Il.

CUBA'S CASTRO:
THE OLD DICTATOR AND THE SEA

Like Qadhafi and Assad, Fidel Castro came from a well-to-do family. His father worked for the same type of American firm that the son later vilified as the personification of economic imperialism. This contrast between his prior background and future policies nests nicely with the dichotomy of images from supporters and detractors.

Castro's propagandists picture him as a bearded, romantic idealist with noble aims. His detractors paint Castro as a scruffy, cynical, communist relic with ignoble goals. Both sides, however, agree that he is a survivor. Physically, he lived through great tumult during his time at the University of Havana and later lived for years as a guerrilla fighter in the jungles of Cuba.

Ideologically, Castro "survived" the background of growing up as a scion of a wealthy landowner. Although Fidel's father took delight in conducting business with American firms like the United Fruit Company, Castro emerged as the communist leader who overthrew Batista.[34] Because Castro endured imprisonment for a bold and foolish assault on the Batista regime's second largest military installation, he is no stranger to hardship.

Like Santiago in Ernest Hemingway's *The Old Man and the Sea,* Fidel Castro's life suggests a struggle both for legitimacy and power.[35] Consider the way that Hemingway, who is Castro's favorite author, deals with legitimacy. For Santiago, legitimacy came in the form of a large marlin; in Castro's case, legitimacy has been a struggle since birth. Born out of wedlock in a Catholic country, he sought legitimacy throughout his troubled adolescence. As a national leader, he has had his eye on power and esteem in the international community. These drives for legitimacy and power have made him into a political opportunist and, later, a paranoid personality. As he has aged, Castro has become less opportunistic, as well as more fearful and suspicious about those around him. These personality factors play an integral role in the politics and policies of Havana.

One way Castro survives is by his effective use of propaganda for maximum political gain. While he was seeking to overthrow the Batista regime, he claimed that his men were only fighting for a democratic Cuba. Supposedly, they only wanted an end to the Batista dictatorship. In order to bolster his identification with American democracy, Castro used his knowledge of major league baseball in the United States. Hence, an association between democracy and baseball became Castro's propaganda tool to present himself as less of a threat to the United States.[36]

Castro even pitched for a baseball team when he was a senior in high school. He had the grand idea of playing in the U.S. major leagues. At issue is whether he was talented enough to make it in American baseball, or whether it was all another propaganda ploy. One scholar of American-Cuban diplomatic relations asserts that Castro was a Cuban baseball phenomenon. By his account, Castro was one of the first foreign athletes to be offered a contract by an American major league baseball team.[37] Legend has it that Castro was chosen as the country's best high school athlete in 1945. A leading biographer of Castro, however, researched Havana's prestigious newspapers and sports pages of every issue for that year and discovered that another young man actually was pronounced athlete of the year. There was no mention of Castro's name anywhere.[38] According to this account, Castro's baseball prowess was just the propaganda of friends, and he was not a promising young baseball pitcher at all.[39] *Rogue Regimes* assumes that the second interpretation is correct: Castro would not have come to the plate to play with the big boys of the American major leagues.

Fidel's dream of playing in the major leagues turned into a nightmare for both the Batista regime and successive American presidents. He has survived a series of them. Upon coming to power, Castro was in a position to toss fast balls and curve balls through nine innings of Presidents: Eisenhower, Kennedy, Johnson, Nixon, Ford, Carter, Reagan, Bush, and Clinton. How did the Presidents react to Castro's antics? They imposed an economic embargo on Cuba, maintained it irrespective of changes in East-West relations, and even tightened sanctions under the pretext of a provocation. But Castro has been able to manipulate the American threat in order to achieve political gains. And by exploiting that threat, he has created an opportunity to endure.

NORTH KOREA'S KIM JONG-IL: WILL THE SON ALSO RISE?

Another relic of the Cold War who seeks to manipulate the American threat for political purposes at home is the would-be dictator of North Korea—Kim Jong-Il. At issue in his ascension to office is whether he will be able to amass as much power as his father, Kim Il-Sung.

Violence and grief marred the son's childhood. In 1949, when Kim was eight, his mother mysteriously died. North Korean "spin doctors" quickly squelched rumors about her death being a suicide. They issued a government announcement that she died of a heart attack.[40]

While his father was alive, Kim Jong-Il blamed him for the loss of his mother. Not only was Kim Jong-Il a difficult son to his parents, he became an even larger problem for soldiers, workers, and teachers in Pyongyang. His destructive rebellion as a child carried over into adulthood. Former teachers, acquaintances, and schoolmates recall Kim's dangerous antics in his Mercedes-Benz, his impolite demeanor, and his obvious pleasure in exploiting his power.[41]

Kim Jong-Il also keeps a group of women to use at his disposal. Approximately two thousand young women are currently "employed" in Kim's "Pleasure Team," "Satisfaction Team," and "Happiness Team."[42] While the pleasure groups are well known in North Korea, the government's propagandists work hard to keep Kim Jong-Il's activities from the light.

Even though his father, Kim Il-Sung, made provisions to ensure a stable succession upon his death in 1993, he ran into difficulties in promoting his son as a successor. In 1982, Kim Jong-Il failed to acquire one of three vice-presidential seats. Yet, because of his birthright, he remained one of the most powerful men in North Korea. However, it took the North Korean government 100 days to declare the intended successor, Kim Jong-Il, Supreme Leader of the Democratic People's Republic of Korea. Trying to downplay the fact that he led a privileged yet tumultuous life, propagandists have tried to create a Weberian image of a charismatic leader.[43] They have even lied about Kim Jong-Il's birthplace, declaring that he was the "Baby General Star" that appeared on the holy Mt. Paekdu. A sacred shrine now marks his birthplace.[44] In reality, this is a ploy to give Kim Jong-Il an image of divinity. He was really born in a Siberian military camp in Watsukoye, Russia.[45] This fabrication was a tool to change his public personality in order to strengthen his control of the politics and policies of Pyongyang.

All of his life, Kim Jong-Il has been running from responsibility. Does this carry over into his political responsibilities to his country? Perhaps so, but an argument can be made that he is still that little frightened boy who is lashing out at the world. At issue is whether he is a greedy, selfish, power-hungry dictator, on the one hand, or a troubled, pampered, socially created, and fear-driven maniac, on the other hand.

ROGUE PERSONALITIES
AND THE NEW WORLD ORDER

Idiosyncratic politics are the order of the day in the post–Cold War era. As the discussion above of key dates demonstrates, stars from less powerful states have walked onto the world stage. Without the checks and balances of a democratic system or the constraints of large-scale bureaucracies, rogue regimes are subject to the whims of charismatic individuals. These leaders may hold the future of international stability in their hands. For about fifty years, the world had been preoccupied with two superpowers battling each other for dominance. A few regional powers remained on the periphery of their confrontation. As the twentieth century closes, the United States faces a new world order of regional challengers to its global hegemony. Whether the challengers represent threats or opportunities depends upon the values and perceived interests of status quo powers like the United States and its European allies.

THREAT VERSUS OPPORTUNITY

In the forest of East-West politics, the West slew a dying Soviet bear. In the aftermath, the United States perceives itself in a woodland teeming with additional beasts—fresh threats to the Washington-dominated post–Cold War world. Viewed through an American prism, they are the rogue elephants of the international system.[46] In dispute is why America's Western allies view these same states as opportunities to be embraced and accommodated rather than as hazards. As threats, rogue states need to be contained or confronted.[47] If they are a combination of both opportunity and threat, the United States could balance accommodation with confrontation.

The Chinese ideogram for "crisis" contains characters that mean both threat and opportunity.[48] In this respect, peril and promise are two faces of a similar problem. But what is a threat to national security for some leaders may be a domestic economic opportunity for others. This peril and promise competition occupies a central role in a great debate during the transition from the Cold War to the post–Cold War era. Two questions characterize the controversy. Are there new threats or additional opportunities in the global village, and, if so, how should the industrialized democracies react to these risks or rewards?

In addressing these questions, two schools of thought divide the Western allies. One theme that cuts across these perspectives is the nature of threat perception. Both camps acknowledge that there are threats in the world. They differ, however, in their perceptions of danger and what to do about the menace. Sometimes threats are overestimated; at other times they are underestimated. Those who misperceive threats do so because they see what they want to see and/ or what they expect to see.

Threat misperception derives from the misleading influences of biases on perception. Biases come in two types—motivated and unmotivated. If you see what you want to see, that is a motivated bias. If you see what you expect to see, that is an unmotivated bias. These two cause threat misperception.[49]

The American school perceives high dangers from rogue states and imposes sanctions in order to deter and coerce them.[50] The European school does not perceive much of a threat from these same states and resists the imposition of trade restraints. Indeed, this school would embrace rather than confront. By embracing America's "rogues," they are less likely to become Europe's problems later. Twin issues addressed here are why certain leaders see outlaws and others perceive opportunities; and conversely, why particular leaders choose to contain the perilous possibilities, while others decide to embrace the promising prospects. Those who select containment via economic sanctions do so despite evidence that this approach often fails to coerce. And those who choose to embrace by means of trade incentives do so in spite of indications that dialogue frequently fails to reduce misbehavior.

As a result of its high threat perception, the United States imposes trade restraints on its newly found beasts. When there is allied consensus, Washington prefers multilateral action; in the absence of accord among the allies, Washington imposes unilateral penalties. Both collective and individual trade restraints reflect the approach of the pro-sanctions school of thought.

Europe, leader of the anti-sanctions school, strongly resists unilateral U.S. sanctions and is even cool to multilateral trade penalties.[51] While Americans perceive outlaws abroad, Europeans foresee lost opportunities at home. Not having businesslike relations with less-than-perfect nations abroad makes little sense. Viewed through the European prism, American-defined rogues are not only areas for business opportunity but are also candidates for democratization through economic development. Due to Europe's propensity for appeasement and engagement over antagonism and confrontation, it tends to avoid the American approach of applying restraints on trade. European nations would rather buy off and engage potential rogues with goods and services, instead of confronting them with threats and sanctions. And even when threat perceptions are similar on both sides of the Atlantic, Europeans prefer cooperation to coercion.

Indeed, the Brussels-based European Union acknowledges concern about the threat to the West from countries like Libya and Iran. But in contrast to Washington, Brussels pursues a multilateral approach to achieve change and strongly objects to unilateral measures imposed by the United States.[52] European countries hold that it makes sense to keep lines of communication open to those states with which there are political, ideological, and religious differences.

Therefore, when Washington chooses to magnify the misbehavior of comparatively small states like Libya and discount the violations of large states like China, Europeans accuse the United States of inconsistency. They charge U.S. presidents with being guilty of selling American foreign policy in bipolar terms. The public then encourages decisionmakers to follow policies that isolate the "good guys" from the "bad." Europeans do not view the world in bipolar terms and hence are inclined to incorporate all states into an overall trade system. The debate is between emotional American idealism and cynical European realism.

Europeans question the U.S. assumption that it can sit in judgment on the moral fitness of other states. They challenge America's self-designated right to instruct Europe as to which countries are suitable for trading relationships. Europeans ask why they should not have business relations with a country like Libya, which has over five million people, most of whom are not politically active, anti-Western, or terrorists. Europeans also reason that it is absurd to imagine a nation inducing another to change its ways unless open communication exists. Moreover, they contest the assumption that negative measures are capable of exerting a positive influence on a rogue state.[53]

And even if an isolationist policy contributes to financial and monetary instability, the question arises as to whether the existence of unstable countries on the European periphery is in the interest of the West. If, for example, sanctions on Libya destabilize its regime, one result might be a flood of refugees. Such emigration would transfer instability from North Africa across the Mediterranean into Europe.

In other words, Washington perceives threats from miscreant states, while the members of the European Union see ongoing relationships with a potential for expansion. Washington considers these states as rogues, wandering out of control, meriting isolation, and deserving punishment. By not adhering to international standards of conduct, the rogue-elephant state separates itself from the herd of nations and roams alone. But once isolated from the herd, most rogues find that re-admission is a difficult task; because the United States chooses to ostracize them even further, they find themselves prey to a cumulative isolation.

The question for the United States is which nations it will accept as part of the herd, and which it will exclude as rogues. Those that cross an American threshold of perceived threat prompt Washington to push them even further from the pack. Through its own behavior, a rogue state is a vulnerable nation on the verge of isolation; sanctions then reinforce the separation. The question for Europe is whether to accept America's exclusionary approach or to press for an inclusionary policy. But the downside of inclusiveness is that Europe risks dividing the Atlantic alliance. Pragmatic Europe has a higher threshold of threat perception than does ideological America. With a longer history of dealing with states that fit America's rogue image, Europe is more tolerant of deviant behavior than the United States.

European governments and businesses generally speak with one voice when it comes to their preference for engagement over confrontation with potential rogue states.[54] In contrast to Europe, there are differences both within the U.S. government and between it and the American business community. Consider a split within the government among departments and agencies that dealt with Nigeria during the mid-1990s. The military regime in Lagos hanged a writer, Ken Saro-Wiwa, and eight other political activists in 1995. Advocates for strong sanctions included National Security Adviser Anthony Lake, Assistant Secretary of State for Human Rights John Shattuck, and Undersecretary of State for Global Affairs Timothy Wirth. As a pro-sanctions group, these three pressed for even tougher measures than the Clinton Administration already had imposed on Nigeria. They were opposed by representatives from the Department of Commerce and other business-oriented cabinet departments. These officials argued that unilateral sanctions would only succeed in increasing the price of heating oil for Americans.

Regarding the split between a U.S. administration and the American business community on sanctions, the former often chooses sanctions while the latter generally opposes them. Business considers sanctions a blunt tool of last resort. Like their European counterparts, businesses from Wall Street to Main Street belong to the anti-sanctions school of thought. American firms believe that commercial engagement should be used before governments impose sanctions. They assume that sanctions designed to place pressure on the economies of a target nation damage U.S. interests abroad, hurt the people, and fail to punish the elite.[55]

Mobil Oil typifies the attitude of American firms toward international economic sanctions.[56] It allows that unilateral sanctions may be gratifying—punishing an offender's behavior makes Americans feel good. But despite this positive feeling that comes from dispensing "retributive justice," Mobil Oil emphasizes the negative aspects of sanctions, which usually fail to accomplish what they set out to do—deter and rehabilitate. The corporate sector holds that democratic elections may be facilitated more through dialogue with the offending government than through punishment of its citizens by sanctions. American-based firms operating abroad contend that they reinforce American values and oppose sanctions on the grounds that they prevent the firms from spreading the values.

If there are to be sanctions, corporate America prefers the effective rehabilitation of a target nation rather than punishment for retribution. Allowing American firms to operate in rogue states provides an opportunity to demonstrate such values as protection against human rights abuses in the workplace; an assumption here is that values learned on the job will be incorporated into the wider culture.

The American private sector also stresses other negative consequences of sanctions, especially unilateral restraints. Such actions may cause states to view U.S.-based companies as potentially bad risks, a perception that could result in a decrease in sales, investment opportunities, and foreign trade earnings.[57] Commercial engagement should be used instead to rein in nations that wander outside accepted moral boundaries. The bottom line of American business is that engagement offers the chance for a "critical dialogue," which in turn inspires change in what Washington would call a rogue state.

Threat and opportunity are different aspects of comparable situations; politics, moreover, reinforce threat perception or perceived opportunities and provide a setting out of which policies emerge.

POLITICS AND POLICIES

In contrast to New York's business-oriented Wall Street, Washington's Pennsylvania Avenue views sanctions in a positive light. From Capitol Hill to the White House, government officials are willing to use sanctions. They are midway between doing too much, such as sending in the troops, and doing too little, such as making empty threats.[58] This intermediate position attracts supporters on the Main streets throughout the country.

American political leaders accuse Europeans of opposing U.S. sanctions while offering little in the way of containing the threat posed by the likes of Iran, Iraq, Libya, Syria, Cuba, and North Korea. They charge that these rogue states manipulate the Europeans' critical dialogue approach in order to advance the development of weapons of mass destruction. In a harsh accusation, a former American diplomat explains what he terms "Euroblindness." He defines it as an unwillingness of Europeans to see threats to their own interests and to prefer cooperation over confrontation with rogue states. Why? Because, ". . . Europeans have never lost faith in appeasement as a way of life."[59]

Unlike their counterparts across the Atlantic, American political leaders see sanctions as historically successful. In contrast to business leaders, these politicians want to win elections; hence, they view sanctions as a means of appealing to the values of their domestic political constituencies. The pro-Israel community in New York applauds the Clinton Administration's hard-line approach toward four of Israel's enemies: Iran, Iraq, Libya, and Syria. The anti-Castro community of Cuban-American exiles in Florida praises the Administration's tough stand toward Castro. Preferences of politicians, decisions of diplomats, and lobbying by interest groups converge to produce a policy of sanctions. In other words, the vectors of American politics line up with those of U.S. diplomacy. Politics reinforce the morally motivated grounds for American foreign policy.

But domestic politics, international diplomacy, and human rights idealism may not always converge, as in the case of Nigeria during the mid-1990s. The regime hanged several of its opponents. These hangings led to international pledges for strong punitive measures against the military regime in Lagos. But the campaign for international sanctions stalled. Along with international oil companies, the Nigerian government launched a lobbying effort that took the wind out of the sails of sanctions. But Lagos not only aligned with the international oil industry; the regime also had its local American allies. This alliance defeated the American opposition to Nigeria led by a civil rights coalition.[60]

Following the hangings in Nigeria, the coalition of American human rights, environmental, black, and labor groups had launched a campaign. TransAfrica, an organization devoted to enhancing ties between Africa and the United States, initiated a letter to President Clinton signed by 54 prominent American blacks. It advocated strong sanctions against the military regime in Lagos. As a result of this lobbying effort, Senator Nancy Kassebaum (Rep.-Kansas) and Representative Donald Payne (Dem.-New Jersey) introduced bills in the Senate and House that would have both cut off most investment by American firms in Nigeria and laid the basis for an international oil embargo. But Senator Carol Moseley-Braun (Dem.-Illinois) and the Nation of Islam leader Louis Farrakhan returned from their respective trips to Nigeria with a call for the Clinton Administration to give the regime a chance to enact democratic reforms before imposing sanctions. This split within the liberal coalition gave the Clinton Administration a pretext for shelving strong action against Nigeria.

The Administration had imposed only modest prohibitions against Nigeria. These consisted of a ban on sales of military equipment, a reduction in humanitarian aid, the recall of the U.S. ambassador, and a broadening of an existing ban on visas for Nigerian officials and their families. And following a review at the State Department, officials said that the United States would take further steps in collaboration with European and African states and did not exclude an embargo on Nigerian oil sales.

But the government of Nigeria countered by purchasing services of nine American public relations and lobbying companies for about $10 million.[61] Mobil Oil, Amoco, Chevron, and firms with involvement in a $3.8 billion liquefied natural gas project in southeast Nigeria joined the effort. A central group in the lobbying on behalf of Lagos was the 107-member Corporate Council on Africa, a private, nonprofit organization dedicated to promoting business relationships between African countries and American corporations. The Corporate Council held that dialogue rather than confrontation was more likely to produce political reforms in Nigeria.[62]

In leading the anti-sanctions school, the business community trumped American ethnic politics and the traditional commitment to idealism. The effect was to stop the momentum for imposing strong sanctions against Nigeria. One of the reasons why the business community triumphed was because human rights concerns did not converge with strategic or intrinsic interests. In the case of Iran and Libya, however, ideals, interests, and politics do intersect. Hence, Washington imposed weak sanctions on Nigeria and strong sanctions against Iran and Libya.

Here is the argument for the pro-sanctions school of thought. Strong measures would place regimes like Nigeria's on the defensive. Sanctions would lessen the ability of rogue regimes to wreak havoc abroad and would demonstrate international outrage with the targeted regime's policies. Meanwhile, sanctions would strengthen the domestic opponents of targeted regimes. Through their experience with Cuba, Iraq, North Korea, and Serbia, American political leaders believe that consistently applied pressure in the form of sanctions weakens rogue regimes and facilitates change. Perhaps as a result of sanctions, Cuba is no longer in a position to destabilize other regimes across the Caribbean and in Central and South America, as it did in the first years under Castro.

Regarding Iraq, the U.S. resolve to maintain sanctions helps to contain Saddam Hussein's regime. Although sanctions against Baghdad have indirectly hurt the Jordanian economy, King Hussein has been impressed by the steadfastness of their implementation. The maintenance of sanctions despite international clamor to lift them may have facilitated the King's shift in his position from passive neutrality to active opposition regarding Saddam.

Faced with unremitting American hostility, including the imposition of sanctions and the use of force, Libya is much less adventuresome in its dealings with neighboring states like Egypt, and appears to be more hesitant in its support of terrorist operations abroad. For Serbia, the Clinton Administration insisted on maintaining sanctions, despite pressure from its European allies to lift them prematurely. According to representatives of the pro-sanctions school, sanctions and a preponderance of military power by NATO forces ultimately brought Serbia's Slobodan Milosevic to the table. While there, Serbia and its allies were in a position to deliver on their international obligations under the Dayton Peace Accords.[63]

SANCTIONS FOR REHABILITATION

Given the competing claims of the pro-sanctions and anti-sanctions schools, the question arises whether sanctions are effective. The issue is whether sanctions are rehabilitative; that is, do they coerce target states. In addressing the consequences of sanctions, consider a description of which states initiate them, where they occur, and to what effect. The United States initiated more than two-thirds of all sanctions between 1945-1982. Since 1990, there has been a sharp increase in the use of multilateral sanctions.[64]

Here is a breakdown of 63 sanctions and threats issued by the United States from 1945 to 1982: Latin America, 28; Western Europe, 11; Eastern Europe and the USSR, 5; sub Saharan Africa, 6; North Africa and Middle East, 10; South Asia, 8; East Asia, 11. In this respect, American penalties against Cuba, Iran, and Syria have been unilateral, while Washington has joined the international community in imposing multilateral sanctions on Iraq, Libya, and North Korea. Unilateral sanctions are rarely effective, while multilateral penalties have a better record of success.

As the world moves from the certainty of Cold War threat perceptions to the uncertainty of a new world in disorder, sanctions are of increasing importance for implementing coercive and retributive policies. In the stable bipolarity of the Cold War, the focus of the West was on influencing the external behavior of fairly unitary actors like the Soviet Union. Because vital interests were clear, the U.S. strategy of containment bound European, Asian, and other regional allies in a multilateral effort to deter the Soviet bloc and China. Coercive diplomacy during the Cold War made use of sanctions in an effort to compel relatively unitary states to cease undesirable behavior or take an action favored by the United States. Western multilateral sanctions, in the form of export controls, were a defining element of the containment strategy.

In the unstable multipolarity of the post–Cold War era, trade controls are still in vogue. But those subjected to controls offer new dangers. Absent the Communist threat, rogue states continue to cross an American-defined threat-perception threshold and subsequently receive a large proportion of sanctions. The United States uses export and import controls to contain and coerce rogue states. But coercive sanctions are less likely to be effective against rogues as they once were in the Cold War. In the post–Cold War era, there is less of a consensus on the definition of vital interest, the allies have different perceptions of threat, and they differ regarding the nature of the response to a situation. While the United States is still militarily powerful, it is less politically influential. In periods of declining influence, unilateral sanctions reflect a decrease in the ability of a Great Power to lead.[65]

Absent the Soviet threat, the diminished capacity of the United States as a leader makes it difficult to achieve consensus in the West on multilateral sanctioning. And consensus is problematic on the selection of measures to address threats. Not only are group decisions harder to effect than those of a single state, but concerted action requires harmonizing the policies of nations with varying interests, ideals, and prior commitments.[66]

One of the reasons it is difficult to achieve consensus is that the targeted state may develop defensive measures that would affect sanctioning states differently. For example, Italy resists participating in a multilateral regime—a set of international norms—against Libya because Tripoli's reaction to such sanctions would harm Rome more than Washington.

Another reason why consensus formation is difficult to achieve concerns the difference in threat perceptions in relation to the capabilities of the target state to withstand sanctions. Washington perceives threats and is less concerned with the targeted states' capacity to absorb the penalties. Brussels perceives the same situations as only potential threats: they lie dormant unless exacerbated by Western sanctions or military intervention.

A further reason why international consensus is problematic is that defensive measures taken by a targeted nation may result in the establishing of ties to non-sanctioning states. These links may disadvantage sanctioning states. Thus, Germany resists taking part in American-imposed sanctions against Iran, arguing that German firms stand to lose too much Iranian business to Japanese companies if Berlin participates in Washington-initiated sanctions against Tehran. International accord is difficult when countermeasures damage sanctioning states differently.

Additionally, the breakup of empires and emergence of "failed" nations causes the Western coalition of democracies to have less of a coercive effect on the rest of the world. In particular, failed states, for example, the "Somalias" of the world, are less "state-like" in nature. And hence, they are less amenable to strategies of economic threats and actual sanctions. Normal nation-states have capitals on maps and employ standard communications devices that are subject to intelligence means, such as electronic interception. Nations in disarray lack these accoutrements of state. Their leaders are overridden with fear, isolated from the international community, with too much to lose domestically to be concerned about foreign threats. They may fear losing domestic standing as a result of compliance more than the effects of sanctions imposed by an outside power.

In other words, it may be futile to threaten economic sanctions against a warlord who lacks a foreign ministry building and has no fax machines or mobile telephones to receive threats. But the warlord may have enemies at home whom he fears more than the threats of external powers like the United States. Hence, coercion is virtually impossible when dealing with failed states like Somalia. Rehabilitative punishment is difficult to justify when taken against failed states that have degenerated beyond the capacity to cause further mischief.

However, coercion for rehabilitation is more likely to be effective when addressing a developed state that is a product of a disintegrated empire, such as the former Yugoslavia. Serbia—a product of this collapsed empire—is an entity whose leaders are amenable to coercion and deserving of retribution. One reason that states like Serbia are vulnerable to coercion is that its leaders have sought gains from neighbors more than attempting to protect against losses from domestic or international opponents.

SANCTIONS FOR RETRIBUTION

Irrespective of the instrumental effectiveness of sanctions, there is the retributive punishment aspect to consider. In addition to coercion as a goal, a power may seek retribution—punitive action without regard to behavioral change.[67] Punishment inflicted for retribution deserves some discussion, as it may appear to be a less rational means to achieve a policy goal. Retributive punishment is simply a means to an end. The ultimate goal is to satisfy the desire for payback for previous misconduct, rather than to coerce changes in behavior. Retributive sanctions are a politically safe route to take—success is virtually guaranteed. As soon as the sanctioner inflicts harm, sanctioning as a tool of retribution is immediately effective. For the United States, such punishment is gratifying because of an American belief that sinners should receive their just desserts.[68] Sanctions not only send a symbolic message to the wrongdoer abroad but also to the relevant domestic constituency that wrongs will be righted.

Punishment for the sake of retribution pays scant attention to the future behavior of wayward states. Sanctions against Iraq combine castigation to change future behavior as well as retributive justice; that is, deserved punishment for evil done. Because Iraq committed an evil deed in its invasion of Kuwait in 1990, retributive justice demands castigation beyond that which is necessary to coerce. About seven years after the invasion, Iraq was in virtual compliance with international demands to destroy its weapons of mass destruction and to allow inspections, yet retribution justified continuation of sanctions to right the initial wrong. Retributive sanctions, however, may backfire.

When Washington imposes sanctions for retribution and leaders of the target state believe that they are being wronged for no good reason, they may feel compelled to act in the manner that the United States was originally trying to deter. When imposing retributive sanctions, one should weigh the expected benefit of "feeling good" against the prospects and costs of backlash. When retribution derives from ideals, however, it is difficult to employ a cost-benefit standard.

When leaders of states hit by retributive American sanctions feign surprise and shock about their graduation to rogue status, it is a clear sign that they do not understand an America defined by its ideals. The *mythos* of the patriot who goes to war for the ideals of life, liberty, and the pursuit of happiness is a core element of U.S. history. *Democracy in America,* the prescient work of the French political theorist Alexis de Tocqueville, abounds with passages lauding the idealistic motives of the American people.[69]

Alexis de Tocqueville attributes high idealistic standards in the United States to widespread political discourse. Although Americans have usually focused their discussions on matters of religion, such activity has had the net effect of increasing both their awareness and their moral standards. Consequently, when the United States evaluates the conduct of other nations to determine whether economic sanctions should be imposed, ideals jump-start the decision-making process. In contrast to American moralizing, however, European nations are largely devoid of idealistic concerns. To draw again on de Tocqueville, the states of Europe lack that quintessential sense of moral right and wrong he saw so often in the American mindset.

Given such a broad base of moralizing throughout the culture, it is no surprise that American ideals play such a large part in the decision-making process regarding the application of sanctions. But idealism alone lacks consequence; it is the convergence of idealism with other vectors that carries weight and causes a change in behavior.

The convergence of idealism and international politics is most strikingly observed through U.S. relations with Cuba. Despite immense support by the American business community to lift economic sanctions and reenter the Cuban market, every president since John Kennedy has held the line on restricting economic interaction with Castro's regime. In the spring of 1996 corporate giants, the United States Chamber of Commerce, and the Association of Exporters and Importers clamored for President Clinton not to tighten sanctions. But when business interests go up against the multiplicative effect of politics and idealism, economic interests be damned; as a result of such interaction, President Clinton proposed instead to strengthen United States sanctions. How can one account for such a gap between interests and politics? On a cursory level, it can be argued that Clinton was merely kowtowing to the Cuban-American community, whose support he needed in the 1996 presidential campaign.

But it must be understood that Cuban-Americans are influential when their behavior coincides with American ideals. For a domestic lobby to make an impact, it must line up its vectors in such a fashion that they seem to intersect seamlessly within the larger picture of the Old Glory version of the Red, White, and Blue. When this interaction occurs, the doors to power close on the "greedy hands" of powerful multinational firms, such as Mobil Oil, and the doors open up to local constituencies like Cuban-Americans.

The conflict between ideals and interests may be peculiar to America. A French official would justify a sale to a nation on Washington's hit list of rogues by simply saying, "France wishes to sell technology, roads, and lorries." Whether the customer was a key player in the serious game of state-sponsored terrorism would be a concern to an official from Washington but not from Paris. For example, the French give rhetorical opposition to Iranian involvement in terrorism, but then they continue to cut business deals with Tehran. Meanwhile, they shower the Congress with lengthy letters opposing the Iran and Libya Sanctions Act because of its "extraterritorial application of U.S. jurisdiction."[70] The French serve as a telling example of the difference in perceptions between the United States and its allies regarding the nature of the threat from rogue regimes and application of sanctions on them.

Most Americans do not want to trade with Iran because they consider what that country is doing to be fundamentally wrong. Profits are well and good, but the sight of charred and broken bodies from Iranian-sponsored terrorism remains a powerful image even after the money from oil trading has been spent. Money is fleeting, and while America is a land of staunch capitalists, it is also a land of principled moralists. Americans qualify capitalism; they do not want to have dealings with evil men and women—those who traffic in human suffering. The Founding Fathers created the United States on a principle that all are created equal and deserve a life free from tyranny, which allows for the pursuit of personal endeavors. Iranian-sponsored terrorism threatens those principles, and accordingly, the United States imposes sanctions to counteract that threat.

But the concept of practicing what you preach, a popular American colloquialism, has simply not struck a chord among the French. They would rather build roads for any nation that can pay the bill. They are inadvertently assisting those who not only hold a set of ideals the French claim to oppose, but actually possess the will to apply those ideals—with force against the French. Practicing what you preach is an approach that leads Americans to impose retributive punishments unlinked to interests.

SANCTIONS AND INTERESTS

In contrast to the imposition of sanctions based on ideals, those levied to further American interests prove far easier for other nations to comprehend. Both European nations and rogue states readily understand such actions because they fall within the normal rules of *Realpolitik*. Yet even within the realm of interests there is confusion.

Ideals often coincide with strategic interests, such as the American reputation for being the champion of the Free World. Ideals, however, may not converge with intrinsic interests—tangible assets like trade, natural resources, and financial capital.

Illustrative of the clash between ideals and economic interests is the debate in the Congress about how to treat nations that have poor records for religious freedom but that also are economic powerhouses. China and Saudi Arabia are two such examples. On the one side are human rights advocates who would use trade sanctions in order to induce Beijing and Riyadh to cease their persecution of religious minorities. On the other side are business interests that oppose the use of sanctions to transform China and Saudi Arabia.

The Clinton Administration is torn between these two sides regarding religious oppression abroad. But because fighting religious persecution is a hot-button issue in Washington, the Administration may have to take a stand one way or another. In this respect, there are proposals before the Congress to punish nations that oppress religious minorities.

Senator Arlen Spector and Representative Frank Wolf introduced companion bills in the Senate and the House during 1997.[71] Their bills are part of a concerted effort to fight religious subjugation abroad. The Spector-Wolf Bill would ban all exports to foreign government entities that carry out religious persecution, cut off non-humanitarian assistance to the persecuting nation, and require the United States to consider a country's record on religious oppression in deciding whether to support its membership in the World Trade Organization.[72] Such proposals imply a tradeoff of intrinsic economic interests in favor of ideals.

Subsumed under the category of strategic interests are prior commitments to American friends such as Israel. In this respect, consider the unlikely trio of the United States, Israel, and Iran. As the Arab-Israel conflict winds down, the pro-Israel community in the United States perceives a new threat on the horizon. The fresh menace is an Iran that each year is increasingly capable of delivering nuclear weapons. The community also views Tehran as a fountainhead of terrorism directed at Jews in general and Israel in particular. American citizens are also under attack, and Washington is responsive to the pro-Israel community as a loyal ally of Jerusalem. Consequently, the United States increases the severity of economic sanctions against Tehran. Washington imposes such sanctions even at the cost of intrinsic interests to American oil firms like Conoco and to U.S. strategic interests in the Gulf. America prides itself on committing blood and treasure to the defense of its friends against its foes, so that the light of liberty can survive, to paraphrase President John Kennedy's inaugural address.[73]

Similarly, prior commitments not only refer to international obligations, but pledges also imply domestic political constituencies. Because the United States is a democracy, assurances to interest groups are often made to secure support. The degree to which these interest groups influence U.S. policy, however, stems from their ability to associate their aims with American strategic interests and ideals. The pro-Israel community is powerful to the extent that its activities reinforce other vectors. In this respect, it is increasingly influential in shaping legislation to counter the Iranian threat to Israel and the United States.

SANCTIONS IF LEADERS
ACT FROM WINDOWS OF OPPORTUNITY

When deciding whether to impose sanctions against regimes like the one in Tehran, consider a distinction between windows of opportunity and basements of fear. Underlying the discussion of which states are most likely to be coercible is the mindset of leaders of pariah states and which type of "sanctions regime" might control them.[74]

When rogue actors focus on possible gains, it is as if they were standing in front of windows of opportunity poised to act. Yet, because opportunists concentrate on profiting, they also focus on possible consequences. Rogues encountering windows of opportunity work cautiously in order to avoid punishment. Rehabilitative sanctions are appropriate because such leaders are less willing to accept possible risks to attain gains. Approximately rational actors should think twice about pursuing a goal in the light of possible punishment, such as economic sanctions. Retributive sanctions, however, are suitable, because one can justify punishment when portraying rogues as mercenaries.[75]

In other words, when rogue actors behave in order to maximize gains, they want to attain their goal, but they cautiously proceed in order to avoid possible negative consequences. They need to calculate carefully the risks of action and inaction. Coercive sanctions are relevant measures to confront such opportunists. Sanctions in this context are like "No Trespass" and "Warning" signs to deter crimes of opportunity by individuals from tough neighborhoods who happen to be in the vicinity of wealthy areas.

During the Cuban Missile Crisis, Moscow was an opportunist in Uncle Sam's backyard, seeking to change the strategic nuclear balance of power in favor of the USSR. By attempting to place nuclear-armed missiles in Cuba, Moscow was taking advantage of an opening that could have been closed if Washington had the presence of mind to reinforce deterrence. Rehabilitative threats were in order to cause the Soviets to think twice about their goals of overturning the balance.[76]

SANCTIONS IF LEADERS ACT FROM BASEMENTS OF FEAR

When rogue actors behave in order to avoid losses in either domestic or international affairs, it is as if they were trapped in a basement of fear. To escape the trap and avoid the loss, leaders are willing to take enormous risks.

Rehabilitative sanctions are less appropriate for fearful individuals because those who concentrate on expected losses tend to engage in risky behavior, regardless of the likely punishment. Retributive sanctions are harder to justify imposing on actors who are misbehaving out of fear. If rogues in front of a window of opportunity are mercenaries, then actors in a basement of fear are paranoids who lack the capabilities to make rational or cost-effective choices. Sanctions may even be counterproductive, leading to additional feelings of frustration and helplessness and to further aggression.[77]

The process of escalation through miscalculation demonstrates the counterproductive aspects of threats when used in the context of interlocking fears. For example, because of a fear of losing the mobilization race prior to World War I, nations were caught up in such a process. Mutual accommodation could have calmed their joint fears and perhaps avoided a war that no nation wanted. The lesson coming out of World War I, however, was learned too well and misapplied to the events prior to the outbreak of World War II.

There were fears of unintended escalation prior to World War II. The Allies incorrectly characterized Hitler's situation as being a basement of fear rather than his window of opportunity. They falsely believed that Hitler's motives and goals were limited and defensive rather than broad and offensive. In order to accommodate and appease him, the Allies sacrificed Poland and Czechoslovakia. Appeasement was inappropriate, for Hitler's goals were not limited only to Poland and Czechoslovakia. As a result of their miscalculation, the Allies found themselves in another world war.

SANCTIONS IF LEADERS ARE MOTIVATED BY A COMBINATION OF FEARS AND HOPES

In analyzing the decision-making processes of various world leaders, it is necessary to acknowledge that they may be influenced by a combination of fears and wants. Deterrence theory views leaders as either "rational" or "irrational," operating at windows of opportunity or from basements of fear. But rationality is a matter of degree. Both opportunity and fear influence individuals. When it comes to decision making, however, either one or the other will dominate.

Consider the case of rogue leaders motivated by both opportunity and fear. Washington should be confident that its threats will deter the opportunistic side, but not exacerbate the fearful side to the point where threats become counterproductive. To achieve such a balance requires the use of containment and engagement, a combination of both the American and European schools of thought.

Germany at the close of the nineteenth century serves as a prime example of a state with mixed motivations. Berlin possessed a considerable but diminishing military advantage over its continental rivals, France and Russia. In 1891, those two countries had agreed to an alliance, which Berlin feared was a harbinger of a two-front war. Moreover, Berlin saw the alliance as an opportunity for Moscow to gain advantage.[78] Leaders in Berlin believed that by attacking Russia before it could mobilize fully, Germany's strategic disadvantage could be limited.

Berlin was in the peculiar position of being in a basement while faced with an open window. The window of opportunity recognized by the German government was its decisive military advantage over Berlin's rivals. Such advantage had to be used quickly before it disappeared. Hence, the time was ripe to squelch its adversaries.[79] Simultaneously, however, Berlin was in a basement of fear. The impending change in the regional balance of power caused by the Franco-Russian alliance frightened German leaders. Time worked to Germany's disadvantage, and Berlin recognized the threat of inaction. However, the Germans did not act until forced into war by their Austrian ally. In short, the Kaiser was neither fearful enough nor desirous enough to act.

CLASSICAL DETERRENCE AND PROSPECT THEORY

With respect to the Cold War, an assumption was that leaders stood in front of windows of opportunity. Only by slamming these windows shut on the fingers of would-be intruders could status quo powers deter unacceptable behavior by others. Deterrence by threat and by denial were the order of the day, according to classical deterrence theory. Deterrence by threat of punishment operated on the motivations and intentions of potential challengers. Deterrence by denial acted on their capabilities. In both cases, defenders closed windows to force target states not to take an action.[80]

In the post–Cold War era, classical deterrence assumptions are less valid. Deterrence is more or less likely to be effective, according to the situation of the target. If within leaders' dual motivations, fear of loss influences more than desire for gain, deterrence is not likely to be effective. Consider the case of Cuba. Sanctions are less appropriate tools when initiators act out of fear. And sanctions for rehabilitation are less effective because fearful individuals are willing to accept punishment to avoid other losses.

Classical deterrence theory assumes that leaders of target states are able to perceive threats and act in an approximately rational fashion. If they misperceive threats because of biased information processing, compliance is unlikely. The theory presumes that if a defender has greater capabilities, resolve, and is able to prevent a challenger from controlling and calculating risks, then compliance is a given. But if there is misperception on the part of the target, compliance is not likely.

Classical deterrence also presupposes that challengers act to maximize their gains and that they weigh gains and losses equally. In this regard, defenders can simply increase the expected cost (risk) of noncompliance so that it is greater than the expected gain from noncompliance. Doing so should assure submission. Classical deterrence either assumes that leaders weigh gains and losses equally or that they desire gains more than they fear losses. Leaders of "broken" or failed states are likely to be so bounded in their rationality that they fear losses more than they desire gains. Because deterrence is more likely to be effective if leaders seek gains more than they fear losses, deterrence is less likely to be effective against leaders of failed states.[81]

ROGUES' GALLERY: TICKET FOR ADMISSION

Iran, Iraq, Libya, Syria, Cuba, and North Korea are the American-defined renegades in this study. Outlaws include Ayatollah Khomeni and the militant mullahs' successors, Saddam Hussein, Muammar Qadhafi, Hafez al-Assad, Fidel Castro, and Kim Jong-Il. Theirs are the photographs that would adorn the walls of the world's post offices, like images of common criminals that appear on the walls of the U.S. Postal Service.

The question is why these leaders, and not others, appear in this book. Initially, I considered the term "LISA" as a device for inclusion of cases. During my service in 1981-1982 on the senior staff of the National Security Council at the White House, members of our office used the acronym LISA as a device to recall four of the nations then on the State Department's terrorism list: Libya, Iraq, Syria, and Aden (South Yemen). Using this criterion would have included Aden, which is now a part of a unified Yemen, and excluded Iran, Cuba, and North Korea.

The standard used was the State Department's annual list that appears in *Patterns of Global Terrorism*. It contains a description of those countries where significant terrorist acts occurred and nations about which the Department notified Congress pursuant to the Export Administration Act of 1979. The report details countries that have repeatedly provided state support for international terrorism— premeditated, politically motivated violence perpetrated against noncombatant targets by subnational groups, usually intended to influence an audience.

By 1994, seven nations had made the terrorism list: Cuba, Iran, Iraq, Libya, North Korea, Sudan, and Syria. All of these states, except for Sudan, qualify for *Rogue Regimes*. Sudan fails to make "the cut" because Iran is Sudan's mentor for international terrorism, and Tehran is certainly in the hunt. Although Lebanon is not on the terrorism list, it makes the narcotics list. Syria, however, is the power behind Lebanon's participation in drug trafficking. Because the present study includes Iran and Syria, there is less need to include Sudan and Lebanon, respectively.[82]

Practicing terrorism, possessing a large-scale conventional force, and seeking weapons of mass destruction qualify a state for admission to the showroom of miscreants. Terrorism conducted by a state with conventional forces and ambitions to join the nuclear club combine to constitute a threat to American citizens abroad and at home. Because of American ideals, interests, and prior commitments, a large conventional force, terrorism, and proliferation are unacceptable and hence deserving of punishment. In effect, these criteria justify inclusion of states into the gallery of rogues.

Foremost among criteria for incorporation into the gallery is a violation of American ideals. Strategic and intrinsic interests in geographical regions of the world form a second broad band of standards. Lastly, prior commitments to allied states and domestic constituencies are a reason to impose sanctions.

Serbia is no longer a rogue, because of its cooperation in the U.S.-led Bosnia peace process. During part of 1996, however, sanctions on Serbia remained. As a result, Slobodan Milosevic warrants mention for his prior misdeeds. But Syria's President Assad merits more than a mention; he deserves his own chapter. His on-again, off-again cooperation in the U.S.-led Israeli-Syrian peace process, moreover, may serve to enhance the perception of him as a threat. American sanctions on Syria are likely to remain as long as Assad allows for continuing conflict in territories under his control.[83] Nevertheless, both men deserve attention here because of their role in activities that led to the imposition of sanctions in the first place. Serbia was responsible, in part, for the violent actions of local Serbs in Bosnia and Croatia, eliciting multilateral sanctions. Washington also placed unilateral sanctions on Damascus, due to Syria's history of international terrorism and drug trafficking.

While most nations accused by the United States of international terrorism are in this book, many states charged with drug trafficking do not qualify for inclusion. On March 1, 1996, the State Department classified 140 countries according to whether they were drug-producing or drug-transit. In addition, the Department classified nations by their relative degree of cooperation in combating the drug trade. State classified Colombia as one of 31 nations identified as major drug-producing or drug-transit countries. President Clinton certified 22 of these states, including Mexico, as working sufficiently to solve drug problems.[84]

Colombia, however, joined Afghanistan, Burma, Iran, Nigeria, and Syria on the State Department list of countries judged to be uncooperative in the fight against international drug trafficking. Because Bogota did not take sufficient steps to curb the illicit drug trade, President Clinton decertified Colombia and subjected it to U.S. sanctions. American firms seeking to invest in Colombia could no longer qualify for credits from the Export-Import Bank or the Overseas Private Investment Corporation. Washington plans to vote against any loans requested by Bogota from six development banks, including the International Monetary Fund.[85]

There is quite a difference between the type of narco-corruption that results in decertification of Colombia and the directed drug activities of Syria. Through purposeful state action, Syria uses Lebanon as a platform for producing and shipping drugs. During 1992-1993, Syrian-controlled Lebanon produced and refined over 700 tons of marijuana and 15 tons of heroin, yielding some $3-4 billion in annual revenue to Damascus. In response to American pressure, however, President Assad of Syria took strong yet ultimately futile action against growers and distributors based in Lebanon.[86] As a result of Damascus' control over Lebanon, and its continued production and distribution of drugs, Syria qualifies for inclusion in this book, while Colombia does not.[87]

The idea of a world outlaw assumes a code of conduct similar to the rule of law in domestic affairs. However, the international system's enforcement mechanisms are not as extensive as the counterparts in national courts. Concerts of nations, nevertheless, coordinate their international trade policies, and in so doing, they create multilateral regimes to regulate the actions of others.

The Coordinating Committee (COCOM) associated with the North Atlantic Treaty Organization was a Cold War tool to keep strategic Western exports from falling into Soviet-bloc hands. While there was Western consensus about the Soviet menace, there is no such accord on the nature of the post-Soviet threat. Hence, there is no comparable organization in the post–Cold War era to align policies of the West with respect to exports to American-defined outlaws abroad. Moreover, it is difficult to even conceive of a COCOM-like body in the late 1990s, with the lack of international consensus on who's in and who's out of the rogues' gallery. On the basis of the analyses of the six cases in this book, there is a need to coordinate policies of the West against the new threats to world order.

In summary, the United States perceives post–Cold War threats from Iran, Iraq, Libya, Syria, Cuba, and North Korea and imposes sanctions on them. With the exceptions of Iraq and Libya, the allies see greater future dangers if U.S. sanctions destabilize these American-defined rogue states. Hence, a transatlantic schism in threat perceptions and policies between America and Europe is a problem facing the Alliance.

Four themes cut across *Rogue Regimes*: threat perception, opportunities, politics, and policies. These themes primarily concern terrorism and weapons of mass destruction. Regarding threat perception, the transition from the Cold War to a post–Cold War age has ushered in a grand debate about the nature of threats in the international system. Two issues characterize that debate: different perceptions of threat and opportunity among the industrialized democracies; and policies that are appropriate for the democracies to meet these perceived dangers or opportunities.

CHAPTER TWO

IRAN: BALANCE OF POWER VERSUS DUAL CONTAINMENT

OLD FRIENDS AS NEW ENEMIES

THE 1970S CLOSED WITH THE FALL OF THE SHAH, and Iran shifted in American eyes from ally to adversary. With the rise of the Ayatollah Khomeni, Washington went from being Tehran's mentor to being its menace. The Islamic revolution had ousted the Shah, installed Khomeni, and reversed mutual perceptions between Iran and the United States. At issue was how Washington should treat its old friend, Tehran, which had become a new enemy. Two possible approaches surfaced: the United States as "balancer" between Iran and Iraq; or Washington as "container" of both Tehran and Baghdad. These approaches are balance of power and dual containment, respectively.

On the one hand, balancing consists of applying principles like "The enemy of my enemy is my friend."[1] When Iran and Iraq are adversaries, a balancing approach will play one against the other. In order to deter Iran, the United States would make use of Iraq; in order to restrain Baghdad, Washington would use Tehran. Such a sequence of alternating alignments is the core of a balance-of-power approach. On the other hand, dual containment is an effort by Washington to counter the threats of both Baghdad and Tehran at the same time.[2]

Irrespective of whether the United States is containing both rogue states in sequence or in tandem, their leaders perceive themselves locked in security dilemmas. As a result, it is very difficult to choose accommodation over confrontation. Terrorism from Tehran follows on the heels of containment by Washington.

Security Dilemma: Terrorism and Containment

Tehran and Washington perceive that they are on the horn of a security dilemma.[3] What one side sees as action to increase its security, the other views as a decrement to its own security. There are incentives to take the offensive in a race to obtain a margin of safety. Increases in Iranian terrorism follow escalation in American containment, a policy of isolating Iran through a combination of measures that includes economic sanctions.

After several terrorist incidents, President Clinton signed the Iran and Libya Sanctions Act on August 5, 1996.[4] He called terrorism, "the enemy of our generation" and said that the United States would fight terrorism alone, if necessary.[5] Two days earlier, Secretary of Defense William Perry had laid the national security groundwork for the presidential signing of the act.[6] Perry said that Saudi Arabia was conducting an investigation to find the source of a June 25, 1996 bombing of a U.S. facility in Dhahran that killed nineteen American military personnel. He speculated that Riyadh would find an "international connection" in its search for causes of the bombing. Perry also surmised that the likely connection would be Iran and that the United States would be prepared to take forceful action if the evidence were compelling.

In discussing the possible involvement of Iran in the killing of Americans in Saudi Arabia, Perry made a statement on August 2, 1996 to National Public Radio.[7] He said that the United States would take strong action against any country proved to be involved in the June bombing. He would not say what action would be taken. The secretary, however, backed away from his initial tough stance against Iran. Perry claimed that he welcomed a chance to clarify his initial comments. Perry said that he only had repeated Iran's own threat to support terrorism against the United States. However, if Iran were proven to have committed the bombing, he said that imminent action still might not be taken.[8]

With respect to the link between his initial comments on Iran and terrorist training camps there, at issue was whether Washington might launch a military strike against these sites. Rather than answering the question directly, Perry said that was a classic case of adding two and two and getting twenty-two.[9] On August 15, the Saudi Minister of Interior, Prince Nayef, said that the suspects were Sunnis, born in Saudi Arabia, and veterans of the Afghan war. Nayef seemed to be stressing the internal origin of the suspects in order to refute suggestions by Perry that Saudi evidence might point to an Iranian connection.[10]

The Ayatollah Ali Khameni, Iran's spiritual leader, accused the United States of trying to isolate Iran from the world community.[11] He said that Washington was trying to separate governments and nations from the Islamic Republic of Iran. In other words, Khameni perceived the threat implicit in the U.S. policy of dual containment, the Clinton Administration's isolating Iran and Iraq from the international community. The threat behind that containment approach is the flip side of a Cold War–born interest that first prompted the United States to make contingency plans for the defense of Iran on anti-Soviet grounds.[12]

Even before Tehran entered a rogues' gallery of enemies that sponsor international terrorism and/or engage in trafficking in weapons of mass destruction, there were contingency plans for an assault on Iran in order to save it from the Soviet menace. In the Cold War Pentagon, a defense "of" Iran from Soviet attack could warrant an attack "on" Iran. Whether Iran was friendly or not was irrelevant to whether it should be saved from Soviet attack.

A Soviet invasion of Iran was one of the major Cold War threat contingencies. The Pentagon considered such a Soviet invasion almost comparable to Moscow ordering an invasion of a NATO country. Realignment in Europe without war would be a consequence of a Soviet invasion of the Gulf. Soviet control of the Gulf oil on which Western Europe depended made this contingency very serious, even though it was not very probable. Also, if there were a war on the central front in Europe, there could be a diversionary military move by Moscow in the Gulf. The contingency of a Soviet invasion of Iran produced a worse-case scenario for the Pentagon, especially in the context of war along the central front in Europe.[13]

During a war with NATO, Gulf oil facilities could have been prime targets for Moscow. Simultaneous crises in Europe and the Gulf would have delayed a Gulf buildup by about two weeks. Regarding an invasion of Iran by Soviet combat forces or a combination of Soviet and Iraqi troops, the Pentagon considered the ground and air military balance, the effect of deployments by the United States in a simulated NATO buildup, as well as American-Iranian versus Soviet-Iraqi resupply capabilities.

With respect to Gulf contingencies and Soviet projection forces, the Pentagon was well aware that Soviet troops were closer as the crow flies; that is, they were some 7,000, versus 15,000, nautical miles from the Gulf area. Also, they maintained seven airborne divisions at a high state of readiness. But the United States in the first 30 days of a crisis could have projected by air and sea more capable ground forces than Soviet troops. Only after the sealift began would the Soviets have enjoyed the benefits of proximity. A constraint on the Soviet sealift, moreover, was that it would have been sensitive to the availability of the Turkish Straits and either the Suez or land routes via Syria.

Other Cold War threats included the most important one—a Soviet incursion into the heartland of Western Europe via the Fulda Gap of a divided Germany. Even as American forces anticipated these major threats, Pentagon analysts began to plan for new dangers of an indirect nature. Pro-Soviet regimes in Afghanistan, Cuba, and Libya acted as surrogates for Moscow and thus were fair game for Pentagon planners.

The Reagan doctrine was a rationale for providing military assistance to friendly challengers who sought to shoot their way into closed regimes that carried out Moscow's wishes. In Afghanistan, Reagan analysts dubbed them "freedom fighters," for these Islamic combatants had become surrogate foot soldiers for the United States in its conflict with the USSR over Afghanistan. In addition to backing Islamic fighters against Soviet forces in Afghanistan, the Reagan Administration tilted toward Iraq in 1982. Although Iraq had been a traditional enemy, Washington made an opening to Baghdad as a means to balance Tehran. In other words, the enemy (Iraq) of my enemy (Iran), is my friend.[14]

Iran and the United States have acted as if they were on the threshold of a security dilemma. What Tehran saw as an action to increase its security, Washington viewed as a decrement to its own security. Each had incentives to take the offensive in a contest to obtain a margin of safety. Increases in Iranian terrorism followed escalation in American containment. With the fall of the Shah and the rise of Khomeni, Washington and Tehran inverted their perceptions from friends to enemies. The question arises as to the origins of Washington's changed attitudes.

ROOTS OF AMERICAN PERCEPTIONS ABOUT IRAN

The principal sources of American threat perception regarding Iran are campaign politics and national security, domestic and bureaucratic politics, intrinsic and strategic interests, alliance politics, as well as idealism.[15]

Campaign Politics and National Security

At issue is the effect of campaign politics on the formulation of threat perception. As a member of the Republican National Committee (RNC) National Security Advisory Council during 1979 and 1980, I had the occasion to observe the effect of campaign politics on threat perception. I served with officeholders from previous Republican administrations in a virtual shadow government, that is, one poised to take control in Washington after the 1980 presidential election. Indeed, many of those on the council later assumed high-level positions in the Reagan Administration. The council's chair, Richard Allen, had requested nominees from the American Israel Public Affairs Committee (AIPAC) to serve on the RNC Council. Through my years of association with the pro-Israel community, I became acquainted with Kenneth Wollack of AIPAC, who subsequently nominated me to Allen. He, in turn, appointed me to the council. By suggesting members to the council, AIPAC is able to reward loyal supporters; by accepting nominees, the RNC is able to curry favor with a politically active interest group.

With AIPAC's political support, I had an opportunity to witness the politics of national security from the inside of a presidential campaign, and subsequently, from within the government. I had the occasion to join Reagan's foreign policy and defense advisory group. During the Republican primaries, that group had a meeting on March 10, 1980, in Atlanta, Georgia.[16] Because the Soviet Union had invaded Afghanistan in 1979, the invasion was a topic of discussion. And due to the fact that Americans had been seized as hostages in Tehran in 1979, hostages also were on the Atlanta agenda.

Regarding the Soviet invasion of Afghanistan, the Atlanta group discussed the idea that the United States could threaten the Soviets where Washington had the capability to hurt them. The United States should strike in Cuba, where America was strong, rather than in Afghanistan or in the Gulf, where the United States lacked immediate military capability. In effect, some members of the advisory team favored horizontal expansion across geographical regions rather than vertical escalation within a region.[17] Reagan, moreover, mused that if the Soviets threatened to intervene militarily in the Gulf from their perch in Afghanistan, he could initiate a new arms race that the USSR could not afford to match.

With respect to the Iranian hostage crisis, the Atlanta group discussed an "ultimatum to Iran" option.[18] As president, Reagan could issue a secret threat: "Release the hostages, or else." Because he did not have the authority to act in March 1980, there was no need to specify the "or else." Given the militantly anticommunist nature of the Islamic Republic of Iran, the advisory group discounted the likelihood that Tehran would align with Moscow against Washington. Thus, there seemed to be little risk for issuing an ultimatum.

The purpose of the Atlanta meeting of the foreign policy and defense team was to brief Reagan on national security themes for his campaign. At this briefing, he asked about the 1979 Soviet invasion of Afghanistan and the Iranian hostage crisis. Both events had preoccupied the Carter Administration's national security planning, and the hostage crisis may have doomed the Carter presidency.

Because of a concern that the Carter Administration would effect a release of the Americans held hostage in Iran before the November 1980 presidential election, the Reagan-Bush campaign also set up a group of ten national security experts under Allen's direction, dubbed the "October Surprise Committee." Allen designated former American ambassador to Saudi Arabia and Afghanistan Robert Neumann to be the official "Iran-watcher" for the committee.[19]

After the March 1980 foreign policy briefing, Reagan was to give a speech to the Council on Foreign Relations. As a theme for the speech, the advisory group suggested "peace through strength." Reagan adopted this slogan as his national security theme throughout the campaign and during his first term. He pledged presidential leadership to reverse the downhill slide in American prestige that had occurred during the Carter Administration. Reagan's vision was of a future based upon pride in America's past greatness. The advisory group wanted Reagan to convert the Carter window of vulnerability into a Reagan window of opportunity.

A second meeting of the foreign policy advisory group occurred after Reagan had secured the presidential nomination at the Republican convention in Detroit. On October 4, 1980, the group met with him in Virginia at Wexford—ironically, a former Kennedy estate near Middleburg. Reagan was to receive a briefing about the Iran-Iraq War from Admiral Stansfield Turner, then Director of Central Intelligence in the Carter Administration.[20] Reagan was to receive a "prebrief" in order to prepare him for the Turner briefing.[21] Several members of the advisory team had prior or current high security clearances through government service; hence, Reagan received a briefing of the highest order.[22]

As a result of the hostage crisis and the outbreak of the Iran-Iraq War on September 22, 1980, the October briefing at Wexford focused on the Gulf. The meeting discussed the hostage crisis, oil supplies transiting the Gulf, as well as implications of the war for the Arab-Israel conflict zone.

Henry Kissinger said that the strategic importance of the Gulf area was so great that the United States could not afford to remain hostile for long with any of the countries there. He took the position that there was no reason why a Reagan Administration could not work with Iran once the hostages were freed. Iran was such a vital country that hostility between Tehran and Washington should not be permanent. Admiral Thomas Moorer explained that Iran was the most populous of the oil-rich Gulf states and that it stood in the path of the search by the Soviet Union for warm-water ports to the south.

Kissinger added that the continuation of fighting between Iran and Iraq was in the American interest. As long as it did not facilitate enhanced ties between Moscow and either Baghdad or Tehran, the war served United States goals. The Iran-Iraq War prevented both countries from dominating one another or Gulf states like Saudi Arabia. In effect, Kissinger believed that the United States should capitalize on the continued hostilities.[23]

Kissinger not only blamed the Soviets for taking advantage of the Iran-Iraq War, he also implied that Moscow's activities may have been one of the causes of the war. Sensing a nod from Allen to take Kissinger to task, I challenged him regarding Soviet involvement in the fighting: "Document the intelligence to show that Moscow was the source of the initial conflict or cause for continuation of the war." Moreover, I argued that there were incentives for the Soviets to seek a role as interlocutor between Iran and Iraq. Just as Moscow had sought a mediator role in the hostilities between India and Pakistan, likewise the Soviets had a vested interest to be a peacemaker between Iran and Iraq. Kissinger strongly disagreed with my analysis. And then Reagan said, "I've never heard anyone defend the Russians!" The room erupted with laughter.

After the laughter subsided, we returned to the serious subject at hand: whether Moscow was behind the Iran-Iraq War or simply taking advantage of the fighting. Looking straight at me, Reagan portrayed the Russians as "burglars running down the halls of a hotel, searching for unlocked doors to enter." He turned to Alexander Haig, switched the metaphor, and cast Soviet leaders as "fishermen in troubled waters." Communists were always on the lookout for political instability that would provide an opening into strategically important countries like Iran. A nation that had just undergone a civil war and was experiencing an international conflict was ripe for Soviet intervention.

Pointedly ignoring Kissinger and focusing his eyes directly at Reagan, Haig weighed in with cogent remarks: Baghdad's successes in the Iran-Iraq War were driving Damascus closer to Moscow. In light of the historic enmity between Iraq and Syria, Damascus was aligned with Tehran. Baghdad's victories over Tehran drove Syria in the direction of the USSR for security and political support. Haig's bottom line was that the Soviets could gain a foothold in the Gulf not by subterfuge but by location and by prior support to radical regimes in Baghdad and Damascus. By siding with me against Kissinger, Haig may have bailed me out with Reagan.

Sensing that he was losing the support of Haig, Kissinger appealed to him directly, stating "I am sure that General Haig will agree with me that the Soviets were up to no good in the Gulf, and that they also were poised to exploit the instability there." Kissinger and Haig stared at each other in a standoff that surprised no one who knew their hostility toward one another. Finding no support in that corner, Kissinger appealed to Moorer. And the former chairman of the Joints Chiefs of Staff cheerfully clobbered the Communists for the sake of his old friend, Henry.

To persuade Reagan that, although the Soviets were seeking to take advantage of the fighting, they were not the source of it, I reminded the group of Kissinger's role as a mediator between Egypt and Israel in the 1970s. Then, Washington was not a source of the fighting but sought to gain strategic advantage by facilitating a peace process. I compared Kissinger's activities in the Middle East with the Soviet role in helping to settle the Indian-Pakistan War of 1971.[24] Regarding both cases, the United States and the USSR enhanced their influence with regional belligerents by furthering a peace process between them. In the context of a movement toward peace, neither the United States nor the Soviet Union had to choose between two strategically important states. Moscow could have good relations with Islamabad and New Delhi, while Washington could maintain close ties with Cairo and Jerusalem.

Appealing to his ego, I called Kissinger "the great peacemaker" whom the Soviets sought to emulate. Such flattery temporarily threw him off guard and caused him to grant the validity of a portion of my argument. With his usual self-deprecating humor, he said that he was forced to agree with at least one thing I had said—my characterization of him as "great." Whereupon Bush said, "Golly, this debate reminds me of a Yale seminar." Kissinger then commented that Harvard was a more apt reference, and I countered that, "This is a Michigan seminar conducted by a University of Michigan professor!"

After the laughter waned, Reagan raised the possibility of an arms-for-hostages trade. He asked about a potential trade of Iranian assets in the United States in exchange for American hostages in Tehran. This subject became politically explosive in his second term. Because Haig sat on the Board of United Technologies, his colleagues there asked about the possibility of sending military supply parts to Iran. And Moorer added that Vietnam had begun to sell Iran spare parts for American-origin F-4 aircraft. These parts had been left at the United States base in Danang after the hurried evacuation of American forces from Vietnam in 1975. Not one of the participants spoke out against the idea of arms for hostages, but the proposal did not seem so outrageous at that time. However, in view of the failed Iran-contra deal six years later, arms for hostages should have been a cause for alarm at the Wexford briefing.

Using Kissinger's remarks as a point of departure, Moorer discussed the likelihood of oil interruptions as a result of Gulf War fighting. He said that it was logistically impossible to close the Strait of Hormuz. The Wexford team then discussed sea lines of communications—the Strait of Hormuz as the "choke point" in the Gulf between Oman and Iran. Few believed that Tehran had the capacity to close down the Gulf to Western shipping. Whereupon, Kissinger quipped that President Carter was seeking political credit for keeping open what no one could close. He explained, "Carter has a tendency to discover what is not going to happen and then to act strongly to prevent it from occurring. And in resisting the unlikely, Carter creates an artificial crisis that provides a pretext for arguing that this is not the time to change presidents."

The attack on Carter took the immediate pressure off of me and provided a segue into the Arab-Israel conflict zone. I led the discussion on the 1973 war (Israel versus Egypt and Syria). Using the need to balance force and diplomacy as a theme, I began to compare the Iran-Iraq War with the 1973 war. But Kissinger cut in with the remark that in 1973, the United States had both force and diplomacy; in the 1980 war in the Gulf, the United States had less force and no diplomacy. Heads nodded in agreement, offering me another opening to complete the analysis. I pointed out that a year after the 1973 war, there were both oil-production cutbacks and a Saudi oil embargo of the United States, which led to a fourfold increase in the price of oil. When the Shah fell and Khomeni rose to power in 1978-1979, the price of oil only doubled. We surmised that the Iran-Iraq War could result in an increase in the price of oil. In fact, oil prices did go up by about 25 percent, but in nine months fell back to prewar prices.[25]

Former Ambassador Neumann also weighed in on the linkage between the Iran-Iraq War and the Arab-Israel conflict zone. He said the unresolved Palestinian issue was a barrier to good relations between the United States and Arab Gulf states. Kissinger, however, added that the Saudis were more afraid of Iraq and a radicalized Palestine Liberation Organization (PLO) than Israel. Kissinger thought that an Arab-Israel solution had to be a result of an American peace initiative, not the consequence of Arab radical military action like an Iraqi victory over Iran. Such a victory over Tehran could gain allies for Baghdad in its struggle against Jerusalem.

Kissinger also suggested an American military buildup in the region and an arms transfer policy that would restore the balance of power in Washington's favor. A favorable balance of military power would provide Riyadh with confidence to play both the Arab nationalist game of alignment with the radicals and the pro-Western game of aligning with Washington against Moscow and regional threats. Along the same lines, I said that Saudi Arabia provided funds to Arab radicals and oil at low prices to the United States as a form of risk insurance. Riyadh thought that paying off the PLO insured Saudi Arabia against terrorist attack. Selling oil to the United States and permitting Washington to defend them insured the Saudis against Soviet and Iraqi assault.

The Wexford team was also concerned about the long-term stability of Iran, irrespective of its capabilities and short-term intentions. Because of our emphasis on the Cold War, Reagan advisors saw Iran as a strategic asset. Despite animosity from Tehran, we still considered Iran to be on the U.S. side of the East-West divide. If Iraq succeeded in its goal of a de facto partitioning of Iran, that contingency could provide an opening for Moscow to intervene on the side of Tehran.[26]

Two schools of thought emerged at the October 1980 Wexford briefing. One mainly feared the contingency of an Iranian triumph; the other mostly feared an Iraqi victory. If Iran were winning the war, that would be an opening for the Soviet "burglars" on behalf of Iraq. That is, Baghdad would call on Moscow for military assistance, or even intervention. If Iraq were winning the war, this would not provide an opening for Soviet intervention on behalf of Iran. We believed that the Islamic Republic of Iran would not call upon Moscow. Tehran's anticommunist stance follows the principle, "Better green [Islamic] and dead than alive and red [Communist]." But the group also believed that Baghdad had accepted and would continue to accept assistance from both Moscow and Washington.

If Iran were winning the war, some former officials in the Wexford group expected that Baghdad would call upon Moscow and Washington for assistance. In order to prevent Soviet deployments from arriving first, the United States would need rapid deployment forces for Gulf duty. But, severe transit problems inhibited the movement of heavy American armor across the Atlantic, through the Mediterranean via the Suez Canal to the Arabian Sea, and through the narrow Strait of Hormuz into the Gulf. If called upon to defend Iraq without a conventional ground combat presence in the Gulf region, the United States would be in a difficult position. The group preferred that Washington defend Gulf states without relying on nuclear weapons. In short, the United States needed to have sea- and airlift capabilities for rapid deployment of conventional forces before the Soviets became entrenched.

Those in our group who feared an Iraqi victory more than an Iranian triumph were concerned with the Arab-Israel conflict zone. Former officials in the advisory group who favored a tilt toward Iraq wanted Baghdad to emerge victorious with American assistance.[27] Their eyes were on the effects of the Iran-Iraq War on the East-West struggle. I had the principal action to articulate the consequences of the war on the Arab-Israel zone. At that session, Allen had asked me to speculate on the impact of that war on Israel in particular. I said that Israelis preferred that no single power should exercise hegemony within the Arab world. Jerusalem did not want Baghdad to win a war against Tehran and then to dominate the Arab nation with what would have been a well-deserved high status. In this respect, I disagreed with those briefers who preferred an Iraqi victory with American assistance. Kissinger and I finally found common ground: an Iraqi triumph would not be in the American interest.

While elaborating on the negative consequences of an Iraqi suc-cess, I took the position at Wexford that the likelihood of an eastern front war against Israel declined to the degree that Iraq was preoccupied with its war with Iran. But if Iraq were successful against Iran, Baghdad might be in a position to mobilize rejectionists in the Arab world against Israel. Although there were major political problems between Baghdad and Damascus, Jerusalem considered both as threats on an eastern front. This front included the Palestine Liberation Organization, Syria, Jordan, Iraq, Saudi Arabia, and other Gulf states.[28]

I said that Jerusalem followed the principle, "The enemy of my enemy is my friend." Tehran and Istanbul as adversaries of Baghdad and Damascus should be friends of Jerusalem. Iran and Turkey were two states on the outside of the immediate confrontation arena of the Arab-Israel conflict. Israel historically has sought to maintain good relations with both as a counter to hostile Arab states on its borders. In this doctrine of the periphery, Israel tried to have good relations with non-Arab Muslim states on the perimeter of the Arab-Israel conflict zone. Israel's doctrine required that it cultivate an arms supply relationship with radical Iran, without jeopardizing its alignment with the United States.[29]

In the context of the discussion of collusion between Iran and Israel, Henry Kissinger discussed how he had directed the American tilt toward the Kurds of Iraq. The Nixon Administration, along with Israel and Iran, had supported the Kurds of Iraq as a way to pressure Baghdad, beginning in May 1972.[30] But Kissinger failed to say that in March 1975, as secretary of state in the Ford Administration, he had given blessings to a reduction in the tacit alignment that the coalition had with the Kurds. At that time, Saddam Hussein had met with the Shah of Iran in Algiers in order to sign a border accord. It called for Baghdad and Tehran to refrain from any further interference in the other's domestic affairs. Such an agreement meant that the American-Israel alignment with the Kurds of Iraq had ended. As a result, Iraqi Kurdish resistance to Baghdad collapsed on March 22, 1975. Thousands of Kurds who had trusted the American commitment died at the hands of Saddam as a result of the flip-flop in U. S. support.

The 1980 presidential campaign provided Kissinger with a forum to give his spin on history, perhaps in a bid to enter the Reagan Administration. The bottom line of his exposure to candidate Reagan at the briefings was that the president-elect asked Haig to be Secretary

58

of State, and Kissinger did not receive an offer to join the new administration. In order to bolster his anticommunist bona fides, however, Kissinger may have magnified the Soviet threat, toned down the danger from Iran, and made a persuasive case for a balance-of-power approach to the Gulf.

Campaign politics had a definite effect on the formulation of threat perception. During the 1980 campaign, the American sense of threat from the Middle East was even higher because dramatic events abroad coincided with the presidential political season. The electoral clock coincided with the aftermath of the Soviet invasion of Afghanistan, the fall of the Shah and rise of Khomeni, Americans held hostage in Iran, the Iran-Iraq War, East-West tensions, and stalemate in the Arab-Israel conflict. As an anti-Soviet campaigner who also seemed to take a harder line against Iran, in contrast to Carter, Reagan was able to take political advantage of the increased threat perception of the American people.

Domestic Politics Prevail Over Economic Profits

Executive-legislative branch conflicts are par for the course in the formulation of American foreign policy. But in the case of Iran, there is remarkably little disagreement between these two branches of government. As a result, the Iran and Libya Sanctions Act became law in a unanimous vote in the Congress, with only minor dissent after the vote. One voice was that of the Chairman of the Subcommittee on International Economic Policy and Trade of the House of Representatives.[31] He acknowledged that Iran was a rogue state; but he doubted if economic sanctions against foreign firms that invest in Iran were the best means to change its behavior. The Chairman claimed that sanctions intended to hurt Iran should not have the effect of targeting America's allies. Without their support and cooperation, sanctions would not be effective and might provoke allied retaliation. But he failed to realize that allied support is necessary in the context of sanctions for instrumental, not symbolic, goals. Insofar as symbolic objectives are paramount, the test is whether sanctions please domestic constituencies. And there was no doubt that they were satisfied by U.S. sanctions against Iran.

With respect to the role of interest groups in American foreign policy, ethnic and business groups clash in the formulation of policy toward Iran. The pro-Israel community and the American business sector represent the pro-sanctions and anti-sanctions schools of thought, respectively.

In the aftermath of the fall of the Shah and the rise of Khomeni, the pro-Israel community pressured successive presidents to magnify what might be called Israel's "enemy of the year." At various times, the main antagonist was Iraq, the PLO, Syria, Libya, or Iran. The Iranian threat was not a constant because Israel has had an on-again, off-again relationship with Iran. Even after the fall of the Shah and the takeover by militant anti-Zionist mullahs in Tehran, Jerusalem has formed occasional tacit alliances of convenience with Iran. Because the pro-Israel community is not as engaged in the nuances of a balance of power strategy as the government of Israel, that community has been more consistently and strongly anti-Iran than Jerusalem.

The bottom line is that the pro-Israel community perceives Tehran and Jerusalem as each other's enemies.[32] During the height of the Arab-Israel conflict, the main mission of the pro-Israel community was twofold: first, to facilitate the flow of economic and military assistance to Israel; second, to restrain the stream of aid to Arab regimes hostile to Israel. With the decline in intensity of the Arab-Israel conflict, there is less of a need to lobby for foreign aid just for Israel. Indeed, one task that interest groups friendly to Israel have initiated is to lobby Congress for aid to Arab states and the Palestinian Authority. As former enemies are being transformed into friends, so the pro-Israel community has become an advocate on Capitol Hill of assistance to an emerging "peace bloc."

In the post–Cold War era and as the Arab-Israel conflict winds down, U.S. foreign economic aid and military assistance budgets are becoming harder to justify. With Israel's comparative wealth, it has less of a need for American economic assistance.[33] To the extent that the threat from Arab confrontation states decreases with successes in the peace process, it is increasingly difficult to make a case for American military assistance to Israel.[34] Two developments occur as the Arab-Israel peace process reduces the traditional threat facing Israel. First, Jerusalem suggests Iran is its new "threat of the year."

Second, taking the lead from Jerusalem, the pro-Israel community in the United States pushes Capitol Hill to focus on the Iranian threat to both America and Israel.

The most influential representative of the pro-Israel community on Capitol Hill is AIPAC. In a paradoxical fashion, AIPAC uses crisis as an opportunity for increasing its clout. During 1981, it lost a major fight with the Reagan Administration over the transfer to Saudi Arabia of Airborne Warning and Control System (AWACS) aircraft. The loss on AWACS jolted AIPAC to become a superlobby. Its budget went up by a factor of eight in nine years, while its membership multiplied from 9,000 households during 1978 to 55,000 in 1987. AIPAC's leadership steered $4 million in campaign contributions to candidates friendly to Israel.[35] In other words, AIPAC's loss on AWACS was an opportunity for growth.

AIPAC used a second crisis as an occasion for change: the success of the peace process with the Palestinians. With the Oslo Accord of 1993, the Israeli government and the PLO began an exchange of autonomy for the Palestinians in return for peace to Israel. Following on the heels of Oslo was a peace treaty between Israel and Jordan. During the transition from the Arab-Israel conflict to a comprehensive peace settlement, AIPAC assists Jordan in obtaining foreign economic aid and military assistance from the Congress. AIPAC sought a new mission. Enter Iran. Although different from the traditional Arab-Israel threat, Tehran nevertheless is a useful tool for AIPAC's survival.

The Iran and Libya Sanctions Act sailed through Congress in 1996 because of AIPAC's lobbying and its new image as an "Iran-basher." AIPAC used the following argument in lobbying for the act. The organization claimed that Iran needed to be contained until Tehran moderated its behavior and ceased behaving like an international outlaw. American sanctions would impose a cost on the rogue behavior of Iran. The Tehran regime would be less able to devote resources to the export of international terrorism and would have less capital available for the development of weapons of mass destruction. Quarantined by the world, Iran would lack international legitimacy. The regime then would have to explain to the Iranian people how its policies have resulted in such adverse world reaction.

In addition, AIPAC argued that sanctions on Iran would escalate dissatisfaction with the Iranian regime. Economic problems had already contributed to growing discontent. Sanctions also would diminish the regime's ability to buy off or placate its internal opponents. Export and import controls would undermine support for the government by the military. A military deprived of contemporary equipment and technology might diminish support for the Islamic regime. Iran would have fewer resources for terrorism, the export of its Islamic revolution, building up its military forces, developing weapons of mass destruction, and opposing the Arab-Israel peace process.

Consider the relationship between AIPAC and the oil industry in regard to Iran. A noted private oil consultant, Christine Helms, director of country analysis for the Petroleum Finance Company, described the conflict between AIPAC and the industry over Iran. After President Clinton's Executive Order of May 1995, which banned most trade with Iran, she stated "U.S. companies—sensing that Clinton was strumming American chords in the countdown to elections—merely hunkered down in their trenches."[36]

Oil industry sources admitted to Helms that in light of AIPAC's role in formulating anti-Iran legislation, business groups were reluctant to join the battle. "Given AIPAC's involvement in stirring political waters," she wrote, "oil industry sources acknowledge they are reluctant to wade in too deep."[37] Why would businesses be afraid to take on an ethnic lobby? Perhaps the reluctance stems from fear of being accused of anti-Semitism and/or being on the wrong side of counterterrorism.

Shying away from a frontal assault on the pro-Israel community, oil analysts attack the Administration's policy of containment of Iran. The main line of argument is that in order to lower the price, more oil has to flow from as many sources and through as many different routes as possible. They reason that because of the American embargo of Iran, there is too great a dependence on oil from Arab Gulf states like Saudi Arabia and Kuwait. With flat production and increasing demand, prices are on the rise. Hence, there is a need to free the Iranian market from the constraints of the U.S. embargo. And regarding transportation of oil, the embargo makes it difficult for the West to tap the large oil reserves in the Central Asian states of Azerbaijan, Kazakhstan, and Turkmenistan. This oil would have to be shipped across the Caspian Sea, through Iran, then via the Gulf to emerging markets in Asia.[38] Despite the lobbying efforts of American firms and industry consultants, however, ethnic politics triumph over business economics. But the business community has had an impact on policy making.

Before the adoption of the Iran and Libya Sanctions Act, Undersecretary of State Peter Tarnoff repeated an argument of American business. He said on March 17, 1995, that the State Department was concerned about the effect of unilateral restrictions on Iran for American firms. He felt that such controls "could hurt Americans more than the government of Iran."[39] In other words, because the sanctions are unilateral, they are ineffective against the target but considerably risky for American firms. U.S. businesses believe that unilateral sanctions diminish their market opportunities and place them at a competitive disadvantage.

While AIPAC is a formidable foe of Iran in the war for Washington, there are business associations willing to work against anti-Iran legislation. Mobil Oil exemplifies the prevailing views of American firms toward international economic sanctions.[40] Mobil opposes sanctions because it contends that they fail to achieve their goals. The Petroleum Industry Research Foundation and the Middle East Institute are organizations in Washington that also were on the losing side of the Iran sanctions legislation. In discussing the oil market and economic sanctions, John Lichtblau, the chairman of the foundation, echoes the Mobil Oil argument concerning the ineffectiveness of punitive, unilateral American legislation regarding Iran.[41]

The business community concerned with American sanctions against Iran held a conference sponsored by the Petro-Hunt Corporation during May 1996 in Dallas, Texas. Several former Bush Administration cabinet officials were very critical of the Clinton Administration's approach of containing Iran because of the unilateral nature of the policy.[42] In addition to the tepid effort by the American business community, a convergence of domestic and bureaucratic politics reinforces the likelihood that politics prevail over profits. But politics also converge with counterterrorism ideals in the battle over whether to impose sanctions on rogue states and foreign firms dealing with them. Not surprisingly, politicians seek the moral high ground on rogue regimes, even if they leave American businesses "high and dry."

Bureaucratic Politics Prevail Over Economic Profits

To illustrate the political roots of American attitudes about Iran, consider an anecdote told by President Reagan. During a visit to the Department of Interior, he came across a bureaucrat from the Bureau of Indian Affairs who was crying. "Why are you crying?" asked Reagan. "My Indian died," answered the bureaucrat, "and now what am I to do with my life?" Imagine a Pentagon bureaucrat crying. Why? The threat from Moscow has waned. The USSR died, Russia was reborn, and the former constituent Soviet republics emerged as independent states. What does this official do in the absence of the Soviet threat? Enter Iran. Although less than a Cold War threat, Tehran nevertheless is a useful tool in bureaucratic battles over budget allocations.

The question arises whether the Pentagon engages in a deliberate and systematic overestimation of the Iranian threat for budget purposes. Under the psychological principle that motivated biases cause leaders to see what they want to see, that process would explain why American defense officials would magnify the Iranian threat.

According to the reasoning of those who accuse the Pentagon of threat magnification, the military needs a pretext to defend its budget. It is nonsense, however, to imagine that the Pentagon created an Iranian threat out of thin air just to serve its bureaucratic needs. Nevertheless, Michael Klare makes the case that the Pentagon virtually invented the Iranian threat, among others.[43] In discussing the nature of American post–Cold War strategy, Klare argues that the Pentagon manufactured a rogue state threat. He assumes that the policy of containment against the USSR shifted to containment of rogue states simply to maintain the approximate levels of defense spending of the Cold War years.

Without much evidence, Klare presumes that the Pentagon magnifies the rogue state threat for its own bureaucratic purposes. He holds that some officials seek "to invent a new *raison d'être* for the military establishment."[44] Congress and the public no longer support a Soviet-oriented military posture at a time of decreasing Russian capabilities. Therefore, Pentagon officials have developed an alternative strategic outlook based on non-Soviet threats to American security. He acknowledges that some rogue states do threaten global peace because of the proliferation of weapons of mass destruction and terrorism. But they were, in fact, engaged in these activities even before the rise of rogue state terminology. Consequently, he is on weak ground in suggesting that the Pentagon invented the rogue state threat and on even weaker ground in suggesting that rogue regimes only seek weapons of mass destruction and partake in terrorism because the United States singles them out.

Klare labels deliberate overestimation of threat, coupled with the desire to disrupt a peaceful status quo, as a rogue state doctrine. An alternative policy he prefers is "rogue state marginalization," a policy that would diminish the perceived importance of rogue states. In so doing, the United States would deny them the ability to serve as role models for potential rogue states. In order to induce outlaws to change their ways, Klare favors a policy of holding out increased rewards—economic assistance, trade, and investments.[45]

Because of Washington's practice of "demonizing the alien Other," says Klare, the United States overestimates the rogue state threat.[46] He may be correct that the Pentagon overestimates the Iranian threat somewhat and gains some budgetary advantage; he goes too far in stating that the Pentagon "invents" that threat. In any event, the psychological concept of motivated bias would explain threat magnification: you see what you want to see. Pentagon officials saw what they wanted to see—a threat that would fit the size of their budgetary needs.

RETRIBUTION TRUMPS REHABILITATION

In addition to bureaucratic and domestic politics as sources of decisions to impose sanctions, consider the rehabilitative and retributive goals of an embargo policy. Besides politics, idealism adds to the tendency of presidents to choose sanctions. Ideals provide an incentive for rehabilitation: American presidents believe they have a virtual fiduciary responsibility to change the behavior of foreign leaders, that is, to rehabilitate them. This tradition derives from the idea that occupants of the Oval Office have a right to sit in judgment over, and change the behavior of, their counterparts abroad. Presidents from Carter to Clinton have believed they were entrusted with the charge of transforming Iran's behavior. At least, however, they have not sought to remake the Iranian regime the way they intended for Cuba.[47] Presidents have accepted the Islamic nature of the Republic of Iran, but opposed the export of its revolution.

Regarding idealism and retribution, American presidents think they have the moral obligation to punish wrongdoing. In addition to using coercive sanctions against Iran, the United States has sought retribution—punitive action without regard to changing Tehran's behavior. In terms of domestic politics, retributive sanctions against Iran are gainful and risk-free: as soon as Washington inflicts harm on Tehran, sanctioning as a tool of retribution is effective. Such punishment has proved immediately gratifying to the presidents as well as to the pro-Israel community. But with regard to international politics, retributive sanctioning jeopardizes alliance unity.

In short, the U.S. embargo not only had an instrumental rehabilitative function—to change Iran's behavior—but also a symbolic retributive purpose—to signal Tehran and the pro-Israel community that wrongs were being righted. The only legitimate basis for imposing rehabilitative sanctions on Iran would be if it were acting "opportunistically," that is, because of a window of opportunity; rehabilitative sanctions would then be appropriate. But if Tehran were motivated by fear, then rehabilitation would be inappropriate. The only legitimate basis for punishing a person acting out of fear is retribution.

In the context of symbolic goals like retribution, it is unnecessary to evaluate the effectiveness of economic sanctions in changing a regime's behavior. They are effective because sanctions make interested domestic groups "feel good." While it is not mandatory to invoke a rehabilitative test, if one were to do so, the issue would be whether a policy that makes the American people feel good makes the regime in Tehran feel bad enough to alter its ways. Congress designed the Iran and Libyan Sanctions Act to achieve both retributive and rehabilitative objectives.

When leaders act because of a "window of opportunity," that is a metaphor for assuming that their conduct approaches the standards of "bounded rationality."[48] The window signifies freedom of choice for an actor to pursue expected gains. And when leaders act from a "basement of fear," that is a metaphor for assuming that their conduct is less rational. The basement psychology suggests restricted choice and minimization of expected losses. If leaders emphasize loss avoidance over gain, tools like economic sanctions may have counterproductive effects.

With this overview of retribution and rehabilitation, consider now an analysis of historical sanctions.

President Carter imposed sanctions on Iran during the hostage crisis of 1979.[49] His goal was to coerce Iran, that is, force the government to crack down on the so-called students who held U.S. citizens hostage in the American embassy in Tehran. Carter's sanctions were intended to be rehabilitative: they sought to change Iran's behavior. But because of the Iranian revolution, there was no "Iran" to coerce: the Shah was on the run, the government was in disarray, and mullahs were assassinating pro-Western military officers.[50] Because Iran lacked the quality of a unitary actor, American economic sanctions for rehabilitative purposes were irrelevant. Retribution for holding American hostages was the only legitimate basis for economic sanctions.

President Reagan imposed sanctions on Iran in 1987 during the Iran-Iraq War.[51] He wanted to compel Tehran to end its attacks on Gulf-bound Kuwaiti ships that had been reflagged as American vessels. In contrast to the disorganized Iran of the Carter years, Tehran then was more or less a unitary actor seizing a window of opportunity. As a result, Reagan's rehabilitative sanctions were an appropriate means to change Iran's aggressive behavior toward Kuwait. But once Iranian behavior became less offensive, the rehabilitative aim withered, leaving only the retributive goal of righting a wrong. Even after that first Gulf War ended in 1988, the Reagan sanctions remained. When controls stayed in effect after the attacks against Kuwaiti shipping ceased, these sanctions retained a retributive purpose. The persistence of sanctions when a threat has diminished suggests that retributive purposes are given greater weight than rehabilitative goals. In effect, retribution trumps rehabilitation.[52]

As a result of state-sponsored terrorism by Iran and its accelerated acquisition of weapons of mass destruction, President Clinton tightened the Reagan sanctions. Clinton issued two executive orders in the spring of 1995. And on August 5, 1996, he signed the Iran and Libya Sanctions Act, which institutionalized his 1995 executive orders into legislation and also expanded the sanctions to include firms from third countries.[53] Clinton prohibited American oil firms like Conoco from engaging in commercial transactions with Iran without an export license. In this regard, he designed these prohibitions as a deterrent to American investment in the oil and gas sectors of Iran. And the Iran and Libyan Sanctions Act of 1996 served as a deterrent to investment by foreign firms.

In addition to goals of retribution and rehabilitation, another aim is to weaken a rogue state challenger so that it is less able to carry out behavior deemed undesirable by a defender. Weakening an actor is equivalent to deterrence by denial, a method of diminishing the capabilities of a challenger in order to enhance the prospect for compliance.[54] There is little doubt that Iran is less capable of threatening its neighbors as a result of American sanctions.[55] In this respect, one of the achievements of the sanctions against Iran has been to force it to curtail its ambitious 1989 plan for the acquisition of a large-scale modern military. Tehran had proposed to purchase $10 billion in armaments during 1989-1994, mainly from the USSR. Hard currency military expenditures had to be cut in half during 1992-1994, when sanctions imposed by Washington hurt Tehran in the world capital markets. A reduction in military expenditures slowed down Iran's program to develop weapons of mass destruction, including ballistic missiles. Indeed, writes Iran expert Patrick Clawson, " . . . cash constraints explain why Iran was not able to take delivery on a submarine for two years, as well as the delays in acquiring more missile launching boats and modern mines."[56]

Designed to coerce Iran into ceasing its sponsorship of terrorism and stopping the development of nuclear, biological, and chemical armaments, the Clinton sanctions also had a domestic political bonus for him: they sent a signal to the pro-Israel community that wrongs were being righted. While the Reagan sanctions were retributive, Tehran provided Clinton with a rationale for a return to rehabilitative sanctions.

Clinton signed the Iran and Libya Sanctions Act less than a month after the midair explosion of TWA Flight 800 over waters near New York. Although there was no evidence at the time to link Iran to the downing of the aircraft, the conventional wisdom on Capitol Hill was to assume an Iranian connection. A bias toward inferring Iranian involvement suggests that retribution influenced decision making. Because the predisposition was to presume the worst of Iran, members of Congress blamed Tehran without waiting for proof. Furthermore, these politicians received domestic political kudos from the general American public and especially the pro-Israel community for tightening the sanctions on Iran.

Interests Under Siege: Intrinsic and Strategic

Intrinsic Interests at Stake. Contrary to the assumption that the pro-Israel community "invented" the Iranian threat, there indeed is a perceived danger from Iran as seen from within the United States government. American leaders believe that Iran threatens both intrinsic and strategic interests, which are two sides of the same coin under assault.[57] The Iranian menace threatens American civilians and military personnel in the Gulf—intrinsic interests. Iran also is a risk to other inherently valuable targets like Western petroleum products transiting the Gulf and other sea-lanes of communications.

An incident in Saudi Arabia exemplifies the Iranian threat to civilians as well as U.S. military personnel and installations. A fuel truck exploded on June 25, 1996, outside the northern fence of an apartment complex near an air facility at Dhahran, close to the eastern Saudi coast. The explosion killed 19 people and injured about 160 others. The facility housed F-15 and F-16 aircraft belonging to the anti-Iraq coalition's Joint Task Force, Southwest Asia, which includes American, British, French, and Saudi Arabian combatants. Besides U.S. Air Force personnel in the housing area, there were Army technicians who operated a Patriot missile air defense unit.

About 2,000 Americans were stationed at the Dhahran air facility.[58] They helped enforce the UN No-Fly-Zone over southern Iraq. Operation Southern Watch is intended to protect Shiite Muslims against Saddam's Sunni Muslim air force.[59] After the Gulf War, the

Shiite Muslims of southern Iraq challenged Saddam's rule, and he cracked down on the insurgents. Consequently, Washington designed Southern Watch in order to deter any further move by Baghdad against the south.

Iranian agents working with Saudi dissidents have intrinsic motives for attacking Americans in Saudi Arabia. U.S. civilian and military personnel are innately valuable to Washington. Hence, Tehran's motive could be to destroy what is of such inherent importance. But the same event can be of both intrinsic and strategic value. In this respect, a strategic aim is what would be gained from publicizing the bombing of U.S. military facilities in Saudi Arabia. Attacking such a facility calls attention to the American presence in the Kingdom and places pressure on the United States to reduce its postwar "occupation forces."

But the paradox of the Gulf War victory is a requirement for a semipermanent American combat presence in Saudi Arabia to monitor the No-Fly-Zone in southern Iraq. While triumph in the Cold War reduced the need for an American combat presence to contain the Soviet Union from penetrating the Gulf region, victory in the Gulf's "hot war" reinforced the need for deployment in Saudi Arabia.

Strategic Interests at Stake. Irrespective of the termination of the Cold War, the U.S. strategic interest in the Gulf is about the same— preserving the uninterrupted flow of petroleum to the world market at prices that are compatible with the economic growth of the industrialized democracies. The post–Cold War era only changed the source of danger; the strategic interests at stake remain constant. The external threat of the Soviet Union gave way to a regional threat from Iran and Iraq.

While there is a threat to intrinsic interests, there is also an Iranian danger to U.S. strategic interests. These include the credibility of America's threat to use military force; its resolve to remain engaged in the world; as well as the commitment to defend its friends against its foes.[60] To the extent that Tehran stands up to Washington, it challenges U.S. credibility, resolve, and commitment. One means by which Tehran confronts Washington is through state-sponsored terrorism. Not only does Iran target American citizens, it also directs terrorism against the Iranian political opposition at home and abroad. Insofar as the domestic opposition derives from Iranians who were associated with the Shah's regime and thus tarred by the American brush, Tehran's attacks are assaults on U.S. strategic interests.

After the rise of Khomeni and the seizure of American citizens as hostages in Tehran, occupants of the Oval Office perceived Iran as an "evil" nation of international terrorists. This perception constitutes an unmotivated bias that associates Iran with malice, irrespective of its behavior. Thus, any president perceives Iran's current conduct as malicious without evaluating that behavior on its own merits. Such misperception is an overestimation of the threat posed by Iran's behavior.

Threat magnification notwithstanding, Iran deserves its status as a repeat offender on the annual Department of State list of nations that sponsor global terrorism.[61] In order to export terror throughout the global village, the regime formed the Supreme Council for Coordination of the Islamic Revolution. Activities of such an Islamic council may have been discussed during a meeting in Paris during mid-June 1996.[62]

There were reports from Paris that Egyptian President Hosni Mubarak presented a confidential file to French President Jacques Chirac. The file supposedly contained information on a secret conference in Tehran between leaders of terrorist organizations and Iranian intelligence. Reports indicated that the participants discussed plans to carry out systematic attacks directed mainly at American targets. Hezbollah's senior leadership used the conference to establish an organized international terrorist association that would incorporate all of its branches in approximately 15 countries.[63]

Iran's Supreme Council may have been behind several incidents abroad that endangered American strategic interests. With respect to the threat to Iranian opposition forces, several defectors have been assassinated in countries throughout the region, such as Pakistan.[64] And concerning the threat against American allies, Iranian-sponsored Hezbollah combatants in southern Lebanon periodically launch rocket assaults on northern Israel. Iran provides arms, training, and money to the Lebanese Hezbollah, which, in turn tries to derail the Middle East peace process.[65] In addition to being the leading suspect in the October 1983 bombing of the American Marine barracks in Beirut, and the 1994 bombing of a building housing Jewish organizations in

Buenos Aires, Argentina, Hezbollah may have been involved in the bombing of Iranian dissidents in Pakistan.[66]

Iran, furthermore, encourages Palestinian groups that reject the peace process with Israel, such as Hamas.[67] Additionally, there is the Popular Front for the Liberation of Palestine-General Command (PFLP-GC).[68] U.S. intelligence officials reported on a June 1996 meeting in Tehran of suspects in airline bombings, at which representatives of the PFLP-GC reportedly requested permission to carry out terrorist attacks against U.S. interests. This meeting occurred one month prior to the July 17 midair explosion of TWA Flight 800 departing from New York for Paris.[69] Because of Iran's role in slowing down the Arab-Israel peace process, Tehran poses a threat to United States strategic interests in furthering it.

In addition to supporting the PFLP-GC, Tehran provided a safe haven to the Kurdistan Workers' Party (PKK) after various attacks against Turkey and Westerners traveling there. The Islamic Republic of Iran also supported Turkish Islamic groups suspected of assaults against secular Turks and Turkish Jews. And the State Department surmises that Tehran is guilty of using terrorism to destabilize friendly regimes in Algeria, Egypt, and Tunisia.[70] To the degree that Washington is unable to provide security for its allies and friends from the Iranian threat of terrorism, Tehran poses a threat to United States strategic interests in the Middle East.

In addition to the worldwide confrontation between Iran and the United States over international terrorism, there is a direct confrontation in the area lying between Bosnia and Baghdad. A strategic aim of both Iran and the United States is to extend their separate authorities in this geopolitical sphere. This "region" is the only part of the world where American military forces are on the increase. The U.S. military has conducted operations in support of Bosnian and Afghani Muslims. Tehran has interpreted the American military presence on behalf of the Muslims under siege as a direct threat to its own authority. As the presumed leader of a supposedly emerging Islamic empire, Tehran believes that it, not Washington, has the responsibility to protect Muslims. Rather than acknowledging the American contribution to Muslim security, Tehran berates Washington as the "Great Satan," who acts on behalf of "Little Satan," Israel.

Yet, in two Muslim wars, Washington and Tehran had a tacit alignment. Both sponsored the Islamic Mujahadeen in Afghanistan against the Soviet occupation. Both Iran and the United States supported the Bosnian Muslim regime against Christian Orthodox Serbia and the Bosnian Serbs. In Afghanistan, the CIA provided covert assistance to Islamic rebels fighting against the Soviets. So did Iran. In the former Yugoslavia, the United States supported the Bosnian Muslims. So did Iran.[71] Washington gave a green light for Zagreb to receive arms from Tehran en route to Sarajevo.[72] Despite rejecting the American role in Afghanistan and Bosnia, Iranian Revolutionary Guards and their Saudi brethren fought in Muslim wars against the Soviets in Afghanistan and against the Serbs in Bosnia.

But Iran was not only at war with the USSR via proxies in Afghanistan. During February 1982, there also was growing cooperation between Tehran and Moscow in the field of arms trade. When Western nations showed a reluctance to deal with the religious extremists of Iran, the Soviets began to make inroads. Unable to find a secure source of Western arms, Tehran sought arms wherever it could find them. In addition to approaching American arms merchants on a regular basis, Iranian representatives also made the rounds of arms bazaars in Eastern Europe. And there were some 2,000 Soviet advisers in Iran, as well as about 75 Cubans. Iranians were increasingly confident that they could handle such Soviet ties and still export their own revolution to places like Riyadh and Mecca.

Upon returning to Saudi Arabia from the Afghanistan war against the Soviets and from the Bosnian crusades, the Saudi fighters became dissidents. They used the presence of non-Muslims in Saudi Arabia as a means to challenge the Saud family dynasty. The Saudi dissidents opposed both Saudi Arabia's close ties with non-Muslim countries and its failure to observe Islamic tenets. The primary non-Muslims under fire in Saudi Arabia are American military personnel. The dissidents are ardent readers of the London-based Saudi, Mohammed al-Masari, who publishes reports documenting human-rights abuses and excesses of the Saudi ruling family.

Initially, Riyadh accused Saudi dissidents of being responsible for a prior bombing of the Saudi National Guard installation in Riyadh on November 13, 1995. In the next year, Saudi Arabia pointed fingers at both Iran and Syria as sources of assistance for the Saudi dissidents. That assault was the first political attack against the American military in Saudi Arabia. The Kingdom "convicted" four dissidents and beheaded them. One motive for the June 25, 1996, attack was to avenge these beheadings.

In addition to protecting friends against the threat of Iranian terrorism, American strategic interests include coercing Iran to cease its development of weapons of mass destruction, including nuclear, biological, and chemical armaments. A purpose of such weapons is to enable Iran to deter attacks from states like Iraq. The two neighbors fought a war of the cities from 1980 to 1988, in which they both employed weapons of mass destruction. Additionally, possession of nuclear, biological, or chemical armaments would allow Tehran to coerce neighbors like Saudi Arabia. The two explicitly negotiate or tacitly bargain over issues like Iranian pilgrims visiting Saudi holy sites, oil production quotas, as well as the presence of U.S. combat personnel in the Kingdom.

Tehran seeks to import sophisticated weapons systems and expand its own internal capabilities. Iran has the ability to obtain a nuclear device from a former Soviet republic, such as Muslim Kazakhstan, which possessed nuclear weapons. But to acquire such a device on its own could take some five years.[73] Whether with outside assistance or not, there are Central Intelligence Agency reports to indicate that Iran may have a nuclear weapon by the year 2000.

Iran has a larger stockpile of chemical weapons than nuclear or biological armaments. Chemical weapons, however, are not as lethal as either the nuclear or biological hazard. Tehran began acquiring chemical arms in its war with Baghdad. The Islamic Republic stockpiled mustard gas as well as blood and nerve agents. But Tehran has also initiated limited production of biological weapons. It is creating an infrastructure to sustain biological arms at places ostensibly engaged in pharmaceutical research.[74]

Regarding systems to deliver weapons of mass destruction, Beijing and Pyongyang are selling ballistic missiles to Tehran. While the Islamic Republic has the ability to produce its own ballistic missiles, it prefers to import them from sources like China and North Korea. Iran's inventory consists of about 450 Scud-B and Scud-C missiles. Not satisfied to rely on these limited-range systems, Tehran is obtaining longer-range, solid-fuel missiles. Intelligence analysts expect Iran in 1996-1997 to take delivery on North Korea's Rodong ballistic missile, which has a range of about 800 miles, thus bringing most of the Middle East into Tehran's missile envelope. This range, coupled with the capacity to deliver weapons of mass destruction, will enable Tehran to emerge as a world-class strategic threat to the United States.

In short, in order to counter the coercive potential of Iranian armaments, Washington has a strategic interest in preventing Tehran from acquiring weapons of mass destruction. Presidents have acted upon this strategic interest, whether directed at Iran, Iraq, or other rogue regimes. In the history of American-Iranian relations, several presidents have formulated what might be called doctrines regarding the Gulf in general and Iran in particular. A discussion of these approaches should assist in the process of understanding the use of economic sanctions as a tool of choice by American presidents in their relations with the Islamic Republic of Iran.

A Tale of Presidential Doctrines

Although presidents do not label their policies as doctrines, it is possible to outline the defining characteristics and label them as such. Here is a brief overview of these policies toward the Gulf, with special emphasis on Iran.

Presidential doctrines vary according to the extent to which American regional allies act as proxies, the degree of U.S. resolve, and the overall balance of military power in the area. As Cold War Presidents, Nixon and Carter focused on the external threat from the Soviet Union. During the transition to the post–Cold War era, Presidents Reagan, Bush, and Clinton emphasized the internal threat from the Gulf region.[75]

Nixon Doctrine—Containment of the USSR with the Twin Pillars. In view of the 1971 British military withdrawal from the area east of Suez, the Nixon aim was to reinforce American strategic nuclear deterrence of the Soviet Union. The method was to strengthen U.S. regional proxies—Iran and Saudi Arabia.[76] A twin pillars policy provided justification for supplying arms to Tehran and Riyadh so that each could act as props to hold up Western interests in the Gulf. In 1969, Nixon acknowledged the declining ability of the United States to take unilateral action in defense of its regional allies. Consequently, he put them on notice that they would have to shoulder more of the burden. Military assistance was the tool of choice in order to facilitate allied defense initiatives. Faced with fighting the Vietnam War, Nixon formulated a policy that would encourage U.S. allies to participate in their own defense and minimize the American role.

Carter Doctrine—Containment of the USSR Via American Resolve and Rapid Deployment Force. President Carter issued a statement of intent to intervene in the event of a Soviet military move in the Gulf. With the withdrawal of the British and the Soviet invasion of Afghanistan in 1979, the USSR had an imbalance of power in its favor in the Gulf region. Moscow could stage combat aircraft from airfields in Afghanistan. In the contingency of a Backfire bomber attack on U.S. naval forces in the Arabian Sea, Soviet use of Afghanistan would extend the range of fighter protection for that aircraft.[77]

Consequently, Carter said that he would act to prevent a takeover of that region by any hostile outside power.[78] The President's aim was to show resolve in order to deter a Soviet move into Iran from the Caucasus or Afghanistan.[79] The problem was, however, that the United States lacked the capability in the Gulf region to implement the Carter Doctrine.

During the summer of 1980, tensions increased between Iran and Iraq. But the United States focused on the possibility of a Soviet military intervention of the Gulf area. Washington downplayed the likelihood of an Iran-Iraq War. In effect, Carter held that he would not allow the Soviets to do to Iran what they had done to Afghanistan.

Reagan Corollary—Balance of Power Between Iran and Iraq to Preserve Stability of Saudi Arabia. The fall of the Shah of Iran in 1978 and the subsequent rise of the Ayatollah gave Reagan an occasion to issue what analysts later dubbed the Reagan Corollary of the Carter Doctrine. The United States would use military force in the Gulf region not only to make sure that oil flowed freely but also to ensure that the regime in

Saudi Arabia would be safe from internal and external threats. It was important that American-supplied armaments, such as the Airborne Warning and Control System (AWACS), not fall into unfriendly hands. The Iranian scenario should not be repeated. When the Shah fell, American military equipment came into the hands of anti-American Iranian radicals. Reagan vowed to use military force if necessary to foreclose the Iranian scenario.

In short, the Reagan Corollary stated that President Reagan would not allow the Iranian revolution to spread to Saudi Arabia. He would not permit Riyadh to move away from Washington because of a change of regime.[80] Reagan would not allow Saudi Arabia to go down the same path as Iran, e.g., for a revolution to overthrow a friendly regime and for the successors to oust the United States from a position of influence.

But just as President Carter asserted the Carter Doctrine to protect the Gulf area without the military forces to back it up, President Reagan asserted a commitment to Saudi Arabia without having the political or military capabilities to back up that undertaking. Although the Saudi monarchy is more stable than the Shah's regime, the forces that assassinated Sadat of Egypt during October 1981 were operating in Saudi Arabia two decades later. If there were a coup in Saudi Arabia and the new rulers wanted to slow down oil production and accommodate Islamist opponents, there would be little justification for United States military action to save the regime. Additionally, a commitment to the Saud regime commits Washington to shore up a family whose future is bleak in light of the social and economic forces that are on the rise there. And the United States lacks the capability to stop a coup from opposition groups, including a military coup of competing elites within the Royal family.

One way to protect Saudi Arabia from Iran or Iraq was for the United States to act as a "balancer" between the two. The United States provided tacit support to either so that neither could dominate the Gulf. However, once Iran became hostile to the United States and Iraq invaded Iran in 1980, Washington acted as the "holder of the balance" in the Gulf. It initially tilted toward Iraq.[81] But when Reagan sent U.S. arms to Iran in exchange for American hostages held in Lebanon by terrorist allies of Tehran, Washington tipped toward Tehran.

Bush Doctrine—Balance of Power between Iran and Iraq to Preserve Security of Saudi Arabia. In the post–Cold War era, the Bush Administration continued the Reagan policy of acting as holder of the balance between the two enemies. Bush first leaned toward Iraq by selling it dual-use equipment, removing it from the terrorist list, providing import subsidies, and encouraging the country to play a major role in the Arab-Israel peace process.[82] With the Iraqi invasion of Kuwait, Bush "drew a line in the sand," with the deployment of American ground combat forces to the Arabian peninsula.[83]

Bush, in effect, stated that he would not allow the Iraqis to do to Saudi Arabia what they had done to Kuwait. Following the defeat of Iraq, American ground troops remained in order to deter Baghdad and monitor the terms of the cease-fire. Although the purpose was deterrence, American combat forces created a predominance of military power that could be used to contain either Baghdad or Tehran.

Clinton Doctrine—From Balance of Power to Dual Containment. The United States will refrain from the Reagan-Bush balance of power approach of tacitly supporting either Iran or Iraq in an attempt to thwart expansion by the other.[84] The basic purpose of dual containment is to counter the threats of both Baghdad and Tehran. The Administration has sought to fashion an approach specific to each country, as separate threats.[85]

A balance of power assumption is that the "holder" should keep its options open regarding whether to have political relations with states in a region. Depending upon the balance in the area at any particular time, the balancer may intervene to prevent either state from dominating third parties. Iran's traditional aspirations to become a regional hegemon have in the past been kept in check by a rough balance of power with Iraq. Baghdad could count on the support of its Arab neighbors in any conflict involving Arabs and Persians.[86] U.S. policy under Reagan and Bush was in the British balance of power tradition of preventing the emergence of any hegemonic power in the Gulf capable of controlling the production and pricing policies of the oil-producing states.

Contrary to the Reagan-Bush balance of power policy is an approach that rules out political relations on ideological grounds. The Clinton doctrine of dual containment rejects the balancing assumptions in favor of an ideological approach to Iran and Iraq. This ideological rigidity contrasts sharply with the flexibility of the balancing approach. But the principal flaw of dual containment is the assumption that it is possible to contain both Iran and Iraq at the same time, without making use of the hostility of the one against the other.[87]

Isolation of Tehran assumes a comparatively powerful and united Iraq on the Islamic Republic's extensive western frontier; if not, Iraq becomes a tempting location from which Tehran can seek to escape containment. Likewise, isolation of Iraq assumes Iranian complicity. In this respect, multilateral economic sanctions on Baghdad would not be very effective if Tehran refused to enforce the embargo. Indeed, during the summer of 1996, these two states had a de facto economic alignment that allowed some Iraqi oil to be shipped across Iranian borders contrary to United Nations restrictions against such shipments.

Additionally, dual containment encourages Iran and Iraq into a de facto political alignment against the United States. But a rogue state alliance is precisely not the goal of American policy; the Clinton Administration's aim is to separate and isolate Iran and Iraq not only from the rest of the world, but from each other. Paradoxically, the Clinton policy pushes Tehran and Baghdad together. Fortunately for the Administration, local forces work to separate these two states.

With respect to local populations, Iran and Iraq compete for allegiance of the Kurds along their borders. But the Kurds in northern Iraq divide into two competing groups. The Patriotic Union of Kurdistan and the Kurdistan Democratic Party have appealed for assistance from Iran and Iraq, respectively. As a result of Iranian intervention on the side of the Patriotic Union in the Iraqi city of Irbil, Saddam's ground troops attacked that city on the weekend beginning August 30, 1996. In launching this assault, however, Iraqi forces violated the Western-protected safehaven above the 36th parallel. The United States responded with a cruise missile attack.[88]

In light of the dual containment policy, it would be hypocritical for the United States to intervene on behalf of Iranian-supported Kurds in Iraq. This approach does not permit Washington to align temporarily with Tehran in order to thwart Baghdad. Because of dual containment, the Administration is on the horn of a dilemma. On the one hand, acceptance of Baghdad's violations would leave Iraqi forces in control of a portion of a haven that was supposed to be safe from them. On the other hand, American attacks against Iraqi forces in the safehaven would aid Kurds aligned with Tehran, contrary to dual containment's requirement to isolate Iran.

In order to avoid these unacceptable options, the Administration chose to launch cruise missile strikes against Iraqi defense installations in the south. In doing so, Washington sought to avoid either rewarding Baghdad or aligning with Tehran. But in fact, the attacks only weakened Iraqi capabilities in the south and left Saddam's forces in control of the safehaven. Despite Clinton's claim that the cruise missiles were a success, they did not resolve the dilemma.

Dual containment also places a disproportionate political problem on Saudi Arabia. By housing the American forces that implement the military aspects of the containment policy for both states, Riyadh assumes the burden of retaliation from both neighbors. The number of troops required to enforce the No-Fly-Zone in southern Iraq is fewer than the number needed to monitor it and to deter Tehran. And if there were an Iranian connection to the June 1996 bombing of an American military installation in Saudi Arabia, that could be payback for Riyadh's collusion with Washington.

Dual containment is a flawed policy. It is indicative of the failure of the Clinton Administration to come to grips with regional and local factors that sustain conflicts in the Gulf, absent the external threat from the Soviet Union. As Cold War presidents, Nixon and Carter successfully dealt with the external threat posed by the USSR. And during the transition to the post–Cold War era, Presidents Reagan and Bush managed the internal threat from the region. A return to the flexibility inherent in the balance of power policy of the Reagan and Bush years would allow Washington to make use of changing circumstances in the Gulf. Dual containment does not permit external actors to take advantage of future political instability in the region. A balance of power approach would permit the United States to make flexible adjustments in policy by temporarily siding with either Iran or Iraq.

While the United States sought to build consensus within the international community and regional allies to contain both rogue states, it succeeded only in the case of Iraq. Containment of post–Gulf

War Iraq is an international strategy based upon UN resolutions. Containment applied to Iran, however, is problematic because the allies are reluctant to isolate Tehran.

In short, another assumption of the Clinton doctrine of dual containment is that the allies would help enforce it. Failure to persuade the allies to boycott Iran has led to a situation in which they must accept the American approach or be in public dispute with the United States. By punishing foreign firms that invest in Iran above a threshold determined in Washington, the United States seeks in vain to compel its allies to accept dual containment.

American Politics and Idealism Trump Alliance Obligations

There is a convergence of bureaucratic and domestic politics with idealism and perceived interests. As a result, alliance obligations have less influence on American policy regarding terrorism and weapons of mass destruction. In this respect, the Pentagon's threat perceptions, the pro-Israel community, counterterrorism ideals, and principles against proliferation prevail.

Even though the allies oppose designating countries as rogues, opposition was comparatively mild when Secretary of State George Shultz placed Iran on the list of states that sponsor international terrorism on January 13, 1984.[89] He thereby subjected Tehran to a set of antiterrorism laws, which included the Anti-Terrorism and Effective Death Penalty Act of 1996. In a prohibition of assistance to terrorist states, this Act imposes penalties upon U.S. "persons" (individuals or firms) who engage in financial transactions with a country knowing, or having reason to know, that it has been designated under the Export Administration Act as a country supporting international terrorism.[90]

Because Americans are the subjects of the 1996 antiterrorism law, the allies have little problem with its prohibitions. What is at issue for them in the Iran and Libya Sanctions Act is that Washington applies its laws to "any person," for example, either people or foreign firms trading or investing with Iran or Libya.[91] In response to the act, the European Union voiced its strong opposition. It claimed that the Iran/

Libya legislation was a case of extraterritorial application.[92] The Union criticized the act under the assumption that it would allow a president to impose sanctions, even if the relevant parties were located outside of the United States and the transactions involved no American financial instruments or technology.

The act is a secondary boycott, a ban against firms that fail to comply with a primary sanction like the United States boycott of Iran.[93] But the Iran and Libya Sanctions Act may be more like the Arab League boycott of Israel than it is like the Cuban Liberty and Democratic Solidarity Act against Cuba.[94] It gives U.S. citizens the right to sue foreign companies that traffic in Cuban property formerly owned by Americans. Because foreigners who acquire confiscated property are liable to prosecution under American laws, the act is an illustration of extraterritoriality.[95] Therefore, the Cuban Liberty and Democratic Solidarity Act may be a more extreme application of extraterritoriality than the Iran and Libya legislation, due to the involvement of U.S. courts.[96]

In connection with the imposition of penalties against foreign persons, there are previous cases in American laws. Here is legislation that contains precedents for the application of sanctions against foreign persons: the Foreign Relations Authorization Act of 1994 and the Arms Export Control Act of 1967. The Missile Technology Control Regime (MTCR) provisions in the Arms Export Control Act apply to foreign persons. The penalties deny future U.S. government contracts to persons in violation of the MTCR. In addition, they lose the right to export goods and services to the United States.[97]

Other precedents for imposing sanctions against foreign persons include the Anti-Economic Discrimination Act of 1994 and the National Defense Authorization Act for 1993. They penalize foreign persons who support the Arab boycott of Israel.[98] These two acts restrict the departments of State and Defense from doing business with foreign persons who are in compliance with the Arab boycott of Israel.

Because of the U.S. assertion of legal precedents for its secondary boycott regarding Iran and Libya, the European Union passed its own regulations, which make it difficult for its member states to comply with the American boycott. In addition, the Union threatened to mount a legal challenge to the United States through the General

Agreement on Tariffs and Trade (GATT) and the World Trade Organization (WTO). The European Union Council of Foreign Ministers called for a WTO dispute settlement panel that would deal with the issue of extraterritoriality.[99] But the American view is that because the GATT permits a signatory state to adopt measures to protect its national security, the GATT allows economic sanctions by member states.[100]

Legal issues notwithstanding, the European Union, " . . . fails to see why the United States needs to hit out at its friends while targeting its adversaries."[101] It is because of a convergence of politics, idealism, and perceived interests that Washington hurts its friends while targeting its enemies. Despite Iran's attempt to divide America from its allies, however, the battle is still mainly between Washington and Tehran.

SCENARIOS

Three broad scenarios are relevant to an understanding of the future of American-Iranian relations: limited war based on dual containment, differentiated containment, and a grand bargain.

Limited War: Dual Containment

Washington could find Tehran to be responsible for the bombing of American citizens in Saudi Arabia. The president might order retaliatory air strikes against terrorist bases in Iran. Tehran might answer with naval attacks against U.S. assets in the Gulf, American citizens abroad, and installations within the United States. Because of the constraint on American policy due to dual containment, Washington would be unable to play off Baghdad against Tehran. But Iraq might take advantage of a limited conflict between its two adversaries to move against the Kurds in the north or the Shiites in the south. Also, Iran and Iraq might confront each other over Iranian dissidents in southern Iraq. Violations of the No-Fly-Zone in the south could result in Coalition attacks against Iraqi aircraft and U.S. strikes against Iran. The cost of even a limited war is so great, however, that both Tehran and Washington are likely to take steps to limit escalation and expansion. While the likelihood of a war scenario is low, skirmishes over the No-Fly-Zone are likely.

Differentiated Containment: Balance of Power?

In addition to limited war, differentiated containment also is plausible. There is a growing dissatisfaction with dual containment and a reluctance to accept an explicit return to balance of power. How is it possible to achieve the national security benefits of balance of power without incurring its domestic political costs? The answer: differentiated containment.[102]

Leaders in the move away from dual containment include two former national security advisors and a former assistant secretary.[103] Their argument in favor of differentiated containment is simple: contain Saddam, but take actions regarding Iran in order to keep the anti-Saddam coalition united. The nuanced approach would acknowledge that Washington's efforts at unilateral isolation of Iran are costly and ineffective. Differentiated containment concerning Iran would include tradeoffs.[104] Those who advocate differentiated containment, however, divide into two camps. One approach would be to deny Iran an unconventional weapons capability. The other approach would relax opposition to Iran's nuclear program. The second school would pay less attention to the Iranian nuclear threat in exchange for Tehran's agreement to comprehensive international inspection and control procedures. The possibility of a tradeoff in the nuclear area suggests prospects for a grand bargain across the entire spectrum of American-Iranian relations.

A Grand Bargain:
Capital for Terror and Arms Control

Both Washington and Tehran use weapons of choice in confrontations with one another. Export controls on investments are tools of the capital-rich to take advantage of the susceptibility of the capital-poor; the export of international terrorism is a weapon of the weak to exploit the vulnerability of the strong. Because the United States is a primary source of global capital, it employs economic sanctions to constrain international investment in Iran. Tehran is a regional power with a capacity for exporting its revolution worldwide; it engages in state-sponsored terrorism against the United States. Exporting terrorism is an Iranian tool of choice befitting its aspirations to become a fountain-head for the Islamic revolution.

While exporting terrorism is a way by which Iran can spread the ideology of its revolution, importing equipment for the develop-ment of weapons of mass destruction is a means for the country to catapult its way into Great Power status. The acquisition of nuclear, biological, and chemical armaments is a method to achieve an equality of deterrent and coercive potential with the United States, at least in the Gulf region. Just as revolutionary ideologues are reluctant to give up the option of resorting to state-sponsored terrorism, so the more secular-oriented officials may be hesitant to give up what Iranians may perceive as a great equalizer—weapons of mass destruction.[105]

The currency for Washington is capital for investment and relief from its embargo; the currency for Tehran is cessation of its campaign of terrorism and weapons proliferation as well as a commitment to keep its oil production and pricing free from politics. At issue is whether there can be a currency exchange—a grand bargain between the two confrontation states. Is there a potential for an accord that would trade a piece of capital for a piece of peace? Doubtful. As long as each state derives both national security and domestic political benefits from confronting the other, there is little prospect for such a bargain. Idealism motivates both Tehran and Washington. Hence, there is scant potential that these new enemies can resume their old friendship. And within Iran, revolutionary ideologues may have reached an accommodation with their secular competitors: the reli-gious faithful can export the revolution; the secular military can have its weapons systems.

The Iran and Libya Sanctions Act, moreover, also contains seeds for an exchange. For a cessation of Iranian terrorism, conventional military buildup, and acquisition of weapons of mass destruction, there is an implicit promise of a removal of American sanctions. In the currency exchange proposed here, there would be an explicit pledge of sanctions removal. More important, there would be a promise of capital investment. For its part, Iran would have to cease the practice of terrorism, reduce its conventional armaments, and dismantle its rudimentary nuclear, biological, and chemical components.

On the one hand, the allies would be somewhat optimistic regarding the prospects for a currency exchange between Tehran and Washington. Iran projects a moderate image of itself to the allies in order to enhance the prospects of business relations with them. The State Department views this quest for respectability as an explanation why Tehran reduced its attacks in Europe during 1995: "Tehran wants to ensure Western capital and markets."[106] The Europeans claim that their "critical dialogue" with Iran yields dividends. They take a critical posture toward Iran's misbehavior, while they maintain normal commercial and political relations. The allies would argue that if Iran decreases its terrorist assaults in order to gain access to European and Japanese capital and markets, perhaps Tehran would be willing to do the same with respect to Washington.

On the other hand, the United States would be pessimistic concerning the possibility of a bargain. For Washington, there is no question that Iran is disingenuous regarding its moderate posture and should not be trusted. American officials believe that Tehran is making a tactical, short-term reduction in its practice of terror in order to gain capital and market access.[107] Iran still retains its long-term use of terror as a strategic weapon, while making a tactical accommodation for the moment. Washington assumes that Tehran's moderate posture is a ploy to gain short-term advantage with the European Union, Japan, and Canada in their disputes with the United States over Iran.

Because of Iran's subterfuge, critics may view the idea of a currency exchange as appeasement. In contrast to the appeasement policy implicit in the arms-for-hostages tradeoff, the exchange of investment capital for a cessation of terrorism and proliferation is more demanding on Tehran. The arms/hostages arrangement gave Iran an incentive to seize hostages in order to gain additional armaments. A capital-for-terrorism/proliferation arrangement would place the ball in Tehran's court: only in the context of a reduction in terrorism and arms acquisition would there be a corresponding cutback in economic sanctions. The pain would remain before Iran received the gain.

In the arms-for-hostages swap, there was no new pain for Iran but a high prospect for a weapons gain. In the capital-for-terrorism/proliferation bargain, the gain would only come after the terror ceased and the pain ended. In short, an incremental reduction in terrorism and proliferation would be a necessary condition for a gradual decrease in sanctions; success of this tit-for-tat process would mean an end to the Iranian terrorism threat and weapons buildup. Only then could investment capital flow freely to Iran from capital-rich Europe, Japan, and North America.

As the emerging markets of Asia require more oil to fuel explosive growth, Iranian oil could help meet the demand and keep prices low. Such an achievement could allow new enemies to rekindle their old friendships. Furthermore, the inflexible policy of dual containment should revert back to the flexible balance of power approach. America can act as a balancer between Iran and Iraq and contain both better than it can contain one or the other at the same time.

Recall the four themes that cut across *Rogue Regimes*: threat perception, opportunities, politics, and policies. For Iran, bureaucratic and domestic politics reinforced by idealism are the key factors that explain Washington's sanction policies toward Tehran. With respect to the debate about the nature of threats in the international system, a rogue regime does occupy Tehran. It is a fitting substitute for the Soviet threat. But given the different perceptions of threat and opportunity that divide the United States from its allies about Iran, it is difficult to fashion policies to change the regime's behavior or to punish it for misbehavior. A continuation of punishment is justified only on retributive grounds.

CHAPTER THREE

IRAQ: ACCOMMODATION OR CONTAINMENT

WASHINGTON MOVES THE GOAL POST; SADDAM CHEATS ON COMPLIANCE

TWIN QUESTIONS DOMINATE THE DEBATE in American-Iraqi relations. Why does Washington interpret as disingenuous Baghdad's reputed efforts to comply with international sanctions imposed during the Gulf War? And, why does Iraq fail to conform fully with the international sanctions regime that requires it to dismantle weapons of mass destruction, verify their eradication, and cease being a threat to regional peace and stability? To anticipate the conclusions below, the United States seeks retribution on Saddam for his evil deeds, and seeks his ouster from power; Washington is not interested in rehabilitating him. Likewise, Baghdad is not willing to comply fully with the international sanctions regime: Saddam has not given up his vision of uniting Kuwait with Iraq and becoming the all-powerful ruler of the Gulf region.

Underlying these two questions is the issue of whether or not international sanctions should be lifted in the event that Iraq complies with them. But before determining whether to lift sanctions, it is useful to infer motivations of leaders in Washington and in Baghdad.

Two schools of thought are relevant to understanding the reasons behind their respective actions. The first accuses U.S. politicians of "moving the goal post."[1] With each act of Iraqi compliance, Washington shifts the criteria for adherence. The United States seeks to punish Iraq for punishment's sake, not for rehabilitation. Washington also endeavors to overturn the regime in Baghdad rather than reform it. Because there is no consensus in the international community for the overthrow of Saddam, however, Washington is itself following a deceitful policy: the United States "pockets" Iraqi concessions, does not reciprocate with conciliatory gestures, and fails to recognize genuine acquiescence on the part of Iraq, according to this school. It suggests that Saddam Hussein acts from a basement of fear. He defies the United States in order to avoid other losses. Saddam resists the United States because he feels he has nothing to lose. If America is intent on destroying Iraq or removing Saddam from power, he has nothing to gain by compliance. Critics of this persuasion would reassure, embrace, and accommodate him.[2] They would engage him in a "critical dialogue," in order to rehabilitate him. Also, they would refrain from retributive punishment, avoid forcing Saddam into a corner, and reassure him that the West is not out to topple his regime.

This "embrace Saddam" school assumes that he is not deterrable but may be amenable to assurance and persuasion. Because he believes that the United States is determined to undermine his regime no matter what he does, Saddam is relatively immune even to reassuring statements. According to the first school, he is a vulnerable leader motivated by need, rather than an opportunity-driven aggressor motivated by greed. Irrespective of Saddam's actual behavior, reassurance would have to take into account his acute sense of vulnerability.[3] In addition, there has been little promise of reward for compliance with American demands. Deterrence is unlikely to be effective against Saddam, whereas assurance, while also problematic, is the more feasible option.[4]

Saddam also fears that the United States, through economic warfare, is conspiring to destroy him. His suspicion has given rise to aggressive behavior that the United States cannot ignore. The United States intensified its economic sanctions against Iraq, which led Saddam to believe that the United States was conspiring against him.[5] These sanctions only exacerbated the precarious economic situation in Iraq, further threatening Saddam.

As stated in Chapter One, Saddam's suspicion led him to feel slighted by his Arab brethren. He felt that his accomplishments as the "Knight of the Arab Nation" were not being appreciated.[6] Kuwait added to his feelings of persecution by refusing to forgive Baghdad's war debts incurred in the Iran-Iraq War. By siphoning oil from a shared field in a disproportionate amount and by overproducing contrary to oil production quotas, Kuwait added to Iraq's mounting economic difficulties. Saddam saw Kuwait as a threat to his status and power base.

In short, three misperceptions intersected. Washington misperceived Baghdad's capabilities, intentions, and motives. Saddam misperceived the reactions of the United States. And he expected, but did not receive, respect as well as debt forgiveness from his Arab brothers. As a result of these interacting misperceptions, Saddam became virtually nondeterrable. It was also difficult for American leaders to assure him.

Assurance would have been extremely difficult before the invasion of Kuwait. By the time Saddam had decided to risk invading his neighbor, he was already certain of the American desire to topple his regime. The United States was unable to entertain the notion that Saddam was afraid of a grand conspiracy to oust him. Washington discounted information about Saddam's fearful motives.[7] Perhaps assurance would have been more likely to succeed if Saddam had thought U. S. leaders could empathize with him.

Despite the problem with assurance, the first school of thought would advocate major efforts to quell Saddam's fear of domestic turbulence. In order to comfort Saddam, Washington would have to acknowledge that Saddam is operating out of need instead of greed.

In contrast to the fear-based explanation, the second school accounts for Iraq's behavior with the assumption that Saddam is an aggressor. Although he probably is a mixture of an opportunity-driven Machiavelli and a need-based paranoid, the Machiavellian part dominates. His decision to go to war with Iran was partly a matter of being provoked, but mostly his own opportunism explains his choice to invade.[8] In this respect, he does not act just on the basis of short-term issues that divide him from others; rather, his actions stem from long-term goals.

With respect to long-range aims, consider again Saddam's ascension to power. At the age of 26, he returned to Baghdad after four years of exile to take part in a revolution that began his successful climb to power. For 11 years, Saddam waited patiently and schemed behind the scenes. Then, in July 1979, Saddam succeeded in seizing ultimate power—the presidency of Iraq. The second school of thought interprets Saddam's rise to power as evidence of his long-term aggressive tendencies. On his way up the ladder of opportunity, nothing could stop him. He kept his eye on the prize—to be recognized as the absolute ruler of Iraq.[9]

Regarding Iraq's invasion of Kuwait, Saddam saw an occasion to assert his long-standing claim to Kuwait and to control oil pricing. The short-term issues that divided Kuwait and Iraq included Saddam's demand for debt forgiveness and Iraq's claim for a renegotiation of the disproportionate oil levels Kuwait was siphoning off from a field that cut across the Iraq-Kuwait border. These short-term needs were not as important for the opportunity-driven Saddam. He used them only as a point of departure for achieving the long-term goal of exercising suzerainty over the Gulf, solving the border dispute with Kuwait as a first step.

Saddam saw the contemporary borders of Iraq and Kuwait, which were drawn up in 1922 by British High Commissioner Sir Percy Cox, as an injustice brought about by outsiders.[10] Believing that Kuwait was rightfully Iraq's, Saddam saw an opportunity to right a wrong.[11] He invaded Kuwait, declared it the nineteenth province of Iraq, and renamed Kuwait City "Kadhima."[12]

Besides dramatic moves like the invasion of Kuwait, Saddam also practices the politics of incrementalism. Indeed, the second school assumes that when confronted with opposing power, Saddam achieves his opportunity-driven goals by engaging in "salami tactics." By taking a slice at a time, Saddam may believe that he can get away with individual actions and eventually erode the overall international commitment to sanction Iraq. Each step is too small to cause the coalition that defeated him in the Gulf War to come together again. In total, however, the steps constitute a massive challenge to the resolve of the victors by the vanquished. Hence, Saddam makes incremental challenges to the sanctions regime.

To ignore incremental Iraqi challenges would be an invitation for Saddam to move once more against the Iraqi Kurds, Kuwait, and perhaps against Saudi Arabia as well. The second perspective holds that Saddam acts on the basis of a window of opportunity, and he seeks to gain advantage from noncompliance. Proponents of this school would contain and confront Iraq, and if possible, destabilize his country in order to depose Saddam.

At issue is the relative validity of these competing schools that seek to explain the same behavior: noncompliance. The need-based explanation competes with an opportunity-driven account of Saddam's behavior. The bottom line is that Washington does not accept Saddam's efforts to comply because it perceives him as a wrongdoer. Once the image of the enemy is set, the behavior of the actor is of little consequence. Hence, Washington interprets as disingenuous Baghdad's reputed efforts to comply with international sanctions imposed during the Gulf War.

Similarly, Saddam perceives American leaders as wrongdoers. Again, the image of the enemy is a filter through which actors interpret information. Iraq, therefore, fails to comply fully with the international sanctions regime. As long as images of enemies confront one another, nothing will change: Washington's sanctions will remain, and Saddam will be defiant.

Examining American-Iraqi relations over time is one means of highlighting the interplay of fear-based and opportunity-driven explanations as well as changes in images and behavior.

BAGHDAD AND WASHINGTON:
FRIENDS IN THE 1980s, ENEMIES IN THE 1990s

American-Iraqi relations have been on a roller coaster of ups and downs over time. While the two countries were on friendly terms, the dominant explanation for Saddam's rogue behavior was that he was afraid of losses and in need of Western understanding. In the 1980s, the image of Saddam was that he was capable of being a friend. Sanctions can be lifted on a rogue who is paranoid; although they may be retained for reasons of retribution, such punishment is hard to justify.

When problems arose in the relationship, Washington explained Saddam's outlaw behavior as a consequence of his Machiavellian desire for gain. If true, he would not deserve Western empathy. Indeed, sanctions as punishment could rehabilitate him. Rehabilitation notwithstanding, sanctions could be justified on the basis of retribution. As an aggressor in the 1990s, the image of Saddam was that he was an enemy. Saddam was a thug who deserved to be mugged.

Empathy coincided with an upswing in American-Iraqi relations in the 1980s; intolerance accompanied a downswing in the 1990s. In response to one specific downturn, Washington ordered a cruise missile attack against Iraq on September 3, 1996.[13] The assault was in retaliation for Iraqi military attacks against the Kurds in the north. American warships and B-52 bombers launched missiles against airdefense sites, as well as military command and communications facilities in southern Iraq.

U.S. officials had warned that Iraqi President Saddam Hussein must pay for ignoring American warnings not to attack the Kurdish population north of the 36th parallel of Iraq. U.S. aircraft had been policing No-Fly-Zones north of the 36th parallel in northern Iraq and south of the 32nd parallel in southern Iraq. The goal was to keep Saddam's forces from attacking the Kurds in the north and the Shiite Muslims in the south. Saddam had sent three tank divisions composed of 30 to 40 thousand elite Republican Guard troops into northern Iraq to help one Kurdish faction involved in a bloody power struggle with another.

The downward spiral in relations represented by the air strikes was typical of the way Washington treated Baghdad in the mid-1990s. There was a general expectation that Saddam was driven by a desire for gain, that he constituted a severe threat and had to be met with American force.[14] Not only should sanctions be maintained, but also military force needed to supplement economic warfare.

There are four main indicators that Saddam seized a window created by external circumstances. First there was an internally focused United States, with its 1996 American presidential campaign in full swing. Second, there was a sympathetic government in Turkey with an Islamic prime minister. Third, there existed a divided Kurdish region where Iran had been interfering. And, fourth, the Arab-Israel peace process was on the rocks, and a new right-wing government in Israel looked as if it were responsible for the diplomatic stalemate.

With respect to the American presidential campaign, Saddam may have surmised that he could strike against the Kurds when no one was looking. But someone was looking. Indeed, Republican presidential nominee Bob Dole said he hoped President Clinton's missile assault against Iraq marked the start of decisive action to curtail Saddam's power and end his atrocities against the Kurdish minority in the north. Dole said the goal of the U.S. action should be the withdrawal of Saddam's troops from the Kurdish-populated north, release of Kurdish prisoners, and a halt to interference in the Kurdish civil war by both Iran and Iraq. In addition, Dole called for a reestablishment of UN weapons inspection efforts and an end to Saddam's support of international terrorism.[15] In short, because of consensus in Washington, American air strikes failed to cause a domestic political stir in the 1996 presidential campaign. There was a virtual "ho-hum" response to the use of force against Iraq.

In connection with Turkey, Saddam may have calculated that Ankara would have been less likely to authorize Coalition air attacks against his forces than the previous, Western-oriented government there. Again, he was wrong. The government of Prime Minister Erbakan was displeased about the use by the allies of Turkey's southern airbase at Incirlik to protect Iraqi Kurds from Baghdad. Nevertheless, the United States continued to use Turkish bases to monitor the No-Fly-Zone over northern Iraq, even though allied unity was under strain.[16]

Taking advantage of the traditional disunity among the Kurdish population of northern Iraq, Saddam saw a window of opportunity through which to move against one Kurdish faction that was supported by America's enemy, Iran. If the Kurds in Iraq had been in accord, Saddam would have been less likely to make a military move.

With respect to the Arab-Israel talks, Saddam seized a moment to move against the Kurds in northern Iraq when the peace process had hit a roadblock. The international community held the new government of Prime Minister Netanyahu in Israel responsible for the deadlock in talks with the Palestinians and Syrians; hence, Saddam may have calculated that the time was right to pounce on the Kurds.

While there was a consensus in Washington that Saddam acted on the basis of opportunity, a case may be made that he also acted out of fear. The move against the Kurds could have been the gasp of a desperate and failing ruler. Confronted with dissent in his military, Saddam Hussein decided that this was the time to move. Analysts and Iraqi dissidents agreed that one of the most significant factors pushing Saddam to act was his discovery in June 1996 of a network of key midlevel officers in Baghdad who supplied his opponents abroad with information; they were preparing to overthrow his regime.

Saddam's intelligence organization had discovered a CIA-supported coup attempt that was directed from northern Iraq. He wished to destroy the CIA presence and their collaborators in Irbil. The U.S. preoccupation with the presidential elections and the small possibility of serious military intervention made this low-cost action attractive to the Iraqi regime. Having arrested hundreds and executed scores of conspirators, Saddam wanted a show of strength both to discourage other would-be plotters and to create a cause for celebration in the ranks of the Iraqi military. The move on Irbil, which is in principle under allied protection in the northern No-Fly-Zone, offered a chance for a weak leader to boost his prestige.[17]

But routine mutual hostility during the 1990s in American-Iraqi relations was quite different from perceptions two decades earlier. As stated in Chapter Two, the 1970s closed with a crescendo of multiple crises that converged on the Middle East. Their effects ricocheted against the padded walls of the White House Situation Room and caused a reassessment of the American policy of sanctions against Iraq. These crises enhanced the American perception of dangers from the Gulf area, and they provided an incentive for the United States to acquire a new friend—Iraq—to compensate for new a enemy—Iran. On the one hand, Washington interpreted Saddam as a fearful leader in need of U.S. aid. On the other hand, U.S. leaders perceived the Ayatollah Khomeni of Iran as a ruler to be confronted with American power.

The crises included the fall of the Shah in 1978 and the rise of Khomeni the following year. Additionally, there was the 1979 Soviet invasion of Afghanistan and the Iran-Iraq War in 1980. After entering Afghanistan, Soviet military forces in the USSR Southern Theater of Military Operations conducted in 1980 a command post exercise (CPX) simulating an invasion of Iran. The simulation set off alarm bells in the White House, transforming President Carter from a dove to a hawk. He had sought accommodation with Moscow, but became a leader who accepted the possibility of a Soviet-American confrontation over Iran. The Soviet CPX for an invasion of Iran also drew attention to the need of keeping Iraq out of Soviet hands. In this respect, the Carter Administration sought to widen the gap between Baghdad and Moscow.

These multiple crises in the Gulf had a potential for spilling over into the Arab-Israel conflict zone. In addition, Ethiopia and Syria began to emerge as large recipients of Soviet arms. The United States threat perception rose as Washington bureaucrats noted Soviet arms transfers to the Middle East as a danger to American friends and allies in the region.

After the Soviet invasion of Afghanistan, Gulf Arab states like Saudi Arabia became less concerned about too close an identification with the United States. They had been reluctant to align publicly with Washington because of a lack of resolution of the Palestinian issue and a sense of vulnerability that the Arab elites felt in regard to their domestic political foes. Nevertheless, Saudi Arabia still wanted the United States to be out of sight—just over the horizon, but available in case the Arab states needed help against external threats.

Following the Islamic revolution in Iran, Riyadh perceived less of an external threat to the Arab states from Moscow than from a neighbor—Tehran. Muslim, non-Arab Iran intervened in the Arab world and tried to destabilize conservative Arab states. Tehran gave an Islamic dimension to the Palestinian fight, and thus maintained pressure on the reactionary Arab states for militant action against Israel on behalf of the Palestinians.

Baghdad and the PLO shared a joint dependence on Moscow; but the PLO had strained relations with Iraq. The Iran-Iraq War also exacerbated tensions between Baghdad and the Palestinian mainstream leadership. Contrary to the PLO's preferences, Baghdad had tried to destabilize Tehran by encouraging the Arabs of the Khuzestan province of Iran to revolt. But Iraq's efforts to destabilize Iran failed. The so-called Persian Arabs considered themselves more Iranian than Arab.

The first Gulf War (1980-1988) gave Washington an occasion for an opening to Baghdad. The explicit issue between Baghdad and Tehran was the location of the Iran-Iraq border along the Shatt-al-Arab waterway. An implicit issue between these two neighbors, though, was the political instability of Iran and hence its vulnerability to attack. In Tehran, the fall of the Shah and rise of the Ayatollah gave Baghdad an occasion for a favorable revision of the border. Iran's vulnerability also gave Iraq a chance to assert its suzerainty over the Gulf area. Because of Khomeni's Islamic revolution and Saddam's attack on Iran, Washington faced the question of whether or not to contain or accommodate Baghdad.

Those who explained Saddam's assault on Iran as being driven by his fears favored accommodation with Iraq. Others who explained the attack as a consequence of his innate aggressive drive preferred containment and confrontation of Baghdad.

The Islamic revolution in Iran reversed mutual perceptions between Tehran and Washington.[18] Additionally, the revolution presented the United States with a need to retain a foothold in the strategically important region of the Gulf. Hence, the United States had an incentive to improve its relationship with Iraq as relations with Iran deteriorated. Historically, the Cold War had been an impetus for Washington to maintain good ties with both Baghdad and Tehran. Hostility from Iran forced Washington policymakers concerned with Iraq to choose between East-West interests and stakes in the Arab-Israel zone.

At issue were Washington's treatment of its old enemy, Baghdad, in light of a new adversarial relationship with Tehran; continued conflict with Moscow; and the perceived threat from Iraq by Israel. During the Cold War, there was consensus within the United States bureaucracy over the need to contain the USSR. But that understanding failed to carry over from the global East-West arena to Iraq, because of its hostility to Iran, Israel, and Egypt.

In short, the Iran-Iraq War highlighted the split between domestic political groups versus economic associations and the national security bureaucracy over whether to contain or accommodate Baghdad. The pro-Israel community favored containment, but the business and bureaucratic preference was for accommodation.

SOURCES OF AMERICAN THREAT
PERCEPTIONS ABOUT IRAQ

Underlying the issue of accommodation or containment of Iraq are sources of American threat perception of Baghdad. They include politics versus business and the bureaucracy. American decision-makers' preferences are sources of motivated biases that affect their estimation of the Iraqi threat.[19]

Ethnic Politics versus Business Interests

Interest groups clash in the formulation of policy. One traditional lineup for the Middle East is the conflict between the pro-Israel community and firms that profit from doing business in the area. Ethnic groups with ties to an area may overestimate the threat, in order to protect the country with which they have links; business associations with economic interests in a region tend to underestimate the threat, in order to do business there.

Regarding the Middle East, the pro-Israel community had more of an impact in the Reagan Administration than did the business sector. The opposite was the case for the Bush Administration. Ethnic politics had a major impact on the threat perception of Iran in the Reagan years and had less of an effect on the threat perception of Iraq in the Bush years. The composition of their campaign staffs might explain the different threat perceptions.

In the 1980 campaign, candidate Reagan had a pro-Israel reputation, and he had excellent ties with the pro-Israel community; so did those around him. Richard Allen chaired the campaign's Foreign Policy and National Security Advisory Council, and I served as co-chair of the Middle East Task Force, having been recommended by AIPAC to Allen. After the election, White House National Security Advisor Allen was able to make good use of his well-deserved reputation of being staunchly pro-Israel. One area in which he benefited from his reputation was to minimize the political costs to the Reagan Administration of arms sales to Arab states. But in the 1988 campaign, candidate Bush did not display a pro-Israel stance, nor did he attract a staff with the views of the Reagan team. Allen's counterpart on the Bush team was the distinguished General Brent Scowcroft (U.S. Air Force, retired). Although he had a sterling reputation, Scowcroft had no known standing in the pro-Israel community comparable to that of Allen.

And who was my counterpart in the Bush campaign? Richard Fairbanks, a paid registered lobbyist on behalf of the government of Iraq. He headed up the Middle East Policy Task Force for Bush. While I had the support of AIPAC, Fairbanks served on the board of the U.S.-Iraq Business Forum. It was a pro-Baghdad lobbying group that had quite an impact on Washington policy making as a result of having former national security personnel on its board.[20]

Although Fairbanks had served earlier in the Reagan Administration as one of the Secretary of State's Middle East envoys, it would have been inconceivable for him to be on the staffs of the Reagan campaign or the National Security Council. His pro-Iraqi views would not have been compatible with the dominant pro-Israel mindset. Although there were no pro-Iraq American citizens who were as influential in the Bush campaign as the pro-Israel community was in the Reagan campaign, there were business groups that had the ear of pro-Iraq American national security professionals such as Fairbanks.

Despite the views of the Reagan campaign staff, once the Administration began to govern, it came under the sway of the bureaucracy and began to lean toward Iraq. The clout of the business community and bureaucracy rose. There was little domestic political opposition to the embrace of Baghdad. With the hostage crisis still foremost in the mind of the American populace, there was much hostility toward Iran. Iraq had not seized Americans and held them hostage, while Iran had done so. Moreover, the profit motive from the prospective sale of grain and dual-use technology provided incentives for a policy of accommodation with Iraq. American business interests, however, had to contend with the influence of an ethnic lobby—the pro-Israel community, which was anti-Iraq.

Led by AIPAC, the pro-Israel community favored containment of Iraq. While it worked to retain Iraq on the State Department's list of nations that sponsor international terrorism, the effort was not very strenuous.[21] Thus, when anti-Iraq sanctions came before the Congress in 1988, AIPAC did not work against that legislation as much as it worked on the Iran and Libya Sanctions Act.[22] Perhaps as a result, the anti-Iraq legislation of the 1980s failed.

One reason AIPAC gave a less than maximum effort against Iraq is that Iran had gained major military advantages in the 1980-1988 war. As a result, there was a growing consensus within the bureaucracy for a tilt toward Iraq. The pro-Israel community was reluctant to suggest to Washington that it sacrifice influence with Baghdad against both Moscow and Tehran. Despite the fact that counterterrorism against Iraq was a major concern of the community, its top priority at that time was economic and military assistance for Israel.

With progress in the Arab-Israel peace process in the 1990s, AIPAC has turned its attention to the threat from non-Arab Iran against Israel. In the 1980s, the community's tepid opposition to transfers of dual-use equipment to Iraq was insufficient to turn the tide of the American business community and national security professionals. Although the community still also gave attention to efforts by Iraq to acquire weapons of mass destruction and applauded Israel's successful air strike against Iraqi nuclear facilities, AIPAC did not organize political opposition against Baghdad.

AIPAC also paid little attention to Tehran in the 1980s. The organization was aware of Jerusalem's arms-supply program to Iran. The government of Israel had a covert program of arms transfers to Iran. This program led to a similar arms sales policy by the Reagan Administration, which in turn culminated in the arms-for-hostages fiasco.[23] Although a debacle, the policy of American arms to Iran was consistent with the balance of power approach of the Reagan-Bush era, and it was compatible with Israel's arms for Iran policy.

Politics and National Security

Not only did Reagan attract professionals who had good ties with ethnic interest groups; he also recruited analysts with excellent links to the national security community. As a result, these professionals had access to intelligence that proved of use in the 1980 presidential campaign.

In addition to being co-chair of the Regan-Bush Task Force, I also was on the Chief of Naval Operations (CNO) Civilian Executive Panel, an advisory committee to the Chief. Membership on his panel provided access to information that was useful for briefing the candidate. With respect to Iraq and the Gulf, a celebrated strategist, Albert Wohlstetter, headed the Strategy sub-panel. He also was a Reagan advisor. His company, Pan Heuristics, had just completed a major study of the Gulf for the Pentagon.[24]

The impetus for the Wohlstetter study came from a concern at the Department of Defense that a growing preponderance of Soviet power in the Gulf area coincided with a comparative weakness of the West. He highlighted a paradoxical reassurance that dominated conventional wisdom of the early 1980s: the Soviets would never attack in so vital an area where the West was at a disadvantage. To do so would mean World War III, the prospect of which would deter Moscow. Wohlstetter was critical of this sunny scenario. He extended it to show how absurd this scenario was. If the Soviets would not strike at vital points where the West was weak, they also would not attack where the West was strong. And regarding nonvital areas, the Soviets would be irrational to risk attacking for marginal gains.[25] Thus, according to the wishful thinkers, a Soviet invasion of the Gulf area was inconceivable.

In conjunction with analysts at Pan Heuristics, the Pentagon had conducted its own study of Gulf security.[26] It dealt with topics like American strategic stakes in the area, allied interests, Soviet objectives, Great Power rivalry, sources of instability in the Gulf and the Arabian Peninsula, Soviet military options, and military threats to United States interests. American objectives included protecting Western oil supplies, restoring the flow of oil if there were an interruption, and minimizing Soviet influence over the policies of oil-producing states.[27]

Among the U.S. goals were to contain radical Arab states, such as Iraq, and to prevent them from using military power to coerce moderate Arab nations like Kuwait and Saudi Arabia. Iraqi control of the Arab Gulf states would have placed too much power in the hands of Saddam. Also, radical Arab domination of the Middle East could lead to another Arab-Israel war, oil embargo, and superpower confrontation.

A specific problem debated at the Department of Defense during the early 1980s was the threat to Kuwait from Iraq. In addition to Iran, the Iraqi threat involved a direct invasion of Kuwait and the use of implicit Iraqi power to coerce Kuwait and the Arab Gulf states. Regarding non-Soviet Gulf contingencies, the threat from Baghdad to Tehran was the most serious and probable. Iraq and prerevolutionary Iran were in approximate balance. But the postrevolutionary situation found Iraq militarily preeminent in the Gulf. The role of Iraq was critical for a successful Soviet invasion of Iran. In a scenario with Iraq and Soviet projection forces against Saudi Arabia and projection forces from the United States, overall force ratios would have been very unfavorable to the United States.

To address the problem of unfavorable force ratios and thus meet non-Soviet Gulf contingencies, there was a need to wean Baghdad from Moscow. One of the advocates of a tilt toward Iraq in the Carter Administration was National Security Advisor Zbigniew Brzezinski.[28] In this view, Washington should seek to moderate Iraq's policies regarding Iran while balancing Baghdad's power. In addition, there was a need to meet the threat in the Gulf on its own terms.[29] To do so would have required joint consultations with the allies. At issue was how to create an allied force to confront a combined Soviet-Iraqi threat without compromising the Western capability needed outside of the Gulf and without destabilizing host countries like Saudi Arabia.

Such goals required achievement of the following tasks: an upgrading of the American forces in the Indian Ocean and deployment of United States and allied forces through the Indian Ocean, and insofar as was politically feasible, into the Gulf. Other tasks included the conduct of military exercises separately and jointly with local forces; a year-round presence of at least one carrier task force group, as well as prepositioning of equipment and supplies to facilities that could handle a rapid buildup of ground forces and tactical aircraft. Such a combat presence had to be politically acceptable, able to defend itself against land-based attacks, and capable of projecting enough firepower ashore to deter an Iraqi-Soviet military move in the upper Gulf.

During an October 8, 1980, meeting with the Chief of Naval Operations, our panel discussed general global challenges and threats to the Gulf. At issue was Moscow's general aim for the Gulf area, given the Soviet presence in Afghanistan, the Iran-Iraq War, and possible Soviet military moves in Poland to quell labor unrest. The chief, Admiral Tom Hayward, spoke about the opportunity that the Iran-Iraq

War created for the United States: enhanced prospects for deploying American military forces in Saudi Arabia. He reasoned that because Iranian advances against Iraq threatened Riyadh, the Saudis would be more amenable to an American force deployment in the Kingdom. But he also expressed great concern that an unraveling Iran could be pretext for a Soviet military move into that troubled country.

But if Soviet forces did deploy in Iran, Hayward suggested that such an action would be a constraint on Moscow's prospective crackdown against striking Solidarity union members in Poland.[30] From our discussion about threats to the Gulf, it was clear that we saw the global Soviet danger to the Gulf to be more important than the threat from regional powers like Iran or Iraq. While we focused more on the external Soviet threat to the region than on an internal danger, Saudi Arabia paid more attention to the menace indigenous to the area—Iran. Indeed, American intelligence attributed close ties between Riyadh and Baghdad to be a means by which Saudi Arabia felt that it could ensure its security against the threat from Iran.[31]

While both Saudi Arabia and Iraq worried about the Iranian threat, Baghdad also was concerned about the threat from Moscow via Afghanistan. Iran was alarmed about CIA reports regarding the Soviet need for oil in the near future. Saddam interpreted Moscow's oil requirements to mean a potential Soviet military move against Iraq for the purpose of securing its oil. In this respect, he felt that the two superpowers were the main source of uncertainty and instability in the Gulf.

Saddam opposed plans for an American rapid deployment force because it provided the Soviets with an incentive to match that force. Joining Saddam, the Saudis also expressed great fear that an American rapid deployment force would give the Soviets a pretext for similar deployment in the Gulf area. Consequently, both Iraq and Saudi Arabia thought that United States protection against a potential Soviet invasion in the future could cause a deployment of Soviet forces in the present. In this respect, they did not perceive the supposed benefit of American protection of the Gulf to be worth the potential price.

Intelligence reports in the summer of 1980 indicated that Iraq wanted to maintain its independence from the USSR, but not enough that it would throw itself into the hands of the West. At that time,

Saddam strongly disapproved of Moscow's decision to invade Afghan-istan and was equally opposed to Washington's use of the Soviet presence there as a pretext for bringing in American military forces. Until the invasion of Afghanistan, he had taken it for granted that the Soviets were nonexpansionist in the Middle East. After the Soviet move into Afghanistan, however, Saddam increased the distance that he had begun to impose in Iraq's relations with the USSR. While maneuvering was taking place in the Middle East, another balancing act was occurring in Washington.

The battle between ethnic politics and business interests was a war for the White House and Capitol Hill. In the case of Iraq, economic views triumphed. Businesses with ties to Iraq lined up their vectors with those of national security bureaucrats. While the firms wanted to make money on Iraq, the professionals desired to leverage Baghdad against both Moscow and Tehran. They sought an opening to Iraq in order to balance Soviet forces in Afghanistan with Iranian combat units across the waterway.

While Baghdad was winning the war for Washington, it was losing its war with Iran. Thus, there was a great incentive from professionals in the national security community in Washington to reconcile with Baghdad. Even with incentives to placate Iraq, full-scale accommoda-tion with it was politically risky. Because Iraq had been designated as a state that sponsored terrorism, it was a risk to embrace Baghdad. Hence, there was a need to bring the American business community's power to bear on behalf of Iraq. Its role was to downplay the Iraqi threat to the American public, while profiting from the sales of dual-use equipment to Saddam's military. Economics provided a cover for professionals to slide away from a policy of isolating Iraq. Ordinarily, moving closer to a rogue state would have been a controversial policy and not advisable in an election year.

In the run-up to an election, containment of a rogue state is less risky than accommodation . Pressures to continue containment often rise in even years and fall in odd years, while the reverse is true for reconciliation. Ethnic groups reinforce the politics of containment during an election, while business groups buttress the politics of accommodation in off-election years. During the 1980 presidential primary campaign, the pro-Israel community bolstered the politics of containing Iraq. After the election, however, the business community dominated the policy-making process regarding Iraq. Momentum for the Reagan Administration to take Iraq off of the list of states that support international terrorism began during late 1981, an off-election year, and culminated the following year in Baghdad's removal from the list.

Bureaucratic Politics and Threat Perception

Washington's accommodation with Baghdad commenced when the Reagan Administration deleted Iraq from the list of states that sponsor terrorism on February 26, 1982. The Administration's public explanation was because of Iraq's improved record on terrorism, but the implicit reason was to assist Baghdad in its war against Tehran.[32] The significance of eliminating Iraq from the terrorism list was that the enumerated nations are subject to export controls on the sale of arms and high technology equipment. And because Iraq was losing the Iran-Iraq War, there was a great incentive for it to obtain American arms and dual-use technology.

In March 1984, President Reagan's Special Envoy to the Middle East, Donald Rumsfeld, began a process of shifting the American interest from a primary focus on the Arab-Israel conflict zone to the Gulf region. Because of Iranian successes in the Iran-Iraq War, he was able to persuade Riyadh and other Arab Gulf states to initiate joint contingency planning and prepositioning of supplies and equipment at their military facilities.

In addition to deleting Iraq from the list of states that support terrorism, the Reagan Administration took other actions that favored Baghdad. During 1984, the president signed a directive that authorized a limited intelligence-sharing program with Iraq. Another directive called attention to the need to counter Soviet influence as a rationale for expanding ties with Iraq. There was a chance that Washington could take advantage of strained relations between Baghdad and Moscow. Baghdad had denounced the Soviet invasion of Afghanistan, and the USSR had been an inconsistent arms supplier for Iraq.

Even before the Iran-Iraq War began in September 1980, Iraqi-Soviet relations were strained. The war exacerbated tensions between

Moscow and Baghdad and thus provided an opening for Washington. The first Gulf War also furnished an occasion for advocates of Iraq to lobby within the American national security bureaucracy on behalf of Baghdad.

The 1980-1988 Gulf War also highlighted the globalists versus regionalists split in the American bureaucracy across the Carter and Reagan administrations. Despite political differences between these administrations, both contained globalists, who saw conflicts in East-West terms, and regionalists, who perceived the same conflicts through the lens of the region in which they occurred. Globalists preferred an alignment between the United States and Arab states on the periphery of the Soviet Union. Regionalists preferred leaving some distance between these states and Washington, for fear that too close identification would be a source of instability for their fragile regimes. Globalists wanted to move closer to Iraq and the Arab Gulf states, while regionalists were concerned that such alignment would be destabilizing. They also had reservations about too great a focus on the Gulf at the expense of the Arab-Israel zone in general and Egypt in particular.

Regarding the bureaucratic politics of containment versus accommodation, two approaches toward Iraq surfaced within the Carter, Reagan, and Bush administrations. The "Arab-Israel first" perspective suggested discontinuation of a policy of containment of Iraq in order to use Baghdad as a facilitator of the Arab-Israel peace process. A "Gulf first" group advocated détente with either Iran or Iraq, for the sake of containing the Soviet Union. Given that the Iranian option was unrealistic, this group gravitated toward Iraq. Bureaus at the State Department found common ground with economic units, such as Treasury and Commerce, which preferred a conciliatory Iraqi policy as a part of their pro-business perspective.

The State Department's European and Canadian Affairs (EU) and the Politico-Military Affairs (PM) bureaus contained officials who perceived United States options in East-West terms. The Bureau of Near Eastern and South Asian Affairs (NEA) tended to view the Iran-Iraq War according to its implications for the Arab-Israel conflict and the balance of power between a hostile Iran and friendly Arab Gulf states.[33] NEA wanted to use the good offices of Baghdad in order to move the Arab-Israel peace process forward. Although PM took a harder line on Iraq, the outcome of bargaining between the two bureaus was for a tilt toward Baghdad.

The slant toward Iraq became manifest in National Security Directive 26, signed by President Bush on October 3, 1989. It states: "Normal relations between the U.S. and Iraq would serve our long-term interests and promote stability in both the Gulf and the Middle East. The U.S. Government should propose both economic and political incentives for Iraq to moderate its behavior and to increase our influence with Iraq."[34] Clearly, the Bush Administration as a whole had made a strategic commitment to accommodate Iraq.

But there were dissenters within the Administration. It may be useful to trace the interest expressed by the Department of Defense in the Gulf area in order to place the Bush Pentagon's views within a historical setting. Not until the fall of the Shah and Soviet invasion of Afghanistan did the Pentagon manifest a major interest in the Middle East. Before then, the American military had paid more attention to the European and Asian threats. "Palestine" had been on the periphery of Pentagon policy making. The Department of Defense had focused on containing Moscow and Beijing, in order to restrain them from attacks on Berlin and Tokyo.

Earlier, as the Cold War spread to the Middle East, the region became an important part of national security planning. With the extension of the anti-Soviet policy of containment eastward—the Eisenhower Doctrine—there came a need to sign up countries on the periphery of the East-West divide. In this respect, Iraq, Iran, Pakistan, and Turkey were in demand as allies.[35] The 1955 Baghdad Pact aligned the United Kingdom and the United States with such states on the periphery of the USSR.

On the one hand, in the 1980s, officials at the White House and the State Department who wished to focus on the Gulf prevailed over "Egypt-firsters" at the Central Intelligence Agency. These individuals worried about whether Cairo would drift toward Moscow if Washington did not pay enough attention to Egypt. On the other hand, some officials at the Department of Defense reinforced the bureaucratic consensus toward Iraq. Those in the Secretary of Defense's Office of International Security Affairs (ISA) leaned toward Iraq in order to balance Iran.[36]

Richard Armitage, Assistant Secretary of Defense/International Security Affairs, seemed to favor accommodation with Iraq. But his counterpart at Defense, Richard Perle, opposed the embrace of Saddam Hussein. In March 1985, Perle tried without success to require a nonnuclear-use assurance agreement from Baghdad as a condition for exporting two advanced computers. Perle lost the battle to a coalition that included his colleague Armitage and officials from the White House and the Department of State.[37]

In addition to International Security Policy at Defense, other dissenters in the rush to embrace Saddam Hussein were in the office of the Joint Chiefs of Staff. Many military officers were wary of Iraq's military buildup. Indeed, during the early 1980s, a growing number of them began to see Iraq as a threat to the United States, even while other government agencies perceived it as a candidate for membership in an American alignment. Due to the fact that Baghdad had been an ally against Moscow until the Iraqi revolution in 1958, the Reagan and Bush national security bureaucracies hoped to restore this alignment in the 1980s.

Saddam and his ilk in Baghdad saw a White House leaning in their favor, a split State Department, a divided Pentagon, and a tilt on their behalf from Treasury and Commerce. The net policy effect of the bargaining among the departments, however, was for the United States to pursue accommodation with Iraq and to continue the containment of Iran. From the point of view of American planning for possible war with Iraq, the Defense Department's views were on the rise; from the perspective of planning for peace in the Arab-Israel conflict, the White House and the State Department seemed to be in control.[38] And with respect to economic planning, Treasury and Commerce were in ascendancy.

Because of a tendency to see what you want to see, Saddam interpreted the friendly signals from the White House as the valid representation of American foreign policy and discounted the Pentagon's hostile signals. Also, Saddam expected that the White House view would be dominant, just as the executive branch was the sole factor in the governance of Iraq. Because Saddam did not want to see a deterrent threat, he paid more attention to the White House and the State Department than to the Pentagon. Indeed, officials at the White

House and the State Department communicated their reassuring views to Baghdad on a regular basis, while the military officials at the Pentagon kept their secret planning documents to themselves.[39]

A minority within the American bureaucracy favored containment of Iraq. I belonged to a small group of officials during the early 1980s committed to containment of Iraq. We perceived Baghdad to be a threat to Israel and a competitor of Egypt. Iraq was a leader of the rejectionist front against Jerusalem, a rival of Cairo and Damascus over leadership within the Arab world, and a threat to the United States because it was engaged in international terrorism and proliferation of weapons of mass destruction.[40] Hence, we vainly sought to contain Iraq within its own borders. Because successive regimes in Baghdad had made a cottage industry of being anti-Israel and anti-American, it was simple to justify a continuation of a containment policy to the American people. Iraq was an easier sale on Capitol Hill than within the national security bureaucracy: Baghdad was an enemy of Israel and an adversary of the United States, attributes that made Iraq loathsome to the American people, but acceptable to the bureaucracy.

On the one hand, politicians on the Hill were sensitive to ethnic interest-group pressures and ideals regarding the Arab-Israel zone; they thus favored containment of Iraq. On the other hand, professionals at State, Treasury, Defense, and Commerce emphasized American interests in the Cold War and Gulf oil; consequently, this consensus view wanted accommodation with Iraq. The bureaucrats reasoned that Iraqi setbacks in the 1980-1988 war against Iran required Washington to tilt toward Baghdad so that neither Tehran nor Moscow would reign supreme in the Gulf area.

With its Cold War orientation, the Gulf-first school split into two groups: one focused on Iran, the other on Iraq. Both shared an antipathy toward the Soviet Union. This anti-Soviet attitude was a common lens through which to perceive the Middle East. The Iran camp in the United States saw Tehran as the key to preventing a Soviet invasion of the Arab Gulf. Although Iran was anti-American, its long border with the USSR made it a gateway through which the Soviet Union could make inroads into the Arab Gulf.[41]

From a balance of power perspective, Iraq bordered on hostile states that posed a threat to Baghdad: Iran, Syria, and Turkey. Pro-Iraq officials at the White House and State Department were inclined to follow a balance of power approach rather than a policy to contain Iraq; Pentagon officials tended toward a containment approach, and they prepared for a worst-case scenario—war with Iraq.

The Iraq camp of the Gulf-first school was motivated less by the USSR and more by the Arab-Israel conflict. It had a desire to solve the Palestinian problem and secure economic profits for American corporations and farmers. This faction assumed that Saddam could be accommodated with both American-origin dual-use equipment, such as trucks, machine tools, and computers, as well as Midwestern wheat. A satisfied Saddam then would be active in Palestinian diplomacy, less belligerent toward Israel, and would serve as a bulwark in the conflict with Iran.

Regarding the peace process, the aim of the Iraq camp of American bureaucrats was to enhance diplomatic, military, and economic ties with Baghdad. They wanted to bring the PLO into direct negotiations with Israel. But because of the Iraqi threat to Israel, this camp sought to deny Baghdad sophisticated American-origin military equipment while providing it with the capability to quell domestic unrest and deter Iran. With respect to economic motivations, Iraq sought the assistance of congressional allies, and it lobbied the United States national security bureaucracy in order to gain American technology.

INTERESTS UNDER SIEGE:
INTRINSIC AND STRATEGIC

Intrinsic Interests at Stake

American leaders believe that Iraq threatens both intrinsic and strategic interests. These interests are two sides of the same coin under assault.[42] The Iraqi menace threatens American civilians and military personnel in the Gulf—intrinsic interests. And before its defeat in the Gulf War, Iraq also was a risk to other inherently valuable targets like Western petroleum products transiting the Gulf.[43] But in the mid-1990s, Iraq still had 2,000 tanks and 300 combat aircraft. As a result, Saddam had the largest military force in the Gulf region.[44] Hence, while his military was diminished by the Gulf War and UN sanctions, it nevertheless still constitutes a threat.

Besides the intrinsic interest highlighted by the Iraqi threat to American military personnel in the Gulf area, Baghdad is also a danger to American citizens in general via its support for international terrorism.[45] According to the State Department, Saddam probably ordered the assassination of former President Bush in Kuwait during April 1993. The group arrested for the assassination attempt was also planning a bombing campaign to destabilize Kuwait in general.

Iraqi-sponsored terrorism has become a routine fact of life in northern Iraq. Baghdad probably has been responsible for attacks on UN and other international relief agency staff as well as humanitarian aid convoys.[46] Although Iraq has not recovered its capability to launch terrorist attacks outside its borders after the deportation of Iraqi intelligence agents from several states during the Gulf war, Baghdad has begun to deploy agents in search of Saddam's adversaries who resided abroad. Iraqi-backed surrogates were probably responsible for two attempts to bomb the Kuwait Airways office in Beirut and another attempt to bomb the Kuwaiti Embassy, also in Lebanon.

Although the Iraqi government agreed in 1992 to comply with UN Security Council Resolution 687, which requires that Iraq not allow any terrorist organization to operate within its territory, Baghdad still maintains contacts with or provides sanctuary to several groups and individuals that have practiced terrorism. For example, the Kurdish Workers Party, which has killed hundreds of people in attacks inside Turkey and has mounted two separate terrorist campaigns against Turkish interests in Europe in 1993, has training camps in Iraq. Baghdad supports an opposition group that carried out several violent attacks in Iran from bases in Iraq. Baghdad also harbors members of several extremist Palestinian groups, including the Arab Liberation Front and the Palestine Liberation Front.[47]

Strategic Interests at Stake

The U.S. strategic interests regarding Iraq are related to objectives for the Gulf as a whole. Washington has an interest in continuing the flow of oil to the world market at prices that are consistent with the economic growth of the industrialized democracies. With the end of the Cold War, the regional menace from Iraq (and Iran) replaced the Soviet threat.

The Iraqi threats to American strategic interests include Baghdad's challenge to U.S. threat credibility, the American resolve to remain involved in global affairs, and the U.S. commitment to defend its allies against its adversaries. One means by which Baghdad confronts Washington is Iraq's failure to comply with United Nations Security Council Resolutions 686 (March 2, 1991) and 687 (April 3, 1991). These two resolutions specify the terms of reference for the end of the Gulf War.

Resolution 687 intended to prevent Iraq from once again becoming a threat to the Gulf region. It mandated the destruction, removal, or dismantlement under international monitoring of Iraq's nuclear, biological, and chemical armaments, as well as ballistic missiles with a range over 150 kilometers.[48] The United Nations formed a special commission to implement Resolution 686, which demanded that Iraq implement its acceptance of all twelve previous resolutions and specified the necessary measures to be undertaken that would end hostilities.[49] To the extent that Iraq fails to comply with these two resolutions, Baghdad is a threat to international credibility in general and American credibility in particular.

Another strategic threat concerns nuclear weapons. Iraq remains a nuclear proliferation threat despite its lack of fissile material and production facilities in the post–Gulf War era. Baghdad had constructed a large nuclear weapons program with the assistance of Western suppliers and may seek to do so again. Although Operation Desert Storm damaged those facilities and UN sanctions make it difficult to reconstruct them, Saddam has not abandoned his nuclear weapons goals. And he has taken steps to thwart the process of international inspections.[50]

MILITARY FORCE VERSUS
ECONOMIC DIPLOMACY

Once Baghdad ordered the invasion of Kuwait in August 1990, there was no doubt that Iraq constituted a threat to American interests.

There was a spirited debate within the bureaucracy, however, over how to meet that threat. As tensions mounted after the Iraqi invasion, at issue was whether an impending war involving the United States was to be an instrument of first or last resort.

The Bush Administration split into two camps. One proposed the use of air power even before there was a ground war capacity in place.[51] The first camp would have used air power prior to exhausting other remedies like sanctions and before the capacity was deployed to conduct combined combat operations.

The chairman of the Joint Chiefs of Staff during the Gulf War, General Colin Powell, represented the second camp, and his position became American policy. He advocated economic sanctions while building up for possible offensive action. If and when the President decided to liberate Kuwait, Powell proposed using combined air, naval, and ground forces to oust the Iraqi army.[52]

Powell's views are consistent with a doctrine of just war, which says warfare is legitimate to the extent that leaders can show that other solutions, such as economic sanctions, are found to be inadequate. In this respect, Secretary of Defense Caspar Weinberger provided a series of "tests" in a 1984 speech on the use of military power at the National Press Club. One principle was that the commitment of U.S. forces to combat should be a last resort.[53] The American policy during the Gulf War reflected the Weinberger-Powell principle. Other aspects of the Powell view include the hope that economic sanctions work, the preparation for war by assembling an overwhelming amount of firepower, and the delay of ground war until there is a force in place that guarantees victory.

Powell denies that he was an advocate of either sanctions or war options. His goal was to make sure that the president had the opportunity to consider both, "fully and fairly." Even before the air war began in mid-January 1991, Powell told President Bush that sanctions had serious disadvantages: "Sanctions left the initiative with the Iraqis to decide when they had had enough. And . . . sanctions take time, if they work at all."[54]

The issue posed by Powell is not either military force or economic warfare; it is how to combine force and diplomacy in ways that secure compliance at minimum costs. To have used air power prior to exhausting other remedies like sanctions and before the capacity was deployed to conduct combined combat operations would have lessened both the legitimacy of the coalition war effort and diminished allied effectiveness once war began. As the Gulf nations maintained an uneasy cease-fire, economic warfare continued during the mid-1990s.

As Washington sought to balance force and diplomacy, the balance of power on the ground began to change. Consider the history. As the 1970s closed, the Arab Gulf states were increasingly fearful of a growing threat from Iran. As the decade of the 1990s ends, the Arab Gulf states are again worried about Iran. In the earlier era, Arab states in the Gulf region doubted that the Carter Administration had the resolve to defend them against either a Soviet or an Iranian threat. Likewise, these Gulf states believe that dual containment punishes Iraq more than Iran. Consequently, they wonder if the Clinton Administration has the resolve to defend them against Iran.[55]

Perceptions of threat differ among Arab Gulf states that are members of the anti-Saddam coalition. Consider in this regard the threat perceptions of the Gulf Cooperation Council members.[56] There is both support and opposition for Washington's dual containment policy toward Iran and Iraq among the leadership levels in the Arab Gulf. But there is much less support among the informed elites and on the "Arab street," that is, the general public. And there are differences in threat perception between Saudi Arabia and Kuwait. Elites and the Arab street in Riyadh perceived an Iraqi mobilization along the Saudi border during October 1994 as less of a threat than did their counterparts in Kuwait City and in Washington. Saudi Arabia saw Saddam's military move as a diplomatic means to highlight Iraq's economic plight brought about because of UN sanctions. In this respect, Saudi elites and the Arab public believed that the United States overreacted with its military response.

While there is support for dual containment, there also is quiet opposition. Some Arab Gulf states view dual containment in a dubious light because of its equal treatment of Baghdad and Tehran. On the one hand, Iraq is more of a short-term menace that stems from the continued reign of Saddam. UN sanctions, hence, are an unintended prop for Saddam to use in order to maintain his power in Iraq: the sanctions bolster Saddam and prolong his rule while turning the population against the Arab Gulf states that support the sanctions.

On the other hand, Iran is the long-term threat to the Arab Gulf states. Even though there is a high perception of threat from Iran, there also is reluctance to antagonize Iranian leaders. U.S. measures, such as trade sanctions, cause anxiety about the prospects for a potential military confrontation between Tehran and Washington. There exists a clear preference among the Gulf states for a balance of power approach instead of dual containment. A balancing policy has the potential for accommodating both Iran and Iraq.[57]

Just as is the case at the turn of the century, the 1980s found Arab moderate states pressuring the United States to move closer to Baghdad as a counter to Tehran; and Washington followed that advice. As the twenty-first century approaches, the same pressure may provide the seeds for a change in American policy toward Iraq.[58] A weakened Iraq seems less of a threat to the Arab states than a growing Iran. Also, there are Iranian efforts to destabilize the Arab-Israel zone with increased levels of arms transfers to Hezbollah combatants in Lebanon. These arms transfers suggest that Tehran may be up to its old tricks.

The increased Persian threat to Israel may forge an unholy alliance of moderate Arab states and Israel in tacit alignment with Iraq against Iran. And because Syria is aligned with Iran, Damascus serves as a convenient transshipment point for Iranian weapons for Hezbollah in Lebanon. As the 1990s close, consider war scenarios for the future of the Gulf region, which will determine in part whether the United States continues to pursue a posture of containing and confronting Iraq.

SCENARIOS

Kurdish Civil War Resumes: Coalition Cracks Down on Saddam

A first scenario is the most likely and perhaps easiest to handle with containment, confrontation, and perhaps rollback of Iraqi combat forces. It is a resumption of the Kurdish civil war in northern Iraq, followed by tit-for-tat escalation and expansion of fighting between Iraq and coalition forces in both northern and southern Iraq.[59] This scenario implies some tacit cooperation between Tehran and Washington to contain Baghdad.[60]

Iran Attacks or Subverts Arab Neighbors

A second set of scenarios consists of Iranian attempts to destabilize Arab states like Saudi Arabia, Kuwait, the United Arab Emirates, Bahrain, and Oman. In this event, Washington would have to consider whether to embrace Baghdad as a counter to Tehran.[61] These are more difficult to manage than if Baghdad were the culprit. Because Iran's air force poses a moderate threat to high-value targets in the Gulf region, Tehran's warplanes could launch small-scale surprise attacks with great destruction and with even greater psychological impact. Ships and transshipment facilities in Kuwait and the United Arab Emirates would be fruitful targets for Iranian assault. But an attack on Saudi Arabia is the least likely because of the deterrent threat of retaliation. Regardless of damage, an assault on Saudi Arabia would raise the threat of concerted American and Arab Gulf state retaliation on key Iranian facilities.

As a result of enhanced capabilities acquired during and after Desert Storm, Saudi Arabia is better able to engage in self-defense than in times past. But even with American-supplied AWACS, the Saudi air force and ground-based air defense system might not be able to counter a surprise Iranian air strike on Saudi oil installations. The time and distances are just too short. About 100 Iranian F-4 fighter-bombers could strike oil fields anywhere in the eastern provinces of Saudi Arabia from bases in Bandar-e-Abbas, Iran, in just a few minutes. Despite the short time for response to an Iranian air assault, Riyadh considers Iranian-inspired subversion, rather than airstrikes, to be the more likely threat to occur.

Another contingency of concern to Riyadh is for Iraq to be under coalition force assault while Iran strengthens its diplomatic ties in the region. The Saudis would worry about Iranian diplomatic moves to improve Tehran's relations with Turkey and Pakistan, which would be designed to protect Iran's flanks. Tehran also could expand its relations with other third-world countries in proximity to the Gulf. A shield of compliant rulers from friendly neighboring states would help secure the Islamic revolution at home, lower United States influence in the region, and allow for a more vigorous challenge to the Gulf states. Hence, Riyadh would be very concerned about contingencies, such as Iraq under siege from coalition warplanes, while Iran was on the upswing in military capabilities.

In this second scenario, Iranian-sponsored subversion would be directed at the Gulf states in order to foment popular uprisings among their Shiite Muslim population. Had the Iran-Iraq War ignited a broad-based Shiite revolt in Iraq, that instability could have created smaller-scale flare-ups in Bahrain and perhaps even in Saudi Arabia and Kuwait.

Regarding other contingencies that include Saudi Arabia, there could be a recurrence of the July 1987 Iranian-inspired riots in the Kingdom, in which about 400 people died. Shiite pilgrims from Iran clashed with Saudi security forces near the Grand Mosque in Mecca.[62]

In addition, Saudi Arabia has accused Tehran and Damascus of masterminding attacks on American-Saudi military facilities in Riyadh and Dhahran during 1995 and 1996. Such riots and bombings could escalate tensions between Tehran and Riyadh to the point of involving American air strikes against Iran in defense of the Kingdom. Because of the proximity of Kuwait to the borders of Iraq, Iran, and Saudi Arabia, any conflicts involving Saudi Arabia and Iran would threaten Kuwait as well. Consider the contingency of a conflict between Saudi Arabia and Kuwait versus Iran. Washington could deter or defend against such a contingency better if there were an alignment of convenience between Iraq and the United States.

Besides Saudi Arabia, there are tensions between Iran and smaller Arab Gulf states.[63] In December 1982, during the Iran-Iraq War, Iran undertook to induce the United Arab Emirates (UAE) to be more responsive to Tehran and less sensitive to Riyadh. The Emirates responded by seeking a balance between the two. So long as Iran did not defeat Iraq, Iranian efforts to tip the balance in its favor would fail. Iran's approach, however, was disingenuous. It was designed to win support from the Arab Gulf states and pave the way for a reassertion of Iranian influence in the postwar era.

During the mid-1990s, the Emirates have been the most outspoken of the Gulf state critics of the dual containment policy of the Clinton Administration. They feel that Iran will adopt a more aggressive posture toward them if the comparatively pragmatic Iranian President Rafsanjani had yielded to the more radical Speaker of the Majlis—the Iranian assembly—Natiq-Nouri. But, in fact, Khatemi won the Iranian presidency with about 70 percent of the vote. And he has a similar reputation as Rafsanjani. Hence, there is no reason to expect that Iran would adopt a more assertive posture toward the Emirates.

During September 1993, the UAE's regime of Sheik Zayed was involved in a long-standing dispute with Iran over the administration of the island of Abu Musa. The conflict had escalated during April 1992, when Iran declined to permit hundreds of expatriates back onto that island. Iran and the United Arab Emirates under a 1991 accord jointly administer it. And to make matters even more difficult, the UAE has had other conflicts with Iran over the two Tunb islands in the Gulf. In the context of enhanced tensions over Abu Musa and the Tunb islands, this contingency of escalating tension could be met more effectively if there were cooperation between Iraq and the United States.

Bahrain is another Arab Gulf state in fear of Iran. After the Iranian Shiite revolution in 1979, Tehran stimulated instability among Bahrain's Shiite Muslims and revived its claim to islands in dispute between Bahrain and Iran. And during 1981, Bahrain thwarted an Iranian-inspired plot to foment revolution in the Emirate. Similar plots occurred in 1985. Again, détente between Baghdad and Washington would help deter Iranian moves against Bahrain and facilitate the defense of that state in the event of deterrence failure.

Oman has been worried about its security, especially after the Iranian revolution and the Soviet invasion of Afghanistan. And during the Iran-Iraq War, Oman signed defense agreements with neighboring Arab states against the Iranian threat. In order to block first the rise of Soviet, and then Iranian, influence around the entrance to the Gulf, the Sultan of Oman signed a 1980 accord with Washington. The arrangement provided for American military assistance in exchange for U.S. access to Omani bases. Because of the location of Oman at the southern end of the Gulf, there is less of a need for accommodation between Iraq and the United States for its defense.

As a result of scenarios involving hostilities between Arab Gulf states and Iran or Iranian-inspired efforts to destabilize these regimes, they would like to see an Arab counterweight to Iran, and that could only be Iraq.[64] These scenarios argue for Washington to have a tacit alignment with Baghdad as a counter to Tehran.

American attacks in the Gulf on Iranian shipping and U.S. cruise missile attacks on military positions within Iran would imply that Baghdad and Washington would be in a position to cooperate against a common adversary, Tehran. And if Saddam fell from power, that could be a pretext for an incremental reintroduction of Iraq into the family of nations. With Saddam out, tacit alignment with the United States would be a distinct possibility. In fact, Saddam's demise could allow for an explicit alliance between Western countries and Iraq. Such a contingency would be quite worrisome to Israel as well as to Iraq's neighbors.

A Grand Bargain: Iraqi Compliance for End of Economic Warfare

In the event of escalating hostilities instigated by Iran against the Arab Gulf states and in the Arab-Israel zone, as well as the ouster of Saddam, conditions would give rise to the possibility of a deal between Baghdad and Washington. The grand bargain is already explicit in the sanctions regime imposed on Iraq by the UN. Iraq would have to comply fully with UN Security Council Resolution 687, whose main purpose is to prevent Baghdad from becoming once again a military threat to Iraq's neighbors or to the Gulf region as a whole. And Baghdad would have to demonstrate that it would not seek to acquire or develop nuclear weapons or engage in nuclear weapons research and development, support, or manufacturing.

In exchange for full Iraqi compliance, economic warfare against Baghdad would be lifted. In the meantime, Iraq's partial compliance resulted in a temporary arrangement: UN Security Council Resolution 986. It permits Iraq to sell up to $1 billion in oil every 90 days in order to pay for humanitarian relief supplies, reparations, as well as operating expenses of UN monitoring units in Iraq.[65] For Washington to agree to a complete lifting of international sanctions, American leaders would not have to shift their policy from one designed to overthrow the Saddam regime. With another leader in power, the United States goal could change from retribution to rehabilitation. There would be no need to move the goal post as Baghdad approaches compliance.

The likelihood of a grand bargain between Washington and Baghdad, however, is low. It is unlikely that Saddam will be ousted and even more so that Tehran will act militarily against Saudi Arabia, Kuwait, and the Arab Gulf states. Meanwhile, the United States has to remain alert to the danger imposed by both rogue states, Iran and Iraq, while Washington keeps open the option of tacitly cooperating with either one against the other.

Consider the four themes that cut across *Rogue Regimes*—threat perception, opportunities, politics, and policies. For Iraq, politics with the added element of personality are core factors that explain American policy. The last chapter finds that Washington deals with Iran as a nation-state irrespective of who's at the helm in Tehran. By contrast, Washington deals with Saddam as the personification of Iraq. And in connection with the debate about the nature of threats to the international system, Iraq is a fitting substitute for the Soviet menace. There are similar perceptions of threat and opportunity among the allies. Hence, it is easier to fashion joint policy of sanctions against Saddam than for Iran. Punishment against Saddam can be justified, because it appeals to domestic political constituencies, is in line with American idealism, and may even change his behavior.

CHAPTER FOUR

LIBYA: CONTAIN
OR EMBRACE

THE IRAN AND LIBYA SANCTIONS ACT OF 1996

IN A UNANIMOUS VOTE Congress passed legislation that imposed a
secondary trade boycott on the firms of America's closest allies.[1] If
they dared to invest substantial sums in the energy sectors of Iran
or Libya, the businesses could be subjected to stiff penalties. The
unanimity of the vote is an indication of the overwhelming public
sentiment against both countries. As the vote suggests, there were
no advocates of the option of embracing Colonel Muammar
Qadhafi of Libya in order to change his errant ways. Rather, the
opinion of the American public was clear: contain Qadhafi so that
he cannot engage in subversion, terrorism, or chemical weapons
proliferation.

In order to understand why the Sanctions Act passed with no
dissent, one must consider the geopolitical situation in the Mediterranean, the American-Libyan relationship over time, American
objectives and interests regarding Libya, as well as sources of U.S.
threat perceptions. This chapter pays particular attention to bureaucratic political maneuvering during the Reagan years, when the die
was cast concerning the hard-line approach toward Libya. With this
overview in mind, it is possible to understand the effects of
unilateral American as well as United Nations sanctions against

Libya. In addition, the overview provides historical context for the battle being waged by Qadhafi for the "American Street." Finally, there is a discussion for scenarios relevant to the future of American-Libyan relations.

PREPONDERANCE OF POWER
IN THE MEDITERRANEAN

While Iran and Iraq are rogues of the Gulf region, Libya is a geopolitical outlaw of the Mediterranean. The question for Washington regarding Tehran and Baghdad is whether to embrace or contain them, and the answer is less than clear-cut. It requires a determination whether the United States wants to balance Tehran against Baghdad, or vice versa; if so, then accommodation with at least one of these states is conceivable and advisable.[2]

If the leadership of Tehran and Baghdad were waiting to seize windows of opportunity, then containment would be preferable. And, because of indications that these leaders are acting more for gain than to stave off pain, containment is the order of the day. Although there is evidence that fear is a motivating factor, opportunity appears to dominate. And with both rehabilitation and retribution as motivating factors underlying American national security policy toward Iran and Iraq, containment of one or the other can be readily justified.

When Iraq and the United States are on friendly terms, the dominant explanation for Saddam's rogue behavior is that he is a paranoid afraid of losses and in need of Western understanding. As a paranoid in the 1980s, the image of Saddam was that he was capable of being a friend. When problems arose in the relationship, Washington explained Saddam's outlaw behavior as a consequence of his Machiavellian desire for gain, as a result of which he did not deserve Western empathy.

Regarding Qadhafi, his relationship with American presidents has been downhill all the way, in contrast to the ups and downs with Saddam. The explanation is more consistent for Qadhafi's behavior than for Saddam's: Qadhafi has always been a Machiavellian leader out for gain, deserving of United States sanctions, and undeserving of American empathy.

With respect to Libya, therefore, the answer to the question whether to contain or embrace is straightforward: containment and perhaps confrontation are the options to pursue. Hence, the U.S. geopolitical strategy is to surround Libya with a ring of states aligned with Washington and to supplement this with a preponderance of credible American power within striking distance. In this respect, the Gulf of Sidra, an international waterway that borders on Libya, is a flash point of confrontation between Tripoli and Washington.

Unlike the comparatively clear threat posed by Libya and the consensus about how to meet it, there is more ambiguity regarding Iran and Iraq. Because Washington has alternated between a balance of power and a dual containment approach in the Gulf, neither Iran nor Iraq has been the permanent enemy Libya has been.[3] When Presidents Reagan and Bush conducted a balancing approach, there was a move to accommodate Iran and/or Iraq. Upon the adoption of dual containment as Clinton's policy of choice, both regimes were considered rogues. Iran and Iraq were to be isolated until they changed their ways or the offending regimes fell from power.

Balance of power and dual containment are national security policies that focus on the nature of danger from abroad. But what is the menace? Threats depend on perceptions. And perceptions derive from values as interpreted by bureaucratic organizations and political interest groups. A threat to one organization or group may be an opportunity to others.

Economic and ethnic groups clash in the determination of what is a threat and thus in the formulation of policy. In the event of economic interest-group domination of the policy process, there is an inclination for the United States to move closer to Iran or Iraq. When national security and economic vectors line up, they reinforce one another. Hence, a policy of accommodation and even appeasement of rogue states is possible, but often not advisable. But when ethnic-group lobbying magnifies national security threats, this convergence facilitates a policy of containment and confrontation.

Balance of power ideas, however, are not as relevant to the Mediterranean as to the Gulf. It makes no sense to balance Libya and

Syria. There is, however, a perceived need to strengthen countries on all sides of Libya—Morocco, Tunisia, Chad, the Sudan, and Egypt. But such a buildup via economic and military assistance is for the purpose of encircling Libya with antagonist states that are friendly to the United States. Also, there is the belief in Washington that these countries would like the United States to isolate, contain, and confront Libya.

Republican and Democratic presidents have imposed varying degrees of sanctions on Libya. Washington imposed a unilateral arms embargo on Tripoli in the mid-1970s, closed the American embassy in Tripoli in 1980, and closed the Libyan mission in Washington in 1981. Because of Libya's aggressive activities toward America's friends in the Mediterranean, there is bipartisan consensus in favor of a containment policy against Tripoli.

In October 1980, during the Carter Administration, Qadhafi sent Libyan ground combat forces as well as helicopters and aircraft into neighboring Chad, a country due south of Libya. With explicit Soviet approval, Cuban and East German military advisors facilitated Libya's invasion. Long-range, Soviet-built aircraft also carried out bombing raids against Chad. As armored and mechanized units proceeded on the ground within that country, Qadhafi also sent his military across the border into the Sudan, just southeast of Libya.

The Libyan invasion of Chad and its raids into the Sudan were accompanied by subversion of regimes throughout Africa: Cameroon, Gabon, Gambia, Ghana, Liberia, Mali, Niger, Nigeria, Senegal, Sierra Leone, and Uganda. As a result, leaders of these states perceived a growing threat from Libya.

One specific manifestation of Libya's troublemaking involves Egypt in the late 1970s. After a military confrontation in its Western Desert, President Sadat had asked the Carter Administration to cooperate with him against Qadhafi. He wanted to develop a preponderance of power to deter and confront Libyan aggression. Washington, however, refrained from conducting coordinated military planning with Cairo for an attack against Libya. Sadat believed that President Carter lacked the determination to stand up against Colonel Qadhafi. This perception on the part of Sadat would cast a shadow on the credibility of the American commitment to Egypt, which felt endangered by the threat of radical Arab states like Libya.

Egypt is not alone in its aversion toward radical Arab regimes. Despite their differences, Egypt and Israel share a common threat perception of extreme Arab states. Like President Sadat, General Ariel Sharon of Israel was also concerned with the radical threat posed by regimes like Libya, Iraq, Syria, and South Yemen. During 1981, he stated that these regimes had a political/military strategy for the liquidation of Israel. Their approach included Soviet political support, a military buildup via arms transfers from Moscow, and the use of the oil weapon. Sharon also saw the PLO as an element in a Soviet strategy to foster subversion against moderate Arab regimes like Egypt's and build up fanatical Arab regimes like Libya's.[4]

According to Sharon, Soviet goals included attaining a sea-control capability in the Mediterranean, the Indian Ocean, the Gulf, and the Red Sea. Moscow wanted to penetrate key countries in the Middle East and the Gulf from the direction of Afghanistan, Iraq, South Yemen, and Syria. The Soviets wanted to outflank NATO's eastern tier through Iran, Iraq, Syria, and Lebanon. In addition, the USSR desired to get around its southern tier in the Mediterranean by aligning with Libya, Syria, and Algeria. Moscow also wanted to gain control over critical states in Africa from the direction of Libya, Algeria, South Yemen, Ethiopia, Mozambique, Angola, and the Congo-Brazzaville. Finally, Sharon defined these areas of Soviet interests as "the strategic hinterland of Israel."[5] Although Libya is not an active confrontation state on the front line against Israel, Tripoli constitutes a serious threat to Jerusalem.

While Sharon expressed his threat perception of Soviet-inspired Arab radicalism in the winter of 1981, Sadat had already expressed similar concerns the summer before his death in October 1981.[6] Following Libya's invasion of Chad, Sadat thought that the Sudan would be Qadhafi's next target. And with Soviet assistance, Egypt could be on Libya's hit list after the Sudan. Sadat suspected that Moscow was behind Libya's efforts to envelop Egypt. Because Egypt and the Sudan share a long border, Cairo has a vital interest in its neighbor. Sadat could not afford to let the Sudan fall prey to Libyan and Soviet domination. Radicals then would control one of Egypt's major strategic assets—the Nile River, where over 90 percent of the Egyptian population resides.

Furthermore, Libya also could gain a foothold along the Red Sea because of its alliance with Ethiopia and Aden (South Yemen). During the late 1970s and early 1980s, leaders of Somalia and the Sudan perceived that a tripartite alignment of Aden, Ethiopia, and Libya was directed primarily toward Somalia, Sana (North Yemen), and the Sudan. And the ultimate objective of this collusion was to undermine moderate regimes in Egypt and Saudi Arabia. As a result, Sudanese President Nimeiri welcomed the Reagan Administration's resolve to deter Qadhafi. He wanted the United States to make Qadhafi powerless to deliver on promised assistance to Ethiopia—assistance that was conditional on active Ethiopian opposition to the Nimeiri regime in Khartoum.[7]

An informal league of extreme states composed of Iran, Libya, and Syria began to worry the Arab moderates that the radicals were out to destabilize their mainstream regimes. Tehran had upgraded its links to Damascus and Tripoli in order to acquire additional military supplies during the Iran-Iraq War. Iran was pursuing an overall strategy with three phases: create an Islamic revolution, starting in Tehran; subvert Arab regimes, beginning with Saudi Arabia and the Arab Gulf states; and spread the Islamic revolution to Turkey, Pakistan, and the Arab states of the Fertile Crescent and the Nile Valley.

One of Iran's moderate Gulf targets was the United Arab Emirates, which wanted to mediate between Libya and the United States in order to split Libya off from Iran. The UAE reasoned that the best way to neutralize Qadhafi was to reconcile him with Washington. The Emirates feared Iranian expansionism. Besides Syria, Libya was the only ally Iran had in the Arab world. The rulers of the Emirates understood that the only protection against an Iranian attack was the United States.

Unless there was advance coordination between the moderate Arab states and the United States, protection would have arrived too late to prevent an Iranian takeover. But the fight between Washington and Tripoli made coordination with the United States on security against an Iranian attack all the more difficult. Note that it was not the Palestinian issue that hindered strategic planning with the United

States, but rather Washington's disagreements with Tripoli USSR stood to gain from lack of strategic cooperation between United States and the Arab Gulf states.

The consensus in the Reagan Administration during 1981, its first year of office, was that Moscow was attempting to exploit tensions between Tripoli and Washington in order to forge closer links with Libya. The USSR was stepping up arms sales to Libya in exchange for hard currency. The accord among Libya, the People's Democratic Republic of Yemen, and Ethiopia was a way for the Soviet Union to strengthen its presence in the region. Hence, Soviet arms to Libya would have allowed it to arm Yemen and Ethiopia.

Libya also supplied oil for Eastern European states when the Soviets were cutting back on oil shipments. Enhanced access to Tripoli ports and other facilities provided Moscow with the best strategic position it had had since being ousted from Egypt in 1972. Although somewhat close, however, Moscow and Tripoli were still quite a distance apart regarding policy coordination. The October 1981 Soviet deployment preceded one in July of that year. They represented a substantial plus for Moscow's naval interests in the Mediterranean. Since Cairo expelled Moscow's naval air element in 1972, no Soviet naval aviation shore-based aircraft had flown missions for reconnaissance over the Mediterranean until the July and October 1981 deployments. These were a significant step toward Moscow's aim of establishing a permanent naval air presence on the Mediterranean littoral.

While Soviet-supported Libya was invading Chad and the Sudan, as well as subverting regimes to its south, it was less active in the Arab-Israel conflict zone. Tripoli was even out of step with the main confrontation state against Israel—Syria. Despite the fact that they shared a history of acute confrontation with Israel, virulent anti-imperialism, and unwavering Arab nationalism, Libya and Syria differed with respect to their commitment to the Arab-Israel peace process. As stated in the following chapter on Syria, there is evidence that Damascus has made a strategic commitment to make peace with Israel. Libya has not made such a commitment. Indeed, Tripoli stands outside of the peace process, just as it stands outside of the mainstream of African states, the Arab nation, and the Islamic world.

TRIPOLI AND WASHINGTON:
FRIENDS IN THE 1960s, ENEMIES THEREAFTER

American relations with Iraq and Iran have been on a roller coaster of ups and downs over time. U.S. relations with Libya, however, were friendly before 1969 and hostile thereafter, when a coup removed a pro-American king from power and replaced him with a group of anti-American leaders. On September 1, 1969, a group of young army officers overthrew the royal government and established a republic.

Dominated by Colonel Muammar Qadhafi, the revolutionary government displayed a strong resolve to play a major role in the Middle East theater. Tripoli negotiated with Cairo and Khartoum to coordinate their political, economic, and military policies. And during September 1971, Libya succeeded in forming a political federation with Egypt and Syria. Designed to be an alliance against Israel, this federation was a nonstarter. It lasted only until 1974, because of internal rivalries.[8]

Despite the failure of the federation, Libya's appetite for coordination was still strong. Tripoli sought to coordinate the oil weapon in the struggle against Israel. After Israel's 1973 war with Egypt and Syria, Libya joined an embargo. Tripoli raised its oil prices in order to take advantage of the panic associated with the war.

One of the reasons for Libya's tensions with Egypt concerns the Arab-Israel peace process. While there is some doubt about the commitment that Damascus has made for peace with Israel, there is less doubt about Egypt's commitment. Tripoli opposed Sadat's peace initiatives toward Israel and played a leading part with Syria in the rejectionist front. Tripoli provided strong political and financial support for the PLO in the late 1970s. In addition, during the early 1980s, Tripoli began a campaign of state-sponsored terrorism and assassinations of Libyan dissidents who lived abroad.

Accelerating the descent from friend to enemy, Libya's relations with the United States deteriorated with the coming of the Reagan Administration to power. I had the privilege of serving on candidate Reagan's political campaign and then on President Reagan's National Security Council staff. At the White House, I shared the action on Middle East matters with these colleagues: Geoffrey Kemp and Douglas Feith, and later, with Oliver North and Howard Teicher. Based on the division of labor at the White House from March 1981 to September 1982, I had the principal action on Libya and Lebanon, but shared it with Teicher once he came on board in the summer of 1982.

Teicher was one of the national security professionals who was a holdover from the Carter Administration's Pentagon and State Department. Although during the transition he was a relatively low-level civil servant, he rose rapidly through the ranks with the incoming Reagan team. He represented the holdovers who were delighted with President Reagan's hard-line stance again the Soviet Union and its radical Arab allies like Libya. Indeed, with the invasion of Chad in mind, Teicher and his allies agreed with our description of Libya as the "cat's paw" of Soviet expansionism.

Unlike the Carter Administration, we Reagan officials not only believed that the United States had a strategic interest in arresting Soviet inroads into the Middle East, but were prepared to combine economic diplomacy with military force to achieve that objective in the case of Libya. That is, we wanted the United States to act in accord with its great-power status in the world at large as well as in the Mediterranean vis-à-vis Libya.

AMERICAN OBJECTIVES AND INTERESTS

Washington's aims with respect to Tripoli concern antisubversion, counterterrorism, and nonproliferation. Specific American objectives are to coerce Tripoli to cease its subversive behavior toward neighboring countries that are friendly to Washington, to terminate its sponsorship of international terrorist organizations, and to end the pursuit of weapons of mass destruction, with particular reference to chemical armaments. Underlying these specific aims are strategic interests. They are both more general and more important than the specific purposes just mentioned.

Strategic Interests

As a superpower, the United States has a strategic interest in making sure that it is unchallenged. A perception of invincibility is the glue that holds together the American deterrent system. To the extent that Tripoli stands up to Washington, it challenges U.S. credibility, resolve, and commitments. When a nation like Libya challenges Washington's resolve, the likelihood of deterrence failure elsewhere increases. And if that nation is aligned with another superpower, as Libya was associated with the USSR in the 1980s, then the United States should not tolerate challenges to its will.

Consider the coalition designed to multiply the influence of the radicals and to counter American alliances in the Middle East: the tripartite pact among Libya, the Peoples Democratic Republic of Yemen, and Ethiopia. Signed in August 1981, it was a direct political challenge to the United States and its friends like Egypt, Jordan, and Israel. Also imagine a situation in which Washington took action against Libya and neither Moscow nor its surrogates supported their ally. Such a scenario would constitute a major strategic victory for Uncle Sam over the Russian Bear.

The strategy for achieving American objectives regarding Libya are to challenge Tripoli's claim to territorial waters beyond the normal 12 mile limit, to confront Libya's state sponsorship of international terrorism, and to coerce Libya to cease the development of chemical weapons. Freedom of the seas is not only a strategic interest of the United States, it also is a value that stems from the American principle of free market capitalism. And when ideals reinforce strategic interests, that is a potent brew indeed.

Freedom of the Seas

Libya posed a threat to freedom of the seas when it asserted an extension of its territorial waters beyond the recognized limits of international law. In light of great-power status, Cold War perceptions, international law ideals, as well as antiterrorism attitudes, it is no surprise that Tripoli and Washington were on a collision course in the spring and summer of 1981.

Consistent with its strategic interest in asserting its principles concerning freedom of the seas, Washington initiated a freedom of navigation challenge in international waters in the Gulf of Sidra, an area of the Mediterranean claimed by Libya as being in its territory.

Although the global standard for national territorial waters is 12 miles, Qadhafi claimed that Libyan waters extended 200 miles. Hence, during March 1981, the U.S. Sixth Fleet began to conduct air and sea exercises in the Gulf of Sidra.

With respect to the use of the Gulf of Sidra for military exercises, the Organization of the Joint Chiefs of Staff was neutral concerning the idea of sending a strategic signal to Qadhafi. They did feel, however, that if there were to be military exercises, there ought to be a military benefit. The Pentagon planned to conduct an exercise to fire a missile from an American warship. The Gulf of Sidra was a good location because it was not along the main sea-and-air-lanes of commerce.

On August 19, 1981, the U.S. Navy conducted a military exercise in the Gulf of Sidra. Upon being challenged by Libyan planes, two U.S. F-14 aircraft shot down two Libyan warplanes. The shoot-down occurred after the Libyan pilots had prepared to attack and activated the target-acquisition radars and guidance systems of their air-to-air missiles.

Qadhafi could not accept the downing of Libyan warplanes, because Libya has a strategic interest in not being seen as a compliant nation. He used the shootdown as a point of departure for rallying domestic political support for his faltering regime and for rallying Arab support against the United States. He was more successful in using the raids to bolster his standing at home than abroad, receiving virtually no support in his calls for Arab leaders to retaliate against Washington in the Gulf of Sidra.

Counterterrorism

In addition to interests like reputation, resolve, and freedom of the seas, Libya threatens other American interests. One means by which Libya confronts Washington is through state-sponsored terrorism. American intelligence detected Libyan assassination planning. The notorious "Carlos" may have been involved in plans to conduct terror strikes in the United States, and an Amal hit team had been formed in Libya for operations in the United States.[9] There was to be an attack against the President sometime between December 1 and 15, 1981. And later, on January 21, 1982, there were reports that Libyan assassination teams fled to Mexico and remained there.

Regarding terrorism, Tripoli threatens American civilians and military personnel. Although these lives in and of themselves are of great intrinsic value, the reason for their being targeted by Tripoli is not because of who they are as individuals but that they symbolize the United States as a nation. Consequently, intrinsic and strategic interests coincide in the case of international terrorism.[10]

During November 1991, courts in the United States and the United Kingdom indicted two Libyan intelligence agents implicated in the bombing of Pan Am Flight 103 in 1988 over Lockerbie, Scotland. The United Nations Security Council passed three resolutions demanding that the Government of Libya take steps to end its participation in state-sponsored terrorism, and to extradite the two suspects. Resolution 731 of January 1992 demanded that Libya accept responsibility for the bombing, disclose all evidence related to it, and pay appropriate compensation to the families of the victims.[11]

In April 1992, the Security Council adopted Resolution 748.[12] It imposed an arms and civil aviation embargo on Libya, demanded that Libyan Arab Airlines offices shut down, and required that all states reduce Tripoli's diplomatic appearance abroad. Libya's continued challenge to the resolutions led the Security Council to approve Resolution 883, in November 1993, which tightened existing sanctions, imposed a limited-assets freeze, and placed an oil technology embargo on Libya.[13]

The State Department contends that Tripoli made some minor changes to its terrorism infrastructure after the adoption of Resolutions 731 and 748. But Libya made no further changes to its terrorism network. Although there has been a decline in the regime's sponsorship of terrorism, its apparatus for conducting such actions remains intact. Qadhafi repeated his anti-Western ideas throughout 1994 and 1995, and he offered support to radical Palestinian groups opposed to the PLO's Gaza-Jericho accord with Israel.

Also, Qadhafi threatened to support extremist Islamic groups in the neighboring states of Algeria and Tunisia as penalty for not supporting Libya against the UN sanctions effort. Qadhafi's speeches in the fall of 1993, after a mid-October uprising and subsequent crackdown in Libya, became more hostile. He pledged to retaliate against Libyan oppositionists, those who enforced sanctions against Libya, and individuals who cooperated with Washington.

Not only does Libya target American citizens, it also directs terrorism against its own political opposition at home and abroad. The Department of State accuses Tripoli of the 1993 abduction, and continued detention, of a prominent Libyan dissident and human rights activist, Mansur Kikhia.[14] And throughout 1995, moreover, Libya continued to support groups violently opposed to the Middle East peace process. These groups often express their opposition with acts of international terrorism.[15] In addition to international terrorism, Libya fails to comply with Washington's attempts to discourage the proliferation of weapons of mass destruction.

Anti-Proliferation

While Libya's subversion and terrorism were on the decline, its proliferation of weapons of mass destruction was on the rise. During the late 1980s, Western intelligence agencies held that Libya engaged in chemical weapons development. In this respect, proliferation of chemical weapons in the Middle East became a core concern of United States national security policy during 1988. At that time, three events converged: construction of the Libyan poison gas facility at Rabta, deadly use of chemical weapons by both sides during the Iran-Iraq War, and Baghdad's use of poison gas against its own Kurdish population.[16] As a result of this coincidence of chemical weapons use, the United States called for an international conference. Held in Paris, its purpose was to raise the world's consciousness about these mass destruction devices.[17]

Washington had four main goals for the Paris Conference. The first was to urge the signers of the 1925 Geneva Protocol to restate their commitment to that document.[18] The second was to take multinational steps to discourage chemical weapons use. A third purpose was to conclude a new international treaty prohibiting the production and stockpiling of these weapons. Finally, the United States wanted to apply economic sanctions to those engaging in the use of chemical weapons, but Washington was not able to achieve consensus for their implementation.

Franco-American cooperation was the key to bringing about the chemical weapons conference. Although France did not agree with the United States that Libya indeed was building a chemical weapons facility, Paris joined with Washington in highlighting the dangers of these tools of mass destruction. Contrary to the French and American understanding, Arab nations were dissatisfied with the proposed emphasis on chemical weapons proliferation in the Middle East. From the perspective of Arab states in attendance, they felt that any enforcement actions that might come from the conference could be perceived as pointed at the Middle Eastern nations in general, and Iran, Iraq, and Libya in particular.[19]

Libya was both an attendee of the conference and a target of American accusations. Libya came as a signatory of the 1925 Geneva Protocol. Under the principle that a best defense is an offense, Qadhafi suggested that the conference turn its attention to chemical plants in America, Europe, and Israel. Though few believed him, Qadhafi explicitly declared that Libya was against producing chemical weapons.[20]

As of the late 1990s, the jury was still out as to whether Libya was indeed building a facility that housed chemical weapons. But there is evidence that Tripoli is constructing a facility. Western intelligence agencies believe that Libya is building such a factory at Tarhunah, 40 miles southeast of Tripoli. The plant is reportedly being built into a mountain, which would make it difficult to destroy in a military strike using conventional weapons. Tripoli designed the Tarhunah facility in order to replace the plant at Rabta, which is 55 miles southwest of Tripoli. The Rabta facility was reopened in the fall of 1995, five years after a suspicious fire.[21] Libya insisted that the plant only made material for pharmaceuticals. Western intelligence agencies, however, believed that Libya was constructing it for the purpose of producing chemical weapons.

In retaliation for such accusations, Libya accused the United States of hypocrisy on the issue. Tripoli hoped that Western export controls on Libya would not prohibit the export of technology necessary for the so-called peaceful means of the development of his society. Because of his protests, American national security policy-makers were even more intent than before to contain Qadhafi. But

United States economic decisionmakers were just as intent on not letting national security considerations dominate without a fight.

SOURCES OF AMERICAN THREAT PERCEPTION

Politics of Policy Making

Principal sources of threat perception regarding Tehran and Baghdad are ethnic politics, economic interests of the business community, and bureaucratic differences. For Libya, the battle between politics and business interests also applies. While ethnic politics are more important in the cases of Iran and Iraq, they are of less consequence for Libya. Accordingly, this policy-making section for Libya discusses bureaucratic politics at the expense of ethnic politics.

One split in the bureaucracy is between foreign policy and national security—between State, the CIA, and the National Security Council staff and Treasury, Commerce, and the United States Trade Representative. A second divide is between military and civilians from the Department of Defense versus civilians from the White House and the State Department.[22]

And a third gap is within State, between the hard-line functional bureaus—Policy Planning and Politico-Military Affairs—and the softer-line geographical bureaus—Near Eastern and South Asian Affairs as well as European and Canadian Affairs.[23] A fourth division is between foreign policy/national security and criminal justice agencies.

Momentum for the imposition of sanctions picked up on October 1, 1981, when the State Department chaired a meeting of the Libyan Task Force. On the table was the nature of the threat from Libya to Belgium, Greece, and Italy. European countries tolerated a higher level of threat from Libya than did the United States. Nevertheless, there was considerable evidence presented about a growing perception on the part of these nations for the need to take action to counter the threat from Libya.

There was also a discussion of American objectives toward Libya. These aims included the deterrence-by-denial strategy of diminishing

Qadhafi's ability to carry out terror attacks. In addition, there was the political purpose of enhancing his isolation in the Arab world while minimizing risks to American citizens on the ground. A general objective was to carry out the president's policy of bringing swift and effective retribution against those who engaged in terrorism against the United States.

Specific goals included: demonstrating to Qadhafi that Washington would not tolerate acts of terrorism against U.S. interests, and raising the price sufficiently to deter him from future acts of terrorism—a deterrence by threat of punishment strategy. Items of concern to Qadhafi were Libyan military capabilities, economic interests, his personal prestige, domestic political support, and his image within the nonaligned movement.

Egyptian Vice President Mubarak was in Washington during the October 1981 meeting and said Sadat was concerned as to whether the United States would stand tough against Libya. Sadat had good reason to doubt the American resolve, given the unwillingness of the Carter Administration to take forceful action against Libya or to engage in military planning for the destabilization of Qadhafi's regime. While calling for tougher measures against the likes of a Qadhafi, however, Sadat paid the ultimate price for making peace—he was assassinated six days into the month of October.

The 1981 assassination of Sadat gave a new sense of urgency to the planning process regarding Libya. If there were Libyan foreknowledge of the Sadat assassination, this knowledge would have been reflected in the alert sequence of the Libyan armed forces.[24] They did not go on alert prior to the assassination, and thus Tripoli may not have been aware of it. Notwithstanding the time pressure, there also was a need for caution. In this respect, constraints on contingency planning gave rise to cautious risk-averse planning, which was exceedingly slow. As a result, critics seized upon the delays as evidence that the Administration lacked will.[25]

The aversion to risk highlighted a need to assure the safety of American citizens, and those from countries friendly to the United States, who happened to work in Libya. There also was a requirement to avoid measures that would rally support for Qadhafi on the Arab street and in the nonaligned movement. We officials at the White

House were concerned that the United States not push him into a corner where he felt there was no other option except to escalate. In the language of classical deterrence theory, we surmised that he had to believe that the benefits of Libyan escalation were not as important to him as the costs of further retaliation from the United States.

In view of these goals, there was a consideration of diplomatic, economic, and military responses to Libya. On the diplomatic side, options included an embargo on the purchase of Libyan oil, a prohibition on U.S. companies for operating in Libya, and mandatory withdrawal of American citizens. Additionally, there was a ban on U.S. travel to Libya, a freeze on Libyan financial assets, elimination of Export-Import Bank financing for Libya, a ban on U.S. exports to Libya, and a cessation of U.S. visas for Libyan nationals.

Despite the tendency for there to be splits within State, there was a general accord between the functional and geographical bureaus. The Staff for Policy Planning and Politico-Military Affairs, on the one hand, and the Bureau of Near Eastern and South Asian Affairs, on the other hand, agreed on a joint recommendation to Secretary of State Alexander Haig. The consensus was that authorization be given to warn Qadhafi that the United States would respond to a Libyan attack on American assets. Once American citizens had been ordered out of Libya or had departed on their own, military options would include the following: open assistance to anti-Libyan elements in Chad and suggestions that Egypt consider military action against Libya.

Although there was agreement at State, there was less accord between it and the Pentagon. At an October 2, 1981, meeting of the Libyan Task Force, the representative of the Joint Chiefs of Staff first requested, then demanded, a list of political goals.[26] The Chiefs wanted this list of aims to use as a basis for military contingency planning, in the event of anti-U.S. terrorism by Libya. Pentagon officials did not believe that the political aims had been specified clearly enough. Hence, they withheld their support for tough measures against Libya until such time as they felt that there was sufficient specificity.

Another illustration of the battles between State and Defense concerned the clearance process for terms of reference to impose sanctions on Libya. In the process of coalition formation, on December

16, 1981, State Department Counselor Robert McFarlane called me to discuss the procedure for clearing on an interagency basis a terms-of-reference memorandum for cabinet members. Because of tensions between State and Defense, McFarlane wanted to use the National Security Council as the authority for carrying out the State Department's objectives. That is, he wanted the National Security Council, not the Department of State, to be listed as the authorizing agency in the clearance process.

Deputy National Security Advisor John Poindexter told me that he was unsure of what McFarlane was trying to achieve. I replied that it was clear he wanted to cover his flanks by having the White House provide a shield for State against Defense. I suggested that we work closely with McFarlane, while being careful that we were not being used to our disadvantage.[27]

McFarlane's deputy at State, Howard Teicher, called me during December 1981 to inquire about who should receive the inputs for a paper on sanctions regarding Libya and who should compile them. McFarlane's view was that the State Department or the National Security Council staff should receive inputs, but that State should pull the paper together. Poindexter and I agreed that the reports should go to the co-chairs, Bud Nance and McFarlane. State should pull the reports together, I would have an informal role in the process, and then the National Security Council staff should officially receive the paper. State's goal was to forge a coalition with the National Security Council staff as a way to gain additional leverage over the Department of Defense.

And there are other examples of effective policy coordination between the White House and the State Department. With respect to American citizens working in Libya, the Deputy Assistant Secretary of State in the Bureau of Near Eastern and South Asian Affairs called me to inquire where the White House stood in regard to replacement of American workers with those from allied countries. Most Americans in Libya were involved in the exploration for, but not the production of, oil and gas. In this respect, Italy had queried the American embassy in Rome as to the American reaction if Italian workers were to replace Americans who had left. We agreed that State should reply that the United States was neutral to positive, in order to discourage Tripoli from replacing American citizens with Eastern European or Russian workers. State followed the White House line, the outcome was acceptable to Rome, and Russian workers going to Libya were kept to a minimum.

In the process of coalition formation, there are times when advocates of an option in one department will seek allies in another organization in order to affect the decision-making outcome in their own department. During April 1982, a few American citizens wanted to reenter Libya in order to collect on debts due to them prior to the imposition of economic restrictions on travel to Libya. The bureaucratic lineup at the State Department was as follows regarding the reentry option: The Bureau of Near Eastern and South Asian Affairs favored it, its staff for Policy Planning was neutral, and the bureaus of Consular Affairs and Legal Affairs opposed reentry.

Those favoring reentry asked me to weigh in on their side. McFarlane advised me to say that the National Security Council staff had no problem with reentry, but that those who favored it should be aware that the Secretary of State might not look kindly on the National Security Council staff being used to determine the outcome of a bureaucratic dispute at State. I took the position that I had no difficulty weighing in on the decision-making process in favor of reentry, as long as my name was not used in memoranda going to the Secretary of State.

While the bureaus at State were trying to use the White House to gain advantage, there were incidents that reflected just plain confusion and ignorance at Defense. Consider an anecdote about policy coordination that highlights the state of affairs regarding Libya. A military officer on detail with the Office of the Secretary of Defense (OSD)/ International Security Affairs called me to ask whether OSD had coordinated internally on the Libyan study. My answer was, "Why are you calling the White House to find out what your own department has or has not done?" The officer then said that State had suggested that he call the White House to find out if the Department of Defense had coordinated. I told the officer that he should find out within Defense itself whether it had coordinated.

Another policy coordination issue concerned the likelihood of a Soviet response to potential United States military intervention in

Libya. I told an analyst with the CIA to contact her counterpart with the OSD and share names of those working on the Libyan study. She said, "This makes sense. But do you mean that we're going to have a coordinated product?" I replied, "Sorry if it disappoints you, but yes."

In other words, there was bureaucratic warfare and policy coordination difficulties among State, Defense, and the CIA. Additionally, there were turf fights within the National Security Council staff over who had the action on Libya. At issue was who would be the point of contact at the White House for Libyan contingency planning. I sparred with General Robert Schweitzer over who would represent the White House on the Libyan Task Force. Schweitzer demanded that a meeting of the military subgroup of the interagency group be canceled, because he had not been invited and I was representing the White House. We did not cancel the meeting, and the general and I worked out a compromise for future meetings.

One of the reasons why generals at the White House and at the Pentagon were on edge about military planning was that the possibility of a regional conflict between Tripoli and Washington could escalate and expand to involve Moscow. On December 14, 1981, McFarlane requested that I write terms of reference for the study of Soviet reactions to potential U.S. military action against Libya. As a result, I chaired a working group on Libya. We met in the White House Situation Room. At our first meeting, I thanked Howard Teicher, who worked for McFarlane, for his good interagency group coordination. And at this meeting, I stressed the benefit of a discussion of points at issue as seen from different perspectives. Once our differences were on the table, I would synthesize them into a coherent paper. Even before drafting the paper, there was consensus that Washington should send a message to Moscow about actions to be taken against Libya only at the time of that action, and not beforehand.

Teicher asked about the Eastern European angle: how should the Soviet Union's European allies be factored into a Soviet response to the Libyan sanctions study? Regarding military action, there was concern about bombing Libyan air defenses, because of the likelihood that Soviets manning the facilities would be killed. But the interagency consensus was that because the Soviets were bogged down in possible military action in Poland and in an actual shooting war in Afghanistan, they would be less likely to challenge American action against Libya. In any event, there was little expectation that the Soviets would interpose their forces on behalf of Libya. At issue was the American response if the Soviets moved a combat unit into Libya. There were no advocates for Washington to match Soviet moves, despite the fact that Moscow had very few viable options regarding intervention on behalf of Libya.

During mid-January 1982, the Libyan working group discussed what to do about American citizens in Libya if export controls were imposed and military force used. There were about 400 Americans in Libya during January 1982, and the goal was to evacuate those who chose to depart by mid-February. There were some 300 additional American citizens not working for U.S. companies, some of whom may have been spouses.

In our discussions, the representative of the Office of the Secretary of Defense took a hard-line position against American citizens who might choose to remain in Libya. He said that the purpose of the drawdown was to avoid a hostage situation. The State Department had to inform those who wished to remain that they were on their own. Defense preferred a mandatory order to compel American citizens to depart. An overall purpose of the withdrawal was to provide flexibility of decision making.[28]

In addition to a drawdown of American citizens from Libya, another option considered was the mining of Libyan harbors and waters. But because of the downside of mining—it would take too long to put into effect—it was not a serious option. Defense also expressed an interest in the use of covert operations to destabilize Libya, rather than direct use of American military force. Coupled with an ultimatum listing particulars, covert operations would get the attention of Qadhafi and could have been instrumental in rehabilitating him. A lack of American intelligence assets in Libya, however, made the option of destabilization difficult to achieve. Other forums existed for a discussion of clandestine activities against Libya. Hence, the working group did not discuss the possibility of conducting covert actions against Tripoli.

The State Department was concerned about the presence of about 5,000 Libyans in the United States. State reported how difficult it was to get a handle on them, who was here, and for how long. The Immigration and Naturalization Service was unable to locate people because of inadequate computerization. Of course, that agency then seized upon the Libya crisis as an opportunity to increase the size of their budgetary requests for computers.

Within the White House staff, there were indications of a struggle for power. The setting for it was a draft I prepared on December 10, 1981, for National Security Decision Directive 16 on Libya. It drew upon National Security Council meetings on December 7 and 8 and a checklist initialed by the president. I coauthored the checklist with Admirals Nance and Poindexter on December 7, and the president approved it on December 9. On that day, I met with several officials who had the action: Nance, Poindexter, McFarlane, and Judge William Clark, Acting Secretary of State.

We were to iron out the details on actions toward Libya in the White House Situation Room. There was a morning meeting of principals in the office of Chief of Staff James Baker. The meeting included Baker, Michael Deaver, Clark, Nance, McFarlane, Communications Director David Gergen, and Richard Darman (deputy to Baker). Ed Meese was absent. Meese's deputy, Craig Fuller, and I were in the hallway outside the meeting. Poindexter said to Nance that I should attend, but Nance said no, because Baker had not explicitly invited me. Although I had prepared the draft, shepherded it through the interagency process, and obtained presidential approval, I remained in the hallway, chomping at the bit.

Consider an indication of how bureaucratic power accrues to those who have it, are willing to use it, and courageous enough to deny it to others. On December 9, 1981, Poindexter asked me to send talking points about Libya to Assistant Secretary of Defense for International Security Affairs Bing West for approval. I said that West does not clear his talkers with the National Security Council staff, so why should we clear with him? Poindexter agreed. By not clearing the talking points with the Pentagon, the White House officials retained and perhaps expanded their power.

Here is yet another example of power plays at the White House concerning Libya. Nance told Poindexter to ask me to send a memo to the president via White House Chief of Staff James Baker. It was clear to me that to have done so would have undercut the independent authority of Nance as Acting National Security Advisor. I counseled against doing so because it would downgrade Nance if his memos to the president went via Baker. Poindexter agreed with me, asked me to remove Baker's name, and Nance would then simply show it to Baker. A power play well executed.

Another principle of bureaucratic politics is that power accrues to those in a position to act during a crisis, not necessarily to those who are in a formal channel of authority. Although I was not in the European part of the National Security Council staff, the planning for Libyan contingencies frequently brought me into contact with West Wing principals. That is, I tended to spend a great deal of time in the West Wing of the White House, rather than in my own office in the Executive Office Building, which adjoins the White House proper. Consequently, I happened to be nearby when the Soviets ordered a crackdown by the government of Poland on its own workers. Just being there allowed me to weigh in on the options being considered. Acting National Security Advisor Nance relied on me to assist him on matters relating to Poland, in part because some of the issues regarding the application of sanctions overlapped the cases of Libya and the USSR.

With respect to the intersection of cases, there was a meeting scheduled for February 4, 1982. I wrote the memo for National Security Advisor William Clark on Libya in relation to Poland. The memo asked whether sterner measures could be taken against Libya. Because those American citizens who wished to leave had departed, there was a window open for intense actions against Tripoli. At issue was whether there was adequate legislative authority and political justification to act against Libya in the absence of an overt Libyan provocation. I answered in the affirmative.

The basic paper for the meeting considered Libyan behavior, U.S. objectives, and changes in the international system, including Poland, the world oil market, relations with regional states, Soviet posture, and public opinion. In the context of competing bureaucracies, two executive summaries appeared at the meeting: one from the State Department and mine from the National Security Council.

Contrary to State's summary, which downplayed disagreement within the bureaucracy, I highlighted the consensus as well as the dissent. Treasury had expressed grave doubts about the proposed course of action set out in the State discussion paper on Libya, which had been written as if the only cost of imposing economic sanctions would be friction with the allies. But there also would be substantial economic costs to the United States. Treasury also took the position that Washington should take all effective measures, but also believed that court rulings concerning extraterritoriality in allied nations could make export controls unenforceable.

At issue at the February 1982 meeting regarding Poland was whether expanded export controls on oil and gas equipment for the USSR should be interpreted to include United States subsidiaries and/ or equipment manufactured by U.S. licensees abroad. In June 1982, the United States government decided this issue in the affirmative.

On the one hand, Defense, Commerce, the CIA, and the U.S. Permanent Representative to the United Nations took a position contrary to that of an opposing coalition led by State. They held that economic sanctions should be interpreted to include subsidiaries and licensees. Their reasoning was as follows. Sanctions might be effective in slowing or stopping the development of the Siberian pipeline. If the sanctions were not interpreted to include subsidiaries and licensees, these controls would only harm United States exports and American workers. Even if litigation resulted from the imposition of sanctions, the uncertainty might damage the pipeline project. And not interpreting the sanctions to include subsidiaries and licensees would be perceived as undercutting American sanctions.

On the other hand, the State Department held that sanctions should not be interpreted to include subsidiaries and licensees. Sanctions might be divisive to the alliance at a time when the United States was attempting to obtain allied cooperation. The allies did not accept use of the crisis in Poland to block the Siberian pipeline. And the legal authority to impose sanctions was questionable over technology transferred prior to December 30, 1981.

The interagency consensus was that if a decision were made to expand export controls to include subsidiaries and licensees, this should be done after the United States requested the allies to apply controls themselves on U.S. subsidiaries and licensees in implementation of their promise not to undercut American sanctions.[29] In the midst of the crisis in Poland, some serious humor surfaced. One official said he believed that the "U.S. business community was even willing to sacrifice the Solidarity Labor Union in Poland rather than impose sanctions on the USSR and Poland." Another cracked, "The American business community did not like labor unions anyway."

Because of the crisis in Poland, the Deputy National Security Advisor and Military Advisor to the President, Admiral Poindexter, was overwhelmed and could not supervise me in regard to the Libyan situation. As a result, I assumed additional responsibility in the decision making. I drafted the terms of reference for the interagency process. And in the middle of the crisis over Poland and contingency planning for Libya, Israel made a move to apply its laws to the Golan Heights, seized from Syria during the 1967 war. The actions were moving in a rapid-fire fashion, to say the least.

The White House is not the only building in Washington where power is the currency of exchange. The Pentagon has its share of would-be power brokers. Regarding military planning for Libya, the Joint Chiefs of Staff had resisted conducting civilian-inspired contingency planning. Until there was a specific provocation for which military force might be an option, the Chiefs declined to do the bidding of the White House or the interagency groups that had the action on Libya. A military officer explained to me why. He said, "Preplanning does not get United States assets there any faster." And without a near-term provocation, officials of his ilk were even less inclined to plan.

Despite reservations about contingency planning in advance of a provocation, we were able to persuade the Chiefs to develop a spectrum of options for the application of force against Libya. But there was a precondition on which they insisted. They demanded a good-faith effort for a drawdown of the number of American citizens from Libya to its lowest possible level. As long as those who wanted to leave were required to leave, the Pentagon then was prepared to use force against Libya.

In the midst of bureaucratic warfare over politico-military contingency planning, there also can be some light moments. One occurred in the middle of a discussion regarding whether an American strike against Libya would heat up the border between Libya and Egypt. If the strike provided an incentive for President Mubarak to attack Libya, the United States might have had a full-scale war on its hands. In the middle of this weighty discourse on war, McFarlane leaned over to whisper something of grave import to me. With a twinkle in his eye, he said, "I don't have any Christmas presents, and it is so close to Christmas!" I nodded, knowingly, as generals and colonels imagined that we were commenting on their brilliant briefing about Libyan military contingencies.

In addition to turf battles, there were legal issues surrounding possible military action against Libya. The international legal authority for taking military action was Article 51 of the United Nations Charter, which allows for individual and collective self-defense. With respect to collective self-defense, the State Department's staff for Policy Planning took the position that the original justification for sanctions against Libya came from Egyptian and Sudanese complaints about Qadhafi's efforts to destabilize them. In addition to the defense of friendly countries like Egypt and the Sudan, there were direct threats from Libya to American citizens. The consensus was that any threats to American citizens or efforts to interfere with their departure from Libya would be regarded as grave provocations and would justify equally grave responses—a proportionality criterion. Additionally, the target should relate directly to the threat. Hence, targeting terror camps in Libya was a reasonable response to Libyan support for terrorism against American citizens.

With respect to the proportionality principle, if Libya launched a terror attack that did not cause loss of life, then economic sanctions would be a legitimate response; if terrorism resulted in a loss of life, then military force would be relevant. Although the State Department had pushed for proportionality, the Department of Defense expressed serious doubts about it. Defense also had reservations about State's suggestions to target oil-production facilities.

Another set of legal issues arose as to what kind of legal authority to use in reacting to Libya. Those who wished to impose broad-scale sanctions favored a maximalist legal authority. In a February 1, 1982, meeting on Libya, the topic for discussion, according to representatives from the White House and State Department, was how to punish Tripoli. Officials from Treasury and

Commerce, however, framed the topic differently. They assumed that the purpose of the meeting was not only to consider whether to punish Libya, but also whether there was a Libyan provocation sufficient to warrant use of certain legal instruments.

In terms of bureaucratic politics, the Commerce Department representative took strong exception to the pace at which decisions were being made. He said that a paper prepared for the meeting was couched as if decisions had already been taken. But without Libya engaging in a provocative incident, those decisions had no legal basis. He also charged that the paper assumed that once American citizens were out, economic sanctions were to be implemented, because the decision had already been made to do so. In fact, however, there had been no such decision. He demanded to know what act by Libya would have to take place that would justify invoking the International Emergency Economic Powers Act (IEEPA).[30]

One of the principles of the politics of policy making is that if you think opponents are going to slow down the momentum toward a preferred option of the group, be sure to exclude them from the meeting. Agencies that were involved with the economy tended to oppose sanctions on Libya, and some were excluded from interagency discussions because of their pro-trade, anti-export control position. The United States Trade Representative was not even on the list to receive one of the main papers that contained options for presidential decision on trade controls. Treasury and Commerce could not be excluded, however, but Justice could be cut out, even though the discussion involved legal interpretations.

A principle of bureaucratic politics is to seek to slow down the process of decision making when it is not going in the direction you favor. One method of delay is to cite laws that require consultation with allies. Those opposed to the rapid pace of decision making in regard to imposition of sanctions on Libya also favored the use of authorizing legislation that required consultation.

Because the Export Administration Act required consultation with allies, the Department of Justice was very concerned that consultation, in fact, be carried out. Regarding consultation over the imposition of sanctions on Libya, the question was whether to consult with intent to impose sanctions or impose sanctions with a plan to consult. We made a decision to act with the intention of consulting the allies. Irrespective of whether they were consulted to find out their views before or after making a decision, Treasury held that we needed to be very clear about what the United States was doing. For example, Treasury wanted the allies to know that Washington was not planning any measures of an extraterritorial nature.

The Commerce Department wanted to invite the Department of Justice to conduct a legal analysis of the issues prior to imposing sanctions. Regarding the favored instrument of choice by the foreign policy and national security community, IEEPA, an official from the Commerce Department compared it with a nuclear weapon. He said that if you only intended to use it partially, it should not be used at all. And if IEEPA had been employed when Libya began its state-sponsored terrorism, such use would have been more valid than introducing it after the fact.

Indeed, a Justice Department official, who had not been invited to a planning meeting about export controls for Libya, told me that in the absence of a clear provocation, it would be hard to justify the use of IEEPA. Because it is a drastic measure rather than selective controls, this act requires a provocation before use. Sanctions against the USSR, for example, were in the category of selective controls, and indeed Lyle Brady from Commerce wanted to place Libya in the same category as the USSR regarding high technology equipment. This position would mean proceeding under general licensing and imposing controls regarding oil and gas licensing. The Export Administration Act was the authority for controlling exports to the USSR, and that act could be used also against Libya.[31] Because there was little experience in the use of IEEPA—it might have been used only once before, in the Iran sanctions case—lawyers should have been present when discussing whether to invoke such a law.

Although IEEPA provided a firm legal basis for a broad range of economic measures, there were significant political disadvantages. The president had to find that policies and actions of the government of Libya constituted an extraordinary threat to national security, and he had to declare a national emergency regarding that threat. There was, however, interagency group agreement that IEEPA could have been invoked, given the broad threat Libyan policies pose to United

States interests: international terrorism, subversion of friendly states, and specific threats to target American assets and personnel.

McFarlane acknowledged that confirming the correct legal authority could have strengthened the interagency draft. But that concession did not result in a decision to postpone the move toward adopting drastic measures. And he also insisted on including in the paper that the government of Libya had to change its behavior. McFarlane held that the American public must be brought along to accept the hard-line action he was proposing. Cutting off oil early could set the stage for tougher measures later. He not only concerned himself with influencing the American public. He also focused on bureaucratic politics in Tripoli.

McFarlane thought that U.S. sanctions were necessary in order to influence political change in Libya. He surmised that an oil cutoff would encourage political opposition against a regime that had engaged in terrorism.

McFarlane recognized that there was bureaucratic opposition to the imposition of sanctions against Libya. Hence, he tried to act as if the President had already made a decision in principle to levy sanctions. Leland of the Department of Treasury strongly disagreed and asked what the legal justification was for invoking IEEPA. He questioned Libya's continued support for international terrorism generally or specifically the hit teams that Qadhafi had sent to the United States. That is, Leland wondered if these teams were still in America.[32]

In addition to this discussion of legal authorities, there was another set of legal issues that concerned the application of sanctions on Libya. The issues highlight the split in the bureaucracy between foreign policy and national security, on the one hand, and the criminal justice system, on the other hand. There were fights in the Reagan Administration in areas ranging from arms control to the Middle East.[33] Despite these fights, there was a conscious effort for an interagency group to work out trade-offs and priorities between foreign policy and national security as well as law enforcement. Although there were serious differences among the departments, there was almost a team approach to international terrorism.

By contrast, the Clinton Administration's procedures for managing international terrorism imply a less than unitary government. In the Clinton years, criminal justice agencies have come to the forefront of the decision-making process on international terrorism. There are troubling legal issues surrounding the growth of "globaloney" issues, such as terrorism, proliferation, and drugs. Consequently, there is a good chance that legal concerns may receive increasing weight in regard to sanctions.

Another set of legal issues concerning Libya arose in 1982. At that time, Edwin Wilson, a former CIA employee with sensitive technological information, defected and lived in Libya.[34] His situation illustrates the interplay of legal and foreign policy/national security concerns. The management of Wilson's defection by an interagency team in the Reagan years contrasts with the Clinton Administration's response to the bombing of American military installations in Saudi Arabia.[35] Both cases are at the intersection of national security and criminal justice. As part of my role on the National Security Council staff, I served as a White House liaison to the Department of Justice in the Wilson matter.

Wilson operated under the guise of being an exporter of civilian goods, but in actuality, he was an arms merchant trading in controlled, clandestine goods. He thus became a fugitive from the American legal system. He found refuge in Libya, where he may have been responsible for providing to Libyan agents the same kind of C-4 plastique that was used in the destruction of Pan Am 103 over Lockerbie, Scotland.[36]

The Department of Justice, FBI, and CIA negotiated terms of reference, from a criminal justice perspective, on how to apprehend Wilson. Once they agreed upon the terms, the Deputy General Counsel for Counterinsurgency briefed me. As the point man at the White House on the Libyan Task Force, I was charged with the responsibility to make sure that those in pursuit of Wilson take into account national security issues in the process of apprehending him.

The government of Libya took Wilson into custody on March 3, 1982, and kept him under virtual house arrest.[37] But when the FBI contacted Wilson in Libya, he was unaware that he was under house arrest there or even under restricted movement. In any event, a decision had to be made whether extradition of Wilson by Libya meant that it was following standard norms for criminal prosecution, or whether Qadhafi was trying to send a signal to Washington of a conciliatory nature. The American assumption was that good-faith extradition of a suspect to a third country like Germany would have implied little in the way of a political concession by the government of Libya.

But from the Libyan perspective, the same act of extradition could be seen as a signal that Qadhafi was in the mood to bargain. If he understood that Bonn intended to extradite Wilson to the United States, then Qadhafi thought he was being conciliatory. Tripoli had good reason to pursue a conciliatory policy during the spring of 1982: the United States was in the process of deciding the nature and scope of export controls that could have hurt the Libyan economy. Conciliation on the part of Qadhafi might have carried with it the expectation of reciprocity by the United States.

The Deputy Director for Intelligence at the CIA surmised that Qadhafi was attempting to be conciliatory by sacrificing Wilson. Libya, in fact, had sent its own deputy intelligence chief to the United States in order to sell Wilson down the river. The fact that Libya was willing to turn Wilson over to American authorities indicated that Qadhafi himself was frightened by the prospect of export controls and possible military escalation later. Indeed, the feeling around Libya was that the American marines were coming again to the shores of Tripoli. Although no officials in the Washington had given any indication that extraditing Wilson would result in any softening of U.S. hostility toward Libya, Qadhafi was, nevertheless, ready to make a deal.[38]

One question was whether Tripoli would extradite without a signal from Washington that a conciliatory gesture would in turn engender cooperation. The Deputy Director for Operations at the CIA interpreted Libyan willingness to sell out Wilson as a sign that Qadhafi was afraid and desperate. Justice and the FBI surmised that Libya expected a quid pro quo. In fact, extraditing Wilson may have been a move by Qadhafi to preempt the imposition of sanctions, for right in the middle of the spring 1982 consultations with the allies about Libyan sanctions, Qadhafi brought the Wilson case to a head.

Washington had to decide whether or not seizing Edwin Wilson was worth the risk of opening up a dialogue with Libya. If that entailed the implicit concession of legitimizing Tripoli's engagement in international terrorism, perhaps extraditing Wilson was not worth the price. Another downside of a dialogue would be to slow the momentum for imposing sanctions when the American-Libyan talks leaked to the press.

Justice wanted to open a dialogue with Libyan intelligence officials about getting Wilson, but deferred to State regarding the foreign policy considerations of such a colloquy. The General Counsel on the National Security Council staff told me that law enforcement did not entail diplomatic concessions. Hence, the United States government could cooperate with Libyan authorities to enforce American laws without implying any diplomatic concession to Libya.

But to avoid a foreign policy snafu, Justice contacted Wilson directly and offered to meet with him on neutral ground. Wilson had met with FBI agents before on impartial territory, but it had come to nothing. Wilson had negotiated with Justice about surrendering and entering into a plea-bargaining arrangement, but no agreement was reached.

The bureaucratic state of play in Washington over the Wilson case initially found the CIA and the FBI at odds over jurisdiction, but to its credit the CIA pulled out of the struggle. Just as the sanctions against Libya were about to kick in, the CIA deferred to the FBI.

Because of the legalities and sensitivities involved in the Wilson matter, the legal attaché at the American embassy in Bonn initially had the action, independent of the American ambassador, Arthur Burns. But this procedure conflicted with the established principle that the ambassador was *the* chief of the mission abroad. Because the legal attaché reported to the Department of Justice, State was cut out of the information loop and foreign policy considerations were not allowed to be weighed alongside criminal justice requirements. Subsequently, however, the legal attaché coordinated with the ambassador.

As a result of the need to weigh national security and criminal justice considerations at the same time, an interagency group in Washington was the coordinating mechanism. This procedure minimized bureaucratic warfare without hindering the process of apprehending a fugitive at large.[39] The management of the Wilson case suggests that bureaucratic politics need not hinder rational decision making and that there are, in fact, situations in which bureaucracy can function in the national interest.

In contrast to the Reagan Administration, the response by the Clinton Administration to the bombing of installations used by American military personnel in Saudi Arabia was one wrought with interagency confusion. The Department of Justice and the FBI took the lead in the investigation. But they did so at the expense of both the State Department and an orderly interagency process, either of which could have made sure that foreign policy and national security considerations were taken into account in the search for clues to the bombings. In this connection, in 1997 a newly appointed Secretary of State, Madeline Albright, found herself caught up in a bureaucratic snafu along with Attorney General Janet Reno and FBI Director Louis Freeh.

Reno and Freeh accused the Saudis of failure to cooperate in investigations regarding the terrorist bombings. Not only was it highly unusual for American officials to make public accusations against the main U.S. ally in the Gulf, but there is some doubt that the two Justice Department officials even spoke with the full authority of the administration. Kenneth Bacon, the Pentagon spokesman, and Nicholas Burns, the State Department spokesman, issued statements to the effect that the Justice Department represented the administration's thinking. But Michael McCurry, the White House spokesman, distanced President Clinton from the Attorney General and the FBI Director.[40] The fact that there were no agreed-upon points among press spokesmen from the White House, Justice, and State was an indication of the lack of an orderly interagency process.

NATIONAL SECURITY VERSUS ECONOMIC PROFITS

In addition to the legal aspects of policy making, there are national security and economic battles. The primary fault line is between the White House and the State Department versus Treasury and Commerce. Because of the technical nature of decisions to impose sanctions, the economic departments possess influence well beyond their formal status in the cabinet. Treasury has an impact on the nature of the sanctions because of its knowledge of the sanctions procedures. Treasury officials can use persuasion in the sense that they know the details of the law of sanctions and can suggest unanticipated risks that might accrue from pursuing a course of action they oppose.

Likewise, Commerce can be persuasive to the extent that its officials can make informed estimates of the economic effects of sanctions and can cite industry attitudes on export controls. As with Treasury, officials from the Commerce Department are well acquainted with the technical portions of sanctions regimes, are aware of prior precedents in their application, and are a part of the permanent bureaucracy where rewards accrue to those in the know about arcane matters of fact. It was amusing to see prestigious practitioners of the "high policy" of national security being outfoxed by officials from departments that engage in the "low policy" of economic analysis. What looks like "administrivia" to a national security official may be perceived as a core concern to a person from the Commerce Department.

In the context of the battle between security and economics, return to our discussion on whether to impose export controls on Libyan oil and gas equipment. Treasury held that only in the context of a freeze on Libyan assets was a ban appropriate. Upon understanding this assertion, national security officials quickly agreed to a freeze on assets to go along with the proposal. But then, Treasury officials countered with the observation that freezing assets has two negative implications. First, it creates uncertainty that the United States is a reliable place for investments. And second, it creates problems regarding extraterritoriality with respect to American banks abroad.

Treasury also held that the only way to hurt Libya via economic sanctions was to regulate deliveries by wholly owned and subsidiaries of American companies. The trade-off, however, was that the allies were opposed to a U.S. claim of extraterritoriality, as well as any steps Washington might take that would endanger their oil supplies from Libya to European countries like Germany.

Treasury took the position that the American business community could not figure out what was different now as opposed to before regarding Libya. And Commerce officials favored an effort to persuade the allies to come on board. Without allied support, they were reluctant to move unilaterally against Libya. Commerce also held that whatever the United States decided to do against the allies regarding Libya should be consistent with earlier decisions concerning the Soviets' pipeline and the crackdown against Solidarity by Poland.[41]

But critics of the consensus viewpoint said that the use of embargoes for political purposes presupposed there had been a precise specification of what behavior should be changed before deciding to use force. They charged that the United States had not yet made clear what specific behavior Libya should change. Qadhafi had already yielded to pressure to withdraw troops from Chad, and the assassination team that was supposedly in the United States did not seem to be active when Washington imposed the embargo.

The critics decried the slippery slope of sanctions that would have the paradoxical effect of generating additional revenues for Libya. They charged that taking public action against Qadhafi would strengthen him within the Middle East region. How to proceed boiled down to whether to do so incrementally with limited actions in the absence of an explicit provocation, or to move quickly with comprehensive measures without clear provocation. Less extreme measures were not likely to have inflicted pain on Libya and might have provided Qadhafi with a pretext to expropriate property owned by American citizens. In any event, there was no evidence that any of the measures contemplated would inflict enough pain on Libya to warrant a change in its behavior.

The decision to impose unilateral sanctions on Libya by the Reagan Administration recognized that whether they were effective or not in changing behavior, they had to be imposed. There was a grand debate between foreign policy and national security officials on the one hand, and economic departments on the other. This debate reflected an interagency process that operated well as a means to vet differences and build consensus. While some players tried to suppress dissent about the imposition of unilateral sanctions, others made sure that dissenting opinions went forth to the highest levels of decision making.

EFFECTS OF SANCTIONS AGAINST LIBYA

Rehabilitative aims of American unilateral sanctions against Libya are to compel Tripoli to stop its subversive behavior, terminate support for international terrorism, and cease efforts to procure or develop weapons of mass destruction, especially chemical weapons. Washington has renewed United States sanctions every six months since 1987.[42] These include a ban on the importation of Libyan crude oil into the United States, the freezing of almost $1 billion of Libyan assets, a prohibition on all hydrocarbon imports from Libya, a ban on U.S. oil companies from operating in Libya, and other measures.

Unilateral American sanctions have provided incentives for Tripoli to cease its efforts to subvert other governments. But Qadhafi began to withdraw his military forces from Chad even before Washington imposed sanctions on Tripoli. Nevertheless, the unilateral sanctions did reinforce Libya's decision to withdraw, and there have been fewer efforts on the part of Tripoli to subvert other regimes than before the sanctions. With respect to Libya's support for international terrorism, unilateral American sanctions have raised the cost to Tripoli for sponsoring groups like that of Abu Nidal, who leads a terrorist group that has received funding, logistical support, and instructions from Tripoli.[43] Also, there has been a decline in Libyan state-sponsorship of international terrorism. But that decrease may be attributed more to multilateral United Nations sanctions than to American export and import controls. In regard to Libya's efforts to acquire chemical weapons, American sanctions have been irrelevant at best and perhaps counterproductive at worst.

But sanctions for retribution are always effective. If they make important domestic political constituencies feel good, they achieve their purpose. Embargoes on Libya fulfill a basic American distaste for despotism. Tyrants such as Qadhafi are natural targets for sanctions. Americans feel genuinely satisfied with their detrimental effects on Libya, being staunch moral capitalists who love to retaliate against those who have committed acts of evil. American ideals permit nothing less than counteraction. The manner in which Libya became a part of the Iran Sanctions bill illustrates the role of retribution in the policy-making process.

At the behest of the survivors of the Pan Am 103 bombing, Senator Edward Kennedy inserted Libya into the Iran Sanctions bill while it was on the Senate floor. It later became the Iran and Libya Sanctions Act of 1996. The families of the victims of the Lockerbie crash are the most important political constituency concerning retributive justice in regard to Libya. As a concession to them, Senator

Alfonse D'Amato agreed to include Libya in the Iran legislation. The president invited the families to the signing ceremony in August 1996. This gesture is indicative of the act's political significance.[44]

In addition to retribution, sanctions are designed to have negative economic consequences. But the unilateral trade embargo imposed by the United States has had no major economic effects on Libya. One reason is that the items sanctioned by the United States can be purchased from other nations or sold to other countries.[45] Indeed, American economic sanctions may have had the unintended effect of enhancing the long-term economic performance of the Libyan economy. Since the American trade embargo went into effect, Qadhafi's regime has launched a successful campaign to attract financial investments from companies based in Europe.

Tripoli has provided incentives for European-based oil firms to make massive investments in Libya. After the American sanctions on Libya, Tripoli signed new oil and gas exploration, production, as well as oil development agreements with European oil companies. In addition, the Oil Investments International Company, owned by the government of Libya, purchased a majority interest in several refineries in Europe. As of the mid-1990s, it controlled over 300,000 barrels per day of capacity and owned some 3,300 service stations. A consequence of such control and ownership has been to allow Libya to influence part of its oil market, Europe, which is Tripoli's only importer.[46]

The passage of the Iran and Libya Sanctions Act of 1996 would deny export licenses, loans, and credit guarantees to European and other oil companies investing over a threshold amount—$40 million per year—in the Libyan energy sector. This act is a secondary boycott. It not only punishes firms that invest in Libya, but is also bound to have a great, long-term, negative effect on the Libyan economy. By drying up investment funds from European oil and gas companies, the act will eventually cause erosion in the productivity of the Libyan energy sector.

In addition to unilateral United States sanctions, there are also multilateral United Nations sanctions. These controls are designed to induce the government of Libya to hand over the suspects implicated in the airline bombing over Lockerbie. They have been renewed about every three months. Because the suspects are charged with bombing an airliner, the punishment includes prohibitions on Libyan civil aviation. With respect to the effectiveness of multilateral sanctions, they have had no apparent success in coercing compliance. And regarding their effects on the economic status of Libya, one has to take with a grain of salt the many complaints that began coming out of Tripoli after the United Nations sanctions were imposed. At any one time, Tripoli has had a tendency to announce that it has been severely hurt by whatever penalties happen to be in effect.

Tripoli claims that multilateral sanctions have cost the Libyan economy over $19 billion in trade and more than 21,000 lives due to denied foreign medical treatment. It is difficult to believe these figures because Tripoli has an incentive to inflate the negative effects of sanctions. Because trade continues, mainly with Germany and Italy, sanctions against Libya are, according to one authority, an "inconvenience rather than a serious hindrance."[47]

Regarding the rehabilitative effects of the American sanctions, there have not been any major changes in Libya's behavior. If what has been sanctioned by one country can be purchased from another, unilateral sanctions are bound to be ineffective. If anything, the sanctions have both beneficial long-term economic and political effects for Libya. Implementing a containment policy on Libya has stimulated a self-defense effort. Tripoli has succeeded in attracting foreign investments that have strengthened the regime.

But the Iran and Libya Sanctions Act has a greater negative potential effect on Libya than prior unilateral sanctions. By denying loans, export licenses, and letters of credits to European oil companies that make large investments in Libya, non-American companies have begun to invest less in Libya. Given the overwhelming sentiment of the American business community and European nations, the question arises as to why the act passed the U.S. Congress in a unanimous vote.

Politics and Idealism
Trump Profits and Alliance Obligations

In the clash between foreign policy and national security versus economic interests there is no contest. Foreign policy and national security interests found powerful allies in the bureaucracy who were able and willing to fight in defense of high policy over low policy. But business interests reinforced by the actions of the allies caused Libyan policy to be compromised and/or delayed. The overall direction of a policy of containment via sanctions, however, could not be turned around by an alignment of Libya lovers.

The order of battle in the war for Washington had two sides. On one side was a coalition of business firms interested in making profits from trade with Libya, bureaucrats from governmental agencies concerned with trade, and allied governments. On the other was an alignment of the survivors of victims of Pan Am 103, the pro-Israel community, and idealists who would act retributively to punish the tyrant from Tripoli.

In addition to traditional politics practiced by ethnic interest groups, business organizations also are players in American politics. By contributing to political campaigns, businesses hope that they are purchasing a seat at the foreign policy table. Consider the case of the Occidental Petroleum Corporation.[48] During 1997, this firm sought to negotiate a portion of a $930 million oil-exploration project with the Sudan. But Khartoum is an ally of Tehran and politically close to Tripoli. In addition, the Sudan is on the State Department's list of nations that sponsor international terrorism. Antiterrorism legislation bars American companies from doing business with countries on that list. It names seven countries as sponsors of international terrorism, but only five are subject to comprehensive embargoes—Iran, Iraq, Libya, Cuba, and North Korea. Two states escaped sweeping trade embargo status: Syria and the Sudan.

The Anti-Terrorism Act of 1996 permits financial dealings with Syria and the Sudan if these transactions are found not to have an impact on any potential act of terrorism. Syria was subject to less restrictive terms in the 1996 Anti-Terrorism Act because the United States wanted to encourage that country's participation in the Arab-Israel peace process. There has not been any explanation why these same terms applied to the Sudan, which is not a participant in the peace process. Here is where politics may enter the picture. Occidental is an active player in national politics. The U.S. Federal Election Commission indicates that Occidental donated about $600,000 to the two major political parties in 1995 and 1996, including $100,000 to the Democrats during March 1996. President Clinton signed the Anti-Terrorism Act a month later.

Irrespective of the political influence of the business community, however, ethnic political groups have lined up their vectors with those of American idealism and constitute an effective lobby on behalf of sanctions. Thus, Representatives Bill McCollum (Rep.-Florida) and Charles Shumer (Dem.-New York) introduced early in 1997 a bill to close the loophole that favored Occidental and the Sudan. These two members of the House are politically close to the pro-Israel community, and they acted within the context of traditional American idealism against international terrorism. In this respect, McCollum stated, "The only way we are going to eliminate the governmental support terrorist organizations need is to take a firm stance against economic relationships with these countries."[49]

Foreign policy and national security triumph because they converge with ideals and domestic politics. Strategic interests of antisubversion, counterterrorism, and nonproliferation are not only interests; they are ideals as well. Americans do not support regimes that have little regard for human rights. Despots who murder people, blow up civilian aircraft, and espouse revolutionary violence are ripe for the imposition of sanctions. American ideology revolves around the sanctity of human life. Americans do not tolerate barbarians who scorn these ideals. And when domestic groups buttress ideals and strategic interests, these factors constitute a formidable joint effect on American foreign policy and national security affairs.

One reason politics and idealism are so influential in the Libyan case is the unexpected convergence of two dissimilar interest groups: the pro-Israel community and the families of the victims of Pan Am 103. Libya has allies on Wall Street, who seek to profit from trading with an enemy of the United States. But Libya has few allies on Main Street. Hence, in the war for Main Street, Colonel Qadhafi seeks allies.

THE WAR FOR THE AMERICAN STREET

There are wars in the Middle East and wars in the Middle West. The wars in the Middle East, in part, aim to sway Arab public opinion toward the agenda of ruling elites. Mass opinion is often called the "Arab street." Likewise, there is a war in the United States for public opinion, as Libya fights for the hearts and minds of Muslim-Americans in general and the African-American community in particular.

In the section above on the politics of policy making, there is a discussion of the war for Washington, where there are battles between national security officials and those in economic organizations. In addition, the section concludes that bureaucratic politics and idealism are more important than economic profits and alliance obligations in explaining Washington's decisions to impose sanctions on Libya.

Despite American and United Nations sanctions, Qadhafi remains noncompliant. He tries in vain to reassert himself as a major force in the mainstream Islamic community. But due to his notoriety, even among fellow Arab leaders, Qadhafi has been shut out of the many circles of influence. Attempted assassinations and abortive conflicts with neighbors like Egypt and Chad have rightly cast him as a pariah. As such, Qadhafi has turned to nonconventional means of remaining in the spotlight. He knowingly harbors the two suspects in the bombing of Pan Am 103. These two Libyan intelligence agents top the FBI's most wanted list. They are optimal prizes to keep sequestered within Libya's borders.

In addition to harboring suspects from the international community, Qadhafi engages in a search for allies within the American community. He has a history of lending rhetorical and financial support to various dissident groups in the United States. He gave over $300,000 to the Black Panthers during the 1970s.[50] Furthermore, Qadhafi has made contact with the Nation of Islam, headed by Minister Louis Farrakhan.

Farrakhan is an American Muslim to whom Qadhafi has offered $1 billion. Ostensibly, the money is for the purpose for helping the Nation of Islam to work in poor African-American communities. But because of U.S. sanctions against Libya, the Department of Justice ruled that Farrakhan could not accept the offer. The Department monitored his visits to Libya, Iraq, and other rogue regimes while on a tour of pariah countries. Farrakhan visited sixteen nations on a so-called World Friendship Tour.

In entering Libya during his tour, Farrakhan broke the American sanctions regulations. By law, all transportation-related transactions involving Libya by American citizens are prohibited. These consist of the sale in the United States of any transportation by air that includes any stop in Libya. For Farrakhan, the junket had been one to foster unity among Muslims on a global scale. By simply allowing the American "leader" into Libya, Qadhafi purchased political unrest in American domestic politics.

The response to Farrakhan's visit was outrage in Washington. Members of Congress referred to it as a "thugfest tour."[51] White House spokesman McCurry said, "He met with some of the most brutal dictators and leaders of nations that the United States considers pariah states." According to the State Department, Farrakhan was "cavorting with dictators" who had "American blood on their hands."[52]

Allegations abounded that Qadhafi was looking to disrupt American politics. Representative Bob Barr (Rep.-Georgia) said it all when he stated, "Muammar Qadhafi pledged $1 billion to Mr. Farrakhan's Nation of Islam to be used here in this country to . . . improperly influence the American political systems."[53] The Justice Department responded by sending Farrakhan a letter asking him if he planned to register as an agent of Qadhafi as defined by the Foreign Agent Registration Act.

In response, Louis Farrakhan played exactly the role Qadhafi intended by taking a defiant, disruptive stance. He replied to government statements and inquiries by daring the United States to stop him from taking the money. He asserted that he would use the money to build homes and schools, yet there have been no definitive instructions as to how the money would be used. If he is expected to perform any services in return for this "gift," those have not been reported either. As seen above, there is suspicion that Farrakhan will use the money in support of Libyan policies in the United States. But Farrakhan denies any charges that the money is not legal. In open challenge to the U.S. government, he stated, "We're using the money to clean up the mess that you made. Whatever Qadhafi gives me, I'm going to ask you to match it." Farrakhan also paraphrased the Prophet Muhammad in his own defense, "He [Qadhafi] is my friend. He is my brother. Your enemy ain't mine unless I'm your slave."[54]

Farrakhan's aims and objectives are to further Muslim unity and prosperity. In and of themselves, these objectives seem legitimate. But to use the assistance of a Libyan regime dedicated to the use of terrorism against the United States is illegitimate. By choosing to associate himself with Qadhafi, he undercuts his own legitimacy with the American people. He acts as a "useful fool" for Qadhafi, disrupting domestic American politics in a manner that puts the legal responsibility on Farrakhan while giving Qadhafi much needed attention.

The U.S. government may not be able to prevent Qadhafi from giving Farrakhan $1 billion. Qadhafi knows this constraint and so offers the money to a man who calls Judaism a "gutter religion."[55] The offer forces the United States to choose whether or not to violate its own sanctions. Should the government uphold the sanctions, Farrakhan can claim racism and gain political capital and the moral high ground in the American Muslim community. If the government allows the donation, Colonel Qadhafi wins the high ground of having successfully evaded the sanctions. His political agenda is served by Farrakhan's collaboration.

In the war for the American street, Qadhafi seeks to separate the black American Muslim community from other Americans. What he does not understand, however, is that American society is based on a vision of the future that acknowledges religious and racial differences yet transcends them in the pursuit of the American dream. From our origins as observed by de Tocqueville to the contemporary beliefs of Martin Luther King, Jr., Americans judge one another on many different levels. As such, the hateful rhetoric of Farrakhan and Qadhafi falls short. The future of the American street will remain American as long as Qadhafi and his ilk are kept at bay.

A SCENARIO

Historical Precedents for Renewal of Military Action

Consider prior confrontations between Tripoli and Washington as a basis for creating scenarios for the future. The Colonel is in "good company" in trying to deter the United States from taking military action. That crowd includes the likes of Saddam Hussein. He promised the world a "mother of all battles" as a means to frighten away challengers from across the seas.[56] And Qadhafi drew a mythical line in the water—the "Line of Death"—across which American warships would pass only at great risk.[57] Neither Saddam Hussein's battle nor Muammar Qadhafi's line proved to be so frightening as their rhetoric implied.

With respect to Libya, the American navy successfully challenged the international waters of the Gulf of Sidra in August 1981. And in January 1986, the United States initiated another challenge based on the 1981 model when the navy began a series of escalating military exercises in the Gulf of Sidra. The goal was to increase pressure on Libya. And on March 24, 1986, the enhanced compulsion took the form of a freedom of navigation challenge. Libya responded with force. But the Pentagon's rules of engagement allowed American commanders on the scene to make a disproportionate retaliation. This encounter in the Gulf of Sidra in March 1986 resulted in the destruction of two Libyan ships by U.S. navy vessels.

On Saturday, April 5, 1986, a bomb exploded in La Belle disco in Berlin, a club frequented by American troops. My former colleagues in the White House, Howard Teicher and Oliver North, reviewed a transcript of two electronic intercepts from the People's Bureau [Libyan Embassy] in East Berlin to Libyan intelligence headquarters.[58] As a result of this evidence of Libyan complicity, President Reagan gave the order to retaliate against Libya. And on April 15, 1986, United States warplanes bombed sites in Libya declared by the President to be "terrorist centers." The planes damaged one of Qadhafi's homes at one of the barracks and unfortunately killed his infant daughter. But they inflicted major damage on other sites that were military in nature.

If Qadhafi were deterrable, Washington's 1986 air strikes could have served to deter him from further adventures. He would have tempered his desire for anti-American actions, his sponsorship of international terrorism, and his development of weapons of mass destruction. The world would have seen a reformed, quieted Qadhafi.

Though the air strike crippled his morale, Qadhafi's anti-Western fear and hatred still served to strengthen his political base. In 1986, there was growing opposition against Qadhafi, but the American air strikes rallied the Libyan people around their symbol against imperialism. His personal defiance tapped into the collective national experience of being dominated by outside forces. Qadhafi learned to hate the West through watching the imperialist powers "pillage" his country. By personally defying Washington, Qadhafi is trying to bolster national unity behind him. In this respect, Washington's sanctions paradoxically encourage the Colonel to resist the United States at any cost.

Just as the Colonel is isolated in the world community, he is slowly being shut out of the Arab world.[59] If Qadhafi were shunned by other Arab nations, then his goal of pan-Arabism would be unrealized. In this regard, Qadhafi may be motivated by fear of loss. His fear of losing prominence may cause him to act in defiance of the West in a pathetic attempt to increase his importance on the world stage.

Before launching assaults against Libya, the United States inter-agency process analyzed at least two options. As described by Howard Teicher, a senior player at the White House in that confrontation, here is what took place.[60] By early 1985, Vincent Cannistrato, a CIA officer detailed to the National Security Council staff as head of the Intelligence Directorate, had the action on devising new methods to increase pressure on Qadhafi. He had been head of the CIA Libya task force and wrote a paper on U.S. vulnerabilities and opportunities in attempt to influence Qadhafi via covert actions.

Option one of the Cannistrato paper called for a limited, phased strategy to resume air and naval challenges in the Gulf of Sidra. This option assumed that there would be increased restrictions on American citizens doing business in Libya. The paper did not rule out joint planning with Egypt, but focused on how to respond to Libyan actions. Option two intended to oust Qadhafi from power and assumed military planning with Egypt and Algeria as well as covert support that included assistance to Libyan dissidents.

Vice President Bush, Secretary of State Shultz, Director of Central Intelligence Casey, and National Security Advisor McFarlane supported option two. Secretary of Defense Weinberger and the Joint Chiefs of Staff opposed any strategy that would entail the use of force. Their reasoning was that the purposes were too unclear and that not enough attention had been given to a likely Soviet response to American attempts to destabilize Libya.

Washington adopted option one—working with Cairo to destabilize Libya and unseat Colonel Qadhafi. But President Mubarak of Egypt vetoed this option in a meeting during 1985 between him and Poindexter. Libya had given support for the Abu Nidal terrorists who skyjacked an Egyptian airliner in 1985 and had conducted massacres in the Rome and Vienna airports. On the basis of this evidence, President Reagan decided to retaliate, but Mubarak declined to join the initiative.

During the late 1970s, there was a military confrontation between Libya and Egypt. President Sadat had asked the Carter Administration to cooperate with him to unseat Qadhafi. Carter, however, vetoed the option of conducting coordinated military planning with Cairo for an attack against Libya. Because Mubarak was Sadat's Vice President, he should have known that an American president had backed down from a joint Cairo-Washington military initiative against Tripoli. The early 1980s found Mubarak in a position to thwart an American initiative against Libya. Despite the lack of Egyptian support, U.S. military planning moved forward.

With respect to the bureaucratic politics of the 1985 contingency planning, State and Defense were in disagreement. State was in favor of air strikes against Libya, and Defense was not. Secretary of Defense Weinberger opposed retaliation and warned the president that air strikes would endanger the large number of American citizens in Libya and create a hostage-taking situation.

American oil companies continued to operate in Libya. The firms pumped hundreds of thousands of barrels of oil per day. The Department of Defense also expressed doubts about the complicity of Libya in the attacks against the Rome and Vienna airports. In spite of the Pentagon's opposition, the president decided to retaliate.[61]

Renewal of Hostilities

Over a decade later, in the late 1990s, the likelihood of another confrontation is increasing between Tripoli and Washington. In contrast to the 1986 air strikes, hostilities at the close of the century are likely to be on the land and seas. In an implicit threat to use military force, Defense Secretary William Perry said on April 3, 1996, that the United States would not allow Libya to complete an underground chemical weapons facility. Perry made the remark to reporters after discussing the factory with Egyptian President Mubarak.

As opposed to his position a decade earlier, Mubarak was on board the American contingency planning team. Perry said that he had discussed a variety of evidence with Mubarak. "I showed him photographs," Perry said. "They demonstrate that the Libyans are not now producing chemical weapons, but they have an extensive program under way to develop a chemical weapons production facility." In order for serious military contingency planning to go forward, it is crucial for Mubarak to stay on board.

Western intelligence agencies hold that Libya is building a chemical weapons factory at Tarhunah, 40 miles southeast of Tripoli, the Libyan capital. The plant is reportedly being built into a mountain, which would make it difficult to destroy in a military strike. Asked if the United States would allow completion, Perry simply replied: "No."[62] The Tarhunah facility is designed to replace a plant at Rabta, 55 miles southwest of Tripoli. The Rabta facility was reopened in the fall of 1996, five years after damage from a suspicious fire. Libya insists that it only manufactures pharmaceutical agents there.

Renewal of military action might come from an incremental escalation in the Gulf of Sidra or a decision to prevent the completion of the chemical weapons facility. In this regard, it is very likely that there will be a resumption in hostilities between Tripoli and Washington before the end of the century.[63]

In summary, the U.S. perceives post–Cold War threats from Libya and has imposed sanctions on Tripoli. Because the allies see greater future dangers if American sanctions destabilize Libya, there is a transatlantic schism in threat perceptions and policies between America and Europe. Despite the gap between the allies, the United States appears destined to resume military confrontation with Libya.

In light of the high likelihood in the resumption of hostilities, recall the four themes that cut across *Rogue Regimes*: threat perception, opportunities, politics, and policies. On the basis of high threat perception, the United States is willing to trade off economic opportunities concerning Libya. In addition, domestic politics provide incentives for American presidents to devise confrontational policies toward Libya. As was the case for Iran and Iraq, bureaucratic and domestic politics are keys to the American policy process regarding Libya.

And with respect to threats in the international system, Libya is a rogue elephant that is a fitting substitute for the Soviet bear. But given the different perceptions of threat and opportunity between the United States and its allies about Libya, it is difficult to fashion policies that are effective in changing that regime's behavior. Because of the low likelihood that rehabilitative goals can be easily achieved, punishment may be based on the idea of deterrence by denial. That is, Washington takes military steps that weaken Tripoli's capacity to practice international terrorism and develop weapons of mass destruction. Finally, retribution also provides ample grounds for continuing a policy of containment rather than accommodation.

CHAPTER FIVE

SYRIA: CONTAIN
OR EMBRACE

PERSONALITY, POLITICS, AND POLICIES

AS THE 1970S CAME TO A CLOSE, multiple crises converged in the Middle East, and their effects rained down upon the padded walls of the White House Situation Room. These crises enhanced the American perception of dangers from the Middle East. The fall of the Shah and rise of the Ayatollah Khomeni in Iran, the Soviet invasion of Afghanistan, and the Iran-Iraq War threatened Western oil supplies in the Gulf zone. These events also had a potential for spilling over into the Arab-Israel conflict zone. One nation that serves as a link across these two subregions of the Middle East is Syria. It is aligned with Iran against Iraq, is in conflict with Turkey over terrorists based in Damascus, and remains in a no-peace, no-war status with Israel. Hence, it is a state with ties from the Mediterranean to the Gulf. And Syria has an absolute ruler whose forceful personality has a major effect on the foreign policy of his country—President Hafez al-Assad, who took power in 1970.

Besides Israel and Turkey, most of the Arab states of the Middle East are in the grips of absolute rulers. Whether secular like Assad, or religious like the ayatollahs of Iran, these states are personified by their rulers. As president of Syria, Assad is a compelling character. Because the government is for the most part under his sole control, any examination of U.S.-Syrian relations should begin with Assad, the man.[1]

Conventional wisdom about Assad is that he is a rational, patient, and cunning head of state. He rarely makes a move unless he is fairly certain that the outcome is in his best interest. And while his judgments are not always correct in retrospect, the assumption is that he manifests a strong tendency to err on the side of caution. Unlike his main contemporary Arab competitor, Saddam Hussein, Assad is thought to be averse to gambles. According to this interpretation, it would be hard to imagine Assad playing a lottery with its low likelihood of success. Unlike Saddam Hussein, it would be difficult to conceive of Assad ordering the invasion of Kuwait, thereby risking the formation of a Western coalition that could oust his invasion forces and destroy most of them in the process.

But the conditional wisdom fails to take account of Assad's risk-taking propensity in regard to the peace process. Consider the contrasting perspective adopted here. Assad is a leader fearful that the world will accept Israel's occupation of the Golan Heights as permanent; as a result, he may be willing to take risks in the peace process in order to effect the return of the Golan. While the traditional view lets Assad off the hook on making concessions, the alternative assumes that he is able to take chances for peace. The question is whether he is willing to take chances for peace, in light of his aspiration to lead the Arab Nation.

Obsessed with his legacy, Assad yearns to be viewed as the primary leader of the Arab world. Such a role would be a means to the end of restoring the grandeur and respect evoked by the term Greater Syria of past centuries, the exemplar of the pan-Arab ideal.[2] But Assad's vision of himself does not quite jibe with reality. While he may very well be the linchpin in the Arab-Israel peace process, he is hardly its lead voice. But it would be difficult to conceive of a comprehensive settlement between Israel and Syria without Assad's consent in its formulation and implementation, though few expect him to take the lead in the peace process. He is more likely to let the game come to him than to try to take over the game, to borrow a sports metaphor. Assad is no Anwar Sadat, the late president of Egypt who took over the entire peace process with his trip to Jerusalem. In contrast to Assad, who reacts to the initiatives of others, Sadat stimulated an ongoing peace process that led to an accord between Egypt and Israel.[3]

Assad has an impact on policies by dominating the political process. The ayatollahs of Iran, Saddam of Iraq, and Qadhafi of Libya are all ruthless characters who cast a long shadow over their political systems. Because of their ability to operate command systems, they could shift policy almost with a snap of a finger. But even their individual strengths have to overcome domestic political constraints.

A dictator like Assad readily fits in the ranks of rogue rulers who have the ability to make major changes in foreign policy. But he also has domestic political costs to pay for the exercise of power.[4] Assad belongs to the Alawite minority within Syria.[5] Middle East expert Daniel Pipes contends, "An Alawite ruler in Damascus is repugnant to most Syrians."[6] As a result, Assad is constrained from taking bold steps necessary to make a genuine peace with Israel, according to the view of Assad as a risk-averse leader. Other constraints that limit his actions concern the economic dimension. Syria has suffered greatly from the removal of Soviet patronage.[7] And because of the economic cost to Syria due to the collapse of the USSR, Assad should be less willing to take chances in the peace process.

In deciding whether Assad is risk-averse or risk-acceptant, consider his actions in the Arab-Israel peace process. During the decade of 1979-1989, Damascus initially criticized Cairo's peace with Israel. Then Syria abruptly moved back into an alignment with Egypt: following the Gulf War in 1991, Damascus decided to take part in the American-sponsored Arab-Israel peace conference in Madrid.[8] Although there were political protests within Syria about Assad's anti-Saddam policy, he overcame these objections and joined the peace process.

With his reluctance both to take chances and make bold moves, two questions about Assad arise. First, has he made a strategic commitment to the Arab-Israel peace process with its explicit recognition of Israel's right to exist as an independent state in the Middle East? And, second, has he made only a tactical adjustment in a long-term process to weaken Israel as a prelude to its destruction?

On the one hand, if Assad has made a strategic commitment to the peace process, then the United States could build on this shift, accommodate Damascus, and embrace Syria as a partner in the process. On the other hand, if Assad has made a tactical move en route to wearing down and destroying Israel, a policy of containment and even confrontation would be advisable for Washington. Appeasement would occur if Assad were to make a tactical move to weaken Israel and the United States made concessions to him in order to reverse his course of action. Two schools of thought dominate the debate about Assad's intentions. Both assume that his personality has a great impact on the foreign policy of Syria.

The first camp assumes an action-reaction sequence. Syrian policy is more a result of the external environment than its internal milieu. The second camp makes the opposite assumption. The first perspective presumes that changes in the balance of power allow for a shift in Syrian foreign policy toward a political settlement with Israel. The second viewpoint presupposes that domestic politics and economic factors constrain Assad's freedom of action and prohibit him from making concessions necessary for peace.[9] The first camp focuses on international factors as incentives for Assad's risk-acceptant personality. The second camp emphasizes national, political, and economic attributes as incentives for his risk-aversion.

A representative of the first approach is an Israeli scholar, Moshe Maoz.[10] He holds that Assad has made a strategic commitment to make peace with Israel. An emissary of the second approach is an American specialist, Daniel Pipes. He believes that Assad has made only a tactical adjustment in policy as a means to regain the Golan Heights from Israel.[11]

Maoz contends that President Assad has accepted the principle of a political settlement to the conflict with Israel, albeit on his own terms. During late 1973, Syria adopted UN Security Council Resolution 338. It incorporated Resolution 242, which called for peace with Israel in return for withdrawal from occupied territories. But Resolution 338 goes beyond 242 and calls for direct talks among the parties. Since 1988, moreover, Assad has given priority to a political solution instead of a military option.

Assad made a strategic decision in favor of a diplomatic solution because of economic difficulties and changes in Soviet policy that occurred even before the collapse of the USSR in 1991.[12] In addition to changes at the global level, there were regional transitions that prompted a shift in Syrian policy. The elections in Israel were one such change within the region.

Following the 1992 election of Yitzhak Rabin as prime minister of Israel, Assad noted a flexible policy by Israel toward Syria in general and the Golan Heights in particular. With respect to threat perception, Assad may have had an unmotivated bias to see what he expected to see. For example, he expected that the transition in Israel from the Likud to the Labor Party would bring with it a softening of conditions under which Israel would withdraw from the Golan. Because Labor has a reputation of being more flexible in the peace process, Assad may have expected flexibility in the Israeli negotiating stand. Whatever biases operated, Assad acted to decrease the threat from Israel rather than to increase it. As a result of a lower threat perception, Assad has been ready to sign a full peace agreement with Israel, provided it withdrew from the entire Golan Heights and southern Lebanon.

If there is not a political accord reached between Israel and Syria, Damascus is likely to sustain its ideological motivation and military preparation to fight Israel over the Golan Heights. Syria also is likely to enhance its political support for Hezbollah's war of attrition against Israel in southern Lebanon. While strengthening its strategic alignment with Iran, Syria would seek to sabotage Israel's rapprochement with the Palestinians and with Arab states that are contemplating a political settlement.

In contrast, an accord with Israel might reduce the militant intentions of Damascus, weaken its military ties with Iran, and expand Syria's economic development. Additionally, an agreement would foster progress toward peace between Israel and the Palestinians and encourage other Arab states to establish normal relations with the Jewish state.[13]

The Maoz school assumes that Assad not only has made a commitment to make peace with Israel, but that he also has the power and resolve to force an accord upon an unwilling populace. This approach presumes that Assad desires to avoid losing the Golan to permanent Israeli control so much that he would risk his hold on absolute power.[14] This school assumes that Assad focuses more on what he would lose from failure to take part in the peace process than from what he would gain by taking tactical advantage of Israel. Alternatively, he may be willing to run high risks in the peace process in order to avoid domestic political losses: turning his back on the prospect for a peaceful return of the Golan Heights could significantly damage his hold on power.[15]

The Pipes school holds that existence of an enemy, Israel, is a main basis for Assad's rule. If peace with Israel were established, Assad would find himself without a major external threat. The majority anti-Israel Sunni population could turn its hostilities upon the ruling minority Alawites, from which Assad comes. Syria has been in a state of emergency, justified by its war with Israel, since 1963. As a result of the threat perceived from Israel, Assad can justify his oppressive security apparatus. The Pipes approach implies that Assad would magnify the threat from Israel in order to bolster his domestic political position. In this regard, there are motivated biases for threat magnification. Assad stands to gain from overestimation of threat. He sees what he wants to see—a threat from Israel that allows him to sustain his power base.

Remove the potential of war in the Middle East, and it would be nearly impossible, even for Assad, not to lift the state of emergency and refrain from political crackdowns on potential opponents to his rule. If Assad feared domestic pressures as much as losing his chance to regain the Golan Heights, he would not be as cautious in his decisions to make peace, according to the Pipes approach.

But the Pipes approach overlooks the role that Assad's ruthless-ness plays in maintaining his power. Just as Assad ordered the killing of thousands of Islamist rebels in the city of Hama during February 1982, he should be willing to enforce a peace accord with Israel. But Pipes would contend that Assad does not want to regain the Golan Heights so much that he would risk his hold on absolute power.

The Maoz versus Pipes debate raises the issue of Assad's priori-ties—whether he fears permanent loss of the Golan Heights or the possibility of losing office.[16] But Assad may frame the problem in such a fashion that he denies a need to make a trade-off between the peace process to acquire the Golan and continuation of his reign in Syria.[17] For example, Assad may assume that he can engage in a peace process to acquire the Golan Heights and remain in power in Damascus.

This rationale derives from three factors. The dissolution of the Soviet Union, the absence of Moscow as a patron of Damascus, and the presence of Syria in the American-led Gulf War coalition are three reasons Maoz puts forth to explain Assad's strategic commitment to peace. The Pipes approach, however, would downplay the significance of these external events. Rather, for him, the main forces driving Syrian foreign policy are internal political constraints on Assad. When Syria encountered terrorist bombings in December 1996, Pipes would hold that this instability reflected domestic political dissent that would, in turn, explain why Assad would not make peace with Israel.

Consistent with Pipes' reasoning, instead of blaming the opposition, however, Damascus accused Jerusalem of fomenting unrest.[18] These domestic factors are incentives to maintain a state of no-peace, no-war with Israel. Consequently, Assad has not made a commitment to make peace with Israel, according to the Pipes perspective. The United States should refrain from accommodating Syria and should avoid embracing Assad. Therefore, containment and perhaps confrontation would be the best course of action, based on Assad's personality and political constraints under which he operates in Syria.

Pipes also asserts that the Golan Heights is not a key issue for Syria in the peace process with Israel. Rather, maintaining Israel as an enemy is of utmost importance in cementing Assad's hold on power. Maoz, in contrast, claims that the reacquisition of the Golan Heights and southern Lebanon has consistently been demanded in negotiations with Israel. While Pipes contends that it is Assad's fear of losing power in Syria that influences him not to make concessions in the peace process, Maoz suggests that the fear of forever losing the Golan Heights is what influences Assad to negotiate. Despite the anti-Israel majority in Syria and risk of domestic repercussions, Assad is willing to take the chance for a peaceful return of the Golan.

In short, Maoz contends that it is a fear of never regaining the Golan Heights that propels Assad's risk-acceptant attitude in favor of peace; Pipes claims that it is Assad's fear of domestic political losses that encourages him to be risk-averse in the peace process. The Pipes approach is the conventional wisdom about Assad: he is a rational, patient, and cunning politician. In other words, that wisdom assumes that Assad is cautious to a fault, that he is averse to gambles. In fact, however, Assad has been a risk-taker in aligning with the United States against Saddam Hussein and in joining the Madrid peace process with Israel.[19]

Both schools attribute Assad's actions to fears—but different ones. While the Maoz approach is able to justify Assad's risky behavior in the basement of fear, the Pipes approach is less able to explain why he is acting cautiously. The Maoz school is able to provide reasons why Assad is willing to jeopardize political stability in Syria through involvement in the Arab-Israel peace process. The Pipes school, in turn, cannot do so as well.

CONTAIN OR EMBRACE

Given these two contending sets of beliefs regarding Assad's intentions and power to make peace, a dilemma faces the United States in its approach to Syria. On the one hand, Syria supports groups that engage in international terrorism against the United States and Israel, acquires weapons of mass destruction, and has good relations with Iran—an American adversary. On the other hand, Damascus is a potential partner of Washington in the Arab-Israel peace process, has been less of a practitioner of international terrorism since the end of the Cold War, and is an enemy of Baghdad, another of Washington's opponents. Given this conflicting set of problems, at issue has been whether to embrace or contain Syria since the period of the 1980s.

As a member of the National Security Council staff in the Reagan Administration during 1981-1982, I had the occasion to witness from the inside the struggle to resolve the dilemma over Syria. Successive crises over the Golan Heights and Lebanon were laboratories for observing advocates of accommodation and containment of Syria.[20]

DOMESTIC POLITICS OR CONTAINMENT

Washington insiders who wished to contain Syria had the support of domestic political allies in the pro-Israel community. There was a meeting at the White House that I attended on November 19, 1981.

President Reagan met with a conference of presidents of major Jewish organizations to discuss American relations with Israel. At issue was Reagan's commitment to maintaining Israel's qualitative arms advantage, in particular its superiority over Syria.

The president wanted to impress on his audience how committed he was to maintain Israel's security with American arms shipments. Reagan told a story about how during the 1973 war, while he was governor of California, he had called Henry Kissinger at the White House to urge the rapid resupply of aircraft for Israel, which was then fighting against Egypt and Syria. Kissinger said that there was little need for the new aircraft in light of Israel's own figures about losses during the war. Reagan told Kissinger of the press reports based on Egyptian figures; these data showed that Israel had absorbed great losses. Reagan asked, "Why don't you just use the Egyptian figures as a basis for resupplying Israel?" According to Reagan, Kissinger then responded to the governor, "You Machiavellian son-of-a-bitch!"[21]

The president told the story to make clear to the pro-Israel community that he was committed to sustaining Israel's qualitative edge in its conflict with the Arab states, especially Syria. The leadership of the community reasonably inferred from the president's statements that he sided with it in containing rather than embracing Syria.[22]

For Iran and Libya, principal sources of American threat perception are ethnic and bureaucratic politics. These two forms of domestic politics, together with idealism, are more important than alliance preferences. In the clash between ethnic and business interest groups in the formulation of policy toward both states, ethnic preferences have dominated. In particular, the pro-Israel community has triumphed over the business sector in the push for sanctions against Tehran and Tripoli.

For Syria, moreover, American domestic politics reinforce bureaucratic preferences but play less of a role in U.S. threat perception. The pro-Israel community has some effect on perceptions about Syria but does not have to take the lead in seeking to contain Damascus. The business community has virtually no impact on Washington policy making toward Syria, perhaps because of the absence of American business in Syria in comparison to strong and historic economic ties with Iran, Iraq, and Libya.

BUREAUCRATIC POLITICS AND
THE GOLAN HEIGHTS CRISIS[23]

On December 15, 1981, Israel applied its domestic laws to the Golan Heights, which it had seized from Syria in the 1967 war.[24] Those in Washington who wished to embrace Syria used Israel's de facto annexation of the Golan Heights as a pretext for moving closer to Damascus. Secretary of Defense Caspar Weinberger, a leader of the accommodation school, wanted to use the crisis in order to punish Israel for annexing the Golan, while Secretary of State Alexander Haig, a bureaucratic opponent of Weinberger, wished to use it as leverage on Israel, in order to move the Middle East peace process forward. The compromise policy that emerged was for continued sanctions against Syria and mild punishment of Israel.[25] But that middle course neither moved Syria to make concessions to Israel, nor influenced Damascus to soften its hard line toward Jerusalem.[26]

The State Department's position on the Golan Heights crisis was to caution both Israel and Syria to refrain from hasty or emotional actions or statements. Such would only make it more difficult for the parties to act in their own best interests. The department wanted to keep Damascus from repudiating in the heat of the crisis the cease-fire of 1973 between Israel and Syria, their 1974 disengagement agreement, as well as a United Nations mandate to monitor their activities regarding the Golan Heights.

Syria considered Israel's actions concerning the Golan as a move to cancel the 1973 cease-fire, although the assumption seemed to be that Syria canceled the cease-fire accord with Israel. Damascus had stated that by adopting the decision to annex the Golan Heights, Israel had canceled the basis for the cease-fire between the two, United Nations Security Council Resolution 338.

The American embassy in Damascus also belonged to the embrace Syria school. Embassy staffers believed that Syria was playing its hand in a calm manner by opting for UN action. The embassy supported the successful pattern of action used in June 1981, after the Israeli raid on Iraq's nuclear reactor: Washington and Damascus had worked together on a resolution that both could support. The embassy felt that the U.S.

ambassador to the United Nations should not be out front seeking a delay in the United Nations Security Council meeting.

Secretary of State Haig, however, adopted a policy of delay. Notwithstanding the entreaties of the American embassy in Damascus, the position of the State Department was that the U.S. ambassador to the United Nations should take the following stand: declare that formal consideration of the Golan issue ought to await full clarification of the facts. The department's official statement on the Golan was that the United States would be concerned over any unilateral effort to change the status quo of the Golan and would oppose them. The U.S. view was that any unilateral shift in the status of the Golan or any of the territories occupied by Israel in the 1967 war would be contrary to United Nations Security Council Resolutions 242 and 338. The Camp David Accords and all Middle East peace negotiations since 1967 had been based on these two resolutions. Furthermore, any unilateral change in the status quo of the Golan would violate international law relating to belligerent occupation.

Because Haig belonged to the containment school, he sought to soften the impact of Israel's de facto annexation rather than to seek a reversal. He believed that if some means were not found to ease the significance of Israel's law, it could alienate constructive Arab governments and seriously undermine the peace process. Haig wanted Israel to mitigate, explain, or limit the effect of the law regarding the Golan in a public fashion. He stressed to the Israelis the effect that their precipitate action had on the prospects of American-Israel cooperation and coordination and said that it was an affront to a relationship of mutual trust. The secretary's strategy was to play for time while seeking to limit the crisis.

The embracement school in the Reagan Administration held that Israel's annexation of the Golan had taken advantage of developments along two fronts. First, there was the Soviet military intervention in Poland that occurred about the same time. A second front that allowed Israel to act was the need for Egypt to refrain from taking any actions that would lower the likelihood of Israel's withdrawal from the last occupied part of the Sinai Desert. The government of Egypt was not going to take any action in late 1981 that would jeopardize Israel's planned withdrawal on April 26, 1982. The timing of Israel's de facto annexation of the Golan suggested that Prime Minister Begin had made the decision sometime in the past but had awaited an opportune moment. He wanted to implement the decision before Israel's final withdrawal from the Sinai Desert and while the world's attention was on the Polish crisis.

Israel's motives were a blend of strategic considerations related to the peace process and domestic political pressures on the Begin government. Strategically, Israel wanted to accomplish the annexation without jeopardizing the Egypt-Israel peace process. Annexing the Golan in 1981 secured implicit Egyptian acquiescence irrespective of Cairo's denunciations. Domestically, the Golan move simultaneously solved several problems. It countered the political difficulty of evicting Jewish settlers from the town of Yamit in the Sinai. The Golan move also reassured settlers in the West Bank and Gaza that territorial withdrawals would end in April 1982, at the Egypt-Israel border. The Golan action reconfirmed Prime Minister Begin as a decisive leader who would not compromise on issues of vital importance.

Meanwhile, Washington decisionmakers discussed the nature of a statement deploring Israel's actions concerning the Golan. In a fight between Secretaries Haig and Weinberger over whether to sanction or ignore Israel's annexation, Admiral James Nance, Acting National Security Advisor, sent a lighthearted note to White House Chief of Staff James Baker saying, "I'm going to stay out of this one." Baker sent a tongue-in-cheek note in reply, "It is a job of the Assistant of the President of National Security to straighten out these disputes!" Haig had tried but failed to convince the president to avoid harsh criticism of Israel. The Secretary of State had wanted to use the crisis as leverage to move the peace process forward. But after a tough letter from Israel arrived at the White House, the American line stiffened and Haig lost out to advocates of punishing Israel and accommodating Syria.[27]

Meanwhile, the Deputy Chief of Mission of the Israeli embassy in Washington called me to express concern over rumors that unpleasant things were brewing at the White House. He suggested that Washington not blow things out of proportion. Keep in mind that we're talking about Syria, which was the number one enemy of the West in the Middle East. He said that there had only been an application of Israeli law to an area that was devoid of Syrian inhabitants, so that Syrian law did not then apply in the Golan Heights. Clearly, the Israeli representative wanted to reinforce the strength of that part of the U.S. bureaucracy that wanted to ignore the annexation and focus on how to move the peace process forward.

EMBRACE SYRIA; SANCTION ISRAEL

Syria had wanted a United Nations Security Council Resolution against Israel to include the phrase "appropriate measures" in the event of noncompliance, because it would have implied the application of economic sanctions. But Washington held that it could not accept this phrase and would have vetoed any such resolution.

At issue between the United States and Israel with respect to the Golan Heights crisis was the effect of Israel's actions on negotiations for a memorandum of understanding (MOU) between Washington and Jerusalem. The group wishing to embrace Syria called for punishment of Israel for its misdeeds. This meant there would be a suspension of the implementation of the MOU, and that, in fact, did become American policy. But Jerusalem considered suspension of the MOU to be an abandonment of legal obligations.

The U.S. position was that the MOU had not yet entered into force. The two parties had not notified each other of the completion of their respective internal processes, as is required by entry into force of the MOUs provisions. The American statement was that the United States would not be able to proceed with implementation of the MOU. Israel's position was that the MOU related solely to external, Soviet-inspired threats and not to Israel's relations with its neighbors.

Haig's letter to Israel referred to the spirit in which the MOU was concluded. The Reagan Administration had considered that over the past few months, an understanding or spirit had been developed between the United States and Israel that obliged each side to take into consideration in its actions the broad policy concerns of the other. The MOU was one specific formal manifestation of this spirit. It was not intended to limit broader understandings in any way. Israel considered suspending the MOU a serious psychological blow. Jerusalem was trying to put Washington on the defensive. Prime Minister Begin's style in a crisis was to go on the offensive rather than admit error.[28]

During the Golan crisis, the Israel Defense Forces in northern Israel and on the Golan went on high-alert status. But some troops received leave for the Sabbath, from Friday evening to Saturday evening, and tourists once again traveled to the area. Israel had about 25,000 troops in the northern part of the country and on the Golan, as compared to 12,000 before the de facto annexation. Israeli officials had rejected a United Nations Security Council Resolution declaring Israel's annexation of the occupied Golan Heights "null and void," saying no world body can change the decision of a sovereign state or its legislature. The officials said there would no reaction to President Reagan's remarks at a news conference in which he deplored the Israeli move and expressed hope that the actions would be "ameliorated," a term that I wrote into the President's briefing materials.

ALLIANCE POLITICS:
SYRIA BREAKS OUT OF ISOLATION

Those in Washington who wished to isolate Syria were in for a surprise. An unintended consequence of the Golan Heights crisis was to stimulate realignments among Arab states that decreased Syria's isolation. Israel's de facto annexation had the inadvertent effect of reducing Syria's diplomatic isolation within the Arab world.[29] On December 31, 1981, Libya and Saudi Arabia announced that they were restoring diplomatic relations. After Israel applied its laws to the Golan Heights, Damascus and Riyadh decided to restore ties, stop the Iran-Iraq War, and heal divisions between radical Arab states that supported Iran and conservative Arab states that backed Baghdad. Libya and Syria had criticized Iraq for turning away from the struggle with Israel.

Saudi Arabia had broken ties with Syria in October 1981, after Tripoli blamed the Kingdom for allowing four American radar surveillance planes to deploy in Saudi Arabia. Riyadh requested the aircraft for protection in the event the Iran-Iraq War spilled over into Saudi Arabia. Iraq had broken relations with Libya and Syria shortly after the

Iran-Iraq War began. Baghdad accused Tripoli and Damascus of supporting Tehran.[30]

Tehran's military, political, and economic contacts with Damascus had expanded since the Iran-Iraq War began in September 1980. Iranian-Syrian economic ties strengthened with a tentative trade accord worth over $2 billion. Iran agreed to provide Syria oil in exchange for which Syria would supply Iran with refined oil products or proceeds from the resale of crude phosphates, grain, and textiles, as well as Soviet military supplies.

The oil deal was to yield 180,000 barrels of oil per day to Syria, end its need for Iraqi oil, and reduce Iraq's leverage over Damascus in matters affecting the use of pipelines that ran from Iraq through Syria to the Mediterranean at Banyas and at Tripoli in Lebanon. In the spring of 1982, Iraq had shipped about half its crude oil via the pipeline. Because Baghdad earned some $6 billion per year from these shipments, the link to the Mediterranean via Syria was an important one.

On April 8, 1982, Syria sealed two pipelines that carried Iraqi oil, while closing its border with Iraq. Iraq had been exporting 900,000 barrels per day, 400,000 through the two pipelines across Syria. The pipelines had not been closed for political reasons since 1976. Because of the closing of the Syrian outlets, only by shipping via Turkey could Iraq get its oil to the market safely. The Turkish pipeline had a maximum capacity of about 700,000 barrels per day. As a result of the cutoff of pipelines between Iraq and Syria, Baghdad called for economic sanctions against Damascus. Although Turkey stood to gain from the closing of the Syrian routes for Iraqi oil, Ankara also expressed concern about the religious impact of Iranian victories in the Iran-Iraq War. In particular, Ankara worried that Tehran's successes against Baghdad could result in the spread of the Islamic revolution to Turkey via Iraq.

But Syria did not wish to trade total dependence on Iraq for similar dependence on Iran. As the war dragged on, Iran's reliance on Syria increased. Despite the enmity between Damascus and Baghdad, Riyadh wanted Syria to mediate the Iran-Iraq War. In return, Saudi Arabia would help end the dispute between Iraq and Syria. Algeria served as mediator. But the Saudis fretted over the Iranian view that ideological objectives could be achieved by military means. Such a belief frustrated mediation by Algiers, the Organization of the Islamic Conference, and the nonaligned movement.

By concluding an economic deal with Iran in March 1982, Syria had traded off good relations with Arab Gulf states and aligned itself with Iran. One reason for the alignment between Damascus and Tehran was the regional situation facing Assad. Assured of Iranian support, Damascus increased its action against both Iraq and Jordan, two states that were enemies of Syria. Relations between Damascus and Riyadh suffered when Syria improved its relations with Iran. When the Syrian deputy foreign minister called for the overthrow of Saddam in the spring of 1982, it suggested that Damascus had made a long-term commitment to its alignment with Tehran.

While the intention of Israel was to shore up its security with the de facto annexation of the Golan Heights in December 1981, an unintended effect was to reduce the diplomatic isolation of Damascus within the Arab world and hence to strengthen Syria. Israel's actions against Syria also enhanced the influence of advocates within the U.S. bureaucracy of embracing Syria over supporters of containment.

The decade after Syria began to emerge from isolation found it not only back within the Arab world but also at the center of a coalition of moderate Arab regimes and Western allies arrayed against Saddam of Iraq. It was in 1991 that Syria made its most important policy move by participating in the Gulf War coalition. By joining most of the other Arab states in the alliance, Syria sought mainstream status and hence signaled its desire to conform to international standards of diplomatic intercourse. Although not parading its policy intentions, Damascus hinted at potential peace negotiations with Israel and an end to terrorism. The Gulf War coalition marked restoration of economic and diplomatic ties with fellow Arab states and peace talks on the Golan Heights issue, both of which augmented Syria's primary goal of national security. In just five years, Syria had accomplished what it could not achieve after twenty years of state-supported terrorism.

Assad may have changed Syrian foreign policy because the old approach was failing to achieve both Arab influence and reacquisition of the Golan Heights. He demonstrated an ability to learn from his experiences, adapt policy to meet new situations, and correct past failures. Assad additionally chose his political moves for logical reasons—achieving his foreign policy goals—and ended a low-return policy in exchange for a more efficient and effective one.

U.S. POLICY TOWARD SYRIA

Although there are advocates of containment within the U.S. government, there is no official policy to contain Damascus as there is with Tehran, Baghdad, and Tripoli. While Syrian ideology expresses a desire for creation of a Greater Syria that would include Israel, the intelligence estimate in Washington is that Damascus does not have operational plans to carry out this goal. Syria absorbed defeats by Israel in both 1967 and 1973. Then there was the loss of its Soviet patron due to the breakup of the USSR. The end of the Cold War and the hot war in the Gulf left the United States and Syria on the same victorious side. Thus, Syria has the option of playing the American game called "peace process." Whatever ambitions Syria had of destroying Israel are passé. While there is no need to contain Syria per se, there is a wish in Washington to influence Damascus with quiet diplomacy to cease its support for international terrorism.

With respect to another criterion for membership in the rogues' gallery—spread of weapons of mass destruction—there is little evidence that the United States has made much of a public issue about Syria's weapons manufacture. Washington has been almost silent about the chemical weapons production of Damascus in comparison to the warnings issued to Tripoli about its construction of a chemical weapons facility in a Libyan mountain during 1995-1996.

A further rogue state criterion applies to Syria, given its participation in drug trafficking. Again, there is little indication that Washington diplomats care enough about this problem to let it interfere with the felt need to bring Assad into the "family of nations." This phrase stems from the Bush Administration's efforts to appease Saddam for the sake of gaining his support in the Arab-Israel peace process.

Because of the desire of Washington to engage Damascus in the peace process, there is a tendency to discount the Syrian threat. Successive administrations have engaged in bouts of wishful thinking. American officials have imagined that overlooking Syrian "delicts" will result in reciprocity, that ignoring Syrian participation in terrorism will produce concessions from Assad in the Arab-Israel peace process. Furthermore, accommodating Assad's preference to exercise suzerainty over Lebanon will supposedly lead him to reduce the flow of arms from Tehran to Hezbollah in Lebanon via Damascus. In order to get Assad to take part in the alignment against Saddam during the Gulf War, Washington ignored his move to integrate Lebanon into Greater Syria. It has been thought that not taking Assad to task for his housing of suicide bombers in Damascus will moderate Syria in the Golan Heights negotiations.

Assad does take risks by engaging in the Washington-led peace process. And he did participate in the American-led Gulf War coalition. But these risks are insufficient to justify letting him get away with opposing the United States in the Arab-Israel conflict zone. Washington should encourage Damascus to cease being a conduit for Iranian arms for Hezbollah in Lebanon and refrain from housing groups in Syria that commit acts of international terrorism. These three activities constitute a threat to the United States and its allies in the region.

By way of comparison between perceived threats to the United States from Tehran and Damascus, moreover, there is a legitimate dispute among analysts as to whether the pro-Israel community "invented" the Iranian threat.[31] No such dispute pertains to threat perception about Syria. There is an unchallenged consensus that there is danger from Damascus, but the threat is less than that from Tehran and Baghdad. Furthermore, the Iranian menace directly threatens American civilians and military personnel in the Gulf, who are major intrinsic interests of the United States. Iran is also a risk to other inherently valuable assets like Western petroleum products transiting the Gulf and other sea-lanes of communications. Although there are no comparable threats to American intrinsic interests from Syria in the late 1990s, the behavior of its government is a threat to U.S. interests in other areas.

Even though the evidence is strong that Syria is an outlaw state, American officials have been reluctant to name it among the other rogues. President Reagan gave a speech in 1985, in which he named Cuba, Iran, Libya, Nicaragua, and North Korea as being a part of a confederation of terrorist states. He called them outlaws that sought to undermine U.S. interests.[32] The Clinton Administration also provided a list of rogues and conveniently omitted Syria. President Clinton's Assistant to the President for National Security Affairs, Anthony Lake, wrote an article on backlash states that threatened to undermine global security. He listed by name only Iran, Iraq, Libya, and North Korea.[33] The failure of Lake to include Syria is indicative of the vapid policy Washington follows regarding Damascus.

Antiterrorism legislation bars American companies from doing business with countries on the State Department list of nations that support international terrorism. It names seven countries as sponsors of international terrorism, but only five are subject to comprehensive embargoes—Iran, Iraq, Libya, Cuba, and North Korea. Two states escaped sweeping trade embargo status: Syria and the Sudan. The Anti-Terrorism Act of 1996 permits financial dealings with Syria, if these transactions are found not to have an impact on any potential act of terrorism. Syria was subject to less restrictive terms in the 1996 Anti-Terrorism Act because the United States wanted to encourage its participation in the Arab-Israel peace process.

Despite Washington's interest in encouraging Damascus, there are intrinsic interests of the United States under threat from Syria. They include Syrian support for international terrorism and proliferation of weapons of mass destruction, chemical weapons in particular. With respect to terrorism, Syria has a long record. In 1979, the United States officially classified it as a state that supported international terrorism.[34]

Damascus provides safehaven and support for several groups that engage in international terrorism. Hamas, the Palestinian group responsible for suicide bombings in Israel, openly operates a political office in Damascus, where it maintains contacts with Iranian officials. Palestinian Islamic Jihad, which also has claimed responsibility for suicide attacks in Israel, has resident status in Syria.[35] Damascus also provides basing privileges to groups engaged in terrorism or refuge in Lebanon's Beka'a Valley, which is under the control of Syrian armed forces. These groups include Hamas, the Popular Front for the Liberation of Palestine–General Command, the Palestinian Islamic Jihad, and the Japanese Red Army.

Under the authority of Section Six of the Export Administration Act, the State Department established the terrorism list. On it are countries that provide state sponsorship of international terrorism.[36] Once a country is on the list, it cannot be removed without meeting certain requirements, including a presidential determination and advance notification to Congress. States on this list, such as Syria, have trade controls levied against them.

In 1986, Washington expanded economic sanctions against Damascus to include aircraft, aircraft parts, and computers of U.S.-origin or equipment containing such components and technologies. This action was in response to evidence indicating Syrian involvement in the effort to bomb an Israeli passenger airplane at London's Heathrow Airport. Under the 1986 sanctions, Syria is ineligible for the Export Enhancement Program and the Commodity Credit Corporation Program in all agricultural products. The Export-Import Bank suspended its programs in Syria.[37]

In short, American sanctions against Syria include bans on economic assistance and military sales, controls on dual-use equipment that could support terrorism or military activities, and prohibitions on U.S. government support for multilateral economic assistance. The Anti-Terrorism and Arms Export Act of 1989 triggers most of the sanctions against Syria, given its membership on the terrorism list.

Damascus denies charges of supporting terrorism and narcotics trafficking. On terrorism, it claims to use its influence with organizations like Hezbollah—the Party of God—to limit outbreaks of violence on the border between Lebanon and Israel. Also, since 1991, Damascus has actively worked to secure the release of Western hostages held in Lebanon and has removed restrictions on travel by Syrian Jews.[38]

Assad denies claims that Syria is even involved in terrorism. During an October 1994 joint press conference with President Clinton in Damascus, Assad asserted Syria's innocence. "I said in these [peace process] discussions to the American senior officers whom I asked then to mention for me one incident in which Syria has committed a terrorist action, and he was helpless. He was not able to mention one single incident in which Syria supported terrorism."[39] If Assad's statement is true regarding an American diplomat's inability to document Syrian involvement in terrorism, then Washington has not done a good job communicating with Damascus.

Syria also constitutes a threat to the United States through its complicity in international narcotics trafficking. The Foreign Assistance Act of 1961 requires the State Department to publish annually the International Narcotics Control Strategy Report. And section 2346(a) of the Foreign Assistance Act of 1961 requires the termination of U.S. foreign aid to countries implicated in this report.[40] Syria has been a mainstay on the list since the early 1980s, and it appears in the 1995 report, which describes how Syrian military and security personnel personally profited from the drug trade in 1994. It goes on to show how Syrian military protection for drug traffickers persisted in 1994, despite official claims to the contrary.

Syria also engaged in controlled deliveries of narcotics with individuals in Jordan and Lebanon.[41] Moreover, Syria serves as a transit country for Lebanese and Turkish refined cocaine going to Europe and heroin and hashish bound for regional and Western markets.[42] As a result of Syrian complicity in drug trafficking, there is no bilateral narcotics agreement between Washington and Damascus, and Syria receives no U.S. foreign assistance.[43]

Unlike the denials of involvement in terrorism, Damascus does not deny that there is serious international narcotics trafficking in areas under its control. But it does renounce any official assistance or involvement in drug trafficking. Syria also boasts that it is party to the 1988 United Nations Single Convention on Narcotics and its 1972 protocol. In February 1994, Damascus hosted the thirtieth session of a UN Sub-Commission on Illicit Drug Traffic in the Near and Middle East. In addition, Syria publicly reiterated its willingness to pursue all information regarding the possible production of narcotics in Lebanon and Syria. Other important developments include: supposed implementation of stiff drug laws passed in 1993 and joint Syrian and Lebanese eradication efforts in the Beka'a Valley of Lebanon that Syria claims have reduced opium production. Damascus also asserts that there was an increase in the reported number of drug seizures and destruction of drug crops in Lebanon during 1994.[44]

There are political differences over how to handle Syrian complicity in the drug trade. The Clinton State Department lobbied to waive Syria's inclusion on the list of states that do not work hard to stop the drug trade. Officials wanted to remove Damascus from the list as a reward for Syrian participation in the Middle East peace process. Representatives on Capitol Hill strongly objected to the prospective elimination of Syria from the list and threatened to denounce the Clinton Administration for compensating Syria.[45] In opposition to the State Department were not only members of Congress, but also officials of the Drug Enforcement Administration, who contended, with good reason, that Syria had not acted strongly enough to stop the opium trade.[46]

Terrorism and drug trafficking are threats to American intrinsic interests. Syria also poses a danger to U.S. strategic interests. These include the credibility of the U.S. threat to use military force; the American resolve to remain engaged in the world; and the U.S. commitment to defend its friends against its foes.[47] To the extent that Damascus stands up to Washington, it challenges U.S. credibility, resolve, and commitments.

One means by which Damascus confronts Washington is through the provision of safehavens to terrorists who attack American citizens and individuals from allied countries. Subsidizing terrorists is equivalent to state-sponsored terrorism. But the threat to American strategic interests from Damascus is not as great as from Tehran. Not only does Iran target American citizens, it also directs terrorism against the Iranian political opposition at home and abroad. To the extent that the domestic opposition derives from Iranians who were associated with the Shah's regime and thus tarred by the American brush, Tehran's attacks are threats to the strategic interests of the United States.

Given Syria's involvement in terrorism and complicity in the drug trade, the question remains what is the best approach for the United States if it wants to end these dangers? Washington's strategy is to retain sanctions until Damascus ceases its support for terrorism. But what is the best way to maintain pressure on Syria? Two approaches are available: public denunciations and private diplomacy. Washington has given too much attention to private discussions and not enough to public denunciations.

On the one hand, the State Department's Office for Counter-terrorism and the Bureau for International Narcotics and Law Enforcement Affairs follow a public policy of describing Syrian misbehavior. On the other hand, the Department's Near Eastern Bureau is less harsh publicly in its depiction of Syria. Robert Pelletreau, Assistant Secretary of State for Near Eastern and South Asian Affairs, even failed to mention Syria when he discussed American interests to suppress terrorism and the spread of weapons of mass destruction. Although the secretary acknowledges the need "for containing rogue regimes in Iran, Iraq, and Libya," he does not include Syria in his list.[48] What kind of signal does failure to name Syria send to Assad? That it is acceptable to help terrorists, engage in a search for weapons of mass destruction, and take part in drug trafficking.

CLINTON ADMINISTRATION AND SYRIA

The Clinton Administration's approach to Syria reflects the dilemma that faced its predecessors as well. In addition to Clinton's supplications at the Presidential palace in Damascus in October 1994, Secretary of State Warren Christopher made over 20 trips to Syria during the 1992-1996 period. These visits indicate the Clinton Administration's preference to accommodate Assad. But Christopher's retention of Damascus on Washington's list of nations that support international terrorism also shows its inclination to contain Syria. The administration seeks both to engage and contain Syria. As in the past, a central puzzle arises for the United States with respect to Syria: why would the Clinton Administration engage in negotiations with Damascus, despite its participation in international terrorism, proliferation of chemical weapons, and drug trafficking?

An answer to this puzzle lies in the reference point Washington sets for the Middle East.[49] The administration desires peace between Damascus and Jerusalem more than cessation of Syria's terrorism, proliferation, and trafficking. The Clinton Administration fears losing Syria's participation in the peace process more than it values termination of rogue state activity.[50] The United States was willing to take major risks in order to avoid the loss of Syria in the peace process. Hence, Clinton was willing to risk his prestige when he met with Assad in 1994. Because that summit meeting violated the U.S. position of refraining to appear too close diplomatically to states that subsidize groups sponsoring terrorism, it was risky to hold the summit.

SCENARIOS

Whether the United States pursues a posture of embracing or containing Syria depends in part on scenarios that develop between Damascus and Jerusalem. The possibilities are: peace; no-peace, no-war; and war. If Washington would like to facilitate a peace scenario, then the approach of Moshe Maoz seems to be most relevant. He suggests that Assad has made a strategic commitment to peace; hence, Washington should test the validity of his pledge. Not doing so would leave open the possibility of a deterioration of the situation and make the other two scenarios likely.

Peace

A peace scenario stems from the assumptions that both Israel and Syria have made strategic commitments toward a settlement. In this respect, Ze'ev Schiff, a leading Israeli political-military analyst, wrote a seminal essay on the relation of peace to security. Schiff said, "If peace with Syria is the strategic goal toward which Israel is driving, and if the Syrian decision to make peace with Israel and end the conflict is indeed a strategic concept—as President Assad said in Geneva—then the chance for peace is very great."[51]

Schiff's assumption is that commitments by Damascus and Jerusalem are necessary but not sufficient conditions for success of the peace process. The missing ingredient is the American role. The U.S. approach has been like that of a host at a cocktail party, serving the food and drinks but not interfering too much in the conversation among the partygoers. In order to facilitate the peace process between Israel and Syria, however, a more active role on the part of Washington might be required. But an active role need not focus on Damascus.

Ignoring Assad and making progress on the withdrawal of most of the
Israeli military from Hebron may have resulted in a Syrian démarche
to resume negotiations with Israel during December 1996. Indirect
pressure on Syria via progress on the Palestinian front helps to avoid
slippage in the journey toward peace on the northern front.[52]

No-Peace, No-War

Neither peace nor war was the approach adopted by Assad from 1974
to 1991. At that time, there was stalemate in negotiations between
Israel and Syria, yet war did not occur. From the 1974 disengagement
accord between Israel and Syria brokered by Henry Kissinger until the
commencement of the Madrid talks in 1991, there was a freeze in
Israel's relations with Syria. This period was a time during which both
sides "muddled through." Damascus did not choose military action,
however, to unfreeze the political stalemate. Rather, Syria chose to wait
for a change in the strategic situation, which occurred with the end of
the Cold War and the hot war in the Gulf.

At the turn of the century, Assad may calculate that a middle-
ground approach is the best means of keeping the pot boiling without
falling into the hot water of a war with Israel. In this regard, he could
achieve the following objectives. He could extract from Israel a high
price that could include Israeli recognition of the Syrian presence in
Lebanon, disrupt the process of rapprochement between Israel and the
Arab states as well as the Palestinians, and drive a wedge between
Israel and the United States. In addition, he might lay the groundwork
for the renewal of future negotiations under more promising conditions; for example, after the next elections in Israel.[53]

In the no-peace, no-war scenario, Syria could continue its practice
of brinkmanship and tacit support of terrorist groups. Doing so
enhances its bargaining position vis-à-vis Israel. Also, attacks against
Israel by Syrian surrogates help keep the Golan Heights item on the
agenda of the peace process. In the American-led negotiations, Israel
has stopped most negotiations with Syria. The initial impetus for the
cessation was due to a series of suicide bombings. Because of the role
of Palestinians in the bombings and the timetable of the Oslo accords
of 1993, the Israeli-Palestinian dimension has received more attention

than issues concerning Syria. The closer Israel and the Palestinian Authority come to normalizing relations, however, the worse Assad's bargaining position would be when the talks resume between Jerusalem and Damascus. Although Syria needs to keep the pot boiling, it has to be careful not to let the peace process proceed too far without its active participation.

War

In the absence of diplomatic progress on the Syrian front due to Assad's perception that this is the best course of action to get the peace process moving, the parties could head down the slippery slope to war. Assume the persistence of the policy of Israel as a "peace for peace" approach rather than "land for peace," as envisioned in UN Security Council Resolutions 242 and 338. In this event, Ze'ev Maoz believes that the government might as well prepare the country for war in the not-too-distant future.[54] The likelihood of an accord on terms that Assad could accept are lower without the magic of diplomatic momentum.

In the context of stalemate on the Syrian front, Ze'ev Maoz reasons that Assad would face two inter-Arab scenarios, each creating incentives for war. According to the first, the peace process on the Palestinian track would continue, and the Arab world would maintain its rapprochement with Israel. In this scenario, there would be a significant risk of perpetuating Israel's rule over the Golan Heights. A Syrian attack on Israel would pose a dilemma for the Arab Nation. In the best case for Damascus, it would receive military and/or economic support from several Arab states. In the worst case for Damascus, it would still have Arab political support, which manifests itself as pressure on Washington to move the negotiations with Israel forward.

According to the second scenario of Ze'ev Maoz, there would be a radical change in Israel's relations with Arab states because of a stalemate on the Palestinian track and Jordanian disappointment with the dividends of its peace with Israel. In this event, a war with Israel could restore Syria to its position as a leader in the peace process— thus bringing the Palestinians, and even the Jordanians, in line behind the Syrian position. In both scenarios, an inability to ignite the peace process through a military initiative against Israel could exacerbate Assad's domestic political problems.

Yet another possibility stems from the fact that Syrian frustration over the internal political situation might increase to the point where Assad is willing to bear additional risks. The area in which Syria has the capability of causing genuine psychological damage to Israel is to attack its heartland with missiles.[55] Damascus has emphasized massive procurement of missiles in order to balance Jerusalem's air superiority. Syria has over 300 ballistic missiles, including the Scud-C, whose range is more than 500 kilometers. Damascus has even developed an ability to manufacture this missile independently. Syria manufactures these missiles in underground installations that Damascus built with the assistance of China, Iran, and North Korea.[56]

Recall the four themes that cut across *Rogue Regimes:* threat perception, opportunities, politics, and policies. For Syria, bureaucratic and domestic politics are not important elements in the American policy process. Given similar perceptions of threat and opportunity between the United States and its allies, it is comparatively easy to fashion policies to change Assad's behavior or to punish him for misbehavior. The allies are of little consequence in determining Washington's policy of continued sanctions against Damascus. There is little indication of opportunities foregone as a result of maintaining sanctions against Syria. But with respect to the debate about the nature of threats in the international system, the United States does not perceive Syria as equivalent to the former Soviet threat.

CHAPTER SIX

CUBA: CONTAIN AND EMBRACE

PUZZLES AND DILEMMAS

"THE EMBARGO IS A WASTE OF TAXPAYER DOLLARS AND TIME." "I am ready to build the Taj Mahal in Havana." "Isn't there something between dancing with a dictator and sitting passively by while the Europeans invest?"[1] Statements by American business leaders display no fear of Fidel Castro's Cuba. Rather, these businessmen are critical of the U.S. embargo against Cuba, eager to invest there, and hopeful of a compromise that would allow the trade restrictions to be lifted, so that they can be assured a place at the table of profits to be made in Cuba.

They are puzzled by a policy that remains in place even though Havana is no longer on the front line of international communism. Also puzzling are Washington's conflicting goals concerning Cuba. It wants Castro out of power, yet it does not wish to hurt the Cuban people. But Castro uses the embargo as a means of retaining power. His political position has become so untenable that were he to fall, Castro might bring down Cuba with him. Hence, the dilemma: American pressure to oust Castro has the side effects of both strengthening him and facilitating the implosion of Cuban society. Thus, at issue is how to get rid of Castro without reinforcing his grip on power and hurting the Cuban people.

To anticipate the conclusion of this chapter, the dilemma may be resolved if it were possible to contain the Castro regime yet embrace the Cuban population. Because Castro is a "crisis creator," he deserves to be contained.[2] But because the Cuban people are more or less "victims of circumstance," they should be embraced with humanitarian assistance. Consider the origins of the American policy of economic sanctions against Cuba before addressing the central dilemma and the issues of crisis creation and "victimhood."

To solve the puzzles and address the dilemma, here is a discussion of threat perception, domestic politics, and national security. Then there is a treatment of the effects of the American embargo on Cuban trading options, the Cuban-Soviet alignment, ideals and ethnicity versus economics, as well as motivations for economic sanctions and reasons for lifting them.

THREAT PERCEPTION

In U.S.-Cuban relations, misperception of threat derives from distorted information processing and is the order of the day. A concern regarding threat perception in general is why actors perceive each other as threatening. In particular, why does the United States view Cuba as a hazard, and why does Havana see Washington as a danger? Questions about threat perception require an explanation of why people perceive or misperceive threats. While some actors perceive threats as intended, other people misperceive the same actions.

Distortions abound in American threat perception of Cuba. They also occur in Havana's views of Washington. Leaders of both countries tend to overestimate the threat from the other nation. Because of the domestic political benefit derived from standing up to Castro—a motivated bias—presidents magnify the threat. Due to the historical image of Castro as a Communist, there is an unmotivated bias that associates him with "evil." Thus, presidents perceive his behavior as also "evil," without evaluating it on its own merits. Such misperception explains an overestimation of the threat posed by Castro's behavior.

Because of the domestic political benefits to Castro for standing up to the colossus of the North, he augments the threat from Washington. And as a result of Castro's historical image of American leaders as Yankee imperialists, he views their behavior as "aggressive," without interpreting that behavior on its own. Such misperception accounts for Castro's overestimation of the threat posed by American actions. Because leaders in both countries benefit from threat magnification in their respective domestic constituencies, there is little incentive to evaluate behavior independent of historical images of the enemy.[3] The flip side of threat perception is the opportunity posed by a threatening situation.

INTERESTS UNDER SIEGE: INTRINSIC AND STRATEGIC

Threat and opportunity are two faces of the same problem. A threat to national security for some leaders may be a domestic political possibility for others. But only national security is a legitimate justification for a state's international behavior; domestic politics are not. Government actions cannot be justified on the grounds of pandering to constituencies; they must carry the legitimacy of serving the whole populace of a nation—hence, national security is a legitimate means for justifying international action, and domestic politics are not. In the stormy relations between the United States and Cuba, a national security rationale may be a façade for domestic political agendas on both sides.

From the U.S. perspective, at issue is whether Washington perceives Havana as a valid national security threat or simply an unacknowledged domestic political opportunity. Washington explicitly claims that Cuba is a threat, but domestic politics and American idealism account for why the United States continues economic sanctions. Despite the fall of international communism, the embargo remains. If national security pertains, then the American embargo is justifiable. If domestic political games apply, then economic sanctions are less legitimate.

There is a threat from Cuba to American intrinsic values; for example, to the lives of Cuban-American exiles engaged in a struggle for power with the regime in Havana. Intrinsic values include protecting the American civilian population, military personnel and installations, as well as economic concerns like energy supplies. While there is a threat to some intrinsic values, there is a far greater threat from

Cuba to U.S. strategic interests. These interests include the credibility
of the U.S. threat to use military force; the American resolve to remain
engaged in the world; and the U.S. commitment to defend its allies. To
the extent that Castro stands up to Washington, he challenges U.S.
credibility, resolve, and commitments.[4]

DOMESTIC POLITICS
MASKING AS NATIONAL SECURITY THREATS

While Cuba legitimately threatens U.S. strategic and intrinsic interests, domestic political opportunities converge with idealistic motivations to dominate threat perception. For Cuba, domestic politics
also account for national security threat perceptions, but Havana has
a more compelling case than Washington does regarding the primacy
of actual threats over political games.

From the Cuban perspective, at issue is whether Havana perceives Washington's economic sanctions as a national security threat
or a domestic political opportunity. If national security applies, then
Cuban resistance and hostility to the United States are not unexpected and are legitimate. If domestic politics are pertinent, then the
regime in Havana may be using the American embargo as a means to
retain power. For just as Washington politicians can play political
games with national security, so can the Cubans. Though Havana is
threatened by sanctions, the regime still uses this valid threat as a
political opportunity.[5]

Regarding politics in Havana, the question is how the Castro
regime justifies its one-party rule in a world where multiparty
democracy is on a roll. One answer is to keep the American embargo
in place. Dictators facing potential internal challengers may be
pleased to have an external threat to divert the attention of the
population. The American embargo is an external threat that enables
Castro to deny political liberties to his potential challengers and
human rights to the Cuban people. In addition to domestic politics
and national security, a related issue concerns American allies'
perceptions of U.S.-Cuban relations.

LEMONS TO LEMONADE: EMBARGO DIVERSIFIES CUBAN TRADING PARTNERS

The American embargo on Cuba is like handing the Castro regime a bushel of lemons. Rather than drinking the sour juice alone, the regime adds sugar and water to make lemonade—additional trading partners for Cuba. The American embargo is an incentive for the Cuban leadership to seek trade and investments from Europe and Canada, instead of relying solely on the United States. With a termination of the embargo, there may be a return to American economic domination of Cuba. Indeed, it was the American trade in high-demand commodities that initially drew Havana into Washington's sphere of influence.

The United States had subsidized Cuban sugar imports by paying above-market prices. After a break in the relations between Havana and Washington in 1961, the Soviets began their own sugar subsidies for Cuba. Once the Soviet Union disintegrated, Russia dropped the Cuban sugar subsidy. Since that time, Cuba has had to face lower free-market prices for sugar and has absorbed severe financial losses. Because of Cuba's historical economic dependence on the United States, the Castro regime would rather trade off the economic costs of the embargo in order to achieve political autonomy from Washington.[6] Imposing trade restraints on Cuba helped drive Havana away from Washington, first toward Moscow, then toward Brussels and Ottawa. Thus, the American embargo not only serves Castro's domestic political needs, but also promotes Cuba's international economic purposes.

At issue is how Washington can justify sanctions on Cuba to the European allies and Canada. International communism is dead. The allies favor the reintegration of Cuba into the family of Western nations. And they suspect domestic political ploys underlie the American embargo. Also, the allies strongly oppose the U.S. application of its anti-Cuban legislation to their firms.[7] In short, it is difficult for the United States to justify the embargo to allied leaders who suspect domestic political games are determining U.S. policy toward Cuba.

Because Havana is no longer exporting its revolution via international terrorism or weapons proliferation, the allies do not believe that

Cuba is a national security threat.[8] As terror and proliferation are two criteria for classifying a state as a rogue, the allies see Cuba as less of an outlaw in the post–Cold War era. Instead, they view Havana as a relic of the Cold War and a casualty of American domestic politics. And with respect to the economics of the embargo, a final issue for Havana is how to avoid renewed economic dependence on the colossus of the North.

While Cuba claims that it seeks economic autonomy, its prior dependence on the Soviet bloc is hardly indicative of economic independence. The Soviet bloc accounted for 85 percent of Cuba's foreign trade from 1970 to 1989, a figure which hardly suggests economic independence. Cuba received $18.5 billion in economic aid from communist countries, compared to only $710 million from Western countries, between 1970 and 1989.[9]

Politics and economics are two interrelated issue areas. In the Cuban-American relationship, there are political and economic paradoxes. On the political side, the United States designed the embargo to oust the Castro regime; but the sanctions actually help it remain in power. On the economic side, Washington imposed the embargo to isolate the Cuban economy from the United States; but the sanctions actually expand Cuba's trading partnerships with other nations.[10] Since his coming to power on New Year's Eve of 1959, Castro's survival has been a main consequence of these political and economic paradoxes. Indeed, he is a survivor par excellence.

ORIGINAL SIN: DANCING WITH THE DEVIL

Castro's original sin was that he dared to dance with the Soviet devil in the American ballroom—the Western Hemisphere.[11] Contrary to manifest destiny and the Monroe Doctrine, Castro invited international communism to penetrate the Americas. Manifest destiny was the nineteenth-century notion that the United States had a moral obligation to control the area from the Arctic Circle to the Strait of Magellan.[12] The Monroe Doctrine applied the idea of manifest destiny to Latin America, establishing the entire Western Hemisphere as the U.S. sphere of influence.[13] In particular, the aim of President Monroe's 1823 pronouncement was to deter European states like Spain and Britain from reasserting their colonial presence in the Americas. Although manifest destiny and the Monroe Doctrine were nineteenth-century concepts, they still color Washington's perceptions of Havana.

As far as the U.S. perspective, it treated Cuba as a virtual colony. Washington asserted a right to intervene in Cuban affairs by writing an amendment to the Cuban Constitution—the 1901 Platt Amendment.[14] It gave the United States the authority to veto international commitments, intervene in Cuban domestic politics, and oversee the Cuban economy. Although this "right" evoked protest in Havana, Washington compelled Cuba to accept the amendment.

Even after Congress revoked the Platt Amendment in 1934 and President Franklin Roosevelt replaced it with the Good Neighbor Policy, the amendment nevertheless had an impact on Washington's perceptions of a budding Cuban-Soviet alignment.[15] That is, the United States acted as if it retained the right to veto Cuba's commitment to the Soviet Union. In July 1960, President Eisenhower began the process of using economic sanctions to punish Havana when he placed import controls on Cuban sugar. It became illegal for American firms to import Cuban sugar. And by the fall of that year, Eisenhower imposed controls on almost the entirety of American trade with Cuba. Finally, just prior to turning the Oval Office over to President-elect Kennedy, Eisenhower broke diplomatic relations.

The incoming president's anti-Castro campaign rhetoric made him reluctant to veto U.S. government plans to support an invasion of Cuba by Cuban-American exiles. The CIA designed the Bay of Pigs operation to coincide with predicted popular uprisings on the island. The operation became a fiasco when the uprisings failed to occur. After Castro survived that invasion, he endured attempts by the CIA and underworld mobsters to assassinate him.[16] As active measures to depose Castro from power failed, economic sanctions continued. But sanctions alone were not enough to bring him down, in light of Soviet economic support and strategic moves to alter the balance of power in the Western Hemisphere.

In defiance of American hegemony in the Caribbean, the Soviet Union placed in Cuba nuclear missiles capable of striking the United States. President Kennedy demanded their immediate withdrawal and sent American battleships to quarantine that island-nation. Soviet Premier Khrushchev consented to the withdrawal of the missiles under the condition that the United States would not invade Cuba. That agreement precluded American military action, yet permitted economic sanctions. Thereafter, the main tool Washington used against Havana has been the economic embargo.[17] Consistent with the Platt Amendment, the United States vetoed a Cuban international commitment and used economic sanctions as a tool to "oversee" the Cuban economy.

The accord that ended the Cuban Missile Crisis allowed the United States to express its distaste for the Castro regime by imposing economic sanctions.[18] Other aims of the sanctions policy are to remove Castro from power, replace him with an anticommunist leader, and democratize Cuba.[19] These are very ambitious goals—much too grandiose for sanctions alone to achieve. But in order to counter Soviet influence in Cuba, sanctions were the only game in town.

Although economic sanctions are a weak method, they are the midway point between doing too much—invasion—and doing nothing—acceptance of the Castro regime. Despite the gap between a formidable agenda and a weak tool, Washington wanted to lay down a marker that would signal its strong desire to counter Soviet influence in Cuba. Havana acted as Moscow's surrogate in conducting political and military operations in places like Angola and Ethiopia. With Soviet backing, Castro placed about 40,000 ground troops in Angola and deployed some 15,000 troops to Ethiopia. He then arranged for various guerrilla factions to assemble in Nicaragua, El Salvador, and Guatemala. Additionally, Castro sent military advisors or forces to Africa and Latin America.[20]

Castro's original sin of dancing with the Soviet devil confronted American politics and idealism with a choice: either oppose or accept the romantic couple. Neither ethnic-based American politics nor principled American idealism would allow presidents to accept Castro's transgression of dating outside of the Western circle of friends.

IDEALS AND ETHNICITY VERSUS ECONOMICS

There is a convergence of idealism and ethnic politics strikingly observed in U.S. relations with Cuba. Despite tremendous support by the American business community to lift economic sanctions so that American firms can reenter the Cuban market, every president since Eisenhower has held the line on restricting economic interaction with Castro's regime. In the spring of 1996, corporate giants, the United States Chamber of Commerce, as well as the Association of Exporters and Importers clamored for President Clinton not to tighten sanctions. When business interests confront idealism and politics, interests be damned. Clinton proposed instead to strengthen sanctions. How can one account for such a gap between interests and politics? On a cursory level, it can be argued that Clinton is merely kowtowing to the Cuban-American community. Although he needed Cuban-American votes in such crucial states as Florida and New Jersey in the 1996 presidential campaign, politics alone do not explain the success of that community in its influence on U.S. policy making.

Cuban-Americans are only influential in the policy-making process to the extent that their behavior coincides with American ideals. For a domestic lobby to make an impact, its actions should intersect seamlessly within the Red, White, and Blue. At this intersection, the doors to power close on the hands of powerful multinational firms and open for domestic political constituencies like the Cuban-Americans.

In other words, ideals and ethnic-based domestic politics challenge economic interests in the formulation of American policy toward Cuba. Regarding the conflict with economic interests, Cuban-American exile groups confront U.S.-based firms, their subsidiaries abroad, and even foreign businesses that seek to conduct operations within Cuba. Because the business community is not a unitary actor regarding Havana, the Cuban-American community has allies within the American corporate sector.

There are at least two schools of thought concerning Cuba within the American business world: the "realists" would conduct trade as usual, unconditionally. The businessman who opened the chapter with the wish to build the Taj Mahal of Havana represents the realists' perspective. The "idealists" would do business on a conditional basis, that is, if there were a movement toward democracy and Castro were removed from power. Realists would not trade off economic interests for the sake of democratic ideals. The *Wall Street Journal* reflects the sentiment of the idealists.[21] In an editorial, the *Journal* criticized European leaders for favoring so-called trade incentives rather than penalties to encourage Havana to protect its workers. Denying that Cuba allows for free market enticements in general, the editorial questioned whether Havana would respect workers' rights if given incentives to do so. Hence, the idealists would trade off an interest for an ideal. They would give up access to the Cuban economy in order to support workers, for example.

The realists would continue the embargo in spite of Castro's hold on power. During 1996, the Council on Foreign Relations, journalists, and business groups interested in world affairs sponsored a luncheon in New York for Castro. The leaders explored with him in vain the possibility of a compromise that would move Cuba toward free elections, respect for human rights, and market reforms—in other words, a movement toward democracy that would provide the political cover for a loosening of the American embargo. But Castro declined to provide those who favored lifting the embargo any ammunition they might use to bolster their argument.

Regarding ethnic politics, Cuban-Americans use American idealism as a platform from which to oust Castro. In order to achieve their goal of ridding Cuba of Castro, there is a division of labor within the community. First are the militant activists; second the political activists. Because the majority of the community shares a desire to oust Castro from power, activists dominate Cuban-American politics.

Periodically engaged in running battles with Cuban military forces in or about Cuban waters, the militant activists provoke confrontations with Havana as a means to pressure the U.S. government to take a tougher stance against Cuba. Indeed, in March 1996, Cuban military forces shot down a Brothers to the Rescue civilian aircraft in or near Cuban territorial waters. Prior to that incident, other civilian aircraft associated with the Brothers had flown over Havana. These planes had dropped antigovernment leaflets calling for disobedience among the Cuban population.[22] An outcome of the skirmishes between Brothers to the Rescue and the Cuban military was the congressional passage and presidential signing of the Cuban Liberty and Democratic Solidarity Act.[23]

The Brothers to the Rescue represents militant activism under the guise of the ideal of humanitarian relief; the Cuban American National Foundation (CANF) exemplifies political activism, again for philanthropic purposes. CANF is the largest interest group of its kind in the United States.[24] It has ties with the Free Cuba Political Action Committee as a result of overlapping leadership. The president of the Free Cuba PAC is on CANF's executive board. According to Federal Election Commission records, the Free Cuba PAC has contributed over $1 million to candidates for president and both houses of the Congress in about ten years' time. The president of CANF estimates that its directors and trustees have contributed triple that amount under their own names. FEC reports show that the Free Cuba PAC has given more than $175,000 to candidates for Congress in 1993 and 1995. CANF gives special attention to members of Congressional committees who deal with foreign relations.[25]

In short, politicians appeal to domestic constituencies that have stakes in continuing sanctions against rogue regimes, such as Castro's Cuba. Domestic lobbies on behalf of ethnic groups bolster politicians who favor sanctions against rogue states. Lobbies on behalf of business firms clash with ethnic interest groups over sanctions policy. But ethnicity triumphs over economics because of the convergence of ideals and politics. The interest of free trade championed by American business cannot hold a candle to the ideal of bringing democracy to Cuba.

FROM REHABILITATION TO RETRIBUTION

Another aspect of American idealism is the notion that American presidents have a "fiduciary" responsibility to change the behavior of foreign leaders—to rehabilitate them. This obligation derives from the idea that occupants of the Oval Office have a duty to sit in judgment over, and change the conduct of, their counterparts abroad. With respect to Cuba, therefore, presidents from Eisenhower to Clinton believed they were entrusted with the charge of changing Castro's behavior—to rehabilitate him. Failing that, they sought to transform his communist dictatorship into a democratic republic—a retributive goal.

Initially, the American embargo against Cuba aimed to coerce a change in Castro's behavior—to rehabilitate him from his Soviet-sponsored activities abroad. After the breakup of the USSR, however, Cuba lacked the capacity to export its revolution overseas. Moreover, with the fall of the Berlin Wall, there was no longer a market for a surrogate of communist "imperialism." Despite a superficial change in Cuban behavior, sanctions against Havana have remained in place. Persistence of sanctions irrespective of changed circumstances indicates that retribution rather than rehabilitation is a motive for U.S. behavior.

Regarding idealism and retribution, there is a principle that American presidents have the moral obligation to punish wrongdoing. In addition to using coercive sanctions against Castro, the United States has sought retribution—punitive action without regard for changing his behavior. Politically, retributive sanctions against Cuba are risk-free. As soon as Washington inflicted harm on Havana, sanctioning as a tool of retribution was effective. Such punishment was immediately gratifying to the presidents as well as to the Cuban-American community. The U.S. embargo has not only had an instrumental rehabilitative function—to change Castro's behavior—but also a symbolic retributive purpose—to signal to Havana and the Cuban-American community that wrongs are being righted. Retribution and rehabilitation are two pillars of presidential policy toward Cuba. And both are legitimate purposes to the extent that Castro can be held accountable for his actions.

FROM WINDOWS TO BASEMENTS

Castro acted from a window of opportunity during the Cold War when he actively sought, and eagerly received, Soviet backing. His moves were calculating and precise, and he was fully aware what Washington's reaction would be. His actions were driven by the expectation of a prize.[26] When Castro acted opportunistically and to a large degree rationally during his early reign, he could be held responsible for his conduct. He knew what the consequences of his deliberate actions were. Thus, American economic sanctions were an appropriate means of rehabilitation and retribution.

Part of the embargo's rehabilitative function has been overtaken by events associated with the fall of communism and the dissolution of the USSR: Cuba no longer is on the front line of exporting its own revolution or communism's ideals. Yet Castro continues to deny human rights to the Cuban people and does not allow a legitimate opposition to challenge him.[27] Hence, there are major changes that need to be made in the regime, namely, democratization of Cuba.

Castro is in a fearful position in the post–Cold War era. A relic of a bygone age, he is alone and isolated in his dark basement. He is growing more and more frantic to escape. Occasionally, he lashes out, seeking to ward off those entities he perceives as threatening. One result was the destruction of American civilian aircraft that were flying over disputed airspace while searching for refugees.[28] In light of this fearful position in which Castro finds himself, consider some scenarios for the future.

SCENARIOS

Three scenarios are plausible: muddling through, implosion, and a happy ending.

Muddling Through

Castro survives in office and dies of natural causes. The status quo continues under Fidel's clones, such as his brother, Raul.[29] In order to prevent this possibility, the U.S. Congress pushed the president to sign the Cuban Liberty and Democratic Solidarity Act legislation. That act tightened the embargo, and it represents the "status quo-plus." Despite this enhanced pressure, however, the embargo may fail to bring Castro down. He uses it as a means of retaining power. In this respect, economic sanctions that bolster a dictator are of doubtful utility. Despite increased burdens, Cuba as a country also survives. The

Cuban people have a remarkable talent for muddling through the hardships imposed by their dictator and his cronies.

Implosion

The implosion scenario has three contingencies. Cuba collapses, igniting a civil war that results in a military ouster of Fidel Castro. Cuban society disintegrates, but Castro's peaceful retirement avoids civil conflict. Cuba collapses, civil war ensues, and Castro successfully resists attempts to oust him.

The first contingency is that the embargo may succeed in toppling Castro, and he tries in vain to bring Cuba with him.[30] The result is that competing elements in the military oust the Castro brothers in a civil war. Their Cold War alignment with the USSR had constituted a window that could be lowered, if not closed, with U.S. sanctions. The dissolution of the USSR, however, left them in a fearful position.

Sanctions imposed on a nation whose desperate leadership is in a cellar may exacerbate fears and increase the risk of anarchy—an implosion of the social structures of a society. Applied to Cuba, there could be a flood of boat people emigrating from Havana to Miami in an escape from the chaos of the failed state. If the American embargo were to destabilize Cuba, this "success" might only be a Pyrrhic victory—a triumph achieved at excessive costs to Cubans and Americans. Washington's attempts to destabilize Havana could also result in some instability in the United States. That is, the flood of émigrés from Cuba on their way into southern Florida might have the effect of creating a humanitarian crisis here.

Although Castro uses U.S. economic sanctions as a means of retaining power and as a tool to diversify Cuba's trading partners, the net effect of the embargo is negative for the country as a whole. In this connection, the sanctions increase the risk of implosion. If Castro believes that his regime is on the verge of downfall, he may decide to take the rest of the country with him, resulting in civil war.[31] Just as Samson pulled down the pillars in order to destroy his enemies, Castro under the siege of sanctions may pull the pillars out from under his country onto himself and onto his adversaries.

A second contingency in the implosion scenario is that the island-nation's society disintegrates, but Castro takes off and lands softly due to his having a "golden parachute." That is, he retires into an exile with "perks" (perquisites) thanks to the cooperation of a like-minded dictator abroad. Although Cuban society collapses, Castro's benign departure makes civil war unlikely.

A third contingency in the implosion scenario is that Cuba collapses, civil war ensues, and Castro successfully resists attempts to oust him. While overthrow is the least likely contingency, in the implosion scenario, Castro's retention of power is more likely.[32]

At issue is whether the embargo is more likely to facilitate implosion or democracy. Assuming that implosion is more likely than democracy, American sanctions for rehabilitative purposes should be terminated. Regarding retribution, however, the embargo continues to have a positive effect: the sanctions make Americans feel good! Although the embargo has been in place for over a third of a century, there is no time limit on the moral principle that wrongs need to be righted.

But the question arises whether the benefit of retributive justice is more desirable than the risk of failed rehabilitation. Failed rehabilitation—implosion—is less desirable than successful retribution—feeling good. Consequently, sanctions for retributive justice also should be terminated. In other words, one should fear implosion more than one should desire to feel good. Hence, on both rehabilitative and retributive grounds, sanctions should terminate.

Happy Ending

A third scenario is that Castro falls from power incrementally, and democratic institutions arise as he descends. Unfortunately, this scenario derives from wishful thinking. Indeed, the intent of the Cuban Liberty and Democratic Solidarity Act is to raise the costs to Castro in doses that may squeeze but not strangle him. That is, increased economic pressures should result in incremental political moves toward democracy and open markets without leaving a power vacuum in Cuba.[33] Therefore, consider the Cuban Liberty and Democratic Solidarity Act.

The most significant feature is that it is extraterritorial in application. Because of this aspect, the embargo has caused foreign firms to think twice about investing in Cuba. The Act punishes foreign executives and their families who benefit from property the Cuban government confiscated from American citizens, principally Cuban-American exiles. When American law extends to foreigners acting abroad, this is extraterritoriality.[34] The European Union and Canada consider extraterritoriality illegal under international law.[35] Indeed, during February 1997, they threatened to take their case against the United States to the World Trade Organization (WTO). But Washington's opposition helped to postpone the formal presentation of the case.

Reflecting that opposition, Stuart Eizenstat, Under Secretary of Commerce and the president's Special Envoy for the Promotion of Democracy in Cuba, issued a statement attributed jointly to the U.S. Department of Commerce and the Office of the U.S. Trade Representative. The WTO Director General had appointed members to a dispute-settlement panel in Geneva on the Cuban Liberty and Democratic Solidarity Act and other U.S. measures concerning Cuba. The Eizenstat statement said, " . . . the WTO was not created to decide foreign policy and national security issues."[36] That is, Washington claimed a national security justification in order to preempt the free trade standard put forth by the European Union and other Western countries. And one national security goal of the act is to facilitate the decline of the Cuban economy.

As a result of a lack of foreign investment capital, the Cuban economy is likely to continue its deterioration. A Mexican conglomerate that had been the largest foreign investor in Cuba, Grupo Domos, left the island after being burdened by American sanctions. The company had been a minority partner in a $750 million joint venture with Cuba in its telephone monopoly. The government of Cuba had announced the deal at a ceremony in Havana during 1994. Present at the announcement were both Castro and his Mexican counterpart, then-President Carlos Salinas de Gortari. Havana saw the accord as opening the door to future Mexican investment to refurbish and expand Cuba's cement, glass, mining, oil, and tourism industries.[37] A free-falling economy would place incremental pressure on Castro to depart or to be ousted. The happy ending scenario that Castro falls

slowly and Cuba democratizes incrementally, however, assumes without evidence that he would be willing to depart without plunging the
country into political chaos.

In summary, there are three scenarios regarding Cuba: Castro
survives, Cuba muddles through; Castro falls, Cuba implodes; Castro
falls slowly, Cuba democratizes. The first two scenarios are the most
likely and least desirable from Washington's perspective. The contingencies of Castro's survival or sudden demise are not in the interest of the
United States. The most desirable but least likely scenario is that Castro
falls in measured increments, and Cuba moves toward democracy.

PUZZLES, POLITICS, AND POLICIES

This chapter opened with a puzzle: why does the American embargo
against Cuba remain in place despite the end of the Cold War, a
cessation of state-sponsorship of international terrorism and subversion, and a termination of Cuba's role in the proliferation of weapons
of mass destruction? One solution to this puzzle: domestic politics
and idealism interact to sustain and strengthen the embargo irrespective of the behavior of the regime in Havana or the nature of its
international support.

Because American pressure to oust Castro has the side-effects of
both reinforcing his hold on power and facilitating the implosion of
Cuban society, the embargo should be lifted.[38] Given the possibilities of Castro's survival or Cuba's collapse, the United States should
eliminate potentially destabilizing sanctions. Whether based upon
rehabilitation or retribution, these sanctions should end. To terminate the embargo without asking anything in exchange from Castro,
however, is difficult to achieve because of domestic political constraints.

These same restraints provided the environment that facilitated
the passage of the Cuban Liberty and Democratic Solidarity Act. But
it is naïve to expect the embargo to produce democratization without
Fidel or Raul Castro. The intensified sanctions produced a paradoxical windfall for the Castro brothers: the heightened embargo
strengthened their hold on power.

Besides the unlikely democratization called for in the embargo legislation, what else might be a unit of currency between Washington and Havana? An alternative is for Washington to end the embargo in stages in exchange for Havana opening its doors. A first measure could include implementation of the Helms-Burton Act in such a fashion as to refrain from infringing upon the sovereignty of other countries or to hinder normal trading practices.[39] Second, the United States could allow the sale of food and medicine to the island-nation.[40] Third, Washington and Havana could improve and expand not only their telecommunications links, but also their transport of mail. Finally, permitting free emigration and immigration as well as opening Cuba to the Western information age could be the first steps in the democratization of that insular society.[41] Just as democracy followed the penetration of Western ideas into Eastern Europe, so Cuban democracy may grow if there were a free flow of people, products, and information into and out of Cuba.

To return to the dilemma imposed at the beginning of this chapter, at issue is how to contain the Castro regime yet embrace the Cuban population. Because Castro is a "crisis creator," he deserves to be contained. But because the Cuban people are more or less "victims of circumstance," they should be embraced with humanitarian assistance. A relaxation of portions of the Helms-Burton Act to permit an explosion of information onto Cuban society might be a way to prevent its implosion. Likewise, redrafting should be for the purpose of isolating the regime from the population. In this respect, it might be possible to contain Castro and embrace Cubans.

Four themes characterize *Rogue Regimes:* threat perception, opportunities, politics, and policies. For Castro's Cuba, domestic politics are the key to the American policy process. And in conjunction with the debate about the nature of threats in the international system, Castro is a rogue leader, but Cuba is not a rogue state. Absent the Cold War, Cuba no longer sponsors international terrorism, does not engage in the export of its revolution abroad, and is not seeking to acquire weapons of mass destruction. And given the United States and its allies' different perceptions of threat from, and opportunity in, Cuba, it is difficult to fashion policies that are appropriate to change the regime's behavior or to punish its misbehavior in a legitimate fashion. Punishment can only be justified on retributive grounds. But the cost of continued retribution against Cuba may be higher than the domestic political gain. Thus, American sanctions against Cuba should end.

CHAPTER SEVEN

NORTH KOREA: CONTAIN AND EMBRACE

MANIPULATOR OF CRISIS OR VICTIM OF CIRCUMSTANCE

AT ISSUE IS WHETHER NORTH KOREA is a "crisis creator," on the one hand, or a "victim of circumstance," on the other. Pyongyang has a history of creating political crises. The regime, however, may be on its last throes of existence as its economic situation spins out of control. To the extent that Pyongyang is a manipulator of political/military crises, then it should be contained; to the degree that it is a potential casualty on its economic deathbed, then it needs to be embraced with humanitarian assistance.

Pyongyang as a crisis manipulator is a more or less rational actor looking for windows of opportunity through which to jump. These openings need to be closed with deterrent threats by status quo powers like the United States and its allies in northeast Asia. The containment/ deterrence strategy Washington has employed against Pyongyang since the end of the Korean War assumes that the regime is capable of approximately rational action. In other words, when confronted with greater expected losses than anticipated gains, North Korea should be able to make a simple calculation and refrain from attacking South Korea.

In contrast to North Korea as a rational actor, the regime as a member of the walking wounded may not be deterrable. Pyongyang lives in an environment not of its own making and, in effect, resides in a windowless basement of fear. In this respect, Washington and its allies may wish to provide aid and comfort to heal the diseased body lest it become a corpse. They need to reassure the body politic of North Korea that the United States means no harm. In so doing, the United States averts the tragedy of a paranoid North Korea: acting out in acute desperation, factions within the regime would behave like victims that lash out at perceived adversaries.

The threat strategy Washington has used against Pyongyang in the aftermath of the Korean War is irrelevant against a divided regime motivated more by fear than gain. There are no windows to be closed to deter by threat of punishment and few gates to be locked to deter by denial. The military elites in Pyongyang worry about losses over which they have scant control. And when losses are the focal point of decision making, actors have a hard time making simple calculations necessary to be deterred.

Two camps come to mind regarding explanations of North Korea's behavior. The first sees Pyongyang as a unitary actor in control of its own destiny. It invents emergencies as a routine part of a rational negotiating strategy.[1] "Talk to me; I may go nuclear," was the diplomatic marker laid down by Pyongyang during the early 1990s.[2] "Feed me, or I'll kill you," is the North Korean outcry of the late 1990s.[3] Pyongyang has polished a sophisticated diplomatic game of bluff. Threaten, receive rewards; then promise, procrastinate, provoke, and pause in anticipation of further appeasement from the powers.[4] Cite floods, feign famine, and place the West on a guilt trip in order to squeeze concessions that would not otherwise be forthcoming.

The second camp frames North Korea as a divided nation whose destiny is in the hands of forces outside the regime's control. North Korea is fated to be a failed state torn asunder by rival factions. Humanitarian predicaments are the circumstances that force the elites to make choices not of their own making. "Feed me before I die and infect your friends," is the moan of the moment. "Prop me up before I fall and bring down your friends," is the lamentation of the lame. But as North Korea teeters on the brink of falling, this relic of a bygone era may be even more dangerous than in Cold War times.

There is historical precedent for empires and nation states to be healthy while youthful and infirm in old age. But because the North and the South are about the same age—about a half-century-old—and Seoul is healthy, longevity is not the explanation for the deterioration of North Korea.[5] Perhaps what ails the nation is the same malady that afflicted other Communist states at the close of the twentieth century. Because there was no private sector to do the job, these states disintegrated when unable to feed and clothe noncomplacent populations. Contrast the collapse of the Soviet Empire and the coherence of China, a Communist nation in the midst of economic reforms and growth.

On the one hand, a Velcro-like blame clings to those in power when famine derives from the politics of defective distribution: the political system falls under the burden of its own bankrupt policies. On the other hand, a Teflon-like immunity shields politicians when famine stems from the economics of scarcity. The USSR fell apart when its politicians could not survive the consequences of an economic system unable to support its population. The Soviet parent who fathered North Korea in 1948 as a child of the Cold War has gone out of business and filed for a "Chapter Eleven"–type bankruptcy.

Irrespective of whether the government is in control or the society is in free fall, the neighbors may wish to ensure that the political outcomes do not jeopardize their own national interests. When the sick man of Europe—the Ottoman Empire—began to collapse, the Great Powers during the nineteenth century propped it up. Their goal was to keep each other from decimating the Ottoman corpse in a feeding frenzy. By keeping the empire together, the Great Powers avoided conflict over the distribution of spoils. The Powers on the eve of the twenty-first century also see a need to hold up a falling North Korean regime. Fortunately, a Dr. Kevorkian-like assisted suicide is not an option: the patient is in a state of severe denial and unwilling to confront death.[6]

QUESTIONS AND PRELIMINARY ANSWERS

As the North Korean regime proceeds down a slippery slope, either by choice or by circumstance, three questions arise. The first requires explanations of the past; the second demands scenarios of the future; and the third calls for plans for the present. The past, the future, and the present march in that order for good reason. If we can explain the past and project the future, we can formulate effective policies for the present.

Question One. Why has North Korea engaged in brinkmanship with the United States, and what are the prospects for a continuation of this pattern? Answer: Pyongyang went to the brink when it was healthy. One of its goals was to compel Washington to negotiate directly, without including South Korea. The government in the North used "crisis as an opportunity" for diplomatic engagement with Washington.[7] While this pattern dominated prior interactions, it may not last.

As floods and famine vanquish the North, the regime is not able to control its future as it controlled its past. Because North Korea deserves the label of "Sick Man of Asia," it is not able to pursue a more or less rational course of action to use crisis as an occasion for diplomatic success. In short, North Korea has used crisis as an opportunity for gaining concessions, but may not be able to continue to use this strategy in the future.

Question Two. Under what conditions will North Korea implode from within and/or explode across international borders? Answer: massive starvation exacerbated by natural disasters, such as floods, could result in an implosion of civil society in North Korea. As a result, civilians would run for their lives. They could flee over land and via the Yalu River into China, escape by sea to Japan, or dare to run the gauntlet of the "militarized" Demilitarized Zone (DMZ) between the Koreas.[8] Starvation also might prompt a military invasion of the South by dissident elements in Pyongyang. Like Samson's destruction of the Philistines' temple, North Korea could bring down others as it falls. Doing so would constitute a severe threat to regional security. In summary, floods and famine may result in national implosion and/or international explosion. But collapse seems more likely than invasion: North Korea's economic situation has worsened more than the political/military environment for the regime.

Question Three. If implosion is more likely than explosion in the midterm, what policy packages should the United States pursue in the short term? Washington's four options are: to contain (deter) North

Korea, to embrace the Pyongyang regime, to contain and embrace it, or to gradually withdraw from the Korean peninsula.[9]

A POLITICAL AVIARY

A consideration of the past, future, and present warrants a framework for analysis. As a first step in its construction, consider the metaphor of a "political aviary." In the bureaucratic politics of Washington, policy analysts act as if they were in a birdhouse—a virtual international political preserve comprised of hawks and doves. Owls from outside the Washington zoo provide critiques relevant to both sets of policy analysts.[10]

Hawks assume that Pyongyang is in command of its own destiny. Doves presume that North Korea is sliding away into an abyss and dragging others with it. And owls explain the past and project the future in order to discover whether the regime was or will be in command or out of control.

Indeed, owls can strengthen the hand of either hawks or doves, once analysis is complete. On the one side, if owls find the leaders in Pyongyang manipulating crises, this reinforces the position of hawks in the bureaucracy. On the other side, if owls discover that circumstances manipulate the leadership, this conclusion gives doves the upper hand.

Given their assumption that the government in power is responsible for its own actions, hawks prefer containment or deterrence. In light of their presumption that situations have the potential to spin out of hand, doves split between accommodation and withdrawal. And their theory-inebriated counterparts in the academic community, the owls, are willing to accept a variety of policy packages, including a mix of containing and embracing.[11]

Hawks also would allow North Korea to collapse on its own without any assistance from the West. They would permit a hard landing for the regime, irrespective of costs. Because hawks assume that problems in North Korea are intractable, they are willing to refrain from intervention. If pressed to intervene, they would condition assistance to Pyongyang on its implementation of economic reforms.

The bottom line, however, is that hawks follow a policy of using threats to contain, while making humanitarian assistance to the North conditional on economic reforms that could doom the regime.

Doves wish for a soft landing for North Korea. They worry about the risks of a hard landing. They prefer a policy of unconditional assurance and humanitarian rewards. Additionally, doves hope for a happy ending at best or a muddling through at the least. They perceive the problems of Pyongyang to be tractable: incremental economic reforms could produce a peaceful transition and subsequent reunification of the peninsula. While doves would like to see economic reforms, they would not use food as a weapon to force compliance.

Following a further clarification of the hawks-doves-owls framework, there is in this chapter a discussion of ideals and interests in American policy, followed by a treatment of United States–North Korean relations. This historical analysis feeds into a specification of war and peace scenarios for the future. Finally, the chapter addresses policy packages available to the Clinton Administration in light of rival perspectives, ideals and interests, prior history, and alternative futures.

THE WAR FOR WASHINGTON

Hawks: Deterrence and Coercion

Hawks favor policies designed to deter and coerce. They assume that leaders can accurately calculate the balance between gains and losses, equally weigh losses relative to gains, and act to maximize expected gain and minimize expected loss. From this perspective, these leaders are "rational calculators" who rarely believe they make errors. According to hawks, disastrous outcomes like wars are due to a vacuum of power and/or an absence of commitment. Wars result from the actions of power-hungry, "error-free," cold-hearted mercenaries who are not held in constant check by capability and commitment.

In the context of avoiding military conflict on the Korean Peninsula, hawks see the proximate cause of a future war as one-sided weakness. This imbalance tempts an adversary, such as the regime in Pyongyang, to exploit an advantage. The classic example of such exploitation is the case of Munich. It symbolizes the failed British and French attempt to appease Nazi Germany. The two allies sold out Czechoslovakia in 1938, as a way of "buying off" Hitler—but he did not "stay bought." Hitler continued to engage in aggression against his neighbors.

To avoid another Korean War conducted by a modern-day Hitler, hawks suggest a policy of "peace through strength." Paradoxically, a demonstrated will to use force is one way of achieving peace. According to hawks, leaders of threatened states will be deterred from going to war if they perceive the expected costs to be greater than the anticipated gains from fighting. Accordingly, they place a high premium on relative capability and credible threats, irrespective of costs—escalation.

Through the eyes of hawks, an aim of the United States is to make sure that North Korea perceives the costs of war to outweigh the gains. Also, the North should realize that the odds of losing are higher than the chances of success. The United States cannot assume that Pyongyang understands this calculus. In order for the North to be deterred from launching an attack, Washington needs to make it very clear that the risks of going to war exceed the foreseen gains. Issuing credible threats to the regime's leaders is a surefire way to bolster deterrence and coerce successfully.

According to the hawks, it was understandable that North Korea launched a war of aggression against South Korea in 1950. Why? There was an "interest vacuum" and a "commitment void." The United States failed to make clear its interests in protecting the South and its commitment to do so.[12] As a part of an overall containment policy, hawks would announce U.S. commitments to friend and foe alike and not worry about the destabilizing effects that might occur as a result of reinforcing deterrence.

To illustrate the idea of announcing commitments, consider an incident regarding Taiwan that occurred in 1997. The speaker of the U.S. House of Representatives, Newt Gingrich, went to China. He explicitly warned the leadership that Washington would defend Taipei if Beijing attacked. The speaker said that the United States should avoid the kind of situation that led to the Korean War, when ambiguity in the American commitment to defend South Korea provided an incentive for the North to attack.[13] The speaker is clearly a hawk. But what kind? Because in the case of Taiwan he focuses on deterring rather than coercing, Gingrich is a "deterrent hawk" rather than a "compellent hawk."

Doves: Unintended Escalation

The upside of explicit commitments is to reinforce deterrence; the downside of making commitments clear-cut is to provoke escalation: there is a risk that those abroad and at home may read too much into an unambiguous commitment. Such misperception may lead to unintended escalation. Commitments that are too precise may send the wrong signal to multiple audiences. Pledges to support a friend against a foe may inadvertently prompt that friend to take undesired or unforeseen action; the foe then can use this action as a rationale to take military steps against that friend.

American reluctance to incite the pro-independence movement in Taiwan serves as a prime example of a policy of "strategic ambiguity."[14] If Taipei were to affirm its independence, that would be a pretext for Beijing to take military action. Hence, U.S. policy is consciously ambiguous: it implies an American commitment to defend Taiwan without provoking Beijing. Unlike hawks, doves are inclined to focus on such downside risks of policies that reinforce deterrence.

Doves presume that threats to deter and coerce often provoke an already agitated leader to retaliate. This process drags all parties into an unwanted conflict. If there were disastrous outcomes—for example, war—it would not be due to an interest vacuum or an absence of commitment. According to the doves, disaster results from the actions of fear-driven, mistake-ridden, risk-prone paranoids.

For doves, the main cause of a future war on the Korean Peninsula would be the destabilizing consequence of mutual efforts to reinforce deterrence: American threats for deterrence would actually provoke an imperiled state like North Korea to risk preemptive attacks or preventive wars.[15]

On the one hand, preemption is a response to an immediate crisis situation: mutually escalating fears and threats place a premium on offensive action. On the other hand, preventive war involves longer-term premeditated behavior on the part of one antagonist: before a situation deteriorates even further, the threatened nation would rather risk war. In this respect, a goal of preventive war is to forestall a change in the overall balance of power. Doves are concerned with both decreasing incentives for preemptive strikes and reducing provocation for preventive wars.

The doves claim that the lesson of the First World War—reassure at all costs—is applicable to North Korea. Prior to the outbreak of World War I, Dual Alliance members (Germany and Austria-Hungary) and Triple Entente allies (England, France, and Russia) failed to reassure one another. As a result, the alliance members saw efforts to reinforce deterrence as attempts to gain advantage. The principal European powers misjudged how their mobilization schemes would interact. Each feared that delay would allow their enemy to gain a decisive tactical advantage. They felt there was no choice but to escalate in order to avoid losing the advantage of going on the offense. This perceptual security dilemma resulted in provocation and unintended war.

With respect to preventive war, doves hold that leaders may decide to make war to avoid war. Leaders of endangered nations may risk war now to avoid a sure defeat later. An illustration of a preventive war is the attack by Israel on Egypt in the 1956 Sinai Campaign. Because of an arms race between Iraq and Egypt, Cairo began to acquire Soviet-bloc arms. Although they were ostensibly intended for use against Baghdad, Cairo's arms could have been employed against Tel Aviv. Hence, in return, Israel purchased arms from France. To avoid a situation where Egypt could start a war later that Israel could not win, it decided to attack before the situation worsened.[16]

To avoid preventive wars, doves suggest conciliation and accom- modation to reassure threatened nations. Following the lead of doves, Cairo should have reassured Tel Aviv that Egypt's arms buildup was directed at Iraq, not Israel. But given the animosity between the Arab states and Israel, reassurance was not a realistic option for Egypt. Cairo could not reassure Tel Aviv without being criticized by Baghdad, Amman, and Damascus. In addition, Israel would not have believed Egypt's reassurance.

Just as the Middle East offers precedents for illustrating processes that lead to preventive wars, so does the Far East. Like Israel in the

1950s, North Korea in the 1990s may feel itself to be an "endangered species." Perceiving a growing disparity between themselves and South Korea, the rulers in Pyongyang may have incentives to launch a preventive war. In this regard, incentives for prevention and preemption may coincide. A perception in the present that it is better to fight now instead of allowing the situation to degenerate even further could converge with a perceived loss of control in a short-term crisis.

Were Pyongyang to launch a preemptive attack on Seoul, an incentive for this action might be a perception that it had no choice but to strike first in a crisis. This "crisis instability" could result from the vulnerability of Pyongyang's weapons systems to a first strike by Seoul. Furthermore, were North Korea to launch a preventive war against the South, it might be due to its perception that Pyongyang was on the losing side of a long-term trend in a changing balance of power.

Hawks: Deterrent versus Compellent

Hawks split along a passive-active line of deterrence and coercion. Both groups advocate action; the issue is in the application. Deterrent hawks prefer a policy of threats to rewards; they seek to discourage action not yet taken. Deterrence can be achieved with a more passive approach, while compellence requires a more active policy. Compellent hawks advocate a conventional hard-line policy of threats over rewards; they want a target to cease taking an action or to undo an action already taken.[17]

With respect to North Korea, there is little distinction between deterrent and compellent hawks in practice. Deterrent hawks abound: they suggest a policy of threats to prevent North Korea from acquiring weapons of mass destruction. Compellent hawks exist only in principle: they would suggest a policy of threats to coerce North Korea to cease pursuing its nuclear weapons program or to dismantle it. And if rewards are in the policy package, hawks would link the rewards to evidence that Pyongyang has been rehabilitated from its naughty nuclear ways.

In other words, deterrent hawks advocate a linkage policy: any carrots should be tied to a change in North Korea's behavior. Conditional humanitarian assistance would be a carrot to be earned by proper behavior, such as agreeing to negotiate with South Korea. Instead of requiring linkage, however, the Clinton Administration has tolerated Pyongyang's reluctance to deal directly with Seoul.

The administration proposed that North Korea enter four-power negotiations involving Beijing, Pyongyang, Seoul, and Washington. When North Korea refused to come to the four-sided table, the administration continued with its humanitarian assistance.[18] This approach of providing unconditional assistance drives hawks up the trees of Washington's aviary. Indeed, hawks claim that Pyongyang requests food aid to keep the entire population from starving while its military continues to operate and absorb the limited resources of the country.[19]

Hawks assume that Pyongyang's goal of a separate peace with the United States, to the exclusion of Seoul, is a consequence of American weakness, saying in effect that U.S. diplomatic flexibility encourages North Korean belligerence.[20] The Heritage Foundation in Washington is a home for deterrent hawks, dubbed here as "Heritage hawks."

Heritage hawks argue that the strategy of North Korea is the deliberate destruction of the existing armistice structure that ended the Korean War. The goal is to convince the United States to sign a bilateral peace treaty with the North. Pyongyang desires "to cut Seoul out of the loop," for example, to exclude South Korea from a military settlement and facilitate the withdrawal of American forces from Korea. The Clinton Administration insists that the United States will not agree to such a deal; nevertheless, it implies that such a deal might be possible because of a willingness of Washington to engage in separate diplomatic discussions. Any Pyongyang-Washington talks imply a bilateral treaty. That is, when the United States negotiates with North Korea without the presence of the South, there is an implication that a separate deal might be acceptable.

Because the United States and its allies fought the Korean War under the UN flag, Washington should not be involved in negotiations with Pyongyang on its own. There should be multilateral talks followed by a replacement of the existing armistice structure with a peace treaty negotiated and signed by the North and South Korean governments. The State Department should announce that the United States will never consider a bilateral peace treaty with the North. That statement should recall for all parties that in the Reconciliation Agreement ratified

by the governments of the North and South in 1992, the two sides
pledged to negotiate a North-South peace agreement.

Heritage hawks believe that the Clinton Administration's policies
have failed to protect U.S. national interests in the Koreas. One
primary interest is reduction of military tension along the DMZ. In
order to achieve the objective of tension reduction along the borders,
hawks advocate a series of interrelated moves.

The United States should condemn the North's behavior and reiter-
ate to friend and foe alike a commitment to the defense of Seoul. In this
respect, Washington should reinforce American ground troops in South
Korea with radar aircraft and temporarily deploy one additional aircraft
carrier to the Seventh Fleet in the Pacific. The bottom line is this: to deter
the North from undertaking aggression against the South, Washington
needs to augment American combat forces in the Korean Peninsula.

When hawks split along an active/passive dimension, the issue is
whether to deter or coerce. Similarly, doves divide into two camps. The
focus of doves is not whether to deter or coerce; their emphasis is on
short-term and midterm consequences of deterrence and coercion.

Doves: Libertarians versus Activists

Just as the Heritage Foundation typifies deterrent hawks, the Cato
Institute exemplifies one wing of doves. Cato doves are of the
"libertarian" variety. They are generally unwilling to take actions to
avert conflicts. These doves place their faith in the long-term balance
of political and economic power to avoid unwanted escalation.

Cato doves are coming into vogue during the post–Cold War era.
Because the threat is less, it is more "politically correct" to be a
libertarian than during Cold War days. Cato doves are the laissez-faire
analysts of the policy process. They rely on the political-military
balance of power among the parties and the magic of the economic
marketplace to take care of a given situation. If there is an imbalance
in favor of the status quo powers, they can take risks for peace.
Similarly, a favorable balance of power for challengers allows them to
have enhanced degrees of freedom vis-à-vis status quo powers.

To illustrate the libertarian position, consider an actual confrontation
between a Cato dove and an unabashed hawk on an American television

talk show. After Iraq had invaded Kuwait, I had the honor of making a guest appearance on *The Oprah Winfrey Show*, August 16, 1990.[21] My role was to defend the Bush Administration's hawkish decision to deploy hundreds of thousands of combat troops to Saudi Arabia.

A former colleague of mine from the Reagan White House, Doug Bandow, represented the Cato Institute. He took it upon himself to criticize the American deployment in the Gulf. Bandow's argument was that the natural operation of the marketplace would cancel out the negative effects to the United States of the Iraqi possession of Kuwaiti oil. According to Bandow, it does not matter who owns the oil; what counts is the nature of the market for it. In order for oil to have value, it must eventually flow into international markets. Once there, its price is a consequence of economic supply and demand, not political ownership. In light of the operation of the oil market, Iraq's invasion of Kuwait was of little consequence to American consumers and thus was not a threat to American national interests, according to Bandow's logic.

I disagreed with Bandow. The Iraqi invasion of Kuwait was a threat to the U.S. national interest. The United States had made a commitment to the defense of Kuwait during the Iran-Iraq War. To allow Iraq to seize Kuwait would be a blow to American credibility and signal a lack of U.S. resolve. I paraphrased President Kennedy's statement that the United States had to honor its commitments. As the leader of the free world, Washington had to be prepared to go anywhere, to defend any friend against any foe, so that the light of liberty could survive. This broad strategic argument contrasted sharply with Bandow's narrow economic perspective. Of course, my strategic argument carried the day. (But who can recall losing a debate described by oneself!)

The Bandow libertarian position on the Gulf bears close resemblance to the Cato argument about the Korean Peninsula. Narrow economic cost-benefit calculations are at the core for both regions. The libertarian approach sees a South Korea that has twice the population of the North, an economy over ten times the size, and hence a Seoul that has the capability to match Pyongyang in defense spending.[22] Additionally, there is an imbalance of diplomatic clout in favor of Seoul and its allies over Pyongyang. With the possible exception of China, North Korea has no allies as such. Because South Korea can take care of itself, it should do so—such is the libertarian bottom line. Although

Seoul's economy is extremely strong in comparison to Pyongyang's, it may not be strong enough to handle the rush of refugees if and when North Korea implodes.

Regarding the political-military situation on the Korean Peninsula, the Cato doves favor accommodation between Washington and Pyongyang. The reasoning: embracing North Korea with economic incentives would reduce its motivations to harm its neighbors.

Additionally, Cato views the North as less of a threat in the post–Cold War era. And in the absence of a global Soviet threat, libertarians maintain that the American defense of South Korea loses its connection to U.S. security. With the lessening of the danger from the North, moreover, the rationale for Washington to defend Seoul is even less compelling.[23]

These libertarians suggest the following policy package for the United States. Washington should withdraw all American forces from South Korea over a four-year period, offer to transfer to Seoul whatever conventional armaments it desires to purchase, and announce an intention to terminate the United States–South Korea mutual defense treaty by the end of the twentieth century.

Also, libertarians prefer to continue improving relations with Pyongyang. One way of doing so is to meet the obligations Washington assumed under the 1994 Agreed Framework with Pyongyang, under which North Korea was to receive two new light-water nuclear reactors, heavy fuel, liaison offices with the United States, and a reduction in American economic sanctions. Other ways to foster enhanced relations include mediation of territorial disputes between the South and North, expansion of South Korean security cooperation with Japan, and participation of Seoul in regional security organizations.[24]

In contrast to the libertarian position, activist doves prefer to avoid preemptive strikes and preventive wars, regardless of the cost. They favor a policy of accommodation, irrespective of motivation. Libertarian doves advocate a hands-off approach, despite the risks of inaction.

Activist doves would agree to provide economic benefits to North Korea and to enhance political relations with its government, in the absence of any improvement in relations between Pyongyang and Seoul.

Activist doves are few and far between in Washington. During the Cold War, there was an "open hunting season" on activist doves. Only in the post–Cold War era has it been legitimate to argue this viewpoint. Even now, however, they are similar to an endangered species.

Activist doves would assure, embrace, accommodate, and even appease North Korea. They would make promises to gain the confidence of the regime in Pyongyang. They would include North Korea into a regional alliance system and would reconcile past differences with Pyongyang. And in the worst case, they would appease the North Korean regime by buying it off. Doves of an activist feather would also lift economic sanctions on North Korea and provide humanitarian relief for its starving people. They would continue aiding Pyongyang, irrespective of the fact that doing so rescues that noncompliant regime from collapse.

Consider a policy problem to illustrate linkage. At issue was whether the Clinton Administration should provide about $25 million in unconditional food aid. The administration decided to do so. And during the spring of 1997, the *Galveston Bay*, an American-flagged ship, carried its first load of humanitarian assistance to North Korea. Doves ask, "If the people of a faraway country are starving, does the United States have a moral obligation to feed them?"[25] Activist doves would answer in the affirmative. Their ethical principle: "Ought implies can, and can implies should." That is, the United States ought to do good because it has the capability to do so. This self-imposed moral obligation is an inevitable consequence of the doves' vision of "America the good," versus the hawks' vision of "America the brave."

Indeed, because the obligation is moral, it is unconditional. Critics of the dovish approach advocate linking American humanitarian assistance to the North Korean diplomatic position: Washington should condition its supplies to Pyongyang's participation in multilateral talks, which would include Seoul. In answer to this proposed linkage, however, the State Department announced that the United States does not link food aid to peace talks.[26] In effect, the Clinton Administration assumes that floods and famine in North Korea are equivalent to similar events in friendly countries like England, Israel, and Mexico.

American hawks emphasize threats to North Korea over assistance to Pyongyang. Libertarian doves would provide assistance only as a transition toward withdrawal from the Korean Peninsula, while activist doves would give aid to North Korea regardless of its behavior.

Hawks and Doves: Rational "Roosters"?

At first glance, it appears that both hawks and doves share in common an assumption that nations act rationally in their decisions to make war or peace. Both believe that leaders are capable of perceiving threat credibility, imbalance of power arrayed against them, and the likely consequences of their defensive actions. Do they simply "roost" on the same rational branch and argue about the best place on which to sit?[27] No, they do not dwell on the same branch. Because they divide over where on the branch threats cease to deter and begin to provoke, hawks and doves make different assumptions about rationality.

Hawks have more faith in rational action than do doves. Hawks do not even raise the prospect that threats can provoke. When doves ponder the circumstances in which deterrent threats become provocative threats, they imply that misperception is an explanation for the slide from deterrence to provocation. Those who would categorize hawks and doves together presume that perception is not a problem between them. But in fact, perception is at the core of the difference between them.

Hawks and doves focus on the balance of power between challengers and status quo powers. For hawks, imbalance in favor of the status quo actor should facilitate deterrence. For doves, a projection of imbalance in the long term may provoke a preventive war in the short term by the nation on the losing side of the trend.

Hawks follow the precepts of comprehensive rationality more than doves. Both, however, presume that the behavior of a target actor is more a result of the external environment than its internal nature. That is, they take a "billiard ball" approach: nations are like balls that ricochet off one another, driven by some hidden hand holding the cue stick of their national fate. Behavior is a consequence of the actions of others, not the result of attributes of the target actor.

The billiard ball approach ignores the characteristics of people. In this view, it is unnecessary to inquire into their incentives, motivations, and fears; it is enough to assume that people are more or less rational, and would avoid punishments and seek rewards from the external environment. This approach, in effect, "black boxes" the attributes of individuals: it conveniently sets aside human characteristics in order to make inferences about how a stimulus like a threat brings about a response, such as compliant behavior.

Owls: Misperception and Loss of Control

In contrast to hawks and doves, owls take issue with the billiard ball approach. Not only do owls consider external incentives for behavior, they also look within the "black boxes" of individuals. Owls regard threat, reward, and prior reinforcement as candidate explanations for misperception and loss of control. They also take into account attributes of the actors, such as their risk-taking propensity. Owls believe that behavior is a consequence of the policies of an external, status quo power *and* the internal nature of a challenger. In this respect, owls attribute both compliant and roguish behavior to internal predisposition as well as prior reinforcements or punishments from the external environment.

Irrespective of risks, hawks suggest threats and doves favor rewards.[28] Owls, however, prefer either, neither, or both. An owlish approach recognizes that there are two ideal types of leaders: 1) power-hungry, error-free, cold-hearted mercenaries; and 2) fear-driven, mistake-ridden, risk-prone paranoids.[29] For owls, disastrous outcomes are due to a lack of knowledge. Owls might recommend policies of punishment, reward or both, as well as a hands-off approach, depending upon the attributes of the challenger.

Hawks and doves care little about the internal factors driving the actions of the North Korean regime. They explain Pyongyang's roguish behavior as due to the absence, or presence, of threats from Washington and Seoul. In contrast, owls would examine the internal nature of Kim Jong-Il's regime, seek to discover his motivations, hopes, and fears, and then from all of these, develop a suitable policy to influence the regime's actions.

Hawks make the most comprehensive set of assumptions about rationality, while doves make fewer, and owls make the least. Indeed, owls explicitly take into account the inability of some leaders to think rationally. In particular, owls focus on misperception as a constraint on decision making. They do not roost in the tree of rational decision making. Owls depend upon the tree of knowledge to underpin their policy recommendations: they nest on the limb of life rather than the assumed branch of rational action. In short, hawks see the proximate cause of war to be weakness; doves attribute war to provocation, while owls stress perceived loss of control among a package of internal and external factors.

Owls understand that national leaders are people with problems that cut across time and space. One set of issues concerns how humans value their possessions. They do not want to lose what they already have, and if given the chance, would like to possess what they desire. But if the world actually operated this simply, scholars would be out of a job. There are factors that cloud human decision making, namely emotions and motives. Owls accept the fact that emotions are almost impossible to control, and those of policy-makers are no exception.

The bottom line for owls is: people fear losses more than they covet gains. Owls contend that when the prospect of losing approaches, people become frantic to avoid deprivation. Situations become fuzzy, and claustrophobia reigns. When leaders are desirous, they become cautious; when leaders are fearful, they run risks.[30] Threats are effective when directed at cautious challengers; threats are ineffective when targeted against risk-takers. Hence, the owls' principle: accommodate those fearful of losing; confront those desirous of gaining. In contrast, hawks and doves are less concerned than owls with the risk-taking propensity of challengers.

World War II is the hawks' paradigm: confront the Hitlers of the world to deter their future aggressions. World War I and the Sinai Campaign are banner cases for doves: reassure the threatened and so avoid preemptive strikes and preventive wars. Both world wars are the consummate situations for owls: know thine adversary's fears and hopes.

NORTH KOREA: CONTAIN AND EMBRACE

MISPERCEPTION IN THE
POLICY PROCESS OF PYONGYANG

If misperception dominates decision making in North Korea, the regime may see no other alternative but war. If the dictators in Pyongyang misperceive American efforts to reinforce deterrence as attempts to gain advantage in an offensive war, they are likely to choose suicidal military action. Also, if perceived loss of control characterizes the leadership, such fears may force them to choose self-destructive war.

Owls would seek to ascertain whether the leaders in Pyongyang are capable of rational analysis. To the degree that they are, these leaders can be deterred and coerced; to the extent that they are not, Pyongyang can neither be deterred nor coerced. If the North Korean elite is on the low end of a "rheostat of rationality," then the leadership is liable to miscalculate the risk and expected gain of warfare.

In connection with threat perception, hawks magnify threats and rely too much on force as a means of conflict resolution. Doves underestimate dangers and overemphasize diplomacy. Owls seek valid estimations of threat and may advocate a balance of force and diplomacy.

On the one hand, hawks and doves suggest feasible policy recommendations. Their policies may be ineffective, because they disregard the psychology of decision making, but the particular appeal of hawks and doves in the policy process is that their analyses make use of simplifying assumptions about rationality. Presumptions of hawks and doves nest well with policy options.

On the other hand, owls, with their devotion to the richness of human behavior, may offer more valid explanations; yet these may be of little use in policy making. Hence, owls are likely to be theoretically valid but pragmatically bankrupt.[31]

In addition to the political aviary metaphor, another way of analyzing the case of North Korea is to inquire as to the aims of U.S. policy. To what extent are the goals retributive, rehabilitative, and idealistic? Also, to what degree are U.S. interests strategic and intrinsic in nature? The next section on the purposes of American policy addresses these two questions.

THE PURPOSES OF AMERICAN POLICY

Retribution and Rehabilitation

While post–Cold War optimists choose rehabilitation of Pyongyang, it was the Cold War pessimists who opted for a policy of retribution toward this floundering regime. In the past, the United States sought to punish the illegitimate government in the north, with little regard for changing its behavior. By contrast, the Clinton Administration leans toward a change in the behavior of the government, not the regime itself. Hence, Washington implicitly accepts its legitimacy. If Pyongyang plays the accommodation game with Washington, it is conceivable that a full range of conciliatory measures may fall into the laps of power-holders of the North.

If the main purpose of the sanctions is to oppose a regime or to right a wrong, retributive justice is at work. Retributive sanctions act in a punitive manner to change a regime, not its behavior. Rehabilitative sanctions, however, are implemented in response to a particular transgression. American sanctions imposed on North Korea in 1950 were mainly retributive. They demonstrated opposition to the North Korean Communist regime. The sanctions sought to punish North Korea and were targeted generally at the regime rather than its behavior.

Consider sanctions imposed on North Korea ostensibly on the grounds of its participation in terrorism. Although the sanctions are in response to a particular provocation, they derive from a retributive justice motivation. Despite the fact that North Korea has not engaged in any act of terrorism for nearly a decade and has repeatedly indicated its opposition to such activity, the United States still categorizes the regime as a sponsor of terrorism. As such, the sanctions may seek to punish North Korea, focusing on the U.S. government's broad opposition to the Communist regime, instead of on what remains of a former terrorist policy.

Pyongyang plays on Washington's anxiety. The Clinton Administration fears implosion of North Korea, with its population flooding across the border toward both China and South Korea. The administration also worries about military explosion by the armed forces of the North against the South. This anxiety is so pervasive that Washington is willing to take huge risks to give peace a chance, so to speak. Given these concerns, Washington underestimates the threat from North Korea, engages in a flight of wishful thinking, and concludes with a sunny scenario with a happy ending.

But there is a risk in discounting the threat: the regime may misuse American assistance. In preparation for an invasion of the South, Pyongyang could employ U.S aid to prop itself up instead of feeding its starving population. This humanitarian relief could unintentionally prolong the inevitable collapse of the regime. What line to take against North Korea can be understood in the context of a description of the nature of that regime in relation to American ideals and interests in the region.

Ideals

In the first phase of the post–Cold War era, Washington perceived North Korea as a rogue elephant substitute for the slain Soviet bear. But this perception may change if evidence continues to mount that the elephant is more fearful than gainful in nature. Meanwhile, North Korea is unique among the rogue states of the world because of its self-inflicted isolation.[32] The unequivocal American support for North Korea's enemy to the south intensifies the separation.

One school of thought that wishes to embrace Kim Jong-Il assumes that he is not deterrable, but may be amenable to assurance and persuasion. But because he believes that the United States is determined to undermine his regime no matter what he does, Kim Jong-Il may be comparatively immune even to reassuring statements. He is a vulnerable leader motivated by need, rather than an opportunity-driven aggressor motivated by greed. Irrespective of which school provides the most valid explanation of Kim Jong-Il's behavior, reassurance must take into account his acute sense of vulnerability.

In contrast to the fear-based explanation, another school accounts for North Korea's behavior with the assumption that Kim Jong-Il is a would-be aggressor. Although he probably is a mixture of an opportunity-driven Machiavellian and a need-based paranoid, the Machiavellian part dominates. His decision to go to war with South Korea would partly be a matter of being provoked, but mostly his own opportunism would explain his choice to invade. At issue is the relative validity of these competing schools that seek to explain the same behavior: noncompliance.

Consistent with North Korea's intended isolation from foreign influences is a philosophy of self-sufficiency—*Juche*.[33] An emphasis on self-sacrifice and hard work manifests itself through the "Drink No Soup Movement." This so-called movement is a bizarre campaign by Pyongyang to keep factory workers from having too frequent a number of rest-room breaks. The goal is to keep the workers on the production lines rather than in the toilets!

The Drink No Soup Movement illustrates the gap between Washington and Pyongyang. At its core are differences concerning ideals and interests. Both governments believe strongly in conflicting ideals and see their interests in direct opposition to one another. Were Alexis de Tocqueville to visit North Korea, he would likely write about the strong links between values and policy. But while de Tocqueville attributed idealistic standards in America to widespread political discourse, such debate is absent in North Korea. Its values derive from a firm commitment to its *Juche* ideology. Just as America prides itself on committing blood and treasure in the defense of its allies, North Korea prides itself in defending itself against all outside influences.

Strategic Interests

In addition to differences in ideals, there is a profound split between the United States and North Korea in perceived strategic and intrinsic interests. A strategic interest is one that is valuable because it allows for achievement of other ends: reputation, credibility, and alliances permit realization of objectives like deterrence and coercion. An intrinsic interest is one that is valuable in and of itself like lives, oil, and industry. Goals and interests are interrelated. Interests are the driving force behind goals.

A particular kind of strategic interest for deterrent purposes is a commitment to an ally. The North Korean case has become a metaphor for the failure to do so. Consider how Dean Acheson, Secretary of State prior to the outbreak of the Korean War, publicly stated that the U.S. defense perimeter in the Pacific ran from the Aleutians to the Philippines, including Japan and the Ryukyu Islands.[34] He tacitly excluded South Korea from the defense perimeter. The lesson for the future was to refrain from such explicit statements of inclusion or exclusion.

As a superpower, the United States has a strategic interest in making sure that Washington is the place where negotiations take place, and that the United States remains unchallenged. A perception of control and invincibility is the glue that holds together the American deterrent system. To the extent that Pyongyang stands up to Washington, there is a challenge to U.S. credibility, resolve, and commitments. When nations like North Korea confront Washington's resolve, the likelihood of deterrence failure elsewhere increases.

Regarding the Clinton Administration's definition of interests, consider a speech to the National Press Club in July of 1995, by former Secretary of State Warren Christopher. He outlined U.S. goals toward East Asia.[35] The first strategic goal is to maintain and strengthen U.S. alliances with Japan, South Korea, Australia, the Philippines, and Thailand. The second strategic objective is to engage former Cold War adversaries in the region. The third strategic aim is to build a regional system that maintains economic growth, facilitates integration, and insures long-term stability. The fourth goal is intrinsic—to support democracy and human rights, which serve U.S. ideals as well as interests.

In addition to the goals outlined by Christopher, there is another overriding one that is both strategic and intrinsic: nuclear nonproliferation. Assistant Secretary of Defense for International Security Affairs Joseph Nye specified that the U.S. aim was to stem the threat of proliferation of weapons of mass destruction and their means of delivery.[36]

The U.S. strategic interests regarding North Korea are related to objectives for Asia as a whole. Washington has an interest in continuing the flow of goods in the world market at prices that are consistent with the economic growth of the industrialized democracies. With the end of the Cold War, the regional menace from North Korea was a good substitute for the Soviet threat.

Intrinsic Interests

American leaders also believe that North Korea threatens intrinsic interests: American civilians and military personnel in northeast Asia and American military personnel near the DMZ. Pyongyang is also seen as a danger to American citizens in general via its support for international terrorism, even though North Korea has renounced its support in this regard.[37]

In the context of the rival perspectives of hawks, doves, and owls, as well as the discussion of ideals and interests, consider the relationship between Pyongyang and Washington across three broad cases: the Korean War at mid-century, a nuclear crisis of the mid-1990s, and a set of humanitarian crises at the close of the century.

FROM CONVENTIONAL WAR
TO NUCLEAR AND HUMANITARIAN CRISES[38]

A brief overview of the early history of the American–North Korean relationship sets the stage for a discussion of the lessons of the Korean case. That history, moreover, establishes a framework for viewing Pyongyang's nuclear weapons development.[39]

American-North Korean relations have been on a roller coaster of ups and downs. The "down times" of confrontation drove the "up times" of negotiations. A first phase in the 1950s consisted of the Korean War followed by protracted negotiations. A second period between the 1960s and the 1980s included small-scale incidents that did not escalate into full-blown military action because of crisis diplomacy. A third phase in the 1990s saw Washington and Pyongyang go to the nuclear brink only to be pulled back by creative diplomacy.[40]

And as the twentieth century closes, a fourth phase opens. This stage finds crisis as an unexpected consequence of flood and famine. Instead of the pattern of Pyongyang inducing a crisis as an opportunity to squeeze Washington, the new model reverses the process. Just as North Korea used crises as an occasion to obtain concessions from the United States, Washington might be able to employ humanitarian crises to pressure Pyongyang to make concessions to Seoul. In other words, these new crises are an opportunity for Western humanitarian diplomacy. Explicit linkage of crises to concessions, however, might be counterproductive.

While the upside of humanitarian crises may be to provide an opening for diplomacy, the downside could be to increase the likelihood for implosion of North Korea's society and/or military explosion across the DMZ. But before turning to floods, food, and fuel, consider briefly the early period in the relationship between North Korea and the United States.

Korean War: Lessons Learned

In 1948, Moscow established a new Communist state in North Korea; Washington replied with a South Korea aligned with the West.[41] Though the United States played an important role in the region, Washington considered South Korea to be of only secondary strategic interest. Of primary concern were Japan and Formosa. As a result, the United States hoped to keep only a short-term tactical force in the Korean Peninsula, but to deploy strategic forces for a longer term in or near Japan and Formosa. Neither Moscow nor Washington expected to occupy the Korean Peninsula for an indefinite period of time. The division of the peninsula into two countries was to have been part of an interim trusteeship prior to a general election.

Tensions rose during the early 1950s, with two opposing ideologies rising between "brotherly" nation-states. Hostilities broke out on June 25, 1950: North Korean troops attacked South Korea. Prior to that assault, Secretary of State Acheson had publicly announced that the United States would support Seoul through the United Nations. But Pyongyang may not have interpreted Washington's commitment to signal military intervention to save Seoul in the event of an attack from the North. However, in apparent contradiction to the U.S. pledge to take any aggression against the South to the United Nations, the State Department omitted South Korea from a list of countries that were a part of the U.S. defense perimeter in East Asia. But the Secretary of State was not alone in excluding South Korea from the defense perimeter.

The U.S. Joint Chiefs of Staff also considered South Korea to be of minor strategic value in terms of another general war. Because its fate would be decided in other theaters of war, Korea lacked strategic significance for the global pattern of U.S. security. In other words, the Truman Administration considered South Korea to be of minor importance in and of itself and significant only to the extent that it was a part of a war with the USSR. Not only did the Chiefs consider South Korea to be of secondary value, they believed it was a strategic liability.[42]

A Cold War idea that Washington had to oppose what Moscow favored had not yet taken root. Indeed, the Korean War was a threshold event precisely because it established the Cold War principle that neither superpower could afford to lose land to the other or to its proxies.

But another of Washington's allies in Asia had already been defeated in the civil war in China during 1949, when the Chinese Nationalists lost their foothold on the mainland and fled to Formosa. Hence, when the Korean War came on the heels of the defeat of America's Chinese allies, the two events reinforced the interdependency of commitments and the connection between national security and domestic politics.

The United States intervened to protect South Korea because of a convergence of perceived threats to international security and the domestic political security of American presidents. As stated above, the danger from the North Korean invasion of the South had been underestimated because of a focus on the global threat, rather than the regional menace of Communism. On top of the reformulated national security assessment that the Korean Peninsula had regional value as well as global utility, there was the significance of Asia to American domestic politics. During the 1950s, China, Korea, and Indochina became hot-button political issues that Republicans could use to slam Democrats.

President Truman had already made a controversial decision to evade the American commitment to the Chinese Nationalists. Once the Communists had defeated the Nationalists in their civil war, Asian national security affairs became a domestic political liability for Truman. He was hammered incessantly with questions about "Who lost China?" The clear answer was that the Democrats had lost China. Consequently, they had a huge image problem. The Democrats were seen as soft on Communism. Even to raise the question was equivalent to political homicide.[43]

Having already been charged with losing China, the Truman Administration could hardly afford to accept the responsibility of having also lost Korea. After the defeat in China and the war in Korea, the Democratic administration was more willing to help the French in Indochina.[44] Thereafter, successive administrations upped the ante. The net effect of these expanding commitments was the Vietnam War.[45] Domestic political danger of inaction in foreign affairs was a motivation for actions abroad that inadvertently spiraled out of control.

With respect to lessons learned, two sets of principles emerged from the 1950s in general and the Korean War in particular. They concern threat and opportunity as well as politics and policies. With respect to the first set, North Korea uses threat in a crisis as an opportunity for diplomacy. In the phases of the American–North Korean relationship, Pyongyang was the initiator during the mid–twentieth century. It created crises in order to control outcomes involving the United States.

But as the twenty-first century opens, North Korea is losing the capability of initiation; rather, events such as floods and famine are creating chaos instead of control. Because it is not as easy for North Korea to use threats for diplomatic gain, there is an opportunity for Washington to be the diplomatic initiator.

Another aspect of the threat/opportunity nexus consists of perception. In the mid-1950s, the Truman Administration misperceived the regional threat as it focused on the global danger. Yet in defining the threat, the geographical frame of reference was crucial. Because it underestimated the regional threat, Washington omitted Seoul from the American defense perimeter.[46]

This omission then led Pyongyang to miscalculate the depth of the American commitment to South Korea. The Korean War was a defining moment in the expansion of America's security perspective. Perceived regional threats from the "Pyongyangs of the world" then took their positions alongside the global menace from Moscow.

A further aspect of the threat/opportunity relationship involves unanticipated consequences of success. The United States succeeded in establishing South Korea as an independent state. Washington perceived independence for the South under its tutelage as an opportunity to gain a strategic foothold in Asia along the Soviet and Chinese borders. But in setting up this presence, Washington failed to include Seoul in its regional defense perimeter. As a result, North Korea seized this exclusion as an opportunity to attack the South. In other words, Pyongyang saw a window of opportunity to reunite the country under Kim Il Sung.

The bottom-line lesson is that the United States should bring its commitments in line with its obligations. In setting up South Korea, the United States took on an implicit obligation to protect it. But by excluding South Korea from its defense perimeter in Asia, Washington created a gap between obligation and commitment.

The second set of lessons deriving from the American–North Korean relationship consists of politics and policies. Politics divide into domestic and bureaucratic aspects. On the domestic side, the loss of land in Asia made national security policies into domestic political priorities. Consequently, decisionmakers need to be aware of the political costs of both inaction and action in foreign affairs. On the bureaucratic side, the 1950s found hawks and doves at odds as usual.

The Truman Administration's initial hands-off policy regarding South Korea was in line with the globalist, libertarian dove policy-making schema. Policy analysts in that administration advocated a laissez faire approach to the regional threat that North Korea posed to the South and emphasized instead the global threat from the Soviet Union. The Truman analysts relied on the global balance of power to take care of regional threats. In the 1950s, the balance of power worldwide was the focus of what was, in effect, a libertarian approach. But the administration failed to pay attention to the strategic consequences of the regional balance.

Another consequence of the Korean War for politics and policies was to change from the bankrupt libertarian dove approach to a hawkish policy. Doves "flew south" in the bureaucratic war for Washington as the North Korean troops marched south into Seoul. From then on, hawks dominated the U.S. national security decision-making process. In short, hawks presided in the bureaucratic politics of Washington in response to aggression from Pyongyang against

Seoul and because Korea had become a controversial topic in American politics generally.

Nuclear Crisis: Lessons Learned

Following the war in the 1950s, North Korea maintained a large standing army, while the United States continued to deploy troops along the border between the North and the South. On top of these large conventional forces facing one another, the pursuit of nuclear weapons by North Korea created a crisis for the United States and its allies in the region.

Tensions reemerged on the Korean Peninsula in 1984. Intelligence indicated that Pyongyang was pursuing an active program of nuclear weapons development. With the construction of a nuclear power reactor in Yongbyon during the early 1980s, North Korea began to acquire a capability to produce weapons-grade plutonium.[47] In 1985, North Korea joined the Non-Proliferation Treaty (NPT). It officially revealed the existence of the Yongbyon plant.

During 1990, North Korea had a demonstrated capacity to separate plutonium. Doing so indicated that Pyongyang had taken a major step in the direction of nuclear weapons construction. And three years later, North Korea revealed plans to withdraw from the NPT.[48] And although Pyongyang did not officially do so, it created a crisis that resulted in negotiations during 1994. At that time, Pyongyang temporarily ceased operations at the Yongbyon plant to allow for the removal of weapons-grade material. A conservative estimation of the yield potential of the fuel was 7-14 kilograms of plutonium, enough to build one or two nuclear weapons.[49]

The North had claimed that it had withdrawn from the NPT and was hence not bound by International Atomic Energy Agency (IAEA) inspections. But Washington did not accept Pyongyang's claim, holding that North Korea remained a member of the NPT and was subject to its rules. Later in 1994, Pyongyang suspended its nuclear program after signing an accord with Washington, the Agreed Framework.[50]

Two years after signing the Agreed Framework, Secretary of Defense William Perry commented on the accord.[51] He said that the United States reached the agreement with a mixed policy that combined threats with promises; that is, coercive diplomacy. The United States and its allies linked threats to impose economic sanctions with promises of commercial nuclear power.

Perry and other defenders of the accord held that both sides had something to gain from the 1994 Framework. On the one side, it would allow North Korea to acquire two new 1000-megawatt light-water reactors and heavy oil for heating and electricity to suffice until the West built the first reactor. These actions would result from a $4 billion deal over a ten-year period. On the other side, Pyongyang would agree to cease all activities at its nuclear weapons–producing gas-graphite reactors, adhere to the NPT, and allow inspections of suspect nuclear facilities.

Critics contend that Washington should have obtained more from Pyongyang in return for exchanging diplomatic liaison offices and supplying North Korea with fuel oil for dismantling its plutonium-generating reactors. Detractors of the accord hold that the United States was too eager to cut a deal with North Korea. These same critics assume that the regime in North Korea is on the verge of collapse and that the Framework Agreement breathed new life into a dying regime.[52]

In connection with lessons learned, the nuclear crisis of the 1990s reinforced principles from the 1950s concerning threat and opportunity as well as politics and policies. North Korea seized upon the nuclear threat as an opportunity to create a crisis, because the issue was so salient to the United States. Pyongyang accomplished one of its main objectives—bilateral negotiations with the United States.

But contrary to North Korea's hope for institutionalizing its bilateral relationship with the United States, Washington was able to create a multilateral organization in solving its nuclear crisis with Pyongyang. The Korean Economic Development Organization (KEDO) is a multinational organization of American, Japanese, and South Korean officials. Their countries created KEDO in order to carry out the Agreed Framework, and it has become an effective interlocutor with North Korea on nuclear-related issues.[53] Therefore, what is the lesson for threat and opportunity? Namely, that a threatening nuclear crisis became a diplomatic opportunity for the three allies to work together.

A related lesson involves the nexus of politics and policies. Third parties like the United States enter alliances to protect weaker parties like

South Korea. In the politics of alliance management, however, there are times in which the protector has to negotiate policies with the challenger and not just with the protected. In such a case, however, it is crucial to include the protected in the talks. In spite of excluding South Korea in some of the bilateral negotiations with the North, though, it was possible to make diplomatic progress on Korean problems while maintaining an international consensus among Seoul, Tokyo, and Washington.[54]

Humanitarian Crises: Lessons Learned

Using the threat of a nuclear crisis to manipulate the West was supposed to be consistent with the North Korea's philosophy of self-sufficiency—*Juche*. But even the nuclear issue produced a multilateral mechanism in the form of KEDO, an organization that further decreased North Korea's self-imposed isolation. Humanitarian crises involving floods and food in North Korea may effect a similar outcome. There is no institutionalized international tool for managing economic crisis and political instability for North Korea. One result of international involvement in addressing humanitarian issues, however, is that it is likely to decrease North Korea's freedom of action and integrate it within the family of nations more than it intended.

As background for examining humanitarian crises concerning North Korea, consider its economic situation. North Korea has a population, estimated in 1995, at about 24 million people. The average population density is over 500 people per square mile. There has been a rapid influx of North Koreans from the countryside to the cities. Over 60 percent of the population is urban. The annual national budget in the late 1980s was about $16 billion. During the mid-1990s, North Korea's economy declined four years in a row. The decrease was as much as 25 percent between 1989 and 1993. The North's external debt was over $10 billion at the beginning of 1994. Its debt is equal to approximately one half of its annual GDP, which is only about $22 billion. The GDP per capita of North Korea is less than $1,000. In contrast to the North, South Korea's GDP is $424 billion, with a per capita value of almost $10,000.[55]

Floods occurred in North Korea in August 1995, and the food situation there immediately worsened. That summer Pyongyang had already negotiated grain deals with Seoul and Tokyo for over 600,000 tons of rice, and by the fall, there was a sea change in Pyongyang's relationship with the outside world. North Korea requested international assistance for the first time in its almost half century of existence, an event that jettisoned its philosophy of *Juche*. During 1996, the North confronted another grain shortfall of about a million tons. Additionally, a dearth of fertilizer reinforced a premature harvest in that year, worsening the food shortages. Without outside help, the food scarcity would become a famine.

During the spring of 1997, the United Nations World Food Programme stated that North Korea needed about 1.3 million tons of food to avoid a famine, and requested them from the international community. The UN agency also announced that North Korea sought direct donations of about one million tons. For two years in a row, North Korea had to ask for food assistance, suggesting an erosion of its philosophy of *Juche*.[56]

At issue in the humanitarian crisis confronting North Korea is what should be the mechanism by which to address it. Based on the lesson learned from the nuclear crisis, multilateral rather than bilateral approaches are the most effective route. A bilateral approach from the South would give rise to political differences both between the two and within each country about the propriety of the assistance. Similarly, a bilateral solution with the United States in the lead could lead to misperceptions on the part of North Korea as to Washington's intent. The bottom line is that the food crisis is not only a threat to the economic security and political instability of the North, but also an opportunity for the international community to insert itself into the politics and policies of the Pyongyang regime.[57]

On the basis of this journey from war to crisis, consider future scenarios and alternative policy packages by hawks and doves. Although owls prefer to analyze the past and the present, their portraits of future states of affairs also are instructive.

SCENARIOS[58]

Policy-planning hawks and doves expect North Korea to experience one of four scenarios. First is explosion—a desperate bid by Pyongyang to unify the peninsula by force. A second is implosion—an economic and political collapse that would fuel a mass exodus of refugees into China, Japan, and South Korea. A third is a happy ending—diplomatic concessions from North Korea in return for Western food and investment, which might reverse its economic deterioration and maintain the regime in Pyongyang, and result in peaceful reunification. And a fourth is "muddling through," or the continuation of the status quo with minor adjustments.

Hawks would continue to contain North Korea, irrespective of whether such containment exacerbates tendencies toward implosion.[59] They argue that power-hungry, error-free, cold-hearted mercenaries would take advantage of humanitarian aid. Therefore, credible strength and effective force must be available to deter a cool-minded Machiavellian leadership from attacking. One problem with this approach of letting North Korea collapse is that it could result in a civil war among factions in the North, in which nuclear fuel becomes a bargaining chip in the struggle for succession, while the collapse itself could provoke intervention by third parties in a crisis that spins out of control.

Indeed, doves would argue that containment and threats toward a fear-driven, mistake-ridden, risk-prone paranoid would bring about unintended disaster: an explosion by factions within North Korea across the border against the South. In contrast, embracing the fearful will bring about a peaceful resolution, avoiding both implosion and explosion. Humanitarian food aid for flood victims and starving civilians are an option to help Pyongyang avoid implosion while quelling its fears of Western control. In fact, doves are not concerned about where food relief is allocated. Even if aid is diverted to the military, at least the military will not have an incentive to march southward for food relief for themselves, or so the doves argue.

Because owls are not a direct part of the policy-making process, they have the time and temperament to analyze each situation individually. They would assess whether or not the North Korean leadership is comprised of the power-hungry or fear-driven, which would let owls know whether leaders are working from a window of opportunity or a basement of fear. But in the context of a North Korea that is very secretive with respect to information, it is hardly likely that owls would be able to gather the data necessary to perform their analyses.

According to owls, North Korean mercenaries would perceive an embrace by the United States as a window of opportunity to explode against the South. In other words, mercenaries are cold-blooded opportunists who jump at occasions to take advantage of enemies. Owls reason further that if North Korean leaders are fearful, they could misperceive deterrent threats as provocations that would warrant lashing out and escaping the basement of fear. Analytic owls, by refraining from the policy-making process and integrating different situational ideas, are able to come up with mixed policy packages, such as a combination of embracing and containing, which could lead to scenarios of both explosion and implosion.

Explosion

Though both hawks and doves have different opinions as to how explosion might come about, they are in agreement as to the consequences. If Pyongyang explodes, it could start a war with a salvo of 170mm shells from its 240 howitzer batteries along the 38th Parallel. The North Korean army would then make a southward charge using all the means at its disposal. Methods would include land and sea forces, especially submarine units. The goal of the quick strike would be a fait accompli.[60] However, the purpose of the assault would not be the military conquest of South Korea and forced unification of the peninsula, but rather Pyongyang's seizure of Seoul as a diplomatic bargaining chip to play during the peace talks.

If Pyongyang pursues Soviet military doctrine, an assault on the South would include an artillery shower followed by a lightning attack. South Korea's half-million-plus army along with about 37,000 American armed forces deployed along the DMZ would be overwhelmed by North Korea's one-million man army. American counteraction would include stealth attacks by the hard-to-detect B-2 and F-117 warplanes. The tactical aim would be to cut off the eyes and ears of Pyongyang by destroying its command, control, and intelligence. Such a strategy would demolish railroads and bridges, followed by direct American engagement by helicopter, such as the infamous Apache.

During an invasion by the North, there would be an evacuation of all American citizens, as well as those from Japan, Canada, and Great Britain. During a tense period in 1994, this American evacuation plan was 24-72 hours away from initiation.

Doves maintain that explosion would be a result of a hard-line approach that provokes North Korea into a desperate preemptive strike or preventive war. Without provocation, doves believe that quelling Pyongyang's fears would avoid an explosion against Seoul. Hawks hold that explosion would be a result of a soft-line approach by Washington. A policy of accommodation might have too many undesirable consequences for hawks. Therefore, the only option for hawks is containment. As the nuclear crisis gives way to humanitarian crisis, however, the likelihood of military confrontation decreases relative to that of implosion.

Implosion and Unification

If the North Korean regime did little to avert the collapse of its society and government structures, unification with the South could be a result. But Seoul strongly opposes unification because of its economic costs, which might amount to about $1 trillion.[61]

Both Hawks and doves consider the possibility that North Korea may just collapse into a vacuum of power. They agree on how an implosion scenario would evolve. The scenario begins with food shortages, famine, and natural disasters. If there were a deterioration of the economic situation, there could be an escalation of the flow of refugees from the North to the South, with only half the food necessary to feed the population available.

If the regime in Pyongyang collapses, Seoul has a contingency plan to handle the influx of refugees from the North. South Korea would establish "counter-brainwashing centers" where refugees would be deprogrammed of Communist beliefs acquired over a lifetime. But with unification costs so large, Seoul has not budgeted for this contingency.

The implosion scenario has two facets. One is that the refugees from the Pyongyang region will automatically turn to the South, beginning the long walk to a land of milk and honey. The other aspect is that villagers from the countryside will not know where to turn. They have been programmed to believe that North Korea has been better off than the rest of the world. They have also been led to believe that China has always been and will continue to be North Korea's only ally. Hence, it is likely that these uninformed rural refugees will turn northwest toward the Yalu River.

In addition to Seoul, Washington has also engaged in contingency planning based upon the implosion scenario. The American military has geared up to be the lead department in the government for implosion planning. Rather than preparing to fight, moreover, the Pentagon proposes to head up a large international relief effort on the Korean Peninsula. At issue is what to do when large numbers of hungry refugees begin flowing out of North Korea via land and sea— by foot and by boat.

One of Washington's main priorities is to limit the American ground combat involvement inside North Korea. In this connection, the UN would assume a major role in the relief operation, while ground-based military personnel would come from South Korea and other nations. The United States would confine itself to long-range transportation, large-scale communications, and international coordination. One reason for minimizing the American involvement would be to avoid a situation in which North Korean troops, uninformed about the American role in a humanitarian relief effort, might open fire on U.S. personnel and equipment operating within North Korea.[62]

Activist doves argue that continued application of sanctions without food relief would exacerbate the humanitarian crisis and provoke remnants of the North Korean armed forces either to fight among themselves or launch a preemptive strike against South Korea. Libertarian doves contend that an implosion is inevitable. But instead of attributing collapse to a hard-line policy, Cato doves would promote a hands-off approach, perhaps even a withdrawal of the 37,000 American troops from the DMZ. Why should the United State waste resources to prop up a falling regime? According to libertarian doves, Washington should not. Without international aid to keep it alive, Pyongyang will eventually crumble. Libertarian doves advocate a hands-off approach, regardless of the risks of inaction. What they neglect to realize, however, is that withdrawal not only reduces threat credibility, but should the North explode into the South, Washington would take the blame.

Happy Ending—A Soft Landing

A happy-ending scenario implies that North Korea will reform its Cold War Communist economy, increase its economic output, and engage in international trade with other nations, irrespective of ideology. But such reforms would challenge the existence of North Korea as a Communist state. Also, economic reform by North Korea would imply détente with the South, a political realignment that would take considerable negotiation to put into effect.

A negotiated reunification of the Korean Peninsula without war or disintegration of North Korea is indeed a sunny scenario. While Heritage hawks and Cato doves agree that propping up a failing regime would be futile, activist doves have a different vision. They would provide assistance in order to avoid preemptive strikes and preventive war and appease Pyongyang to avoid confrontation. The international community would give assistance in proportion to diplomatic concessions, even at the risk of propping up the regime. Pursuit of such a politically risky policy is why activist doves are few and far between in Washington. One reason this scenario would be the least painful is that it hinges on shaky assumptions regarding North Korea and other nations in Asia.

The first supposition is that Pyongyang will be persuaded into compliance and thus consent to a normalizing of ties. But this presumption has been shown to be false in the past. The second assumption of the soft landing scenario is that other Asian countries, including China, Japan, and Taiwan, will see their interests coinciding and will act in concert. In fact, though, a reunified Korean Peninsula may not be in the perceived interests of these three countries. Economically, they may not want to see Seoul, already a fierce competitor, become even stronger years after unification. Politically, these same countries would feel uneasy with a fast growing, militarily strong Korea.

Should policy toward North Korea be based on the happy-ending scenario, owls would be quick to point out a motivated bias. They would state that activist doves see what they want to see—a North Korea that would comply if the United States would only let them. But in so thinking, activist doves would be ignoring the many contradicting facts that make the happy-ending scenario unlikely.

Muddling Through

With the explosion scenario becoming an unlikely possibility, the two main possibilities are happy ending and collapse. But in between reform and collapse lies "muddling through."[63] China, Japan, and Russia, as well as South Korea, might all desire muddling through in contrast to implosion, which is more likely than reform. In the context of a North Korea that neither reforms nor collapses, there would be less of a threat to the United States and its allies than other contingencies. But just as we should guard against the soft-landing scenario because it is so desirable, so we should be wary of the muddling through scenario. Minimizing a threat is a bias in information processing that often stems from the tendency to see what we desire to see, a bias that raises the issue of threat perception.

THREAT PERCEPTION AND POLICY PACKAGES

In contrast to hawks and doves, an aspect of the owl's approach to the evaluation of policies is to inquire as to the nature of threat perception. At issue concerning threat perception is how people see each other as threatening. Such a question requires an explanation of why individuals validly perceive or misperceive threats. Thus, why does the United States view North Korea as a hazard, and why does Pyongyang see Washington as a danger? While some actors discern threats as intended, others misperceive the same actions and experience threat misperception.

Recall from Chapter Six the discussion of American-Cuban threat perception: Washington and Havana misperceive peril because of biased information processing. When the Clinton Administration views Pyongyang, moreover, there may also be a misperception of threat. But there are differences between the two cases.

Unlike its overestimation of the danger from Castro's Havana, the administration may be underestimating the menace from Kim Jong-Il's regime in Pyongyang. Prior administrations tended to magnify the risk from North Korea. During the Cold War, conventional wisdom rewarded North Korean bashing. It bolstered both domestic political fortunes and national deterrence. Magnification of menace was a motivated bias that brought handsome dividends to politicians and diplomats alike.[64] Washington decisionmakers benefited at home and abroad from hostility toward Pyongyang. Overestimation of threat was strengthened by an unmotivated historical bias against communism.

From about 1950 to 1975, the political landscape was riddled with East-West confrontations. This was a time of tensions between the United States and Asian communist states. Accordingly, American politicians stood to gain a political bounce in the polls for standing up to communists in general and to China and North Korea in particular. When U.S. leaders saw both what they *wanted* to see and what they *expected* to see, they magnified the threat posed by North Korea. But in the post–Cold War era, there is less incentive to play the anticommunist card.

According to the reasoning of those who accuse the Pentagon of threat magnification, however, there is a difference between national interests and those of departments within the U.S. government. For example, critics of the Department of Defense argue that it needs a pretext to defend its budget. But it is nonsense to imagine that the Pentagon created a North Korean threat out of thin air just to serve its bureaucratic needs. Yet with the Cold War over, Michael Klare makes the case that the Pentagon indeed magnified a threat from rogue states in general.[65]

The post–Cold War age finds different dispositions operating in American-North Korean relations. As a result, there is a tendency to minimize the threat because of these inclinations. In terms of motivated bias, the Clinton Administration sees benefits in a happy-ending scenario to the Korean conflict. These include a lower U.S. defense budget that allows for higher domestic spending, good economic relations with China, and enhanced security at lower costs for allies like South Korea and Japan. In other words, the administration sees a comparatively benign North Korea, because doing so serves these three goals. In addition, unmotivated biases regarding communism reinforce Washington's threat underestimation. After the fall of the Berlin Wall, communists simply do not look as threatening as they once did. Hence, if Washington expects to see a less menacing Pyongyang, presto! North Korea is less threatening!

But the dispositions do not always move in the same direction or imply a similar course of action. One reason why U.S. policy toward North Korea continues unchanged after the Cold War has ended is that there is a clash among American biases. As stated above, motivated bias causes underestimation of threat. Such a minimal danger is consistent with an approach of embracing North Korea.

Some unmotivated biases operate at cross-purposes to each other. Due to the historical image of Kim Il Sung as one of the lesser communist enemies of Asia, there was an unmotivated bias that associated him with "evil." Thus, there is a tendency by the American public to perceive his son, Kim Jong-Il, in the same light. Such perception is a drag on the policy process. As a result of the anchoring effect of this unmotivated bias, a shift of American policy from containment to accommodation is difficult. In short, motivated bias rewards a change toward accommodation, but an unmotivated bias reinforces the tendency for containment. As a result of this conflict, American policy remains the same.

Just as American policy resists change, so does North Korea's policy defy alteration. Kim Jong-Il has a motivated bias that causes him to underestimate the American threat. His dire economic situation impels him to see less danger in associating with the enemy; consequently, he does so as a means to acquire food assistance, flood relief, and other humanitarian aid.

Kim Jong-Il also has a motivated bias that causes him to overestimate the American hazard. Because of the domestic political benefits for standing up to the United States, he augments the threat from Washington. And his recollection of the bad old days of the Cold War propels him toward a policy of confrontation. In other words, a historical image of American leaders as enemies pushes Kim Jong-Il to view their behavior as aggressive, without interpreting that behavior on its own merits. Dictators facing potential internal challengers may be pleased to have an external threat with which to divert the attention of the population. The American embargo is an external threat that enables the North Korean leadership to maintain a tight grip on the country.

Owls would suggest dealing out sticks when punishment is warranted. They would distinguish situations where a tough response is called for from those in which it is appropriate to provide humanitarian relief. Pyongyang needs to learn that sending a submarine full of spies into Seoul's territory is unacceptable. In this situation, owls would opt to teach the lesson with a forceful reply.

But owls would also acknowledge the fact that Pyongyang is afraid and faltering. As a result of floods and a famine that has wiped out most of their agriculture, North Koreans have been eating only about one bowl of rice per day. Owls would point to evidence that the mass starvation includes 100,000 deaths just in one year and a whole generation shrinking in height. Also, Pyongyang has been involved with a "dance of defecting diplomats," where top officials have escaped to neighboring countries. Owls take all of these factors into consideration and would couple a policy of embracement to quell the regime's fears and one of containment to deter when warranted.[66]

A combination policy not only addresses individual scenarios of implosion and explosion, but also deals with the possibility that both may happen at the same time. Pyongyang may start to implode and, with a last gasp of air, explode toward Seoul. In the event of the mixed contingency of implosion and explosion, owls would say, deal with the aggression of explosion with an iron fist, but deal with Pyongyang's collapse with a soft hug.

President Clinton shares a sense of optimism with the libertarians. His administration, however, parts ways over the balance of diplomatic carrots over economic and military sticks. Both would provide rewards, but the Clinton Administration takes an owlish approach to include carrots and sticks. Critics of the administration, however, would argue that rewards dominate punishments. However, given the history of North Korea and its present rogue status, it is puzzling that the administration believes that Pyongyang can be influenced by a policy of alleviating punishments and augmenting rewards. Despite its faults, the administration pursues a mixed policy toward the peninsula that is about right in its application.

The mixed approach of the Clinton Administration is a shift away from the approach of the Cold War years. The original American sanctions approach was pessimistic and overestimated the threat from the North. Pyongyang, after all, was a child of the Cold War, and its behavior would change only with the fall of the regime and reunification of the Korean Peninsula under the sovereignty of Seoul. Initial American sanctions sought to destabilize the North Korean regime because of its invasion of South Korea. On top of the Korean War came other egregious conduct, including seizure of an American intelligence vessel and construction of nuclear facilities with a capacity for producing weapons-grade plutonium.

U.S. policy toward North Korea is neither too pessimistic nor too optimistic regarding the estimated threat from the North. Because of the end of the Cold War, Pyongyang's behavior is ripe for change, according to the doves. The Clinton Policy assumes that the post–Cold War era is an opportune time for the regime to mend its naughty ways. The administration also assumes that the ruling clique acts more from a basement of fear than a window of opportunity. Three factors justify this optimistic perspective: an end of the international welfare safety net afforded by the Cold War; the death of a long-time dictator and his replacement by an unsteady hand at the helm; and a series of natural disasters. These three make Pyongyang more vulnerable to reason and reward. Rewards are more effective than punishment of a noncomplying or a frightened North Korea. Additional penalties might frighten it into making counterproductive choices, according to the optimists.

But, according to the owls, the Clinton Administration approach makes sense only if the North Korean regime is driven more by fear than by opportunity. Otherwise, post–Cold War optimists in Washington may lead the United States down a slippery slope to assure, embrace, accommodate, and perhaps even appease the oppressors in Pyongyang.

Whether the United States pursues a posture of embracing or containing North Korea depends in part on scenarios that develop between Pyongyang and Seoul. The option of a military withdrawal by the United States is a nonstarter. With the memories of prior failures and fallen countries due to American inaction, successive administrations have been cautious about the Korean Peninsula. In order to avoid the possibility of being blamed for inaction when disaster strikes, it would be less risky politically to retain the American troop deployment in Korea even in the event of war than to withdraw prior to an attack. If the United States were to withdraw the 37,000 troops from around the DMZ, and the North attacked, the administration in office would receive a well-deserved domestic political blow. This fear of a political loss brands the military withdrawal policy as political suicide.

Cold War hawks criticized the Truman Administration for implicitly excluding South Korea from the American defense perimeter. Post–Cold War hawks would condemn a withdrawal option as a military weakness that provides a window of opportunity for the North either to launch a new Korean War or to collapse as a society. In this respect, military withdrawal and allowing North Korea to collapse are both nonstarters.

THREAT, OPPORTUNITY, POLITICS, AND POLICY

Recall the four themes that cut across *Rogue Regimes:* threat perception, opportunities, politics, and policies. In the case of Cuba, American threat perception is a result of national security, alliance politics, ideals, ethnic politics, and economic benefits. The main elements of United States threat perception regarding North Korea, however, are national security and alliance politics. In the Cuban case, ethnicity triumphs over economics because of the convergence of ideals and politics. But for North Korea, national security trumps domestic politics.

Korean-Americans are neither as numerous nor as influential as are supporters of Israel in the United States. Korean-Americans also are not as significant a factor in East-Asian policy making as Cuban-Americans are concerning the Caribbean. In the bureaucratic politics of Washington, moreover, hard-liners have dominated the policy process. As a result, ideas about bureaucratic politics are of little import in explaining decision making about North Korea.

Nor are alliance politics of great consequence regarding North Korea. There are, however, disputes among Seoul, Tokyo, and Washington over how to approach Pyongyang. The United States is more willing than Japan and South Korea to be accommodative with the North. But the allies agree more than they disagree. Consequently, it is comparatively easy to create joint policies to change the regime's behavior or punish it for misbehavior. And there is little indication of economic opportunities foregone as a result of maintaining a high threat perception toward North Korea. Economic changes, however, are turning former military belligerents into "tigers" in Asia. If political developments in Pyongyang permit, the Korean Peninsula as a whole may fall prey to the pull of a global economy and turn into a tiger itself.

Returning to the main issue that opened this chapter—whether North Korea is a crisis creator or victim of circumstance—Pyongyang does have a history of making crises, but the regime is on its last legs. The days in which Pyongyang could be in command of crises of its own conception are over. As long as it has large military forces, however, containment needs to be maintained, though it could be phased out in proportion to disarmament of the regime. North Korea is a potential casualty on a deathbed of its own making but is unable to arrest the aging process and economic deterioration. The bottom line is that military forces of North Korea need to be contained, but its population should be embraced with humanitarian assistance.

NOTES

Preface

1. Primary criteria for inclusion in *Rogue Regimes* are: large conventional military forces, international terrorism, and weapons of mass destruction. A secondary criterion is appearance on the State Department's *Patterns of Global Terrorism,* a list released annually by the Office of the Coordinator for Counterterrorism. Although Cuba fails to meet the main criteria, Havana appears on the terrorism list. The Sudan is a nation on State's list, but it fails to make *Rogue Regimes* because it is the proxy of another state, Iran, which does appear on the State list and is included here.

2. Nuclear Proliferation Prevention Act of 1994, Part B, sec. 221(a); Title II of the Omnibus Export Administration Act of 1994.

3. Regarding means for delivery of weapons of mass destruction, over 30 non-NATO countries have ballistic missiles. With the exception of Cuba, the other five of our rogue states have missile programs: Iran, Iraq, Libya, Syria, and North Korea possess ballistic missiles. And North Korea has assisted Iran's missile program. And with respect to the missile threat, the Office of the Secretary of Defense states that "The theater threat to our allies and U.S. forces deployed abroad is real and growing. . . . Besides Iraq, we know that thousands of short-range missiles are deployed today with hundreds of launchers in as many as thirty different countries—some of these countries are quite hostile to the United States." Paul Kaminski, "Ballistic Missile Defense Programs," Prepared Statement of the Under Secretary of Defense for Acquisition and Technology to the Military Research and Development Subcommittee, House National Security Committee, in *Defense Issues,* vol. 12, Number 14, March 6, 1997. Available online at:

   http://www.dtic.dla.mil/defenselink/pubs/di97/di1214.html

   A related statement of the missile threat holds that, "*Within ten years, it is possible that every southern European capital will be within range of ballistic missiles based in North Africa or the Levant.*" [Italics in original.] The area in question or missile envelope includes the eastern Mediterranean and its hinterlands, including Syria, Iraq, and Iran. See Ian Lesser and Ashley Tellis, *Strategic Exposure: Proliferation Around the Mediterranean* (Santa Monica, CA: The RAND Corporation, 1996), 32.

4. In a bet of one million dollars, a rational actor desires gain as much as it fears loss. Approximately rational actors weigh gain and loss about equally. An actor lower on a "rheostat of rationality" fears loss more than it desires the gain.

Chapter One

1. The section *Times to Relive* contains dates that reflect the case studies in the chapters that follow: Iran, Iraq, Libya, Syria, Cuba, and North Korea. As a result, the dates are not in chronological order. Chapter One gives a brief overview of each leader, and the chapters on each country provide details on that person, including references to the literature.

2. Is Assad "rational?" In addition to the definition of rationality in endnote 4 to the Preface, rationality assumes that Assad would be able to acquire information to make decisions without the distorting effects of biases, belief systems, or other preconceptions to cloud his judgment. The fact that Assad commits brutal acts is not relevant to his degree of rationality. Chapter Five revisits the issue of Assad's rationality.

3. For information on the destruction of the Syrian city of Hama, see Thomas Friedman, *From Beirut to Jerusalem* (New York: Farrar Straus Giroux, 1989). President Assad ordered tank and artillery fire to level the ancient city of Hama in 1982, resulting in thousands of casualties. Raymond Tanter, *Who's at the Helm?* (Boulder: Westview Press, 1990), 75.

4. The Muslim Brotherhood is an Islamic Organization that promotes a "purified" Islamic state, a position that places it opposite the secular Ba'ath Party that rules Syria. For decades, the Muslim Brothers clashed with the Ba'athists. These clashes escalated from fistfights on playgrounds to terrorism on the streets of Damascus and other Syrian cities. After a 1963 coup that put the Ba'ath Party in power, the Muslim Brotherhood went underground in various places, including Hama. For information about the Muslim Brotherhood, see Daniel Diller, ed., *The Middle East* (Washington, D.C.: Congressional Quarterly, Inc., 1994), 348.

5. For evidence of the complicity of Colonel Qadhafi in the destruction of Pan Am 103, see Steve Emerson and Brian Duffy, *Fall of Pan Am 103: Inside the Lockerbie Investigation* (New York: Putnam, 1990). For information about terrorism in general, see:
   http://www.emergency.com/panam103.htm
   ENN Archives, August 1993. (ENN is the EmergencyNet News Service.)

6. Regarding Libyan involvement in plots to assassinate Anwar Sadat of Egypt, beginning in the summer of 1977, see John Cooley, *Libyan Sandstorm* (London: Sidgwick & Jackson, 1983), 118-22. After the discovery of the early plots, Egyptian and Libyan border forces skirmished for four days, resulting in several dozen casualties on both sides.

7. Christopher Ogden, "Inside Kim Jong-Il's Brain; 'Baffling Outsiders Is What I Do Best'" *Time* 148, no. 15 (October 7, 1996).

8. Kevin Sullivan, "Congressman Finds 'Severe Famine' in North Korea," Washington Post, April 9, 1997, sec. A,24.

9. Anna Vania Song researched the personalities of the rogue leaders. She discovered that there was a great deal more written about some than others. There was an abundance of material about President Saddam Hussein because of the Gulf War, and there was a dearth of information about President Rafsanjani or the Ayatollah Khameni. Perhaps this difference

reflects the perceived magnitude of the events with which these leaders have been associated. There is more information on the Ayatollah Khomeni than on his successors. Because Khomeni succeeded the Shah in post-revolutionary Iran, there was considerable demand for information about him and interest in him as a person. Khomeni, however, discouraged inquires into his personal life.

10. Thekla Fischer, "The Currency of Coercion: For Washington and Tehran" (master's thesis, University of Michigan, Ann Arbor, 1996), 15.

11. Daniel Brumberg, "Khomeini's Legacy: Islamic Rule and Islamic Justice," in *Spokesmen for the Despised: Fundamentalist Leaders of the Middle East,* R. Scott Appleby, ed. (Chicago: University of Chicago Press, 1997), 21.

12. Amir Taheri, *The Spirit of Allah: Khomeni and the Islamic Revolution* (London: Hutchinson & Co., 1985).

13. Mostafa suddenly died in October 1977. Brumberg, "Khomeni's Legacy: Islamic Rule and Islamic Justice," 38. Also see Mark Gasiorowski, *U.S. Foreign Policy and the Shah: Building a Client State in Iran* (Ithaca: Cornell University Press, 1991), 216.

14. Fischer, "The Currency of Coercion," 50-56.

15. Diller, ed., *The Middle East,* 225.

16. Because the term "fundamentalist" also applies to Christians, it is advisable to use the word "Islamist" to depict radical Islam. See Graham Fuller and Ian Lesser, *A Sense of Siege: The Geopolitics of Islam and the West* (Boulder: Westview Press, 1995), 2.

17. Judith Miller, *God Has Ninety-Nine Names* (New York: Simon & Schuster, 1996), 460. See also Patrick Clawson, "Iran's Challenge to the West: How, When, and Why?" *Washington Institute Policy Papers,* no. 33, 1993.

18. Judith Miller and Laurie Mylroie, *Saddam Hussein and the Crisis in the Gulf* (New York: Random House, 1990), 24.

19. Ibid., 36.

20. Ibid., 37.

21. For example, Michael Corleone killed his younger brother, Fredo, for betraying the family.

22. For a description of Saddam's harsh childhood, see Efraim Karsh and Inari Rautsi, *Saddam Hussein: A Political Biography* (New York: The Free Press, 1991), and Miller and Mylroie, *Saddam Hussein,* 25-28.

23. In 1988, Baghdad "initiated a campaign to break Kurdish resistance. This campaign drew international condemnation, in part because of strong evidence that the Iraqi army used poison gas against Kurdish villages and camps in northern Iraq." Diller, ed., The Middle East, 237.

   An opponent of Saddam Hussein, Samir al-Khalil, wrote an unauthorized biography discussing Saddam's tendency toward violence. Saddam's generation (those born around 1937) were " . . . the children of violence for whom violence has become a way of life." Samir al-Khalil, *The Republic of Fear: The Inside Story of Saddam's Iraq* (New York: Pantheon Books, 1989), xviii.

24. Janice Gross Stein, "Deterrence and Compellence in the Gulf: A Failed or an Impossible Task?" *International Security* 17 (Fall 1992): 147-79. Stein takes

264 ROGUE REGIMES

the position that Saddam's motivation was fear more than gain in his decision to order the invasion of Kuwait. An alternative explanation in Chapter Three of the present volume is that gain more than fear motivated Saddam to invade Kuwait.

25. Contrary to some of the other rogue leaders, Qadhafi grew up in a stable family. But his grandfather's murder greatly disturbed his family's stability and collective outlook toward the West. For more on Qadhafi's background see Mohamed El-Khawas, *Qaddafi: His Ideology in Theory and Practice* (Brattleboro: Amana Books, 1986).

26. People cannot be held responsible for actions they cannot control. "Insane" people cannot control their actions; therefore, they should not be punished for actions beyond their control.

27. Friedman, *From Beirut to Jerusalem*, 95.

28. "'Whenever a person is tortured,' the student testified to Amnesty, 'he is ordered to strip naked. Inside the room there is an electric apparatus, a Russian tool for ripping out fingernails, pincers, and scissors for plucking flesh and an apparatus called the Black Slave, on which they force the torture victim to sit. When switched on, a very hot and sharp metal skewer enters the rear, burning its way until it reaches the intestines, then returns only to be reinserted.'" Friedman, *From Beirut to Jerusalem*, 80.

29. "Shaykh Ali Bayanuni of the Islamic Front claims the Syrian government killed 20,000 civilians and lost 10,000 itself in the Hama incident (*Le Matin*, March 22, 1982, translation in Foreign Broadcast Information Service). Diplomatic observers are quoted as believing that 5,000-13,000 lives were lost (*Christian Science Monitor*, April 1, 1992)." Cited in endnote 6 of John Devlin, "Syrian Policy" in *The Middle East Since Camp David*, Robert Freedman, ed. (Boulder: Westview Press, 1984), 123-42; 141.

30. Patrick Seale, *Asad of Syria: The Struggle for the Middle East* (London: I.B. Tauris & Co Ltd., 1988).

31. The American view of nationalism differs from that of the Middle East. In the Middle West, national identity and citizenship are one and the same. In the Middle East, national identity has been molded by ethnic conflicts among peoples within the same nation. Though several groups may share citizenship, they may not share the same national identity. Therefore, a ruling class may not see other groups as citizens but as national rivals.

32. Syria occupies a portion of Lebanon, while Israel controls a small southern section of Lebanon near the Israeli border. Syria's large military presence in Lebanon casts a shadow on Lebanese politics. And if the troops are not enough to compel, Assad uses force to quell political opposition.

33. Friedman, *From Beirut to Jerusalem*, 104.

34. Two American entrepreneurs founded the United Fruit Company in 1899. It is a collection of several banana plantations and transportation networks mainly located in Central America. Because of its great economic resources and political influence, the United Fruit Company gave a pretext to left-wing critics of America to coin the derogatory term "Banana Republic." Marxists argue that the company symbolizes the neo-colonialism and imperialism of American investment in Latin America. For Fidel Castro's

father to do business with the United Fruit Company is like Karl Marx working as a financial advisor for Lloyds of London!

35. In a discussion with journalist Brian McKenna, former Prime Minister of Canada Pierre Trudeau claimed that Castro loved Ernest Hemingway because of the length of his monologues. Brian McKenna, "Comrades-in-Arms" *Saturday Night* (December/January 1994). Available online: http://www.enews.com/magazines/sn/archive/1994/010194.2.html

36. Consider this anecdote regarding Castro and baseball. Senator Bob Kerrey (Democrat, Nebraska) facetiously nominated Castro to become commissioner of the American baseball leagues. Kerrey claimed that, "Cuba wants to get rid of a dictator, and baseball needs a dictator!"

37. Thomas Paterson, *Contesting Castro: The United States and the Triumph of the Cuban Revolution* (New York : Oxford University Press, 1994).

38. Robert Quirk, *Fidel Castro* (New York: W.W. Norton, 1993), 18-19.

39. Research assistant, Anna Vania Song, discussed Castro's baseball history with Quirk. On the basis of research spanning 15 years, this Castro biographer said that Castro never really played in an organized league and that his baseball experience came from pickup games with friends. Telephone interview by Song with Quirk, June 4, 1997, Ann Arbor, MI/Bloomington, IN.

40. Institute for South-North Korea Studies, *The True Story of Kim Jong-Il* (Seoul, 1985). According to an American scholar at the United States Institute of Peace, the Korean media regularly use that institute as a source for information concerning South–North Korean relations. The inference here, then, is that this institute is as good a source about North Korea as the Korean media itself. Telephone interview by Anna Song with Scott Snyder, July 30, 1997, Ann Arbor, MI/Washington, D.C.

　　The literature on the Koreas produced by either North or South is a mixture of propaganda with less analysis than would be found in Western sources about the peninsula. One institute on which the present analysis relies is the Institute for South–North Korea Studies. Because it is in Seoul, the practice is to seek validation from non-Korean sources concerning controversial inferences.

41. Institute for South-North Korea Studies, *The True Story of Kim Jong-Il*, 59-60.

42. According to one source, Kim Il-Sung also used these pleasure groups. The Institute for South-North Korea Studies states that both father and son justify the use of pleasure groups with the claim that being the nation's supreme leader creates an overwhelming amount of stress. " . . . therefore, their mental and physical stress must be given an outlet." Institute for South-North Korea Studies, *The True Story of Kim Jong-Il*, 87-88.

43. Max Weber, a political leadership theorist, believed that there were three types of leadership, among them, charismatic. A charismatic leader portrays the image of having some type of divinity. Through this illusion of divinity, the leader can then motivate the people.

44. See The Institute of North Korean Studies, *The Red Dynasty* (Seoul: The Institute of North Korean Studies, 1982).

45. *The True Story of Kim Jong-Il,* 7-9, 20-21.

46. For the record, elephant herds generally consist of a cluster of females with their young daughters. Male elephants usually travel on their own or with a pair of youthful males. They chase the females from the herd for the purpose of mating with them. The use of the rogue elephant metaphor, however, does not imply that the United States chases rogue nations out of global herds for the purpose of "embracing" them!

47. "Embrace" is a process of forming an alignment, "accommodation" a procedure of compromising with a bargaining partner on issues but not principles, and "appeasement" a method of buying off potential antagonists at the sacrifice of principles. "Containment" is an effort to isolate, for example, through the imposition of economic sanctions. "Confrontation" is a process of issuing threats that may imply military action. Individuals who favor embrace, accommodation, and appeasement should guard against the underestimation of threats; and people who prefer to contain and confront should be careful of overestimation of threats. In particular, appeasement as a set of beliefs about how to deal with challengers is an unmotivated bias. It distorts threat perception and predisposes individuals to choose embrace and accommodation rather than containment and confrontation of rogue states.

48. Chinese characters for danger and opportunity are wei and chi, which together mean crisis.

49. Robert Jervis, Richard Ned Lebow, and Janice Gross Stein, eds., *Psychology and Deterrence* (Baltimore: Johns Hopkins University Press, 1985), 1-12.

50. Gary Clyde Hufbauer, Jeffrey J. Schott, and Kimberly Ann Elliot conducted a study that defined economic sanctions as the deliberate, government-inspired withdrawal—or threat of withdrawal—of customary trade or financial relations. See their *Economic Sanctions Reconsidered: History and Current* Policy (Washington, D.C.: Institute for International Economics, 1985).

51. The United Nations Security Council imposes multilateral sanctions when there is a consensus among the permanent members: China, France, Russia, the United Kingdom, and the United States. In addition to Europe, the anti-sanctions school includes Great Powers in Asia like China and Japan.

52. The United States took two unilateral measures, the Cuban Liberty and Democratic Solidarity (Helms-Burton) Act and the Iran and Libya Sanctions Act. In anticipation of their passage, the European Union stated that if the U.S. Government wishes further measures to be implemented by the international community, it should introduce them for discussion in the relevant international body, such as the United Nations. See "European Commission Reacts to U.S. Announcement on Cuba," *European Union News,* no. 43/96 (July 16, 1996) and "EU Reacts to Iran/Libya Legislation," *European Union News,* no. 44/96 (July 23, 1996).

53. A German foundation representative in Washington gave a succinct summary of the different approaches between Europe and the United States

regarding how to treat Third World states thought to be engaged in terrorism and proliferation of weapons of mass destruction. First, because détente worked to diffuse tensions during the Cold War, it can have similar effects against so-called rogue states as well. Second, Europeans have a long tradition in the practice of classical diplomacy. This tradition entails having diplomatic relations and conducting negotiations with countries with which there are profound differences: "Talk, talk, talk, is better than fight, fight, fight!" Hence, punitive measures like sanctions and the use of force should occur only after diplomacy has been tried and found wanting. Americans, however, are likely to incorporate force and diplomacy together. Third, there is the factor of economic interdependence between Europe and the Third World states like Libya. Europeans are far more dependent on Middle Eastern/North African oil and trade than the United States. As a result, preservation and furtherance of those ties is much more critical to them.

54. Although Europe is mostly a unitary actor in opposition to politically motivated trade restraints, there are differences among states. British Prime Minister Margaret Thatcher acted like an American idealist instead of like a European realist. Even the French may consider sanctions when the threat is small, the action is symbolic, and their domestic constituency is supportive.

55. Although the American business sector opposes political restraints on trade, many firms lobby on behalf of protectionist measures that benefit their particular sector. Of concern here, however, are only political trade restraints, not economic protectionism.

56. Businesses on both sides of the Atlantic are opposed to the imposition of political trade restraints. Mobil Oil, "Sanctions: The Last Resort," *New York Times,* February 15, 1996, sec. A, 15. Mobil Oil runs a series of advertisements opposite the editorial page of the *New York Times* and other national newspapers.

57. In the fierce competition between the U.S.-based Boeing Corporation and Europe's Airbus Industrie over aircraft sales to China, Boeing had delivered 252 planes, while Airbus delivered only 25, by 1996. In reaction to tension between the United States and China over trade and human rights, however, China subsequently delayed renewed ordering from Boeing and pursued options with Airbus. Jeff Cole, Joseph Kahn, Craig S. Smith, and Douglas Lavin, "China Snubs Boeing Again in a Jet Deal," *Wall Street Journal,* April 12, 1996, sec. A, 3.

58. In 1996, I joined a Council on Foreign Relations study group on economic sanctions. Former White House aide Richard Haass, the head of the study group, stated, "Sanctions—ranging from cutting off aid to shutting down all trade and financing—offer U.S. policymakers and members of Congress an attractive compromise between doing nothing and sending in the Marines." Richard Haass, "Sanctions—With Care," *The Washington Post,* 27 July 1997, sec. C, 9. Available online:
http://www.washingtonpost.com/wp-srv/WPlate/1997-07/27/1211-072797-idx.html#TOP

See also Richard Haass, *Intervention: The Use of American Military Force in the Post–Cold War World* (Washington, D.C.: Carnegie Endowment for International Peace, 1994), regarding economic sanctions and the Gulf War and *The Reluctant Sheriff: The United States after the Cold War* (Washington, D.C.: Council on Foreign Relations, 1997).

59. During the Bush Administration, John Bolton was an assistant secretary at the State Department and in 1996 he was President of the National Policy Forum, a Republican study organization. John Bolton, "Appeasement As a Way of Life," *New York Times,* July 28, 1996, sec. E, 13.

60. In Nigeria, Royal/Dutch Shell has large-scale investments and backs the government at the risk of incurring the wrath of worldwide environmental and human rights groups. Paul Lewis, "Nigeria's Deadly Oil War: Shell Defends Its Record," *New York Times,* February 13, 1996, sec. A, 1.

61. As the world's ninth largest oil producer, Nigeria supplied about 600,000 barrels a day to the United States, about 8 percent of total U.S. oil imports during the mid-1990s. And Nigeria earned over $10 billion a year in oil revenues during this period. These funds account for some 90 percent of Nigeria's foreign export earnings and approximately 80 percent of its government revenues. Hence, Glenn Frankel concludes that an international embargo would have caused Nigeria immediate economic pain. Glenn Frankel, "Nigeria Mixes Oil and Money," *Washington Post,* November 24, 1996, sec. C, 1.

62. "We honestly don't believe a unilateral oil embargo against Nigeria would accomplish much except to further concentrate power and wealth in the hands of a few," said David Miller, the Corporate Council on Africa's executive director, as cited in Frankel, "Nigeria Mixes Oil and Money."

63. Neal Sher, "Comprehensive U.S. Sanctions Against Iran: A Plan For Action," in *A Report to AIPAC's Executive Council* (March 20, 1995), and Jim Hoagland, "Money Does Talk," *Washington Post,* February 8, 1996, sec. A, 1, 12.

64. Richard Ellings, *Embargoes and World Power—Lessons from American Foreign Policy* (Boulder: Westview Press, 1985), 126.

65. In this regard, Richard Ellings finds that, "With eroding leverage, the once preeminent state finds weakening capacity to administer sanctions on a multilateral basis. . . . [Sanctions] indicate a residual will to lead, but a diminished capacity to do so." Ellings, *Embargoes and World Power—Lessons from American Foreign Policy,* 124.

66. Margaret Doxey, a leading scholar on economic warfare, finds that it is hard to achieve international accord on the definition of the situation that requires collective action. Margaret Doxey, *Economic Sanctions and International Enforcement* (London: Royal Institute of International Affairs, 1980), 80-81.

67. Retribution derives from the Latin *re + tribuo,* literally "to pay back." The unqualified noun, "retribution," refers solely to a deliberate return of evil for evil. M. Henberg, *Retribution: Evil for Evil in Ethics, Law, and Literature* (Philadelphia: Temple University Press, 1990), 18.

68. Richard Kim Nosily, "International Sanctions As International Punishment," *International Organization* (Spring 1989): 315, and Miroslav Nincic and Peter Wallenstein, *Dilemmas of Economic Coercion—Sanctions in World Politics* (New York: Praeger Special Studies, 1983), 20.

69. "They [the American people] were more conversant with the notions of rights and the principles of true freedom than the greater part of their European contemporaries." Alexis de Tocqueville, *Democracy in America,* trans. Henry Reeve, rev. Francis Bowen, ed. Phillips Bradley (New York: Modern Library, 1981), 31.

70. Extraterritoriality is the implementation of one nation's laws in other countries or the application of one state's laws to the firms from other nations. See Chapter Two, endnote 4, for an extended discussion of the Iran and Libya Sanctions Act and the concept of extraterritoriality.

71. In addition to the Spector-Wolf Bill, Senator Spencer Abraham (Rep.-Michigan) introduced a similar bill targeted at China. His *China Sanctions and Human Rights Advancement Act* would prohibit the granting of U.S. visas to Chinese Government officials who work in entities involved in the implementation and enforcement of China's law and directives on religious practices. The legislation requires an annual report by the president on whether there has been improvement in China's policy of religious toleration and in its overall human rights record. Congress, Senate, *The China Sanctions and Human Rights Advancement Act of 1997,* 105th Cong., 1st sess., S. 810.Available online:
   http://www.access.gpo.gov/su_docs/aces/aaces002.html

72. Gerald Seib, "Clinton is Squeezed in Middle on Religious Persecution," *Wall Street Journal,* July 7, 1997, sec. A, 16.

73. "Let every nation know . . . whether it wishes us well or ill . . . that we shall pay any price, bear any burden, meet any hardship, support any friend, oppose any foe, to assure the survival and the success of liberty. This much we pledge. . .and more." President, Speech, "Inaugural Address of President John F. Kennedy, January 20, 1961."Available online:
   http://users.southeast.net/~cheryl/speech.html

74. Sanctions regimes are norms that specify acceptable behavior. A United Nations Security Council resolution that mandates international sanctions is a sanctions regime.

75. Retributive sanctions serve as a tool to achieve catharsis. From Greek drama through Sigmund Freud, catharsis symbolizes an emotional release, relieving tension. In this respect, applying punishment by retributive sanctions always makes one feel good.

76. In defiance of American hegemony in the Caribbean, the Soviet Union had placed in Cuba nuclear missiles capable of striking the United States. President Kennedy demanded the immediate withdrawal of those missiles and sent American battleships to quarantine the island-nation. Soviet Premier Khrushchev consented to the withdrawal of the missiles under the condition that the United States not invade Cuba. This agreement precluded American military action, yet permitted economic sanctions. Thereafter, the economic embargo was the main tool that Washington directed against

Havana. See Aleksandr Fursendo and Timothy Naftali, *One Hell of a Gamble: Khrushchev, Castro, and Kennedy, 1958-1964* (New York: W.W. Norton & Company, 1997).

77. Elliot Aronson, Timothy Wilson, and Robin Akert, *Social Psychology: The Heart and the Mind* (New York: Harper Collins, 1994).

78. Richard Ned Lebow, "Windows of Opportunity: Do States Jump Through Them?" *International Security* 9, no. 1 (Summer 1984): 150.

79. Prior to the Franco-Russian Alliance of 1891, a "mobilization-gap" existed between the Germans and the Russians. Both due to better physical infrastructure and to more efficient military command and control, Germany could mobilize its forces considerably faster. After 1891, however, the gap closed, as Germany had to account for faster French mobilization. Hence Germany developed the Schlieffen Plan. The strategy was to deal with France's faster mobilization potential by a series of lightning strikes, and then to turn to the slower Russians. See Lebow, "Windows of Opportunity: Do States Jump Through Them?" *International Security* 9, no. 1 (Summer 1984), 160-8.

80. Deterrence is a process of inducing a potential challenger not to take an action; coercion aims at getting an actor to take an action or undo something already in place. Sanctions may be both deterrent and coercive in nature. Alexander George and Richard Smoke, *Deterrence in American Foreign Policy* (New York: Columbia University Press, 1974); Alexander George, David Hall, and William Simons, *The Limits of Coercive Diplomacy* (Boston: Little Brown, 1971).

81. "Window of opportunity" refers to situations anticipated by classical deterrence: leaders are value maximizers who are deterrable, given the right combination of capability and resolve. "Basement of fear" highlights the failure of classical deterrence theory to explain "irrational" decisions. Prospect theory not only supports classical deterrence when explaining opportunistic behavior, but also accounts for paranoid behavior, which classical theory ignores. Political psychologists who study deterrence theory find that states often are very cautious: they refrain from jumping through windows of opportunity when classical theory would expect them to act.

    See also Lebow, "Window of Opportunity": 147-86; Robert Jervis, "Introduction," in Robert Jervis, Lebow, and Janice Gross Stein, eds., *Psychology and Deterrence*, 1-12.

82. In addition to the State Department, others concerned with sanctions include the Department of the Treasury's Office of Foreign Assets Control (OFAC). It administers and enforces economic and trade sanctions against targeted states, terrorism-sponsoring organizations, and international narcotics traffickers. Its mission statement declares that OFAC acts under presidential wartime and national emergency powers, as well as on the basis of authority granted by specific legislation. OFAC imposes controls on transactions and freezes foreign assets under U.S. jurisdiction. Some of the sanctions OFAC administers stem from United Nations and other international mandates; hence, they are multilateral in scope and involve close cooperation with allied

governments. Available online:

http://www.ustreas.gov/treasury/services/fac/fac.html

83. Assad has assumed the position of a proxy warrior in the conflicts between his neighbors and Israel, exploiting all parties involved to his exclusive benefit. Assad accomplishes his feats of *Realpolitik* by simply outsmarting the competition. By forcing both the United States and Israel to return time and again despite broken promises, Hezbollah rockets, and current Israeli politics, Assad emerges as a winner. He is "a rogue of the first order—but a rogue far more subtle and inconspicuous than his peers." A.M. Rosenthal, "The Winner in Lebanon," *New York Times*, April 16, 1996, sec. A, 13.

84. Department of State, *International Narcotics Control Strategy Report* (Washington, D.C.: Government Printing Office, 1996). Also available online:

http://www.state.gov/www/global/narcotics_law/1996_
narc_report/index.html

85. In his February 28, 1997 determination, Clinton denied certification to Colombia and five other countries. He decided that "it is in the vital national interest of the United States" to certify three "major illicit drug producing and/or transit countries," Belize, Lebanon, and Pakistan. See Office of the Press Secretary, The White House, Memorandum for the Secretary of State: "Certification for Major Narcotics Producing and Transit Countries" (Washington, D.C.), 28 February 1997. Available online:

http://www.usembassy.org.uk/drugs3.html

86. "American sources estimate that during 1996 Lebanon exported approximately 60 tons of heroin and 100 tons of marijuana, with a total value of more than $12 billion. It is reasonable to assume that the Syrians pocketed a significant percentage of this sum, probably more than $1 billion." Ron Ben Yishai, *Yediot Ahronot,* June 6, 1997, sec. A, 4-7.

87. Although Colombia does not warrant a chapter in this study, it does merit further elaboration in an endnote. The Colombian drug cartels are responsible for about 80 percent of the cocaine and 30 percent of the heroin entering the United States. These operations produced more than 700 metric tons of cocaine in 1994, yielding over $7 billion in U.S. sales alone. (Jesse Helms, "The Challenge of Colombia," *Wall Street Journal,* March 4, 1996, sec. A, 14). As a result of such shipments, narco-corruption is a threat to U.S. interests. But such a threat is only one aspect of a multidimensional relationship between Colombia and the United States. Along with Colombia, Iran also failed to be certified as working on the drug problem, yet it is a subject of this study. In contrast to Bogota, Washington seeks to isolate Tehran as a pariah.

Chapter Two

1. For a critique of balance of power principles such as "The enemy of my enemy is my friend" as applied to Iran, Iraq, and the United States, see Bruce Jentleson, *With Friends Like These: Reagan, Bush, and Saddam, 1982-1990* (New York: W. W . Norton, 1994), 15 ff.

2. The Clinton Administration rejects the Reagan-Bush policy of building up either Iran or Iraq to counter the threat from the other and favors a policy of "dual containment." Anthony Lake, "Confronting Backlash States," *Foreign Affairs* 73, no. 2 (March/April 1994): 48-51.

   A grand debate rages regarding dual containment. On the one side is the Clinton Administration as represented by Anthony Lake. On the other side are two former national security advisors and a former assistant secretary of state: Zbigniew Brzezinski, Brent Scowcroft, and Richard Murphy, "Differentiated Containment," *Foreign Affairs* 76, no. 3 (May/June 1997), 20. They dismiss dual containment as "more a slogan than a strategy."

3. A structural security dilemma is a situation in which the security of each state requires the insecurity of others. A perceptual security dilemma occurs when decisionmakers overrate the advantages of the offensive or the hostility of others. Jack Snyder, "Saving Face for the Sake of Deterrence," in Robert Jervis, Richard Lebow, and Janice Gross Stein, eds., *Psychology and Deterrence,* (Baltimore: Johns Hopkins University Press, 1985), 155.

4. The Iran and Libya Sanctions Act seeks to deny both countries the ability to support international terrorism and to fund the development and acquisition of weapons of mass destruction. The Act limits their ability to explore, extract, refine, or transport petroleum resources by pipeline. If foreign persons (people or firms) invest more than $40 million, they are subject to U.S. penalties. The act does not require the president to sanction foreign persons, but it allows the president to do so. Furthermore, mandatory sanctions are also applicable against companies that violate the UN Security Council trade sanctions against Libya. Available online:
   http://thomas.loc.gov/cgi-bin/bdquery/L?d104:./
   list/bd/d104sh.lst:493

5. Allison Mitchell, "Clinton Signs Bill Against Investing in Iran and Libya," *New York Times,* August 6, 1996, sec. A, 1.

6. Reuters, "Perry: Iran May Be Suspect in Saudi Bombing," August 3, 1996.

7. National Public Radio interview by Martha Raddatz with Secretary of Defense William Perry, August 2, 1996, Washington, D.C. Available online:
   http://www.npr.org/plweb-cgi/fastweb?getdoc+npr+ npr+
   8729+15+wAAA+August%262,1996

8. See William Safire, "October Surprises," *New York Times* August 15, 1996, sec. A, 19. With respect to the possibility of an Iranian connection, Safire reports that Clinton Administration national security officials secretly tipped the presidential campaign of Bob Dole about the likelihood of a punitive strike against Iran if the evidence of Iranian involvement were compelling.

9. Reuters, "U.S. Defense Secretary Clarifies Iran Comments," August 3, 1996.

10. Youssef Ibrahim, "Saudi Rebels Tied to June Bombing," *New York Times,* August 15, 1996, sec. A, 1, 6.

11. Reuters, "Iran's Spiritual Leader Lashes Out at U.S. Claim of Saudi Bomb Link," August 3, 1997.

12. During 1997, the United States maintained a robust military presence in the gulf region: about 25,000 military personnel, 100 aircraft, 25 ships, as well as prepositioned equipment for at least one heavy armored division. There should be about two divisions by the end of the year 2000. U.S. forces could be used against either Iraq or Iran. Tehran perceives American economic warfare and the U.S. military presence in the Gulf as a threat. Therefore, Iran's perception of a high American threat is not unreasonable.

13. See Joshua Epstein, *Strategy & Force Planning: The Case of the Persian Gulf* (Washington, D.C.: Brookings Institution, 1987), 2-6, for an analysis of a Soviet assault on the oil fields of Khuzestan Province, Iran's principal oil region. Such an attack was the central planning contingency for the Gulf region within the Pentagon during most of the Cold War. A Soviet invasion of Iran would have required some 15 armored division equivalents as well as approximately 700 aircraft. This force could have reached Tehran in about 45 days.

     The Pentagon assumed that a Soviet intervention in Iran could have been conducted under the cover of a peacekeeping role in the event of an Iranian civil war. And there might have been direct attacks on oil facilities by guerrillas as a part of a larger war. In addition, this scenario included attacks on oil sea-lines of communications, such as mining, submarine, or air assaults on tankers. The result might have been Soviet control of the Strait of Hormuz. Office of the Assistant Secretary of Defense for Program Analysis and Evaluation: "Capabilities for Limited Contingencies in the Persian Gulf," unclassified summary, (Washington, D.C.: 1979).

14. Jentleson, *With Friends Like These,* 15.

15. Politics, interests, and values may lead to biases in information processing. All three can result in misperceptions and provide incentives to magnify threats. Motivated biases are those that distort perceptions because individuals see what they want to see. Unmotivated biases distort perceptions because people see what they expect to see. Bureaucratic and domestic politics are sources of motivated biases affecting American decisionmakers in their overestimation of the Iranian threat. For a discussion of biases and threat perception, see Robert Jervis, "Perceiving and Coping with Threat," in Jervis, Lebow, and Stein, eds., *Psychology and Deterrence,* 18-27.

16. I attended the Atlanta briefing along with Richard Allen, William Casey, Joseph Chourba, Daniel Graham, Fred Ikle, Jack Kemp, and Michael Pillsbury. After Reagan's victory in November, some of us served in his Administration. They included Allen as National Security Advisor; Casey as Director of Central Intelligence; Graham as advisor to the President on the Strategic Defense Initiative; Ikle as Under Secretary of Defense/Policy; Kemp as a member of the House of Representatives and later Secretary of Housing and Urban Development in the Bush Administration. And I became co-chair of the Middle East Task Force for the Reagan-Bush Campaign, senior staff member of the National Security Council at the White House, and then personal representative of the Secretary of Defense at security talks in Europe.

17. Some members of the advisory group thought that the Soviets also had options across different regions. In the event that conflict in the Middle East expanded to a NATO–Warsaw Pact war in Europe, Soviet armed forces could engage in selective attacks in Asia against American forces capable of attacking Soviet land-based forces. And Soviet forces could conduct operations to prevent reinforcement and supply of NATO-Europe from the Pacific.

18. Iranian militants seized 52 Americans at the U.S. embassy in Tehran on November 4, 1979, held them for 445 days, and released them on January 20, 1981, the day Reagan replaced Carter as President. Following the seizure of the embassy, Washington blocked the assets of the government of Iran in the United States or in overseas branches of U.S banks. Washington took that action on November 14, 1979, based on the legal authority of the International Emergency Economic Powers Act. Under the Iranian Assets Control Regulations (Title 31 Part 535 of the U.S. Code of Federal Regulations), Washington froze some $12 billion in Iranian government assets. The Carter Administration expanded the assets freeze into a full-scale trade embargo. It remained in effect until Iran and the United States signed the Algiers Accord on January 19, 1981. Office of Foreign Assets Control, "What You Need to Know About U.S. Sanctions: An Overview of O.F.A.C. Regulations Involving Sanctions Against Iran," Washington, D.C.: Department of the Treasury, August 22, 1996.

19. Regarding the politics of the hostage crisis, see Gary Sick, *October Surprise: America's Hostages in Iran and the Election of Ronald Reagan* (New York: Random House Times Books, 1992), 12, and Barbara Honegger, *October Surprise* (New York: Tudor, 1989). Sick was a member of the National Security Council staff and the principal White House aide for dealing with Iranian affairs in the Carter Administration. He and I overlapped on the Council staff during 1981. Sick concluded that elements within the U.S. government worked with members of the Reagan-Bush campaign to delay release of the hostages in order to influence the outcome of the November 1980 election in Reagan's favor. As a member of the Reagan campaign team, I saw no evidence to sustain Sick's allegations.

20. Briefings of nonincumbent presidential candidates are a traditional means of minimizing statements by challengers that could jeopardize national security. With respect to the Wexford briefing, here is the way one former intelligence officer describes the meeting that followed our prebrief.

> Before the election, candidate Reagan received only one intelligence briefing . . . D.C.I. [Director of Central Intelligence] Adm. Stansfield Turner, accompanied by three senior Agency officers, represented CIA . . . Participants in that first briefing remember it as "a circus." The living room of the Middleburg home where the session was held was like a chaotic movie set with chairs scattered more or less randomly about the room and people constantly coming and going. The Governor was an engaging host, but in the impossible setting it was extraordinarily difficult to make effective

use of the briefing aids and other materials that Turner had brought with him. Throughout the meeting, which went on for approximately one hour, the CIA participants had the feeling that the Reagan camp had accepted the briefing simply because it had been offered and they had to do it. There was no evidence that anyone had the expectation that the Governor would engage in an in-depth review of the substantive issues.

Even in these awkward circumstances there was some serious discussion of developments in the Middle East, the agreed focus of the session. Turner discussed the petroleum aspects of the issue and the conflicts between Iran and Iraq and in Afghanistan. National Intelligence Officer for the Middle East Robert Ames briefed on the internal politics of Saudi Arabia and Iran. Richard Lehman, from the National Intelligence Council, elaborated on the impact of the Iran-Iraq war on the region and on the Soviet role.

John Helgerson, *Getting to Know the President: CIA Briefings of Presidential Candidates 1952-1992,* (Washington, D.C.: Center for the Study of Intelligence, Central Intelligence Agency). Available online:
http://www.oD.C.i.gov/csi/books/briefing/index.htm

21. I attended the Reagan prebriefing. In attendance were vice-presidential candidate George Bush; former Secretary of State Henry Kissinger; General Alexander Haig, former Nixon deputy National Security Advisor who subsequently became Reagan's Secretary of State. Also included were Admiral Thomas Moorer, former Chairman Joint Chiefs of Staff; Edwin Meese III, who later became Reagan's Attorney General; and Richard Allen, who subsequently became the President's National Security Advisor. In addition, there was Robert Neumann, former Ambassador to Saudi Arabia and co-chair with me of the Middle East Task Force of the Reagan-Bush campaign.

22. Gary Sick named Reagan campaign advisers to be part of a network of informants throughout the government. They were to alert the campaign about hostage developments. According to Sick, they included, Henry Kissinger, Alexander Haig, Thomas Moorer, and Robert Neumann. See Sick, *October Surprise,* 23, 27, 35, 101.

23. Personal recollection of author from the "prebrief" that prepared presidential candidate Reagan to receive a briefing from the Director of Central Intelligence, October 4, 1980, Virginia, at the Wexford Estate.

24. T. N. Kaul, *The Kissinger Years: Indo-American Relations* (New Delhi: Arnold-Heinemann, 1980), 2.

25. Michael Lynch, "The Next Oil Crisis," *Technology Review* 90, no. 9, Massachusetts Institute of Technology Alumni Association (November 1987): 38.

26. On September 22, 1980, Iraq launched an attack against Iran's southwestern province of Khuzestan. Baghdad falsely assumed that the mainly Arab population of Khuzestan, a large Iranian minority, would rise up in arms against their rulers from Tehran.

27. My assessment was that the Reagan advisers leaned toward Iraq. In contrast, Sick asserts that the Reagan-Bush campaign wanted to come to terms with Tehran on the hostages, even at the expense of entering into an arms-supply relationship with Iran. Sick, *October Surprise,* 143. My inference derives from first-hand experience.

28. See "Case Four: A Jordanian-Syrian Alliance—the Eastern Front," Anthony Cordesman, *Perilous Prospects: The Peace Process and the Arab-Israeli Military Balance* (Boulder: Westview Press, 1996).

29. See also Sick, *October Surprise,* 108, for his assessment of Israel's doctrine of the periphery. With respect to Israel's relations with Iran, moreover, Sick (p. 65) found that the hostage crisis and Iran's vulnerability to Iraq in their war gave Israel an occasion to reopen its ties with the Islamic Republic of Iran. Tehran was desperate for supply parts for its American-origin arms in October 1980, the first month of the Iran-Iraq War.

30. From about 1965 to 1975, Iran and Israel may have trained and supplied arms to Kurdish rebels in Iraq.

31. Congressman Toby Roth (Rep.-Wisconsin), "New Iranian-Libyan Sanctions Will Only Hurt U.S.," *Wall Street Journal,* August 6, 1996, sec. A, 14. A Roth staff aide, who had the action on the Iran and Libya Sanctions Act, explained why Roth wrote in opposition to a law for which he voted. "Along with 414 other members in a unanimous vote, no Member wanted to be on the wrong side of an issue concerning Iran and Libya." Telephone interview with Raymond Tanter, Ann Arbor, MI, August 19, 1996.

32. While engaging in rhetoric of confrontation, Jerusalem also has provided arms to Tehran. The goal is to form alignments with non-Arab Muslim states like Iran and Turkey, which are on the periphery of the Arab-Israel conflict zone.

33. Despite negligible amounts of oil, Israel has a per capita income higher than that of Saudi Arabia's. Israel: population, 5.4 million (July 1995 est.); GDP, $80.1 billion (1995 est.); $15,500 per capita GDP (1995 est.). Saudi Arabia: population, 19.4 million (July 1996 est.); GDP, $189.3 billion (1995 est.); $10,100 per capita GDP (1995 est.). Central Intelligence Agency, "Israel and Saudi Arabia," in *World Factbook 1996* (Washington, D.C.: U.S. Government, 1997). Available online:
    http://www.odci.gov/cia/publications/pubs.html

    With respect to American economic aid and military assistance to Israel, it receives $3.2 billion dollars annually. Dividing that figure by the 1995 population of 5.4 million yields U.S. aid per capita to Israel of roughly $500. Subtracting that $500 per head from Israel's GDP per capita of $15,500 amounts to $15,000, which is still $4,900 greater than the Saudi Arabian figure of $10,100. The bottom line is that it is false to state that Israel's wealth derives mainly from American assistance.

    The per capita income of Saudi Arabia has declined by about 50 percent during the 10 years from the mid-1980s: the population has about doubled while the GDP growth rate has remained essentially flat. And 54 percent of the population is under the age of 24. Finally, Saudi Arabia had 12 years of budget deficits during this period, and the Kingdom paid $120 billion for the cost of the war with Iraq. See also Douglas Jehl, "A Tutorial for Young Saudis On Ways to Toil for Money," *New York Times,* November 21, 1996, sec. A, 1, 4. He cites a Petroleum Finance Company chart to show real per capita GNP for Saudi Arabia just above $8,000 a year for 1996.

34. The good news is that the traditional Arab-Israel conflict, as one of wars between nation-states, is coming rapidly to a close. The bad news is that a new set of conflicts between secular governments and religious radicals vying for political control is emerging. The last decades of the twentieth century no longer experience a bipolar conflict between Israel and the Arab bloc. Rather, Israel focuses on specific threats, such as from Iran or Hezbollah in Lebanon. Because of the changing nature of the threat, Israel now enjoys relative state security. Individuals, however, may be personally less secure as a result of an increase in the rate of suicide bombings and other attacks against Israelis.

35. Hedrick Smith, *The Power Game* (New York: Random House, 1988), 216-31.

36. Christine Helms, "Washington Gains Moral High Ground on Iran, But Leaves US Business High-And-Dry," *Energy Compass Weekend Review* (May 5, 1995): 11-12.

37. Ibid.

38. The chairman of the Petroleum Finance Company said, "Washington must reexamine its strategy toward Iran, the largest and most stable country in the region. Whether we like it or not, Iran's Gulf neighbors must work with it. Besides, our attempt to isolate Iran lacks credibility with European and Asian governments." J. Robinson West, "How to Avert a New Oil Crisis," *New York Times,* November 30, 1996, sec. A, 19.

39. Menas' Associates, "US-Iran: Bad Feelings Made Worse," *Iran Focus Economy and Business* (1995): 1.

40. Mobil Oil, "Sanctions: The Last Resort," *New York Times,* February 15, 1996, sec. A, 15, paid advertisement.

41. John Lichtblau, "Oil Markets and Economic Sanctions," *Petroleum Industry Research Foundation* (April 29, 1996): 2. An ally of the Petroleum Industry Research Foundation is the U.S. Council for International Business, whose Washington representative is Joseph Gavin III.

42. Robert Mosbacher, speech delivered at the "Iran in Transition" Conference, (May 1, 1996); Brent Scowcroft, speech delivered at the "Iran in Transition" Conference, (May 2, 1996).

43. Michael Klare, *Rogue States and Nuclear Outlaws* (New York: Hill and Wang, 1995).

44. Klare, *Rogue States,* 10.

45. Klare, *Rogue States,* 219-20.

46. Klare, *Rogue States,* 24-28.

47. The Cuban Liberty and Democratic Solidarity Act of 1996 (Helms-Burton) made permanent the 34-year-old economic embargo that previously had to be renewed by a president each year. The act gave U.S. citizens the right to sue foreign companies that trafficked in property these people formerly owned in Cuba and denied U.S. visas to foreigners who derive benefits from confiscated property. The act also provided a three-month grace period for

foreign companies to dispose of or pay for confiscated property. The act remains in effect until a president determines that a democratically elected government is in Cuba, presumably without Fidel Castro or his brother Raul. Available online:
http://thomas.loc.gov/cgi-bin/bdquery/L?d104:./list/bd/d104sh.lst:169

48. A comprehensive rational process sets logically exhaustive goals, searches across a full range of alternatives, and specifies consequences of options in terms of cost, benefit, and likelihood of success. In light of such a process, a rational choice is one that promises to yield the highest expected gain or the lowest expected loss. Leaders need not be fully rational to be held accountable for their actions. It is enough that they have "bounded rationality" to hold them responsible. Limited rationality is less demanding of people. In contrast to comprehensive rationality, bounded rational individuals need only search across some goals, specify fewer options, make fewer calculations, and make less than optimal choices. See Janice Stein and Raymond Tanter, *Rational Decisionmaking* (Columbus: Ohio State University Press, 1980).

49. During November 1979, Carter took action against Iran. He prevented the export of $300 million in U.S.-origin military equipment to Iran, deported Iranian students living illegally in the United States, ended all crude-oil imports from Iran, and froze Iran's assets in the United States. See Gary Sick, *All Fall Down* (New York: Random House, 1985), for an analysis of Carter's approach to Iran. In the Carter Administration, Sick had responsibility for Iran as a Special Assistant to the President for National Security Affairs.

50. The memoirs of Zbigniew Brzezinski, Carter's National Security Affairs Advisor, describe the period between the fall of the Shah and rise of the Ayatollah. "Khomeni's return to Tehran created in effect a situation in which two governments were competing for power, with growing turmoil in the streets and with increasing signs of demoralization within the Army." Zbigniew Brzezinski, *Power and Principle* (New York: Farrar Straus Giroux, 1983), 389-90.

51. President Reagan took action against Tehran in response to Iranian-sponsored terrorism and assaults on Gulf shipping. He banned most Iranian imports: " . . . no goods or services of Iranian origin may be imported into the United States. . . ." Excluded were petroleum products from Iran refined from Iranian oil by a third party. Office of the Federal Register, "Prohibiting Imports from Iran, Executive Order 12613," October 29, 1987. Reagan imposed sanctions under the legal authority of the International Security and Development Cooperation Act, which gave rise to the Iranian Transactions Regulations (Title 31 Part 560 of the U.S. Code of Federal Regulations). Office of Foreign Assets Control, "What You Need to Know About U.S. Economic Sanctions."

52. An indication that retribution plays a role in a sanctions policy is whether the stated goal is to change a regime's behavior—rehabilitation—but an unstated aim is to overthrow that regime. There is nothing that some regimes can do that would warrant a lifting of sanctions. At issue is the

existence of the regime, not its behavior. But, it is illegitimate and perhaps illegal under international law to interfere in the domestic affairs of member states of the United Nations. Explicitly calling for revolution in a sovereign state is not an acceptable practice in the affairs of nations.

53. President Clinton issued Executive Order 12957, which was effective on March 16, 1995. And on May 8, 1995, he signed Executive Order 12959, which further tightened sanctions on Iran. The statutory authority was the International Emergency Economic Powers Act and the International Security and Development Cooperation Act. Office of Foreign Assets Control, "What You Need to Know About U.S. Economic Sanctions." Available online:
http://www.ustreas.gov/treasury/services/fac/fac.html
    Clinton prohibited American oil firms like Conoco from engaging in commercial transactions with Iran without an export license.

54. Deterrence by denial seeks to gain compliance by reducing the capability of a prospective challenger; deterrence by threat of punishment endeavors to gain compliance by targeting a challenger's motivation and intention.

55. Patrick Clawson, "The Impacts of U.S. Sanctions on Iran," Unpublished Paper Prepared for the Council on Foreign Relations Economic Sanctions Study Group (January 1997), 9.

56. Clawson, "The Impacts of U.S. Sanctions on Iran," states that during the first year of the Iran and Libyan Sanctions Act, American sanctions reduced Iran's foreign exchange receipts by $2 billion, or ten percent of its foreign exchange receipts.

57. While the same threatened interests may have both intrinsic and strategic aspects, the analysis here treats them as analytically distinct. For a further discussion of intrinsic interests and strategic interests, see Janice Stein, "The View From Cairo," in Jervis, Lebow, and Stein, eds., *Psychology and Deterrence,* 38-39.

58. During 1996, about 40,000 Americans worked in Saudi Arabia, the world's leading oil producer. The U.S. military presence in the Kingdom was some 5,000 personnel.

59. In order to prevent Saddam's forces from attacking the Kurds, the coalition created another zone over northern Iraq for Operation Provide Comfort. During the post–Gulf War era, the Coalition aircraft operated out of Incirlik air facility in Turkey.

60. In making alliance commitments, the United States assumes the responsibility to defend its allies primarily from American foes. If Washington pledged to defend its friends against their foes, the United States would invariably become involved in fighting its own friends.

61. Department of State Office of the Coordinator for Counterterrorism, *Patterns of Global Terrorism,* released annually.

62. A centrist Israeli newspaper, *Ma'ariv,* first reported the meetings in Tehran on July 1, 1996.

63. Hezbollah, or Party of God, began after the 1982 war between Israel and the Palestine Liberation Organization in Lebanon. Iran sent Revolutionary Guards to assist in the establishment of revolutionary groups in Lebanon.

Hezbollah uses southern Lebanon as a platform for launching attacks on northern Israel. Goals of Hezbollah include: establishment of an Islamic Republic of Lebanon, complete destruction of Israel, and Islamic rule over Jerusalem. It also calls Israel "Little Satan."

64. "Iran remains the premier state sponsor of international terrorism and is deeply involved in the planning and execution of terrorist acts both by its own agents and by surrogate groups. This year [1995] Tehran escalated its assassination campaign against dissidents living abroad; there were seven confirmed Iranian murders of dissidents in 1995, compared with four in 1994." Department of State, Office of the Coordinator for Counterterrorism, *1995 Patterns of Global Terrorism* (Washington, D.C.: April, 1996), Available online:
http://www.usis.usemb.se/terror/rpt1995/TERSST.HTM#Iran

65. "Since 1989 [to February 1996], Iran has murdered at least 48 regime opponents abroad, provided up to $100 million annually to the Lebanese Hizballah—a group responsible for the killing of over 250 Americans—and refused to repeal the religious judgment condemning British author Salman Rushdie to death." John Deutch, "Worldwide Threat Assessment Brief to the Senate Select Committee on Intelligence," Washington, D.C.: Public Affairs Staff, Central Intelligence Agency, February 22, 1996.

66. Douglas Frantz, "Looking to History, Crash Investigators Compile a Short List of Jetliner Terrorists," *New York Times,* August 24, 1996, sec. A, 11. With respect to the threat against Iranian dissidents in Pakistan, see Department of State, Office of the Coordinator for Counterterrorism, *1993 Patterns of Global Terrorism* (Washington, D.C.: Government Printing Office, April 1994). Also available online: http://www.hri.org/docs/USSD-Terror/93/asian.html

67. Hamas is the dominant, radical group in Gaza and the West Bank of the Jordan River. Hamas wants to establish Islamic Palestine from the Mediterranean Sea to the Jordan. It challenges Fatah, the mainstream Palestinian group, for leadership of the Palestinians. Hamas defines itself as the Palestinian branch of the Muslim Brotherhood that began in Egypt. Cairo accuses the Brothers of seeking to destabilize Egypt. Hamas stands for total rejection of the Arab-Israel peace process. For an explication of the difference between radical Islamists and mainstream Islam, see Graham Fuller and Ian Lesser, *A Sense of Siege* (Boulder: Westview Press, 1995), 4-6.

68. Palestinian rejectionists formed the Popular Front for the Liberation of Palestine-General Command (PFLP-GC) in 1968. Led by Ahmed Jabril, it emphasizes a military strategy in the struggle against Israel. Sponsored by Libya and Syria, the PFLP-GC may have been involved in the downing of Pan Am 103 over Lockerbie Scotland in December 1988. For an overview of Palestine Liberation Organization factions, see Daniel Diller, ed., *The Middle East* (Washington: Congressional Quarterly, 1991), 28-29.

69. Frantz, "Looking to History."

70. *1993 Patterns of Global Terrorism* (Washington, D.C.: April, 1994). Available online:
http://www.hri.org/docs/USSD-Terror/93/midleeast.html#Algeria

71. James Risen, "Administration Defends Bosnian Arms Policy," *Los Angeles Times,* April 24, 1996, sec. A.

72. In September 1991, the international community decided to impose a UN arms embargo on the former Yugoslavia (Security Council Resolution 713). The goal was to stabilize the situation among the former republics. But the embargo left the Serbs with an unfair advantage vis-à-vis other republics, such as Bosnia. The weaponry from Tito's Yugoslav army remained with Serbia and their Bosnian Serb allies. In early April 1994, Croatian President Franjo Tudjman approached the Zagreb-based American Ambassador Peter Galbraith. The question was whether the United States would object to Croatia acting as a transshipment point for Iranian arms en route to Muslim Bosnia. The United States gave a green light when President Clinton instructed Galbraith to inform Tudjman that the ambassador had "no instructions." Washington, in effect, traded the risk of Iranian penetration into the heart of Europe with Revolutionary Guards for the benefit of keeping the Bosnian Muslim regime afloat. For a further explication of the Iranian connection in arms transshipments to Bosnia, see Kristin McLean "Washington's Green Light to Tehran for Arms to Sarajevo via Zagreb?" Unpublished Paper Prepared for Political Science 472, the University of Michigan, (Spring 1996). Available online:
http://www-personal.umich.edu/~rtanter/S96PS472_Papers

73. The Director of Central Intelligence testified that Iran may be devoting up to $1 billion a year on its nuclear program. U.S. Senate. Committee on Governmental Affairs. *Proliferation Threats of the 1990's* Hearing, 24 February 1993. Available online:
http://web.lexis-nexis.com/cis/retrieve/document/s_witness.
html?_form=s_witness.hmtl&_mode=FULL&_results=
G{H^*KO!WAD!UUB$M[SWAD$UUB$AV!DUB]!BD!ABC$E$]DU]AB]DU$U&_
library=LEGIS&_file=CISINX&_firstdoc=1&_reldoc=8&_
citesper= 25&_maxdocs=9&_md5=11dd2eed24de20c90964f99c4a095e6b

   See also Mark Skootsky, "U.S. Nuclear Policy Toward Iran," Unpublished Paper (June 1, 1995). Available online:
http://xpress.studby.uio.no/toofan/public_html/persian/usiran.
html

74. Iran's chemical weapons program is already the largest in the Third World, claims Michael Eisenstadt. In a paper delivered to the Washington Institute for Near East Studies, he said that Iran can produce several hundred tons of chemical agent a year and may have produced as much as 2,000 tons of agent to date.

   And with respect to biological weapons, Iran is thought to be able to deploy them and disseminate them via terrorist saboteurs, or spray tanks on aircraft or ships, although more advanced means of dissemination—by unmanned aircraft or missiles for instance—may currently be beyond its means. Rick Marshall, "Iranian Military Power Assessed," USIA, March 13, 1996. Available online:
gopher://198.80.36.82:70/OR6423641-6427508-range/archives/
1996/pdq.96

75. See Lenore Martin, "Patterns of Regional Conflict and U.S. Gulf Policy," in William Olson, ed., *US Strategic Interests in the Gulf Region,* (Boulder: Westview Press, 1987), 9-10.

76. Although Nixon receives sole credit for the doctrine, Henry Kissinger provided the intellectual basis. In his memoirs, Kissinger writes, "We remain willing to participate, but we can not supply all the . . . resources. The initiative has to move increasingly into that region." To Kissinger's surprise, Nixon readily accepted the idea of relying less on the United States and more on regional allies. Henry Kissinger, *White House Years* (Boston: Little Brown, 1979), 222-25. See also George Lenczowski, *American Presidents and the Middle East* (Durham: Duke University Press, 1990), 116-17.

77. The Backfire bomber has an unrefueled combat radius of 2,486 miles or 4,000 kilometers. It can perform various tasks, such as nuclear strikes, conventional attacks, antiship strikes, and reconnaissance. U.S. Department of Defense, *Soviet Military Power: 1987,* 6th ed. (Washington, D.C.: U.S. Government Printing Office, March 1987), 36-37.

78. In his State of the Union Address on January 23, 1980, President Carter said the following. "An attempt by any outside force to gain control of the Persian Gulf region will be regarded as an assault on the vital interests of the United States of America, and such an assault will be repelled by any means necessary, including military force." "The State of the Union, January 23, 1980," *Public Papers of the Presidents of the United States: Jimmy Carter 1980-1981: Book 1, January 1 to May 23, 1980* (Washington, D.C.: U.S. Government Printing Office, 1982), 197.

79. After the invasion of Afghanistan in 1979, Soviet military forces in the Southern Theater of Military Operations conducted a command post exercise simulating an invasion of Iran. This exercise set off alarm bells in the White House and transformed President Carter from one who sought accommodation with Moscow to a leader who accepted the possibility of a Soviet-American confrontation over Iran.

80. President Reagan stated, "We wanted to keep the Soviets out of the region as well as prevent the radical, anti-American Iranian revolution from spreading to Saudi Arabia, with all the implications that could have for our economy. To put it simply, I didn't want Saudi Arabia to become another Iran," *Ronald Reagan, An American Life: The Autobiography* (New York: Simon & Schuster, 1990), 411.

81. A former Reagan cabinet member claimed, "That 1981-82 period was pretty grim for Iraq, and we were worried about the imbalance in the war with Iran." By 1982, American agencies used Jordan as a transshipment point for U.S.-origin helicopters en route to Iraq. Alan Friedman, *Spider's Web: The Secret History of How the White House Illegally Armed Iraq* (New York: Bantam, 1993), 17.

82. President Bush ignored Saddam Hussein's human rights violations in order to slant American policy toward Iraq. On January 17, 1990, he signed a waiver voiding a prohibition against providing Export-Import Bank financing. In doing so, he paved the way for Baghdad to acquire equipment that it otherwise could not afford. Friedman, *Spider's Web,* 157.

83. After Iraq invaded Kuwait on August 2, 1990, there was a National Security Council meeting the next day at the White House. General Colin Powell asked President Bush, "'Should we think about laying down a line in the sand concerning Saudi Arabia?' Bush thought for a moment, then said, 'yes, we should.'" Colin Powell, *My American Journey* (New York: Random House, 1995), 462-63.

84. On May 18, 1993, Martin Indyk, Special Assistant to the President for Near Eastern and South Asian Affairs at the National Security Council, gave a speech. He addressed the Washington Institute for Near East Policy. It was the first statement by the Clinton Administration of the dual containment doctrine. Indyk described the threat from Iran in terms of international terrorism and opposition to the Arab-Israel peace process. Tehran opposed the peace process by supporting groups like Hamas and Hezbollah. Iran also subverted friendly Arab regimes and directed a military buildup at the Arab Gulf states. In addition to opposition to the peace process, Tehran has made a concerted effort to obtain weapons of mass destruction. See Washington Institute for Near East Policy, "Special Report: Clinton Administration Policy Toward the Middle East," *Policy Watch* (May 21, 1993). See also Anthony Cordesman and Ahmed Hashim, *Iran: Dilemmas of Dual Containment* (Boulder: Westview Press, 1996).

85. Assistant to the President on National Security Affairs Anthony Lake described the logic of dual containment. The Clinton Administration's strategy toward Iran and Iraq began with the assumption that both regimes pursued policies hostile to American interests. The Administration rejected the Reagan-Bush policy of building up one to counter the other, in favor of a policy of dual containment. Lake, "Confronting Backlash States."

86. Paul Jabber, "Introduction: Western Interests and Gulf Stability," in *Great Power Interests in the Persian Gulf* (New York: Council on Foreign Relations, 1989), 2.

87. See also F. Gregory Gause III, "The Illogic of Dual Containment," *Foreign Affairs* 73, no. 2 (March/April 1994): 60.

88. Steven Lee Meyers, "U.S. Calls Alert As Iraqis Strike a Kurd Enclave," *New York Times,* September 1, 1996, sec. A, 1, 7; Chris Hedges, "Safehaven for Iraqi Kurds Has a History of Violence," *New York Times,* September 1, 1996, sec. A, 7.

89. For a description of Secretary of State George Shultz's approach to terrorism, see Shultz, *Turmoil and Triumph: My Years as Secretary of State,* (New York: Scribner's, 1993), 643-88.

90. The Export Administration Act of 1979 seeks to limit the military capability of a foreign state to sponsor international terrorism. The act contains a list of exports subject to national security controls. These include dual-use items that can be used for both civilian and military applications. Additional laws relevant to anti-terrorism are Section 620 (a) of the Foreign Assistance Act. It prohibits American financial assistance under that act as well under the Agricultural Trade Development Act, the Peace Corps Act, or the Export-Import Bank Act to any country designated by the secretary of state to be a supporter of international terrorism. The Arms Export Control Act

contains prohibitions regarding international terrorism. One restriction requires that decisions to approve an export take into account whether that item would be used in support of international terrorism.

91. The act applies to both a "United States person" and "any person." Thus, it applies to foreign firms trading with or investing in Iran or Libya.

92. "While the EU [European Union] may share some of the objectives underlying such laws, it opposes the extraterritorial application of domestic legislation as a matter of principle, insofar as it purports to force persons present in—and companies incorporated in—the EU to follow U.S. laws or policies outside of the U.S." European Commission, *Report on United States Barriers to Trade and Investments* (Brussels: European Union, May 1996), 3. Available online:

     http://europa.eu.int/en/comm/dgoi/eu-us.htm

     The European Commission acts as the "guardian" of the EU treaties to ensure that European legislation is applied correctly. The European Union (Brussels: 1995-97). Available online:

     http://europa.eu.int/en/comm/c9500/comm9500.html

93. Both Iran-Libya and the Cuban Act are secondary boycotts. A primary boycott bans direct trade between a boycotter and a proscribed nation. A secondary boycott informs third countries that if they trade with the proscribed nation, there will be penalties; for example, a ban on trading with the boycotting country. And a tertiary boycott informs other states that if they trade with nations in violation of the secondary boycott, there will be sanctions; for example, a ban on trading with the boycotter. For the standard legal definitions of primary and secondary boycotts as applied to union management relations, see Henry Black, *Black's Law dictionary,* 6th ed., (St. Paul: West Publishing, 1991), 1190, 1351.

     See endnote 46 for the contents of the Cuban Liberty and Democratic Solidarity Act.

94. Clawson, "The Impacts of U.S. Sanctions on Iran," 10.

95. As defined in Chapter One, extraterritoriality is the implementation of one nation's laws in other countries or the application of one state's laws to the firms from other nations.

96. Personal interview with University of Michigan Professor of Law Jose Alvarez by Brian Clune, August 8, 1997, Ann Arbor, MI.

     But a prominent international law firm in Washington, Fried, Frank, Harris, Shriver & Jacobson, states, "Although Helms-Burton is, at least arguably, not strictly extraterritorial in its application, it is correctly perceived as having the equivalent effect (i.e., imposing the dictates of U.S. law on persons who are not U.S. nationals or residents whose proscribed conduct occurs outside the U.S.)."

     The bottom line, however, is, "Helms-Burton, the Iran and Libya Sanctions Act and the substantial body of other U.S. laws with extraterritorial effect make it probable that U.S. and foreign law will come into conflict." David Birenbaum, Jay Kraemer, and William Taft, IV, "The War of the Laws: Coping With Helms-Burton, the Iran-Libya Sanctions and Beyond," Unpublished Paper Prepared for the Client Memoranda Archives

(Washington, D.C.: Fried, Frank, Harris, Shriver & Jacobson) July 31, 1996.
Available online:

http://www.ffhsj.com/firmpage/cmemos/0086223.htm#32

97. Section 821 of the Foreign Relations Authorization Act of 1994 imposes sanctions on persons engaging in export activities that contribute to proliferation. Available online:

http://thomas.loc.gov/cgi-bin/query/6?c103:./temp/~c103fjIp::

The Arms Export Control Act authorizes a president to control the import and the export of defense articles and services. Available online:

http://samsara.law.cwru.edu/aeca.html

Formed in 1987, the Missile Technology Control Regime (MTCR) has a membership of 28 nations. Its aim is to restrict the proliferation of missiles, unmanned air vehicles, and related technology for those systems capable of carrying a 500 kilogram payload at least 300 kilometers, as well as systems intended for the delivery of weapons of mass destruction. Available online:

http://www.usis-israel.org.il/publish/press/security/archive/
november/ds11118.htm

98. The primary boycott banned direct Arab trade with Israel. The secondary boycott prohibited any non-Arab country from trading with Israel. And the tertiary boycott forbade companies from dealing with persons on the secondary boycott list.

99. European Commission, "EU Reacts to Iran/Libya Legislation."

100. Article XXI of the GATT states: "Nothing in this agreement shall be construed . . . to prevent any contracting party from taking any action . . . it considers necessary for the protection of its essential security interests . . . ." Available online:

gopher://gopher.law.cornell.edu:70/00/foreign/fletcher/
BH209.txt

101. European Commission, "EU Reacts to Iran/Libya Legislation."

102. One of the pioneers who called for a rethinking of American policy towards Iran is Geoffrey Kemp. See his *Control of the Middle East Arms Race* (Washington, D.C.: Carnegie Endowment for International Peace, 1991). See also his co-edited volume, *Arms Control and Weapons Proliferation in the Middle East and South Asia,* (New York: St. Martin's Press, 1992). Especially relevant is Kemp's *Forever Enemies? American Policy and the Islamic Republic of Iran* (Washington, D.C.: Carnegie Endowment for International Peace, 1994) and his co-edited volume with Janice Gross Stein, *Powder Keg in the Middle East: The Struggle for Gulf Security* (Lanham MD: Rowman & Littlefield, 1995).

103. " . . . dual containment cannot provide a sustainable basis for U.S. policy in the Persian Gulf. A more nuanced and differentiated approach to the region is in order, one in tune with America's longer-term interests." Zbigniew Brzezinski, Brent Scowcroft, and Richard Murphy, "Differentiated Containment," *Foreign Affairs,* 76, no. 3 (May/June 1997): 20-30; 29. See also their book, *Differentiated Containment: U.S. Policy Toward Iran and Iraq* (New York: Council on Foreign Relations, 1997).

104. A former Member of President Bush's National Security Council staff, Richard Haass, also makes a case for a change in American policy toward Iran. He concurs with the Clinton Administration that the United States should express a willingness to use force if there is incontrovertible indication of Iranian sponsorship of terrorism against the United States or the allies. Going beyond the Administration's policy, Haass suggests that Washington ask its European and Asian allies to join in a "critical dialogue" with Tehran. The allies should make it clear that it would be unacceptable for a military move by Iran against Iraq. For its part in the dialogue, the United States could offer a temporary suspension of that part of the Iran and Libya Sanctions Act that penalizes others for doing business with Iran. See Richard Haass, "The United States and Iraq: A Strategy for the Long Haul," Washington, D.C.: The Brookings Institution, *Policy Brief* no. 7, 1996. Available online:

    http://www.brook.edu/fp/polbrief/polbrf7.htm

105. For evidence of Iran's acquisition of weapons of mass destruction see Yoav Limor, "Within Two Years, Iran Will Have Missiles Capable of Hitting Israel," *Ma'ariv*, 25 June 1997, sec. A, 10.

106. Department of State, Office of the Coordinator for Counterterrorism, *1995 Patterns of Global Terrorism* (Washington, D.C.: April, 1996). Available online:

    http://www.usis.usemb.se/terror/rpt1995/index.html

107. Iran reduced the number of terror incidents in Europe during 1995 and targeted mainly Iranian nationals. But Tehran did not entirely relinquish its practice of European-based terrorism.

Chapter Three

1. In games like football, hockey, and soccer, there are goal posts in fixed positions. When players cross these boundaries with the ball or puck, they expect to score a goal and thus to win a reward. However, if the officials move the posts every time the players are about to cross them, that would be an unfair change in the rules of the game. Saddam Hussein accused the United States of changing the rules every time Iraq was in virtual compliance.

2. "Assurance" is a way of making promises in order to enhance confidence.

3. In order to reduce fear, misunderstanding, and insecurity, assurance suggests that individuals try to communicate to adversaries their benign intentions.

4. But assurance is also unlikely to result in compliance, because of misperception. One explanation of misperception is "top-down processing" of information: "top" is a metaphor that explains how the "human mind" biases perception; "down" is a metaphor that symbolizes how mental biases influence incoming information. In top-down processing, people use existing beliefs and schema to make shortcut judgments in processing information. "Bottom-up" processing occurs when people encounter information, and their assessment is comparatively unbiased by belief systems. Bottom-

up is less likely to bias perception than top-down, because people gather information from the environment with less reference to their beliefs. With respect to Saddam, the assumption here is that his misperceptions stem from top-down processing of information about the United States.

5. Janice Gross Stein, "Deterrence and Compellence in the Gulf: A Failed or an Impossible Task?" *International Security* 17 (Fall 1992): 147-79. Also see her "Threat Based Strategies of Conflict Management: Why Did They Fail in the Gulf?" in Stanley Renshon, ed., *The Political Psychology of the Gulf War,* (Pittsburgh: University of Pittsburgh Press, 1993), 121-53.

    For a general overview of Saddam Hussein's activities from the perspective of an opponent, see Samir al-Khalil, *The Republic of Fear: The Inside Story of Saddam's Iraq* (New York: Pantheon, 1989).

6. Stein, "Deterrence and Compellence," notes that King Hussein of Jordan believed Saddam to be embittered because leaders in the Gulf seemed indifferent to Iraq's sacrifice of blood and treasure to protect the Arab Gulf against the Persian enemy.

7. Richard Haass, "How Saddam Survives: After Years of Conflict, We still Misread Him," *Washington Post Outlook: Commentary and Opinion,* 8 September 1996, sec. C, 1-2.

8. Bruce Jentleson, *With Friends Like These: Reagan, Bush, and Saddam, 1982-1990* (New York: W. W. Norton, 1994), 41.

9. Saddam Hussein sees himself as a modern-day Nebuchadnezzar, the Babylonian conqueror of Jerusalem during the sixth century B.C.

10. With respect to Sir Percy Cox's role in drawing the borders of Iraq, see Emory Bogle, *The Modern Middle East: From Imperialism to Freedom, 1800-1958,* (Upper Saddle River, NJ: Prentice Hall, 1996), 221.

11. "The foreigner entered their lands, and Western colonialism divided and established weak states ruled by families that offered him services that facilitated his mission. The colonialists, to ensure their petroleum interest . . . set up those disfigured petroleum states. Through this, they kept the wealth away from the masses of this nation." Saddam Hussein, quoted in the *New York Times,* August 11, 1990, sec. A, 6.

12. On August 28, 1990, Iraq declared Kuwait its 19th province and renamed Kuwait City al-Kadhima. Frontline, "The Gulf War," (Alexandria: Public Broadcasting Service, 1997). Available online:
    http://www.pbs.org/wgbh/pages/frontline/teach/gulfguide/
    gwtimeline.html

13. Tomahawk cruise missiles cost $1.3 million, have a payload of 1,000 pounds, have a subsonic speed of 760 miles per hour, have a range of up to 1,500 miles, can fly at low levels—100 to 300 feet—and can be fired as an antiship or as a land-attack weapon. They fly at low altitudes, have low heat emissions, and thus are difficult to detect by infrared devices or by radar. Relative to the 297 cruise missiles fired during Desert Shield/Storm, the 47 cruise missiles launched against Iraq during September 1996 had a minor effect on Iraqi military installations. For information about the attributes and performance characteristics of cruise missiles, see Norman Friedman, *Desert Victory: The War for Kuwait,* (Annapolis: Naval Institute Press, 1991),

and Thomas Keaney and Eliot Cohen, *Gulf War Air Power Survey Summary Report*, (Washington, D.C.: Office of the Secretary of the Air Force, 1993).

14. Because people see what they expect to see, the anticipation that Iraq is a threat may result in an overestimation of that threat. This pattern is an unmotivated bias that distorts threat perception.

15. Statement by Republican presidential candidate Robert Dole, Salt Lake City, Utah, Reuters, September 3, 1996.

16. The government of Turkey may have placed constraints on use of its air space for coalition-force offensive operations against Saddam's forces in northern Iraq. The Erbakan government in Ankara was concerned that the Iranian-backed Patriotic Union of Kurdistan in northern Iraq supported the Kurdish Workers Party, an anti-Turkish terrorist movement. Another Kurdish faction, the Kurdish Democratic Party, invited Saddam Hussein into northern Iraq. That group was locked in battle with the Patriotic Union of Kurdistan. The two factions vied for political control of the region and over the income from oil smuggled across the borders.

    "Nobody is happy with the situation in Kurdistan," lamented Saad Bazzaz, a former aide to Saddam Hussein who defected to Jordan. "As long as the two sides fight each other and the Iranians gain influence, nobody is happy with what is going on there. So Saddam figured this is a suitable minute to catch." Ethan Bronner (reporting from Amman, Jordan), "Iraq's Limited Move Was Carefully Timed," *Boston Globe,* September 2, 1996.

17. "Within the very core of his power base he found rot so he needed to do something as a prestige booster," said Amatzia Bar-Am, a specialist on Iraq at Israel's Haifa University. See Bronner, "Iraq's Limited Move."

    On the opportunity side, moreover, the move against the Kurds also gave Saddam an occasion to settle scores with Iraqi officers. He had sent some of his military there in 1991 to put down postwar unrest, but some of them defected to the Kurds.

18. Because of the Islamic revolution in Iran, the United States had a motivated bias to underestimate the Iraqi threat: in a search for allies against Iran, the U.S. overlooked Iraq's misdeeds in a bout of wishful thinking. That is, Washington saw what it wanted to see—an Iraq that was more a friend than it was an enemy.

19. As stated in Chapter Two on Iran, misperceptions stem from the distorting effects of biases. Politics can bias observation and thus may provide motivation to increase or decrease threat perception. Motivated biases are those that distort perceptions because individuals see what they want to see. Unmotivated biases distort perceptions because people see what they expect to see. Bureaucratic and domestic politics are sources of motivated biases affecting American decisionmakers in their overestimation of the Iraqi threat.

    For a discussion of biases and threat perception, see Robert Jervis, "Perceiving and Coping With Threat," in Robert Jervis, Richard Ned Lebow, and Janice Gross Stein, eds., *Psychology and Deterrence,* 13-24, 18-27.

20. Fairbanks, upon concluding that Baghdad had been circumventing United States export control laws, formally ended his relationship with the Iraqis.

He had been formerly associated with them since the mid-1980s. While at the State Department, Fairbanks had been in charge of administering Operation Staunch, the U.S. attempt to stop the sale of arms to Iran. Richard Straus, ed., *Middle East Policy Survey,* no. 246 (April 13, 1990).

21. The following nations appeared on the State Department list of countries that sponsor international terrorism: Cuba, Iran, Iraq, Libya, North Korea, Sudan, and Syria. Sudan is the only country on that list not included here. Department of State Office of the Coordinator for Counterterrorism, *1995 Patterns of Global Terrorism* (Washington, D.C.: April, 1996). Available online:

    http://www.usis.usemb.se/terror/rpt1995/TERSST.HTM#Iraq

22. The failed Prevention of Genocide Act of 1988 would have prohibited American imports of Iraqi oil, dual-use technology exports to Iraq, and credits to Baghdad from the Commodity Credit Corporation and the Export-Import Bank. The senior middle east analyst at AIPAC confirmed that the organization did not work as hard against Iraq in the 1980s as it worked against Iran in the mid-1990s. Keith Weissman, Senior Middle East Analyst, American-Israel Public Affairs Committee, telephone interview by Raymond Tanter, January 10, 1997, Ann Arbor, MI.

23. The U.S. policy of containing both Iran and Iraq—dual containment—began officially with the Clinton Administration. AIPAC, however, had opposed both countries without the imprimatur of the concept of dual containment.

24. Albert Wohlstetter, *Interests and Power in the Persian Gulf* (Los Angeles: Pan Heuristics, 1980).

25. Albert Wohlstetter, personal interview by Raymond Tanter, July 31, 1980, Washington, D.C. See also Robert Bartley, "A Wohlstetter Life," *Wall Street Journal,* January 13, 1997, sec. A, 16, regarding the impact of his work on strategic thinking in general, as well as with respect to the Gulf in particular.

26. Office of the Assistant Secretary of Defense, Program Analysis and Evaluation, *Capabilities for Limited Contingencies in the Persian Gulf* (Washington, D.C.: Unpublished Paper, June 1979).

27. In connection with deterring attacks on oil facilities, topics debated in the Pentagon included oil facility vulnerability to air attack, threat to oil sea-lines of communications outside the Gulf, and mining of the Strait of Hormuz. Regarding lesser Gulf contingencies, analysts considered local wars as well as superpower and third country interventions. Finally, concerning an invasion of Iran by Soviet or a combination of Soviet and Iraqi forces, analysts discussed the ground and air military balance, effect of deployments by the United States in a simulated NATO buildup, as well as American-Iranian versus Soviet resupply capabilities.

    Note that as of June 1979, the assumption was that Iraq would be on the Soviet side and Iran on the American side. Also, the study assumed Iranian cooperation with the United States in the defense of Iran.

28. Howard Teicher and Gayle Radley Teicher, *Twin Pillars to Desert Storm* (New York: William Morrow, 1993), 61. In addition to Brzezinski, Teicher asserts that Richard Haass, who became President Bush's top Middle East official on

the National Security Council staff, also favored a tilt toward Iraq policy. Howard Teicher and Oliver North replaced me on the National Security Council staff in September 1982.

29. Alternatives to meeting the threat to the Gulf on its own terms were to reduce the American need for imported oil, create a regional security pact, as well as threaten to escalate or expand prospective fighting outside of the Gulf. Wohlstetter rejected all of these alternatives. With respect to a reduction in the American dependence on Gulf oil, even if this were possible, Europe would remain dependent and thus subject to Soviet-Iraqi coercion. In connection with a regional security organization, instabilities were too great and Soviet power too strong for a regional security system to be effective. Regarding escalation, moreover, threatening to go nuclear in light of a Soviet-Iraqi attack on Iran would not be a credible response. And a threat to expand a Gulf War, for example, to the northern flank of NATO, would frighten allies like Norway even more than it would deter a Soviet invasion of Iran. Wohlstetter, personal interview by Raymond Tanter, July 31, 1980, Washington, D.C.

30. On December 12, 1981, the USSR made a move against Solidarity by ordering the government of Poland to launch a crackdown.

31. Following Iranian-inspired riots at Mecca in Saudi Arabia on November 20, 1979, Riyadh moved closer to Baghdad. The Saudis defended their approach to Iraq because of a felt need to balance the growing threat from Iran.

32. As momentous a decision as it was to remove Iraq from the list of states that supported international terrorism, there was little evidence of interagency consideration of the pros and cons for doing so. As a member of the National Security Council staff, I had access to classified information about such a decision, but in the case of Baghdad, I could not locate the origins of the decision to remove Iraq nor the paper trail that justified removal.

33. In the 1990s, the State Department divided the Bureau of Near Eastern and South Asian Affairs into two units: the Bureau of Near Eastern Affairs (NEA) and the Bureau of South Asian Affairs (SA).

34. Representative Henry Gonzalez (Dem.-New Mexico), reprinted part of NSD 26 in the *Congressional Record* for July 7, 1992: H6012.

35. Steven Spiegel, *The Other Arab-Israeli Conflict* (Chicago: University of Chicago Press, 1985), 5, 16 ff.

36. One of the assistant secretaries for International Security Affairs under Reagan, Bing West, was adamantly in favor of accommodation with Iraq. A successor, Richard Armitage, however, may have been less inclined to support accommodation.

Officials within the Carter Pentagon also debated whether to tilt toward Iraq. Howard Teicher wrote a paper on Iraq in 1979, as a young analyst in the Office of the Assistant Security of Defense, International Security Affairs. Because this paper opposed the dominant mindset that favored accommodation with Iraq, it was a nonstarter at the Department of Defense and had virtually no impact within the national security bureaucracy. And by March 1984, even Teicher had come around to the view that the United States "had no choice but to work with Iraq in the short term to protect America's vital interests in the Gulf." (Teicher and Teicher, *Twin Pillars to Desert Storm,* 59-71, 303-4.) In November 1984, there was a normalization of relations between Washington and Baghdad.

37. Richard Perle, American Enterprise Institute, telephone interview by Raymond Tanter, January 27, 1997, Ann Arbor, MI. During 1983-1984, Perle and I were colleagues. As personal representative of the Secretary of Defense to arms control and security talks in Vienna, Helsinki, Stockholm, and Madrid, I reported to the secretary via Under Secretary of Defense/Policy, Fred Ikle. The assistant secretaries for International Security Affairs and for International Security Policy were line officials under the authority of Ikle.

38. Michael Klare, *Rogue States and Nuclear Outlaws* (New York: Hill and Wang, 1995), 37.

39. Civilians at the White House and at the State Department had a motivated bias to perceive Iraq as a potential ally. Military officials at the Pentagon had a motivated bias to perceive Iraq as an adversary. In terms of threat perception, the Pentagon tended to overestimate the Iraqi threat, while the White House and State Department tended to underestimate it.

40. Tensions between Cairo and Baghdad reflect the traditional conflict between leaders of the Nile Valley and those from Mesopotamia—ancient Iraq—over the Fertile Crescent, including Greater Syria. This area includes present-day Lebanon and Syria as well as ancient Palestine.

41. Within the Reagan Administration, Robert McFarlane was one of the officials who was reluctant to give up on Iran, even though Tehran had seized American citizens and held them as hostages. He wrote during 1982, in his first memo to the president as national security advisor, "Our position on the Iran-Iraq War is also extremely sensitive. . . . I do not think we should undertake actions which could be seen as a clear tilt toward Iraq, unless Iraq is on the losing end of the fight. As hostile as the current government of Iran is, that country remains a strategically decisive one; we do not therefore want to burn all of our bridges, particularly to those elements which will be of interest to United States in any post-Khomeni succession struggle." Robert McFarlane, *Special Trust* (New York: Cadell & Davis, 1994), 310-11. This memo gave birth to the idea that Iran was of such importance to the United States that it would be worthwhile to seek an opening to Tehran, even using the secret sale of American arms to effect such an opening.

42. While the same threatened interests may have both intrinsic and strategic aspects, the analysis here treats them as analytically distinct. For a further discussion of intrinsic interests and strategic interests, see Stein, "The View From Cairo," in Jervis, Lebow, and Stein, eds., *Psychology and Deterrence,* 38-9.

43. It is irrelevant that Iraq has a diminished capacity to threaten intrinsic and strategic interests. What matters is the image of the enemy held by American leaders. After the invasion of Kuwait, occupants of the Oval Office perceived Iraq as an "evil" nation. This perception constitutes an unmotivated bias that associates Baghdad with malice, irrespective of its behavior at a given time. Because of the invasion, American presidents perceive Iraq's conduct as malicious, without evaluating that behavior on its own merits.

44. John Deutch, Director of Central Intelligence, "Worldwide Threat Assessment Brief to the Senate Select Committee on Intelligence," (Washington, D.C.: Public Affairs Staff, Central Intelligence Agency, February 22, 1996), 3. Available online:

    http://www.odci.gov/cia/public_affairs/speeches/archives/1996/
    dci_speech_022296.html

45. Department of State Office of the Coordinator for Counterterrorism, *1993 Patterns of Global Terrorism* (Washington, D.C.: April, 1994). The following states appeared on the State Department terrorist list for 1995: Cuba, Iran, Iraq, Libya, North Korea, Sudan, and Syria. Sudan is the only country on that list not included in *Rogue Regimes*.

46. Baghdad continued its war of attrition on UN and humanitarian targets in northern Iraq aimed at driving the foreign presence out of the area and depriving the Kurdish population of relief supplies. Baghdad ordered the assault of UN and relief workers. Iraqi agents threw bombs and grenades at civilian residences and vehicles; and they placed bombs on UN trucks loaded with relief supplies. During September 1993, agents of Baghdad destroyed a UN truck carrying twelve tons of medical supplies with a bomb attached to the fuel tank. The explosion injured the truck driver and twelve civilians.

47. "Iraq continues to provide haven and training facilities for several terrorist clients. Abu Abbas' Palestine Liberation Front (PLF) maintains its headquarters in Baghdad. The Abu Nidal organization (ANO) continues to have an office in Baghdad. The Arab Liberation Front (ALF), headquartered in Baghdad, continues to receive funding from Saddam's regime. Iraq also continues to host the former head of the now-defunct 15 May organization, Abu Ibrahim, who masterminded several bombings of U.S. aircraft. A terrorist group opposed to the current Iranian regime, the Mojahedin-e Khalq (MEK), still is based in Iraq and has carried out several violent attacks in Iran from bases in Iraq." Department of State, *1995 Patterns of Global Terrorism*. Available online:

    http://www.usis.usemb.se/terror/rpt1995/TERSST.HTM#Iraq

48. UN Security Council Resolution 687 of April 3, 1991 requires destruction or dismantlement of Iraq's weapons of mass destruction. The Security Council decided to authorize the destruction, removal, or rendering harmless all chemical and biological weapons, stocks of agents, related subsystems and components in Iraq. Also to be destroyed or dismantled were all ballistic missiles with a range greater than 150 kilometers and related major parts, and repair and production facilities. Furthermore, the Council decided to prohibit Iraq from acquiring or developing nuclear weapons, nuclear-weapons-usable material, any subsystems or components. Finally, the Council banned Iraq from conducting research on weapons of mass destruction. United Nations Security Council Resolution 687, available online:

    http://www3.sympatico.ca/aal/private/un/UN-0687.txt

49. United Nations Security Council Resolution 686, March 2, 1991, available online:

    `http://www3.sympatico.ca/aal/private/un/UN-0686.txt`

50. Deutch, "Worldwide Threat," 3.

51. Air power advocates wanted coalition forces to strike deep into Iraq to destroy the command and control structure of Saddam's war machine, as well as infrastructure and air-defense networks. In addition to attacks on Iraq, air war proponents anticipated the following results with respect to Kuwait: Iraq's army in Kuwait might be effectively destroyed; the reoccupation of Kuwait would be met with minimal resistance; U.S. ground forces could be held in reserve as a "cocked fist." And there might be the "near certain" achievement of the American objective to liberate Kuwait with minimal casualties. Colonel John Warden (U.S. Air Force), classified briefing to Defense Secretary Richard Cheney on the expected results of the air campaign against Iraqi forces, December 11, 1990. See Michael Gordon and Bernard Trainor, *The Generals' War: The Inside Story of the Conflict in the Gulf* (Boston: Little, Brown, 1995), 178.

52. In contrast to the air war advocates, Powell stressed the need for air power in conjunction with a ground force buildup. He held that an air war alone would leave the initiative to Saddam Hussein, which conflicted with basic army doctrine of taking and holding the initiative. To give the coalition time to deploy its forces, Powell favored a strategy of sanctions against Iraq. See Bob Woodward, *The Commanders* (New York: Simon & Schuster, 1991), 342-43.

    In Powell's own words, "Many experts, amateurs and others in this town believe that [the defeat of the Iraqi army in Kuwait] can be accomplished by such things as surgical air strikes or perhaps a sustained air strike. . . . Such strategies are designed to hope to win, they are not designed to win." General Colin Powell, testimony before the Senate Armed Services Committee, December 3, 1990. U.S. Senate. Committee on Armed Services. *Crisis in the Persian Gulf Region: U.S. Policy Options and Implications* Hearing, December 3, 1990. Available online:

    `http://web.lexis-nexis.com/cis/retrieve/document/s_witness.`
    `html?_form=s_witness.html&_mode=FULL&_results=G{H^*KO!WA]`
    `!UUB$M[SWA]$UUZ$AV!ZZUW!AZ!ABA$AA$]DU]AWUWV$U&_library=`
    `LEGIS&_file=CISINX&_firstdoc=1&_reldoc=3&_citesper=25&`
    `_maxdocs=11&_md5=2097e593dd15aff00d6ad0e0fab5b99c`

    See also Harry Summers, Jr., *On Strategy II: A Critical Analysis of the Gulf War* (New York: Bantam Doubleday Dell, 1992), 192-93.

53. Caspar Weinberger, *Fighting for Peace* (New York: Warner, 1990), 442. Powell called Weinberger's rules "a practical guide." Colin Powell, *My American Journey* (New York: Random House, 1995), 303.

54. Powell, *My American Journey*, 480. Backing up General Powell's version of history is Secretary of State James Baker. In his memoirs, Secretary Baker recalls an October 1990 meeting with Chairman Powell. It produced a consensus both in favor of a more aggressive military policy and a diplomatic approach that included sanctions. The goal was to drive the Iraqi

armed forces out of Kuwait. Secretary Baker supports General Powell's emphasis on combining force and diplomacy, as opposed to being a sanctions-only advocate. James Baker, *The Politics of Diplomacy: Revolution, War and Peace, 1989-1992* (New York: G.P. Putnam Sons, 1995), 277, 301-302.

55. Chapter Two discusses dual containment, balance of power, and differentiated containment. See Zbigniew Brzezinski, Brent Scowcroft, and Richard Murphy, "Differentiated Containment," *Foreign Affairs* 76, no. 3 (May/June 1997): 20-30. In addition to these three authors, another critic of dual containment is Richard Haass. He said, "The policy of 'dual containment' of Iraq and Iran gave us a slogan when what we needed was a strategy and sustained efforts to implement it." See Richard Haass, "The United States and Iraq: A Strategy for the Long Haul," *Policy Brief*, no. 7 (1996). Available online:

http://www.brook.edu/fp/polbrief/polbrf7.htm

56. Bahrain, Kuwait, Oman, the United Arab Emirates, Saudi Arabia, and Qatar make up the six-member Gulf Cooperation Council (GCC). This section on threat perceptions draws on the research of Phebe Marr. See Marr, "Differing Threat Perceptions," *U.S.-GCC Security Relations* I, no. 39 (August 1995). Available online:

http://www.ndu.edu/ndu/inss/strforum/forum39.html

See also Marr, *The Modern History of Iraq* (Boulder: Westview, 1985).

57. "Most GCC states see Iran, not Iraq, as the long-term threat (a position closer to that of the United States), and do not want Iraq weakened as a balance against Iran (a position more at variance with the United States). This position is particularly strong at the foot of the Gulf, where the UAE and Oman worry about the long-term intentions of Iran." Marr, "Differing Threat Perceptions."

58. But even if there were American diplomatic moves in the direction of a relaxation of tensions with Iraq, Washington needs to remain on guard as long as Saddam is in power and Baghdad retains its military capabilities. "If Iraq continues to be a threat—and there is every indication that it will be—the . . . [United States] needs to maintain a robust force posture in the Gulf for the foreseeable future." Marr, "Differing Threat Perceptions."

59. With respect to the scenario of a resumption of a Kurdish civil war, Richard Haass states, "Saddam is a serial prober; at some point he will turn on his new Kurdish friends, in the process triggering a large flow of refugees in the direction of the Turkish border." Haass, "The United States and Iraq: A Strategy for the Long Haul."

60. In the Gulf War, there was tacit cooperation between Tehran and Baghdad, although Iran remained officially neutral. Iran provided a "parking lot" for over 100 Iraqi combat aircraft that were about to be destroyed by coalition air strikes. Tehran, however, never returned the warplanes. And following the Gulf War, Iran assisted Shiite rebels in southern Iraq against the regime in Baghdad, which implied tacit cooperation between Tehran and Washington.

61. Another contingency that would suggest tacit alignment between Baghdad and Washington concerns the Arab-Israel zone: Tehran sends increased shipments of arms to Hezbollah in Lebanon and provokes hostilities between Hezbollah and Israel as well as a resumption of fighting between Israel and Syria along the Golan Heights.

62. Daniel Diller, ed., *The Middle East* (Washington, D.C.: Congressional Quarterly, 1991), 392.

63. The Gulf states lie along the Arabian shore of the Gulf. They include Bahrain, Kuwait, and Qatar, as well as the seven former Trucial States of Abu Dhabi, Ajman, Dubayy, Al Fujayrah, R'as al Khaymah, Ash Shariqah, and Umm al Qaywayn, which constitute the United Arab Emirates.

64. Richard Straus, "Outlook," *Middle East Policy Survey* (Washington, D.C., 16 December 1997): 2.

65. UN Security Resolution 986 of April 14, 1995, authorizes states to permit the import of petroleum and petroleum products originating in Iraq. This resolution is an exception to the sanctions levied on Iraq by the United Nations for the invasion of Kuwait in 1990. The purpose of permitting the exception is to allow Iraq to import medicine, health supplies, foodstuffs, and materials for essential civilian needs. Iraq may sell up to $1 billion worth of oil every 90 days. United Nations Security Council Resolution 986, available online:

    http://www3.sympatico.ca/aal/private/un/UN-0986.txt

Chapter Four

1. The President signed the Iran and Libya Sanctions Act of 1996 on August 5. It passed the House by 415 to zero and the senate by voice vote. Available online:

    http://thomas.loc.gov/cgi-bin/bdquery/L?d104:./list/bd/
    d104sh.1st:493

2. In contrast to accommodation, dual containment is an effort to isolate two countries at the same time; for example, Iran and Iraq.

3. Chapter Two discusses dual containment, balance of power, and differentiated containment. See Zbigniew Brzezinski, Brent Scowcroft, and Richard Murphy, "Differentiated Containment," *Foreign Affairs* 76, no. 3 (May/June 1997): 20-30.

4. Ariel Sharon, speech prepared for a conference at the Institute for Strategic Studies, Tel Aviv University, December 14, 1981, in *Foreign Broadcast Information Service,* (December 18, 1981). See also Raymond Tanter, *Who's at the Helm? Lessons of Lebanon* (Boulder: Westview Press, 1990), 56-58.

5. Ariel Sharon, December 14, 1981, in *Foreign Broadcast Information Service,* (18 December 1981).

6. Sadat was worried that Qadhafi was attempting to develop a nuclear weapons capability. During the summer of 1981, an American diplomatic envoy, Robert McFarlane, assured Sadat that the Reagan Administration stood by its promise to prevent Qadhafi and the Soviets from gaining further

advantages in the Middle East. Howard Teicher and Gayle Teicher, *Twin Pillars to Desert Storm* (New York: William Morrow, 1993), 137-39.

7. Richard Straus, "After the AWACS—Constructing a Middle East Policy with Limited Resources," *Middle East Policy Survey*, no. 42 (October 23, 1981).

8. For a general discussion of political coalitions within the Arab world, see Malcolm Kerr, *The Arab Cold War: Gamal Abd al-Nasir and His rivals, 1958-1970*, 3d ed. (London: Oxford University Press, 1971).

9. Ilich Ramirez Sanchez, commonly known as "Carlos the Jackal," is one of the best known "revolutionary terrorists." He reportedly has worked under contract for Qadhafi of Libya, Saddam Hussein of Iraq, Assad of Syria, and Fidel Castro of Cuba. "Perhaps the only international terrorist of greater repute is Abu Nidal (Sabri Banna)." On October 10, 1994, the government of the Sudan arrested Carlos and handed him over to French authorities.

    Amal or the "Shi'ite Movement of Hope," an organization based in Lebanon, serves as the Shi'ite voice within the Arab world. Clark Staten, "Carlos Captured; Revolutionary Terrorist," *Emergency Net News Service*, October 10, 1994. Available online:

    http://205.243.133.2/carlos-j.htm

10. While the same threatened interests may have both intrinsic and strategic aspects, the analysis here treats them as analytically distinct.

11. Security Council Resolution 731 is available online:
    gopher://gopher.undp.org:70/00/undocs/scd/scouncil/s92/6

12. Security Council Resolution 748 is available online:
    gopher://gopher.undp.org:70/00/undocs/scd/scouncil/s92/23

13. Security Council Resolution 883 is available online:
    gopher://gopher.undp.org:70/00/undocs/scd/scouncil/s93/883

14. Department of State, Office of the Coordinator for Counterterrorism, *1995 Patterns of Global Terrorism* (Washington, D.C.: April, 1996). Available online:

    http://www.usis.usemb.se/terror/rpt1995/TERSST.HTM#Libya

15. Department of State, *1995 Patterns of Global Terrorism*.

16. Regarding the plant at Rabta see Associated Press, "Perry: U.S. Won't allow Libya Chemical Weapons Plant to be Built," Ismailiya, Egypt (April 3, 1996). With respect to the use of chemical weapons by Iran and Iraq in their 1980-1988 war see Anthony Cordesman, *The Iran-Iraq War and Western Security 1984-87: Strategic Implications and Policy Options* (London: Jane's, 1987). And in connection with Baghdad's use of poison gas against its own citizens the Department of State reported, " . . . a number of Iraqi oppositionists in northern Iraq were poisoned by thallium." *1995 Patterns of Global Terrorism*. Available online:

    http://www.usis.usemb.se/terror/rpt1995/TERSST.HTM#Iraq

17. Barbara Balaj, "Germany and Libya," in "The Federal Republic of Germany and the Middle East" (Ph.D. dissertation, George Washington University, 1997), 59 ff.

18. The Geneva Protocol of 1925 banned the use in war of asphyxiating, poisonous, or other gases and of bacteriological methods of warfare. See *Major International Instruments on Disarmament and Related Issues*,

"Protocol for the Prohibition of the Use in War of Asphyxiating, Poisonous or Other Gases, and of Bacteriological Methods of Warfare," June 17, 1925. Available online:

http://www.unog.ch/frames/disarm/distreat/warfare.htm

19. Thomas Wiegele, *The Clandestine Building of Libya's Chemical Weapons Factory* (Carbondale: Southern Illinois University Press, 1992), 28.

20. "Journalists' Visit to Libyan Plant Leaves Its Purpose Unclear," *Washington Post,* January 8, 1989, sec. A, 24.

21. In March of 1990, a fire supposedly decimated the Rabta facility. According to *TIME* magazine, the CIA later reported that the fire was a strategic "hoax" to ward off U.S. attack. "In 1990 Gadaffi shut down the Rabta plant after Washington threatened to attack it with warplanes and publicly identified European companies that had provided equipment. But U.S. satellites soon discovered that Rabta's equipment had been moved and stored in underground bunkers a mile away." Douglas Waller, "Target Gaddafi, Again," *TIME,* April 1, 1996.

22. One senior Defense Department official told the *Middle East Policy Survey* in 1981 that the United States was "taking new initiatives" regarding Libya. Other well-informed officials said that the Joint Chiefs of Staff repeatedly vetoed civilian suggestions to conduct military planning against Qadhafi on the grounds of "insufficient resources." Therefore, while there was agreement between State and Defense on the need to "get tough" with Qadhafi, there was no consensus on what practical measures could be taken. In this regard, consider the president's public rejection of an economic boycott of Libya. One unhappy U.S. official commented that a boycott would be "bad for business." The rejection forced State Department officials to come up with alternative plans, including repatriation of U.S. citizens in Libya. Richard Straus, ed., "After the AWACS," *Middle East Policy Survey.*

23. Secretary of State Alexander Haig received hard-line recommendations about Libya from the Policy Planning Staff (S/P) and the Bureau of Politico-Military Affairs, State's "functional" bureaus. (In the 1990s, the Department changed the name of PM to Political-Military Affairs.) S/P and PM called for additional measures to demonstrate the seriousness and consistency of U.S. policy. The State Department's Near Eastern and European bureaus opposed the hard line of maximum economic sanctions. The European bureau was particularly adamant. It argued that imposing sanctions on Libya would have exacerbated relations with European countries during the Polish crisis and after Qadhafi's decision to withdraw his troops from Chad. Richard Straus, ed., *Middle East Policy Survey,* no. 49 (February 12, 1982).

24. Washington had demanded that Tripoli refrain from conducting subversive operations in neighboring countries and cease its state sponsorship of international terrorism. Verbal assurances that Libya had ceased its operations were welcome but unnecessary. United States intelligence had its own ways of knowing when Libyan operations had terminated. Reportedly, American intelligence could intercept Libyan military communications.

25. Expressing uncertainty over U.S. policy objectives and impatience with the administration's year-long debate over Libya, one Arab diplomat summed

up a lot of Washington thinking: "If you're going to do something, do it, don't just talk about it." "The Next Move Against Libya," *Middle East Policy Survey,* no. 49 (February 12, 1982).

Other press commentary was also critical of the delay. "After months of well-publicized indecision, President Reagan has resolved to stop American oil trade with Libya," in "A Mere Gesture Again," *New York Times,* March 7, 1982, editorial page.

26. Personal recollection of author from service as one of the action officers for Libya at the White House, 1981-1982.

27. To illustrate bureaucracy in action, consider the way some meetings occur. I asked the secretary to Acting National Security Advisor Nance to call a meeting in the White House Situation Room on Libya. "Who asked for this meeting?" she replied. I said, "Bud McFarlane at State asked Geoffrey Kemp in my office at the National Security Council staff to ask Paul Wolfowitz at State to ask me to ask Bud Nance at the White House!" She replied, "OK." Outside the beltway of bureaucracy in Washington, such statements are meaningless. But within, they indicate the cover-your-flank mentality of bureaucrats who desire to share the risk of responsibility.

28. In a meeting I attended on December 30, 1981 with White House Counsel Edwin Meese, Secretary of Defense Caspar Weinberger recommended the beginning of more stringent measures against Libya, such as a total trade embargo. He felt that the withdrawal of American citizens was a prudent step but was of marginal economic significance.

29. On March 25, 1982, the departments of Defense and Commerce came out in favor of applying export controls to prevent a French firm from exporting General Electric rotors to the USSR. There was a contract between General Electric and Alsthom Alantique that New York law governed. The contract required that Alsthom comply with all future export control regulations. This type of restriction is common for licenses from American firms to foreign manufacturers. In accepting the restriction, the French firm was aware that sales to the USSR were subject to future prohibition.

30. Legal authorities for potential action against Libya included the Trade Expansion Act (Section 232b), Export Administration Act, and the International Emergency Economic Powers Act, in conjunction with the National Emergency Act. Either 232b of the Trade Expansion Act or International Emergency Economic Powers Act could have been used to effect an oil embargo. The Export Administration Act could have been employed to effect a broad but not total ban on exports to Libya. Only IEEPA, however, could have been used for a total export embargo or transaction controls, including those to bring about a withdrawal of American citizens. There was a constitutional issue raised by restriction on travel implicit in an order for mandatory withdrawal of American citizens. But if the withdrawal were ordered under IEEPA in conjunction with other mandated measures taken under the act, that action would have blurred the constitutional issue.

31. Under the Export Administration Act, Commerce has responsibility with the Department of State to report on export controls, which terminate annually in December. The Export Administration Act has a list of controls.

Libya was on the State Department's list of state sponsors of international terrorism, while State had removed Iraq. The Department determined that Iraq's improved record warranted removal, but the real reason was to justify the transfer of dual-use equipment to Iraq in its war against Iran. See Chapter Three on Iraq.

32. Some State Department insiders warned that a decision by the administration might not have been imminent. They pointed out that following the "disappearance" of the "hit team," President Reagan might have been reluctant to approve further sanctions without further provocation from Libya. "The Next Move Against Libya," *Middle East Policy Survey.*

33. On the bureaucratic politics of arms control in the Reagan Administration, see Strobe Talbott, *Deadly Gambits: The Reagan Administration and the Stalemate in Nuclear Arms Control* (New York: Vintage, 1984). For bureaucratic warfare on Middle East policy making, see Tanter, *Who's at the Helm?*

34. For a general overview of the Wilson case see Joseph Goulden with Alexander Raffio, *The Death Merchant: The Rise and Fall of Edwin P. Wilson* (New York: Simon & Schuster, 1984).

35. Saudi Arabia launched an investigation with the assistance of the FBI to discover whether its own dissidents or foreign powers, such as Iran and Syria, were responsible for a bombing of the Saudi National Guard installation in Riyadh, on November 13, 1995. There was also an attack on June 25, 1996, of an air facility in Dhahran that the Gulf War coalition air forces used for monitoring Iraq's compliance with the terms of the cease-fire. Those assaults were the first political attacks against the American military in Saudi Arabia. The Kingdom convicted four dissidents and beheaded them for the 1995 bombing. One motive for a subsequent assault on the Dhahran air base was to avenge this beheading. The CIA helped train some of the Saudi dissidents in order to fight in the Afghanistan war against the Soviets, and they had also fought alongside Bosnia's Muslim-led army against Bosnian Serbs.

36. *The Nation* (February 6, 1989): 153-54.

37. Personal recollection of author from service as one of the action officers for Libya at the White House, 1981-1982.

38. Personal recollection of author from service as one of the action officers for Libya at the White House, 1981-1982.

39. Working with the Dominican Republic, CIA and FBI agents managed to lure Wilson out of Zurich, Switzerland. Arriving at Santo Domingo, Dominican officials declared Wilson's travel papers to be faulty and compelled him to board an aircraft for New York. FBI agents arrested him after he deplaned. Goulden with Raffio, *The Death Merchant,* 382-91.

40. David Johnston, "Reno Says Saudis Did Not Cooperate in Bombing Inquiry," *New York Times,* January 24, 1997, A1, A6.

41. One Administration critic of an oil embargo caustically asked, "Consistency of U.S. policy? What is consistent about lifting the grain embargo when the Soviet Union is still in Afghanistan and imposing an oil embargo on Libya when it is getting out of Chad?" The implicit assumption behind the query

was that the Reagan Administration was not consistent in its handling of similar cases. "The Next Move Against Libya," *Middle East Policy Survey.*

42. Department of Treasury, Office of Foreign Assets Control, "Libya." Available online:

    `http://www.ustreas.gov/treasury/services/fac/fac.html`

43. "In 1985 Abu Nidal, a terrorist leader who had defected from the mainstream of the PLO, moved his base of operations from Syria to Libya. In December 1985 members of his group attacked the check-in counters of El Al airlines at the Rome and Vienna airports with automatic weapons and hand grenades . . . On January 7, 1986, Reagan announced that there was 'irrefutable evidence' that Libya had sponsored the Palestinian terrorists . . . He ended all economic activity between the United States and Libya and ordered all American citizens to leave Libya." Daniel Diller, ed., *The Middle East* (Washington, D.C.: Congressional Quarterly, 1991), 82.

44. Gideon Rose, "Sanctions Against Libya," Unpublished Paper prepared for the Council on Foreign Relations (January 1997), 23.

45. Suleiman Bengharsa, "Sanctions in the Middle East: The Libya Case," Unpublished Paper prepared for the conference on Sanctions and the Middle East: Political Rationale and Economic Impact, cosponsored by the Middle East Institute and the Petroleum Industry Research Foundation (April 22, 1996), 2.

46. Bengharsa, "Sanctions in the Middle East," 3.

47. "Libya: Life in Qadhafi's Shadow," *EIU Business Middle East,* October 1, 1994, as quoted in Rose, "Sanctions Against Libya," 31.

48. George Gedda, "US May Tighten Sudan Sanctions," Associated Press, February 17, 1997.

49. Gedda, "US May Tighten Sudan Sanctions."

50. Associated Press, "White House Blasts Trip by Farrakhan As 'Thugfest,'" February 27, 1996. Available online: http//www.sltrib.com/96/FEB/27/twr/02314317 htm

    Acknowledgements to Brandi Weaver for her assistance in locating the above citation. See "Libya, the United States, and Louis Farrakhan," Unpublished Paper prepared for Political Science 472, the University of Michigan (Fall, 1996). The Weaver paper is available online:

    `http://www-personal.umich.edu/~rtanter/`

51. Associated Press, "White House Blasts Trip by Farrakhan As 'Thugfest.'"

52. Additionally, the State Department's spokesperson Glyn Davies said, "We don't view Muammar Qadhafi as somebody who is trustworthy and we can deal with. That is why many years ago an embargo was enacted against Libya. The most egregious example of Qadhafi's support for terrorism, of course, was the bombing of Pan Am 103." U.S. State Department Directory, Office of the Spokesman, daily press briefing, Wednesday, August 28, 1996. Available online:

    `gopher://dosfan.lib.uic.edu/`

53. Associated Press, "White House Blasts Trip by Farrakhan As 'Thugfest.'"

54. Associated Press, "White House Blasts Trip by Farrakhan As 'Thugfest.'"

55. Tommy Baer, "The Farrakhan Divide," *B'nai B'rith News,* April 4, 1995. Available online:

    http://bnaibrith.org/pr/farrakha.html

56. "We are not content to hear from present Iranian officials words without deeds, rather they must fulfill their non-negotiable commitments at the forefront of which are the release of Iraqi POW's and the return of Iraqi possessions including civilian and military aircraft which were transferred to Iran with their approval before and during the glorious Um Al-Ma'rik (The Mother of All Battles) and entrusted with them." Saddam Hussein, "President Saddam Hussein's [1997] Speech on the 9th Anniversary of (The Great Victory Day) marking the end of the war with Iran." Available online: http://southmovement.alphalink.com.au/countries/Iraq/victory1.htm

57. Institute for National Strategic Studies, *Strategic Assessments 1996: Elements of U.S. Power,* "Limited Military Intervention," (Washington, D.C.: National Defense University, 1996). Available online:

    http://www.ndu.edu/ndu/inss/sa96/sa96ch13.html

58. Teicher and Teicher, *Twin Pillars to Desert Storm,* 347.

59. Edward Wakin contends that Qadhafi is sidelined in Arab-Israel relations, and that he is not even a significant player. Edward Wakin, *Contemporary Political Leaders of the Middle East* (New York: Facts on File, 1996).

60. Teicher and Teicher, 340-47.

61. Teicher and Teicher, 340-47.

62. Associated Press, "Perry: U.S. Won't Allow Libya Chemical Weapons Plant to be Built," Ismailiya, Egypt, April 3, 1996.

63. In contrast to the case studies of Iran, Iraq, Syria, Cuba, and North Korea, the Libya chapter contains only one scenario—renewed military activity. Happy ending or muddling through scenarios are highly unlikely, given the incentives on each side for limited military activity.

Chapter Five

1. Syria is very much a unitary actor. Despite the existence of some institutions that mirror those of a democratic government, its political system places almost absolute authority in the hands of President Hafez al-Assad and a small group of national security advisors. Assad makes the primary decisions on foreign policy, national defense, and the economy. The Syrian legislature is a parliament in name only. It does not initiate laws but only passes judgment on legislation proposed by the executive branch. See Daniel Diller, ed., *The Middle East* (Washington, D.C.: Congressional Quarterly, 1991), 352.

2. Greater Syria includes Syria, Jordan, Lebanon, Israel, the West Bank, the Gaza Strip, and a portion of Turkey.

3. Thanks to John Post, Steve Hessler, and Anna Vania Song for research on the personality of President Hafez al-Assad.

4. "Like any one-man dictatorship, Syria is dominated by its ruler. President Assad unilaterally issues the country's laws and makes most of the life-and-

death decisions affecting the . . . Syrians he rules." Daniel Pipes, "Is Damascus Ready for Peace?" *Foreign Affairs* 70, no. 4 (Fall 1991): 36.

5. Some 90 percent of Syria's population of almost 15 million are Muslim. Of these, about 74 percent are Sunni Muslim, and the remaining 16 percent are Alawite, Shiite, Druze, and other sects. Assad, as well as the majority of his ruling military and political apparatus, are from the minority Alawites sect. Central Intelligence Agency, *World Factbook 1993* (Washington, D.C.: U.S. Government Printing Office, 1994.) The Alawites are an offshoot of Shiite Islam, in contrast to the orthodox Sunni Muslim sect, which constitutes the majority of the Arab world.

6. Pipes, "Is Damascus Ready for Peace?"

7. "Economically Syria has been stalled for years in the grip of socialism, cronyism, and huge military expenditures. Inept policies have produced an annual inflation rate of some 50 percent, a grossly overvalued Syrian lira and debts of some $6 billion to the West and $9 billion to the USSR. Although 30 percent of the work force is engaged in agriculture, grain has to be imported. Cities routinely experience electricity shortfalls, and ordinary items such as toilet paper are unavailable for long stretches of time." Pipes, "Is Damascus Ready for Peace?": 39.

8. According to Moshe Ma'oz, Assad's efforts to align with Egypt were in order to prevent an Egyptian unilateral agreement with Israel. During the October 1974 Arab summit meeting in Rabat, Assad organized Arab support to disapprove any unilateral agreements between Egypt and Israel that would exclude Israel's withdrawal from the Golan Heights. Moshe Maoz, *Assad, The Sphinx of Damascus: A Political Biography* (New York: Weidenfeld & Nicholson, 1988), 110-11.

9. Moshe Maoz, *Assad,* and Pipes, "Is Damascus Ready for Peace,": 50. See also Moshe Maoz, *Middle Eastern Politics* (New York: St. Martin's Press, 1996), and Patrick Seale, *Assad of Syria: The Struggle for the Middle East* (Berkeley: University of California Press, 1989).

10. Moshe Maoz is a professor of Middle Eastern Studies and Director of the Truman Institute for Middle Eastern studies at the Hebrew Institute of Jerusalem. See Maoz, *Assad, The Sphinx of Damascus: A Political Biography* (New York: Weldenfeld & Nicholson, 1988), *Middle Eastern Politics* (New York: St. Martin's Press, 1996), and *Syria and Israel: From War to Peacemaking* (New York: Oxford University Press, 1995).

11. Daniel Pipes is the editor of the Middle East Quarterly.

12. Some of these changes included Soviet opposition to Assad's central strategic doctrine. That is, the Soviet Union urged Assad to seek a diplomatic solution to the Arab-Israel conflict. It would "provide Syria with the means to deter Israel from attacking, but [it would] not support any Syrian attempt to launch war." Alasdair Drysdale and Raymond Hinnebusch, *Syria and the Middle East Peace Process* (New York: Council on Foreign Relations Press, 1991), 165-67. See also Judith Miller, *God Has Ninety-Nine Names* (New York: Simon & Schuster, 1996), 310-15.

13. See Moshe Maoz, *Syria and Israel: From War to Peacemaking* (New York: Oxford University Press, 1995).

14. Why would Assad be willing to take a great chance regarding his hold on power to avoid losing the Golan Heights to Israel? Prospect theory suggests an answer. It holds that individuals are risk-averse concerning gains and risk-acceptant regarding losses: they fear losses more than they desire gains and hence are more willing to take chances to avoid losses than to secure gains. Losing a million dollars is more painful than a corresponding gain is coveted. Individuals choose risky alternatives when they frame choice as avoiding losses rather than obtaining gains.

15. During the Cold War, Soviet decisionmakers were willing to run high military risks to avoid domestic political losses. Retreat would have harmed the prospects for the ruling coalition to retain power. See Dennis Ross, "Risk Aversion in Soviet Decisionmaking," in J. Valenta and William Potter, eds., *Soviet Decisionmaking for National Security* (Boston: Allen & Unwin, 1984), 237-51.

16. In the field of cognitive psychology, prospect theory defines a reference point as a threshold value above which individuals perceive gains and below which they see losses. See Jack Levy, "An Introduction to Prospect Theory," in Barbara Farnham, ed., *Avoiding Losses/Taking Risks: Prospect Theory and International Conflict* (Ann Arbor: University of Michigan Press, 1994), 7-22, and Robert Jervis, in Farnham, *op. cit.,* "Political Implications of Loss Aversion," 23-40.

    The assumption here is that Assad frames prior Syrian possession of the Golan Heights as his reference point for negotiations. Outcomes falling below that point are losses. Hence, Assad perceives the status quo—Israeli control over the Golan with the application of Israeli law there—as a severe loss. He could opt for a risky gamble that might return the situation to the former status quo, that is, undisputed Syrian sovereignty over the Golan.

    For the Pipes view of how some Arab leaders frame their problems and fears, see Daniel Pipes, *The Hidden Hand: Middle East Fears of Conspiracy* (New York: St. Martin's Press, 1996).

17. For a description of approaches to value conflict with special reference to denial of trade-offs, see Alexander George, *Presidential Decision Making in Foreign Policy* (Boulder: Westview Press, 1980), 28 ff.

18. *Hatzofeh,* January 7, 1997. *Hatzofeh* is an Israeli newspaper of the National Religious Party.

19. Prospect theory supports the Maoz approach better than the Pipes perspective, because it accounts for Assad's risk-taking behavior.

20. I served at the White House from April 1981 to September 1982 as a senior staffer with the National Security Council and reported to the Assistant to the President for National Security Affairs, Richard Allen. He went on administrative leave on November 29, 1981, and William Clark assumed his office on January 5, 1982. For an elaboration of the role of Lebanon in the battle over whether to embrace or contain Syria, see Raymond Tanter, *Who's at the Helm? Lessons of Lebanon* (Boulder: Westview Press, 1990), 73 ff.

21. During the Reagan years in the 1980s, there was a gap between arms quantity, in which Arab confrontation states came out on top, and quality, in which the balance favored Israel. Consider the significance of the July

1980 projected Arab-Israel conflict balance for 1980-1985. Since the 1973 war against Egypt and Syria, Israel had continued to increase its margin of military superiority. Hence, it could exercise a wide range of military options and was capable of decisively defeating its Arab opponents on any or all fronts. Without Egypt, the Arab confrontation states were reduced to Syria, and perhaps Jordan, with Iraq as a main source of expeditionary forces against Israel.

Personal recollection of author from having attended a meeting at the White House on November 19, 1981.

22. During the Clinton era of the 1990s, Syria had some 4,500 tanks, about 4,000 armored personnel carriers, and more than 4,000 artillery pieces. The Syrian air force had 511 combat fighter planes and approximately 120 combat helicopters. Syria had more weapons systems than did Israel in all categories of consequence. An analysis of these data makes it clear that in practice, the qualitative gap in Israel's favor held from the Reagan to Clinton administrations. Most of the Syrian military equipment was relatively outdated. Since the Gulf War, the Israel Defense Forces had invested more than $10 billion in equipment and absorbed advanced American tanks and combat helicopters.

Additionally, Syria invested about $2 billion in military procurement. The weapons systems that the Syrian military absorbed originated in the Eastern bloc. Even the more advanced Eastern bloc armaments, however, were of a lower quality than their Western counterparts. Of all of Syria's combat planes, only around 11 percent may be considered advanced (MiG-29s and Sukhoi-27s), in contrast to a larger proportion of the Israeli air force combat planes. Reuven Pedhatzur, "A New Balance of Terror," *Ha'aretz*, August 15, 1996, sec. B, 1.

23. Before 1967, Syria had harassed Israeli farmers in their Hula Valley settlements. Damascus had undermined Israel's economic development plans and attempts to divert the sources of the Jordan River. These sources were in Syrian territory. Following the 1967 war, the situation was reversed. After Israel captured the Golan Heights, the Syrians were the ones who felt threatened. Their capital, Damascus, is only about 60 kilometers from Israel's front lines, and there is little difficulty in bringing Damascus into range of Israel's artillery. Moreover, Syria perceives the presence of Israel's army in southern Lebanon as a reminder of what occurred in 1982, when Israeli forces advanced in the Beka'a Valley of Lebanon and positioned themselves so as to outflank Syrian forces protecting Damascus.

Personal recollection of author from service as one of the action officers for Syria at the White House, 1981-1982.

24. On June 12, 1969, the Israeli military governor for the Golan Heights applied Israel's military law to the area. The authority of the governor to act in 1969 derived from the Geneva Convention regarding the occupation of territory seized in fighting. In contrast to his action as a military commander of occupied territory, the July 1968 administrative order that annexed East Jerusalem to West Jerusalem was pursuant to an act of Israel's parliament—

the Knesset. Similarly, the de facto annexation of the Golan Heights was an act of the Knesset.

25. Dennis Ross was a member of the Policy Planning Staff of Secretary of State Alexander Haig during the Reagan Administration in 1981, head of that office in the Bush Administration during 1989, and President Clinton's special envoy to the Middle East. He wrote about the Assad regime while he was between tours of government service. Ross held that the regime would be constrained internationally by internal factors that would continue to absorb its attention, energy, and resources. These domestic problems were likely to limit Assad's coercive potential in the rest of the region. Moreover, Assad has demonstrated a willingness to accept tacit or indirect international constraints on his freedom of action if he believes that there is an internal danger. Dennis Ross, "Middle East Policy Planning for the Second Reagan Term," *Policy Papers*, no. 1 (Washington, D.C.: Washington Institute for Near East Policy, 1985): 10-12. The Ross paper not only reflected his awareness of domestic constraints on Assad, it also could be used as a justification for a proactive policy of initiating covert actions to destabilize Syria.

26. Irrespective of how the crisis might be used in Washington, one question was whether or not Israel had actually annexed the Golan or just applied its laws to that area. The Israeli desk officer at the State Department told me, "You may now need an Israeli postage stamp to mail a letter from the Golan, but otherwise there were no legal changes in its status!"

27. In the midst of the Golan Heights crisis between Israel and Syria, bureaucratic infighting seemed to decrease among United States departments and agencies concerned with the issue. This apparent lull was deceptive. Reagan's first National Security Advisor, Richard Allen, went on administrative leave. Admiral Nance had taken over as National Security Advisor. And the military assistant to the president, Admiral John Poindexter, had moved up to be Nance's deputy. Poindexter called me to discuss whether the State Department had been cooperative in the Golan issue. I answered, "Absolutely." He asked, "Why?" I answered, "State is using us to achieve their bureaucratic objectives." Poindexter replied, "Yes, to get rid of Allen, they're making sure that the National Security Council staff looks good!" Press reports appeared in weekly magazines describing how National Security Council staffers were pleased with the way that Nance and Poindexter had been processing the paperwork in the absence of Allen.

   Personal recollection of conversation with Poindexter by author in the White House Situation Room.

28. During meetings in Israel, Begin took the position that the United States government had punished Israel at least three times in three months. First, after Israel's bombing of Iraq's nuclear facilities in June, shipments of F-16s were suspended. Second, after the bombing of the PLO command center in Beirut in July, shipments of F-15s were suspended. Third, after Israel applied its laws to the Golan, Washington suspended implementation of the Memorandum of Understanding (MOU) between Jerusalem and Washington. Begin said that he refused to let the MOU become a hostage for the

United States to secure major concessions on Lebanon or on the peace process. He said, "Jews have lived for 3,700 years without an MOU and can live another 3,700 more without one!"

Personal recollection of remarks made by Begin, from author's service as one of the action officers for Israel at the White House, 1981-1982.

29. In relation to Israel's de facto annexation of the Golan Heights, there is an Arab proverb: "I against my brothers. I and my brothers against my cousins. I and my cousins against the world." Israel's actions rallied support for Syria even among those Arab states that were adversaries of the regime in Damascus. This proverb calls attention to the felt need for cohesion when the Arab nation as a whole is under attack by non-Arab forces.

30. The Golan Heights crisis was of great importance to Washington because it threatened American policy goals for the Middle East. At the regional level during the Cold War, southwest Asia was a focal point of contention. United States policy included prevention of the spread of Soviet influence, elimination of the Soviet presence in Afghanistan, and deterrence or defeat of the USSR and/or its proxy or other radical intervention throughout the region. Goals also included preservation of stability and security of friendly states. In November 1979, the United States perceived large-scale Soviet arms transfers to Ethiopia, Iraq, and Syria as a threat to American friends and allies in the region. Israel's annexation of the Golan Heights provided a further bridge for the USSR into Syria.

31. Michael Klare, *Rogue States and Nuclear Outlaws* (New York: Hill and Wang, 1995).

32. U.S. Department of State, "Address by President Reagan Before the American Bar Association," *Current Policy,* no. 721 (July 8, 1985).

33. Anthony Lake, "Confronting Backlash States," *Foreign Affairs* 73, no. 2 (March/April 1994): 45-46.

34. In Title 22, Section 2656f(d) of the United States Code, there is a definition of terrorism: premeditated, politically motivated violence perpetrated against noncombatant targets by subnational groups or agents, usually intended to influence an audience.

35. U.S. Congress, Committee on International Relations, *Syria: Peace Partner or Rogue Regime* Hearing, 104th Cong., 2nd sess., 25 July 1996. Testimony of Ambassador Philip Wilcox. Available online via Congressional Information Service's Congressional Compass.

36. Department of State, Office of the Coordinator for Counterterrorism, *1994 Patterns of Global Terrorism* (Washington, D.C.: Government Printing Office, April 1995).

37. Department of State Bureau of Economic and Business Affairs, *Syria: 1994 Country Report on Economic Policy and Trade Practices* (Washington, D.C.: Government Printing Office, 1995).

38. Department of State Bureau of Public Affairs, *Background Notes: Syria* (Washington, D.C.: Government Printing Office, November 1994).

39. White House, Office of the Press Secretary, "Remarks at a Press Conference by President Clinton and President Asad on October 27, 1994," in the Great Hall of the Presidential Palace in Damascus, Syria.

40. The Foreign Assistance Act of 1961 requires that the State Department issue on an annual basis the *International Narcotics Control Strategy Report*. The act also mandates that the president identify a list of the major drug-producing and transit countries as defined by law. Syria has been on the narcotics list since its armed forces moved into Lebanon in large numbers during the 1980s. Damascus appears on the 1997 list of major drug producing and transit countries. See Department of State, Bureau for International Narcotics and Law Enforcement Affairs, *International Narcotics Control Strategy Report,* "Syria," March 1997. Available online:
http://www.usis.usemb.se/drugs/Africa/syria.htm

41. Department of State Bureau for International Narcotics and Law Enforcement Affairs, *International Narcotics Strategy Report* (Washington, D.C.: U.S. Government Printing Office, March 1995).

42. Central Intelligence Agency, *World Factbook 1993.*

43. Department of State Bureau for International Narcotics and Law Enforcement Affairs, *International Narcotics Strategy Report* (Washington, D.C.: U.S. Government Printing Office, March 1995). But Syrian participation in the drug trade may be a rational decision, because it allows Damascus to regain some losses due to the cost of American sanctions.

44. There is some confirmation for the Syrian claim to have worked to control the drug trade. One report indicates that illicit opium and cannabis cultivation in Lebanon is less due to strict enforcement and highly effective continued eradication efforts by joint Lebanese-Syrian authorities. Bureau for International Narcotics and Law Enforcement, *International Narcotics Control Strategy Report* (Washington, D.C.: March 1996).

45. There was a May 7, 1996 letter sent to Secretary of State Warren Christopher from Representative Michael Forbes (Rep.-New York). Twenty-nine other members signed the letter. It concerned Washington's role in the Israeli-Syrian talks. The letter referred to reports that the Clinton Administration might be prepared to provide significant monetary, diplomatic, and security benefits to Syria in exchange for a peace agreement with Israel. The letter suggested that because of Syrian support for terrorism, it would be inappropriate to remove Damascus from the list of terrorist nations, even if the administration believed that it would further the peace process with Israel. Available online:
http://www.covesoft.com/afsi/forbes/forbes.htm

46. Thomas Lipman, "State Department Back on Effort to Court Syria," *Washington Post,* March 31, 1994, sec. A, 1.; Steve Greenhouse, "State Department Steps Back on Effort to Court Syria," *New York Times,* April 1, 1994.

47. In making alliance commitments, the United States assumes responsibility to defend its allies primarily from U.S. foes. If the United States pledged to defend its friends against their foes, Washington would invariably become involved in fighting its own friends.

48. Robert Pelletreau, "U.S. Policy Toward the Middle East: Steering a Steady Course," address by the Assistant Secretary of State before the Chautauqua Institution, Chautauqua, N.Y. (August 21, 1996).

49. A reference point is a threshold, much as the status quo, below which are perceived losses.

50. The State Department under Warren Christopher shifted its primary goal or reference point regarding Syria from condemnation and isolation of state sponsors of terrorism to viewing Damascus as an integral part of the peace process with Jerusalem, a "key to completing the circle of peace." See Charles Lane, "A Man of Good Intentions: St. Chris on the Road to Damascus," *New Republic* (July 29, 1996).

51. Ze'ev Schiff, "The Necessary Security Conditions for Peace with Syria," *Ha'aretz,* January 21, 1994, sec. B, 5.

52. In an editorial in the Israeli newspaper *Hatzofeh,* on December 29, 1996, there was a report that Damascus had sent a message via Paris of an interest in resuming talks with Israel. The editors speculated that Assad may have felt that he was liable to miss the train if he continued his delaying policy vis-à-vis the negotiations, while the Israeli-Palestinian negotiations were moving forward.

53. Ephraim Kam, "Warning of War Before Its Time," *Ma'ariv,* August 29, 1996, sec. B, 2.

54. Ze'ev Maoz, "The Probability That Syria Will Go to War Increasing Considerably," *Ha'aretz,* August 18, 1996, sec. B, 3.

55. Syria has developed a military capability to strike at the Israeli rear, at population centers, and at other targets. And during the summer of 1996, Damascus ordered test firing of the Scud-C missile. But Israeli security specialists did not view these tests as cause for concern. Soviet doctrine required such tests to be held at the end of annual training exercises by Syrian ground to ground missile brigades. See Danny Leshem, "Between the Missile and the Katyusha," *Yediot Aharonot,* August 22, 1996, sec. B, 3.

    However, "The Syrians estimate that Israel has no effective response to a missile attack on it. Damascus' intention: to deter Israel for the next few years, until the 'arrow' missile becomes operational. Thus Syria will be able to carry out a limited military operation to revive the peace process. Over the last months fortified launch sites have been built, and the development of chemical warheads accelerated. Experiments with VX gas failed. Israel torpedoed Syrian missile deal with China by diplomatic means." See Ron Ben-Yishai, "Syrian Missiles—The Primary Strategic Threat to Israel," *Yediot Ahronot,* June 22, 1997, sec. A, 8-9.

56. See Aaron Lerner, "Review of Syria's Missile Strategy and Iraqi Biological Weapons?" October 23, 1996. Available online:

    http://www.torget.se/users/g/GaNdAlF/Vapen1.html

    And Eitan Rabin, "Iran Developing Missile with Range of 1,300 Kilometers," *Ha'aretz,* July 13, 1997, sec. A, 2.

Chapter Six

1. Statements are by James Perrela, chief executive officer of the construction giant Ingersoll-Rand and chair of the National Trade Council, an American trade association; real estate and casino owner Donald Trump of New York;

and a member of the U.S.-Cuba Business Council. Their comments appear in Pamela Falk, "Eyes on Cuba," *Foreign Affairs* (March/April 1996): 14.

2. "Castro creates crises because that is what dictators do. They create crises to keep themselves in the world spotlight and, above all, to stay in power." Georgie Anne Geyer, "Never a Crisis with Fidel by Accident," *Washington Times,* February 29, 1996. Available online:

   http://www.cubaweb.com/eng/reference/news/never_a_crisis.html

3. For a description of the nature of threat perception, see Robert Jervis, Richard Ned Lebow, and Janice Gross Stein, eds., *Psychology and Deterrence* (Baltimore: The Johns Hopkins Press, 1985).

4. In other words, the United States wants to avoid injuring not only its international image but also its relations with third countries, encourage a more open system in Cuba, and avoid the results of implosion and civil war—a surge of refugees bound for the United States. Wayne Smith, *Cuba After the Cold War: What Should U.S. Policy Be?* (Washington, D.C.: Center for International Policy, 1993). Available online:

   http://www.us.net/cip/coldwar.txt

5. The Cuban Liberty and Democratic Solidarity Act of 1996 gives U.S. citizens the right to sue foreign companies trafficking in property that they formerly owned in Cuba. Upon learning about this feature of the act, Castro reacted with the joy of a dictator who just purchased an insurance policy on power. He said, "In a country like Cuba where 85% of the families own their housing by virtue of the laws of the revolution, all of those families would lose the ownership of their homes [if the Americans brought suit in Cuba under the Cuban Liberty and Democratic Solidarity Act]. It is something so stupid that we were almost about to send a telegram to Helms and Burton and tell them: 'Hey, thanks very much. You are really helping us.'" Tim Golden, "A Year After Boat Exodus, Threat to Castro Dissipates," *New York Times,* August 15, 1995, sec. 1, 6.

6. From the time Spain established Cuba as an export-oriented colony in the mid-eighteenth century, Cuba has been dependent on the outside world in general and on the United States in particular. Cuba is only 90 miles from the United States, whereas Havana is 4,472 miles from Madrid. The proximity to the U.S. mainland and distance from Spain facilitated the growth of strong trading ties between Cuba and the United States and hindered the development of trade with Spain.

   Coffee, tobacco, and most significantly sugarcane, were export crops on which the Cuban economy relied. By about the mid-nineteenth century, Cuban sugarcane furnished one third of the world's supply and became the main source for U.S. sugar. In relying mainly on a single crop exported primarily to a single nation, Cuba became vulnerable to both that country and to the international market. Thomas Skidmore and Peter Smith, *Modern Latin America* (New York: Oxford University Press, 1992), 254-61.

7. In discussions about the passage of American legislation directed at foreign firms doing business in Cuba, the European Union claimed a right to retaliate. That is, if the United States tried to punish European companies doing business with Cuba, Europe reserved the right to respond in kind.

New York Times, July, 25, 1996, sec. A, 4. See also *New York Times,* June 6, 1996, sec. A, 1; June 23, 1996, sec. A, 9; July 19, 1996, sec. A, 13. In addition to Europe, Canada also announced retaliatory measures against the American 1996 anti-Cuban trade law.

8. Despite the fact that there is no evidence of recent Cuban involvement in terrorism or weapons proliferation, the State Department retains Cuba on its list of states sponsoring international terrorism. While it is true that Castro operates a police state in which terror is an integral part of governing, where is the evidence that Havana exports terrorism abroad like Iran, Iraq, and Libya? Castro is surely a rogue as an individual. But the analysis in this chapter questions whether Cuba is actually a rogue state.

9. See Hon. Mark L. Schneider, "After Castro: U.S. Aid to Cuba," Hearings before the House Foreign Affairs Subcommittee on the Western Hemisphere (Washington, D.C.: Federal Document Clearing House), March 24, 1994. Available online:

```
http://web.lexis-nexis.com/cis/retrieve/document/s_witness.
html?_form=s_witness.html&_mode=FULL&_results=G{H^*KO!
DUA!UUA$M[SDUA$UUA$AZ!W]D]!BEE!A]$Z$]DWUUECZB$U&_
library=news&_file=cngtst,fednew,poltrn,polsum&_firstdoc=
1&_reldoc=2&_citesper=25&_maxdocs=6&_md5=7813dd106e02ae7bca240
373e1a4313e
```

And Central Intelligence Agency, "Cuba," *World Factbook 1993* (Washington, D.C.: Government Printing Office, 1994).

10. In a September 1994 interview, a Cuban economics minister said that while U.S. investment would be somewhat advantageous, Cuba would prefer to be linked with Canadian, European, or Latin American companies. If the blockade were to be lifted, he suggested, part of Cuba's former economic dependence on the United States would be reestablished. Association of Caribbean States and the United Nations Development Program, *The Economist Intelligence Unit* (London: 1994).

11. "For almost thirty years, U.S. interests with respect to Cuba were of a security nature and had more to do with Washington's global rivalry with Moscow than with Cuba itself." Smith, *Cuba After the Cold War.*

12. American journalist and diplomat John Louis O'Sullivan first used the term *manifest destiny* in an editorial supporting the annexation of Texas. The article appeared in the July-August 1845 edition of the *United States Magazine and Democratic Review.* See "Manifest Destiny," *Microsoft Encarta 96 Encyclopedia.* 1993-1995 Microsoft Corporation.

13. The Monroe Doctrine states, " . . . the American continents, by the free and independent condition which they have assumed and maintain, are henceforth not to be considered as subjects for future colonization by any European power. . . ." James Richardson, ed., *Messages and Papers of the Presidents, Vol. II* (New York: Bureau of National Literature, 1897), 778.

14. The Platt Amendment is the popular title of legislation drafted by U.S. Senator Orville Hitchcock Platt of Connecticut. It passed the Congress as an amendment to the Army Appropriations Bill of 1901 and established conditions for U.S. intervention in Cuba. Incorporated into its Constitution,

the Platt Amendment laid the basis for American involvement in the internal affairs of Cuba until 1934. See "Cuba" and "Platt Amendment," *Microsoft Encarta 96 Encyclopedia.* 1993-1995 Microsoft Corporation.

15. The Good Neighbor Policy turned away somewhat from the "big stick" approach of the Platt Amendment. But the Good Neighbor Policy notwithstanding, the United States continued to assume an oversight role with respect to Cuba.

16. President John F. Kennedy authorized the CIA to install a reformist, noncommunist government in Cuba. As a result, the Agency contracted with the Cuban underground during the Batista era in order to remove Castro from power. Also see Quirk, *Fidel Castro,* 360-61.

17. The fact that economic sanctions were not excluded by the American-Soviet accord indicates that it permitted such sanctions. For a discussion of the agreement see Paul Johnson, *Modern Times* (New York: HarperCollins, 1991).

18. In addition to economic sanctions, the Kennedy Administration pledged publicly to refrain from invading Cuba and privately to remove at a later date some U.S. missiles from Turkey in exchange for Soviet withdrawal of its missiles from Cuba. For a description of the crisis from an American perspective, see Ernest May and Philip Zelikow, eds., *The Kennedy Tapes* (Cambridge, MA: Harvard/Belknap Press, 1997). And for a Soviet viewpoint, see Aleksandr Fursenko and Timothy Naftali, *"One Hell of a Gamble": Khrushchev, Castro, Kennedy, and the Cuban Missile Crisis, 1958-1964* (New York: W. W. Norton, 1997).

19. One possible replacement for Castro is Jorge Mas Canosa, head of the Cuban American National Foundation. Senator Jesse Helms, chairman of the Senate Foreign Relations Committee, said in April 1995, "I'm going to do everything I can to make sure the United States stands with you." Larry Rohter, "With Voice of Cuban-Americans, a Would-Be Successor to Castro," *New York Times,* May 8, 1995, sec. A, 1, 12.

20. For a discussion of the role of Cuban forces in Africa and in Latin America, see Sheldon Liss, *Fidel! Castro's Political and Social Thought,* (Boulder: Westview Press, 1994).

21. *Wall Street Journal,* August 5, 1996, sec. A, 12.

22. Kevin Fedarko, "The Cold War is Back," *TIME* (March 11, 1996), 19.

23. The Cuban Liberty and Democratic Solidarity Act of 1996 made permanent the 34-year-old economic embargo that previously had to be renewed by the president each year. The act gave U.S. citizens the right to sue foreign companies that trafficked in Cuban property formerly owned by these Americans. The act denied U.S. visas to foreigners who derived benefits from confiscated property. And it act provided a three-month grace period for foreign companies to dispose of or pay for confiscated property. The Cuban Liberty and Democratic Solidarity Act remains in effect until the president determines that a democratically elected government is in Cuba, presumably without Fidel Castro or his brother Raul. It requires the president to withhold a portion of foreign aid from countries contributing to the construction of a nuclear plant in Cuba or supporting a spy station

there. The act was effective as of August 1, 1996. But the president has the power to suspend it for up to six months at a time. If the president concludes that suspension is in the national interest or will help a transition to a democratically elected government, the president can avoid implementing it. Available online as the Cuban Liberty and Democratic Solidarity Act of 1996:

```
http://thomas.loc.gov/cgi-bin/bdquery/L?d104:./list/bd/
d104sh.lst:169
```

24. ". . . the Cuban American National Foundation, which always wanted Helms-Burton, can claim rightly that it runs American policy toward Cuba and can use it to retake power there." Georgie Anne Geyer, "U.S. Helps Castro Return to the Global Stage," *Universal Press Syndicate,* January 31, 1997. Available online:

```
http://www.uexpress.com/ups/opinion/column/gg/archive/
gg970131.html
```

According to CANF, over 250,000 families have contributed to it, and 54,000 send donations every month, Cuban American National Foundation. Available online:

```
http://www.canfnet.org/english/canf.htm
```

25. Rohter, "With Voice of Cuban-Americans," *New York Times.*

26. Georgie Anne Geyer, a syndicated columnist, calls Castro a "Houdini of international conspiracy, that human radar screen, that Machiavelli of the once innocent Caribbean shores." Geyer, "U.S. Helps Castro Return to the Global Stage." See also Geyer, *Guerrilla Prince: the Untold Story of Fidel Castro* (Boston: Little, Brown, & Co., 1991).

27. "At home Castro's regime has created the most repressive police state apparatus in the Western Hemisphere. Cuba is an Orwellian nightmare set in the tropics with Big Brother sporting a beard and cigar. Cuba has refused to ratify any major international law enshrining fundamental human rights. It has refused to sign the International Covenant on Civil and Political Rights," claims Jose Marti, considered a great writer of the Hispanic world. "Castro's Crimes Against Humanity." Available online:

```
http://www.fiu.edu/~jsuare05/cascrime.html
```

28. For an analysis of Castro's reasons for shooting down the Brothers to the Rescue aircraft, see Fedarko, "The Cold War Is Back."

29. Evidence that Cuba may muddle through is that the Cuban economy in the 1990s already bottomed out and, at the turn of the century, may even see some slight upturn. Smith, *Cuba After the Cold War.*

30. "Should the economic situation deteriorate further, food riots might snowball beyond control. But such violence would have to reach the level of a full-scale civil war before it could possibly result in the ouster of the present government . . . it seems most unlikely that the army, which is Castro's own creation, would move against its commander or, at least, that it would take the initiative to do so." Smith, *Cuba After the Cold War.*

31. Georgie Ann Geyer claims that, "civil war in the army seems the most [plausible] scenario. Castro has named his brother Raul as his successor, but that is another of his . . . jokes, for Raul is highly unpopular and politically

inconsequential." That is, one reason for civil war would be Castro's attempt to impose his unpopular brother onto the armed forces. Geyer, "Castro Cares About Himself, Not Cuba," *Salt Lake Tribune*, August 13, 1996. Available online:

http://www.sltrib.com/96/aug/13/cmt/21381912.htm

32. Smith, *Cuba After the Cold War.*

33. "Change is indeed already taking place on the economic side, as evidenced by the Cuban government's willingness to begin mixed ventures with foreign private capital and to allow individual Cuban citizens to engage in private enterprise, at least in the service sector."

   Furthermore, ". . . in late 1991, the Cuban government seemed open to the idea of change. . . . It promised direct and open elections to the National Assembly and even suggested that a multiparty system was an eventual possibility. Some Cuban officials even suggested that known dissidents could become candidates, provided they complied with registration procedures." Smith, *Cuba After the Cold War.*

34. "[The Cuban Liberty and Democratic Solidarity Act] has poisoned our relations with our major allies and caused them to take at best mischievous—and potentially very nasty and disruptive—actions against us that could haunt us for decades." Geyer, "U.S. Helps Castro Return to the Global Stage."

35. In response to the Cuban Liberty and Democratic Solidarity Act, Canada's government introduced legislation amending the Foreign Extraterritorial Measures Act (FEMA), which would help protect Canadian companies against such measures.

   Minister for International Trade Art Eggleton said, "The Helms-Burton law flies in the face of international legal principles. The FEMA changes will give Canadian companies more legal tools to protect themselves against U.S. court claims under Helms-Burton. We will continue to defend Canadian interests strongly, including through the NAFTA process."

   Furthermore, Foreign Affairs Minister Lloyd Axworthy stated, "Canada shares the U.S. objectives of improving human rights standards and moving to more representative government in Cuba. But we are concerned that the Helms-Burton Act takes the wrong approach. That is why we have been working with other countries to uphold the principles of international law." Available online:

http://www.dfait-maeci.gc.ca/english/news/newsletr/canex/960702ae.htm

36. Department of Commerce, "Clinton Administration Position on EU's WTO Challenge." February 20, 1997. Available online:

http://www.usis-israel.org.il/publish/press/commerce/archive/1997/february/dc20221.htm

37. Larry Rohter, "Mexican Conglomerate Pulls Out of Cuba," *New York Times*, (June 30, 1997). Available online:

http://search.nytimes.com/search/daily/bin/fastweb?getdoc+site+site+10412+0+wAAA+%28Grupo%26%29%26OR%26%28%29%26OR%26%28%29

38. "If the United States wants to help the cause of democracy and human rights in Cuba, the best thing it could do is to drop its efforts to pressure and isolate Cuba and instead begin a process of engagement." Smith, *Cuba After the Cold War.*

39. "Even in the midst of the cold war, virtually no other government, from 1975 forward, cooperated or even agreed with our trade embargo against Cuba. Much less are they likely to do so now, with the cold war a thing of the past." Smith, *Cuba After the Cold War.*

40. "Many Americans believed the prohibition of such sales should not have been imposed in the first place, that the United States should never be in the position of refusing to sell food and medicine to anyone." Smith, *Cuba After the Cold War.*

41. "In principle if not in point of law, denying American citizens the right to travel to another country is an infringement of their fundamental rights that should not be continued by a Democratic administration sworn to uphold basic freedoms. Beyond that, allowing Americans freely to travel to Cuba would be an excellent way of increasing the flow of information and new ideas to the Cuban people."

Furthermore, "Cultural and academic exchanges are an excellent means of increasing the Cuban people's access to information and ideas. Performers, artists and intellectuals from both countries should tour the other. Academic exchanges should be expanded so that Cuban scholars can actually matriculate in U.S. universities and so that Fulbright scholars can study in Cuba." Smith, *Cuba After the Cold War.*

Chapter Seven

1. Scott Snyder, "North Korean Crises and American Choices: Managing U.S. Policy Toward the Korean Peninsula," Unpublished Paper presented at the 1997 International Studies Association Convention, panel entitled "Crisis Forecasting on North Korea: Myth and Reality," Toronto, Canada (March 19, 1997; updated May 1, 1997), 8. See also, Snyder, "A Framework for Achieving Reconciliation on the Korean Peninsula," *Asian Survey* (August 1995): 35, 699-710.

2. "North Korea literally has a gun at our [the United States] head even as it begs for relief." See Robert Manning and James Przystup, "Feed Me Or I'll Kill You," *Washington Post,* February 20, 1997, sec. A, 23.

3. "Pyongyang should be given the choice of keeping its gun or its tin cup. But to allow it to have both is sheer folly." Manning and Przystup, "Feed Me Or I'll Kill You."

4. Karen Elliott House, "Let North Korea Collapse," *Wall Street Journal,* February 21, 1997, sec. A, 14. See also Bruce Cumings, "Divided Korea: United Future?" *Headline Series* 306 (Spring 1994): 25-28.

5. Following the post–World War II Soviet military occupation of the northern portion of the Korean Peninsula, the USSR established the state of North Korea in 1948. In the same year, the occupying forces of the United States established South Korea.

6. People in the North Korean countryside are starving, underweight and "rapidly descending into the hell of a severe famine," according to Representative Tony Hall (Dem.-Ohio). He completed a three-day visit to North Korea in April 1997. "Evidence of slow starvation on a massive scale was plain wherever we made an effort to look," Hall said. He added that conditions had deteriorated significantly since he had made a similar visit in August 1996. The member of Congress said he was allowed unlimited access to villages north of Pyongyang, where few outsiders are permitted. Hall told how he had met an elderly woman making soup from year-old cabbage leaves; he visited an unheated hospital with no medicine that was so cold that he could see his own breath. He saw underweight children. Many of them had become orphans when their mothers died from malnutrition. Kevin Sullivan, "Congressman Finds 'Severe Famine' in North Korea," *Washington Post*, April 9, 1997, sec. A, 24.

7. For an explication of crisis as an opportunity for bureaucratic warfare, see Raymond Tanter, *Who's at the Helm? Lessons of Lebanon* (Boulder: Westview Press, 1990), 120-23.

8. North Korea borders China on the north and Russia on the northeast, the Sea of Japan on the east, South Korea on the south, and the Yellow Sea on the west. The Yalu River is North Korea's longest river, and it forms part of the border with China.

9. The third alternative explicitly calls for combining two options—contain *and* embrace. With about 37,000 in combat along the DMZ, Washington seeks to contain the regime in Pyongyang. By providing humanitarian assistance, Americans embrace North Koreans.

10. Graham Allison, Albert Carnesale, and Joseph Nye, *Hawks, Doves, and Owls* (New York: W. W. Norton, 1985), 206-22. In addition to these three, others have used the hawk-dove framework. A journalist, Jim Mann, adds "hummingbirds" to the classification. They are analysts who believe that North Korea has the strength to ride out floods and famine without extreme changes in their manner of operations. See Jim Mann, "Future of North Korea May Become Clinton's Biggest Foreign Policy Test," *Los Angeles Times*, December 30, 1996, sec. A, 5. Another adherent of the idea that North Korea can ride out its economic crisis is Marcus Noland, "Why North Korea Will Muddle Through," *Foreign Affairs* 76, no. 4 (July/August 1997): 105-19, 114.

     See also Fred Ikle, *Every War Must End* (New York: Columbia University Press, 1991), 60-61, for his analysis of hawks and doves. In contrast to Allison, Carnesale, and Nye, Ikle uses these terms to describe the struggle within a government for how a war should end. In answering the question, "Who are the traitors?," Ikle defines hawks as those who engage in treasonous adventurism instead of terminating the fighting: in search of peace with honor, they fight too much and too long. Doves are those who give aid and comfort to the enemy by retreating in the face of aggression: in a quest for peace at any cost, they would fight too little and for too short a time.

11. In addition to applying this framework to North Korea, a hawks-doves-owls classification is relevant to Iran, Iraq, Libya, Syria, and Cuba. But the

framework is particularly suited to an analysis of the Korean Peninsula. Because of the higher likelihood of deterrence failure, unintended escalation, and loss of control due to misperception in Korea than in the other cases, this conceptual framework is of great heuristic value.

12. Thomas Schelling, *Arms and Influence* (New Haven: Yale University Press, 1996), 53-55. He discusses the relationship among interests, credible commitments, and capabilities.

13. Seth Faison, "Gingrich Warns China That U.S. Would Act If It Attacked Taiwan," *New York Times*, March 31, 1997, sec. A, 1, 5.

    Kenneth Lieberthal, a China scholar at the University of Michigan, said that Gingrich apparently would commit the United States to defending Taiwan, even if Taiwan took provocative steps. Such steps might include making unilateral statements that could be construed as declarations of independence. Patrick Tyler, "Unfazed by Gingrich, China Agrees With Some of What He Said," *New York Times*, April 2, 1997, sec. A, 4.

14. On the one hand, Taiwan and China make claims on each other. In this sense, neither is "independent." Even though the Nationalists fled the mainland because of the civil war in China, their successors in Taiwan have never given up their claim to represent the whole country. Their counterparts on the mainland claim that Taiwan is a part of China and that they are its sole representatives. On the other hand, both countries act as independent states. At issue is whether the pro-independence movement on Taiwan will induce the leadership to make an explicit break from the mainland.

15. Robert Harkavy, *Preemption and Two-Front Conventional Warfare* (Jerusalem: Leonard Davis Institute for International Relations, Hebrew University of Jerusalem, Papers on Peace Problems, 1977), 8. Harkavy distinguishes between preemptive attack and preventive war. In preemption, the threatened actor places a premium on offensive action. But in prevention, that actor does not perceive striking the first blow as crucial. In a decision to launch a preventive war, "What *is* important is the forestalling of a change in the balance of power," *Op. cit.,* 7 [emphasis in original].

16. Edward Luttwak and Dan Horowitz, *The Israeli Army* (London: Allen Lane, 1975), 141.

17. Deterrence is a process of inducing a potential challenger not to take an action; coercion aims to get an actor to take an action or undo something already in place. Sanctions may be both deterrent and coercive in nature. Alexander George and Richard Smoke, *Deterrence in American Foreign Policy* (New York: Columbia University Press, 1974); Alexander George, David Hall, and William Simons, *The Limits of Coercive Diplomacy* (Boston: Little Brown, 1971).

18. During August 1997, however, four-power "talks about talks" began under the auspices of Columbia University in New York. Online Focus, "A Parched Land," August 5, 1997. Available online:
    http://www.pbs.org/newshour/bb/asia/july-dec97/korea_8-5.html

19. "And the chairman of the Joint Chiefs of Staff noted that, famine or no famine, the North Koreans were engaging in more military training than ever. 'If they are in such great difficulty, as they claim they are, and if they

are in need of assistance,' asked Gen. John Shalikashvili, 'why are they spending their resources on this kind of military exercising? You have to ask yourself.'" Charles Krauthammer, "Why Feed a Mortal Enemy?" *Washington Post,* April 25, 1997, sec. A, 27.

20. "The North has chosen a bold and provocative course of action because the Clinton Administration's Korea policy is weak and misguided." Daryl M. Plunk, "Warning to North Korea: Stop Provocations and Talk with South Korea," *Backgrounder Update,* no. 273 (April 12, 1996, Foundation). See also Plunk, "Clinton's Korea Policy Falls Short: A Call to Congressional Action," *Backgrounder Update,* no. 236 (January 13, 1995), and "The Clinton Nuclear Deal with Pyongyang: Road Map to Progress or Dead End Street?" *Asian Studies Center Backgrounder,* no. 133 (November 4, 1994).

21. For a transcript of The Oprah Winfrey Show, "America Speaks Out on the Middle East Issue," number 1024, August 16, 1990, write to: Burrell's Transcripts, Box 7, Livingston, NJ, 07039 or call 1-800-777-TEXT (8398). In particular, see pages 13-14 of the transcript.

22. The approximate 1995 population of North Korea was 24 million. The estimate for South Korea was over 45 million. The GDP of South Korea in 1992 was about $270 billion, over ten times the size of the North Korean economy—estimated for 1995 at $21.5 billion. North Korea is one of the richer nations in Asia in terms of mineral resources. Major reserves include coal, iron ore, tungsten, and graphite. In contrast to North Korea, South Korea is poor in mineral resources. The main resources are coal (mostly anthracite), iron ore, and graphite. And there are reserves of natural gas offshore. See "North Korea" and "South Korea," *Microsoft Encarta 96 Encyclopedia,* 1993-1995 Microsoft Corporation. See also Central Intelligence Agency, "Korea, North," and "Korea, South," *World FactBook 1996* (Washington, D.C., 1997). Available online:

    http://www.odci.gov/cia/publications/nsolo/factbook/global.htm

23. Doug Bandow and Ted Galen Carpenter are two leading advocates of cutting American ties with South Korea. See Doug Bandow, "A New Korea Policy for a Changed World," *Korean Journal of Defense Analysis* (Winter 1992); "North Korea and the Risks of Coercive Nonproliferation," Cato Institute Foreign Policy Briefing, no. 24 (May 4, 1993); *Tripwire: Korea and U.S. Foreign Policy in a Changed World* (Washington, D.C.: Cato Institute, 1996).

24. *Cato Handbook for Congress, 105th Congress,* "Weaning South Korea" (Washington, D.C.: Cato Institute, 1997), 485. Available online:

    http://www.frc.org/heritage/links/

25. Krauthammer, "Why Feed a Mortal Enemy?"

26. "Indeed, State Department spokesman Nicholas Burns enunciated the more general principle: 'We believe countries ought to react to this [famine] the way they would to any other part of the world where there is a serious food crisis. All of us have a humanitarian imperative to help.'

    "We don't want to link food aid to the peace talks, because we want to get the food to the people who need it quickly, without regard to politics and to international negotiations.'" Krauthammer, "Why Feed a Mortal Enemy?"

27. Allison, Carnesale, and Nye, *Hawks, Doves, and Owls,* 210.

28. Doves, however, do not always favor carrots. Doves divide into "activists" and "libertarians." Although activist doves perceive threats from adversaries, they would embrace rather than confront. Libertarian doves discern less of a threat and can justify less accommodation *and* less confrontation.

29. This bipolar classification obscures the overlap between the ideal types. One can envision power-hungry, mistake-ridden mercenaries as well as risk-prone, cold-hearted paranoids. In spite of the existence of these hybrid combinations, the assumption here is that they are exceptions rather than the rule.

30. In the field of psychology, prospect theory defines a reference point as a threshold value above which individuals perceive gains and below which they see losses. See Jack Levy, "An Introduction to Prospect Theory," in Barbara Farnham, ed., *Avoiding Losses/Taking Risks: Prospect Theory and International Conflict* (Ann Arbor: University of Michigan Press, 1994), 7-22, and Robert Jervis, in Farnham, *op. cit.,* "Political Implications of Loss Aversion," 23-40.

31. James Blight, "The New Psychology of War and Peace: A Book Review of Robert Jervis, Richard Ned Lebow, and Janice Gross Stein (with contributions by Patrick M. Morgan and Jack L. Snyder)," *International Security* 2, no. 3 (Winter 1986-87): 175-86. See also Raymond Tanter, "Psychology and Deterrence: A Book Review," *American Political Science Review* 82 (March 1988): 345-46.

32. Senator Craig Thomas, Chairman of the Senate Subcommittee on East Asian and Pacific Affairs, described North Korea as becoming increasingly isolated, paranoid, and violent. He concluded that if any country has come to epitomize a rogue regime, it is North Korea. Senator Craig Thomas, "The United States-North Korea Agreed Framework," Senate Subcommittee on East Asian and Pacific Affairs, February 12, 1995. Available online: http://rs9.loc.gov/cgi.bin/query

33. For explications of *Juche,* see Chaouki Ajami, *Juche, Theory and Application* (Pyongyang: Foreign Languages Pub. House, 1978) and Kim Il Sung, *On Juche in Our Revolution* (New York: Weekly Guardian Associates, 1977).

34. Department of State, speech by Secretary of State Dean Acheson, Washington, D.C.: Government Printing Office, January 12, 1950.

35. Warren Christopher, "America's Strategy for a Peaceful and Prosperous Asia-Pacific," *Dispatch* [Magazine of the State Department], 6, (Summer, 1995): 591-94.

36. Joseph Nye, "Strategy for East Asia and U.S.-Japan Security Alliance," *Defense Issues,* 10, no. 35 (March 29, 1995), 1.

    While the same threatened interests may have both intrinsic and strategic aspects, the analysis here treats them as analytically distinct. For a further discussion of intrinsic and strategic interests, see Janice Stein, "The View From Cairo," in Robert Jervis, Richard Lebow, and Janice Gross Stein, eds., *Psychology and Deterrence* (Baltimore: Johns Hopkins University Press), 38-39.

37. Department of State, Office of the Coordinator for Counterterrorism, *1993 Patterns of Global Terrorism* (Washington, D.C.: Government Printing Office, April 1994). The following nations appeared on the State Department list of sponsors of international terrorism for 1995 (and 1996): Cuba, Iran, Iraq, Libya, North Korea, Sudan, and Syria. Sudan is the only country on that list not included in *Rogue Regimes*.

38. For an overview of scholarship on crisis decision making, see Michael Brecher, *Crises in World Politics: Theory and Reality*, 1st ed. (Oxford: Pergamon Press, 1993). Also see Michael Brecher, Jonathan Wilkenfeld, and Sheila Moser, *Crises in the Twentieth Century*, 1st ed. (New York: Pergamon Press, 1988); Michael Brecher and Patrick James, *Crisis and Change in World Politics* (Boulder: Westview Press, 1986).

39. In between the Korean War and the nuclear as well as humanitarian crises are several incidents of little relevance to the construction of scenarios and policy packages. These events include the North Korean seizure of the USS *Pueblo,* an electronic surveillance intelligence ship. See Michael Brecher and Jonathan Wilkenfeld, *A Study of Crisis* (Ann Arbor: University of Michigan Press, 1997), for a detailed historical account of such confrontations between the United States and North Korea.

40. Under the 1994 Agreed Framework between Pyongyang and Washington, North Korea agreed to contain spent fuel from its five-megawatt experimental reactor. Because such fuel could be used in nuclear weapons development, it was a source of confrontation between North Korea and the United States.

41. Moscow and Washington agreed to divide Korea at the 38th Parallel for the purpose of accepting the surrender of Japan's forces just prior to the termination of World War II in the Pacific theater. But the United States and the USSR then employed their respective military presences to encourage friendly governments in their spheres of influence. Although Koreans in both the North and the South expressed hope for unification of the peninsula, they were unable to overcome their differences in the context of the Cold War. Hence, unification conferences during 1946 and 1947 ended without success. Then in 1947, Moscow and Washington began to set up separate governments. The United Nations adopted a resolution to hold general elections under its supervision. The USSR, however, declined to permit the UN to have access to North Korea. As a result, only the South Koreans held elections under UN supervision. The North's elections took place without widespread international acceptance of their legitimacy. Moscow had supported Kim Il Sung, a Communist who had led anti-Japanese irregulars in Manchuria. Likewise, Washington supported Syngman Rhee, a nationalist who also fought against the Japanese. In the South, Syngman Rhee won the election; in the North, Kim Il Sung emerged as Premier. The UN-monitored and American-sponsored elections in the South during 1948 resulted in the formation of the Republic of Korea in August of that year. A month later, the USSR set up the Democratic People's Republic of Korea (DPRK) in the north.

42. George and Smoke, *Deterrence in American Foreign Policy,* 145-46.

43. Regarding the question of "Who lost China?" Senator Joe McCarthy explained the loss as a product of a great conspiracy on a scale so immense as to dwarf any previous venture in history. He said, "It was not Chinese democracy under Mao that conquered China . . . as Acheson, [and others] contend. Soviet Russia conquered China and an important ally of the conquerors was this small left-wing element in our Department of State." Daniel Ellsberg, *Papers on the War* (New York: Simon & Schuster, 1972), 81. Ellsberg quotes McCarthy from the *Congressional Record,* January 25, 1949, 532-33.

44. A core concern within Indochina from the mid-1950s on was the developing Vietnam War. After the fall of China during its civil war and the Korean War, any American administration would be afraid of losing an Asian country to Communism. This fear trapped successive administrations in a basement of fear. The fear of loss to Communism explains why successive administrations were willing to expend blood and treasure without much hope of success. Such theoretical reasoning stems from prospect theory. See Farnham, ed., *Avoiding Losses/Taking Risks.*

45. Ellsberg explains the incremental commitments that eventuated in the Vietnam War as being a consequence of a succession of American presidents who feared the loss of land to communists on their watch. Because of the domestic costs associated with losing the war, presidents escalated without expectation of winning. In other words, they fought to avoid loss rather than to pursue gain. He calls this explanation the "stalemate machine," in contrast to a "quagmire" explanation. Ellsberg, *Papers on the War,* 42 ff.

   An alternative explanation for why American became involved in the Vietnam War draws on the quagmire metaphor: "Each step in the deepening of the American commitment was reasonably regarded at the time as the last that would be necessary. Yet, in retrospect, each step led only to the next, until we find ourselves entrapped in that nightmare of American strategists, a land war in Asia." Arthur Schlesinger, Jr., *The Bitter Heritage: Vietnam and American Democracy, 1941-1966* (Boston: Houghton Mifflin, 1967), as cited in Ellsberg, *Papers on the War,* 49-50. Later, however, Schlesinger admitted that he had been mistaken in the suggestion that escalatory steps would be the last ones necessary. See Arthur Schlesinger, Jr., "Eyeless in Indochina," *New York Review of Books* (October 21, 1971).

46. In connection with threat perception, at issue is whether the underestimation of threat stemmed from a motivated or unmotivated bias. If the Truman Administration discounted the regional threat because doing so provided a benefit, doing so would be evidence of a motivated bias. Conversely, if it downplayed the menace because of expectations, that would suggest an unmotivated bias. In fact, the Truman Administration misperceived the North Korean regional threat because it expected to confront a Soviet global threat. Such misperceptions indicate that an unmotivated bias dominated decision making.

47. David Albright, "How Much Plutonium Does North Korea Have?" *Bulletin of the Atomic Scientists,* September/October 1994, 46.

48. John Fialka, "Asian Tinderbox," *Wall Street Journal,* September 3, 1993, sec. A, 1, 2.

49. David Albright, "How Much Plutonium Does North Korea Have?" 53.

50. According to the Clinton Administration, the Agreed Framework stops Pyongyang's nuclear program in its tracks. A special focus of the accord is to halt North Korea's separation of weapons-grade plutonium and all nuclear fuel-related facilities. The Agreement requires North Korea to resume full compliance with its obligations under the NPT and IAEA safeguards agreement. The Framework provides alternate energy in the form of heavy fuel to compensate for the projected loss of nuclear energy supplies. It anticipates formation of an international consortium to provide two proliferation-resistant light-water reactors to replace the more dangerous graphite-moderated facilities. In addition, the Agreement neutralizes the threat posed by the spent nuclear fuel already in North Korea by removing it for disposal in a third nation. The Agreed Framework requires dismantlement of North Korea's graphite-moderated reactors and begins a process of normalizing diplomatic and trade relations between Pyongyang and the rest of the world community in steps, as the parties implement the agreement. It also encourages restoration of a dialogue between North and South Korea, whose aim is "denuclearization" of the Korean Peninsula and, ultimately, establishment of a permanent mechanism of peace there. U.S. Congress, Committee on Armed Services United States, *Security Implications of the Nuclear Non-Proliferation Agreement with North Korea* Hearing, 104th Cong., 1st sess., 26 January 1995. Prepared statement by Honorable William Perry, Secretary of Defense, 15-16. Available online:

    `http://web.lexis-nexis.com/cis/retrieve/document/s_witness.`
    `html?_form=s_witness.html&_mode=FULL&_results=G`
    `{H^*KO!DUA!UUW$M[SDUA$UUC$AZ!WVZE!V!V$AA$]DAZDZ]`
    `EZ$U&_library=news&_file=cngtst,fednew,poltrn,`
    `polsum&_firstdoc=1&_reldoc=11&_citesper=25&_maxdocs=11`
    `&_md5=32054202b33b83c0511ffc0ca76a1fc7`

51. William Perry, "Fulfilling the Role of Preventive Defenses," U.S. Department of Defense Publications, Volume 11, Number 44, January 18, 1996. Available online:

    `http://www.dtic.dla.mil/defenselink/pubs/di95/di1144.html`

52. Scott Snyder, "The North Korean Nuclear Challenge," Unpublished Paper for the U.S. Institute of Peace: Special Report (September 4, 1996).

53. Scott Snyder, "A Coming Crisis on the Korean Peninsula? The Food Crisis, Economic Decline, and Political Considerations," Unpublished Paper for the U.S. Institute of Peace: Special Report (September 17, 1996).

54. "In the summer of 1994, many [in Washington] feared that military measures might be required to halt the North Korean weapons program. The challenge at that time was coordinating policy with regional neighbors—Japan, South Korea, and the People's Republic of China—which were reluctant or unwilling to apply economic sanctions to prod North Korea toward full observance of the Nuclear Non-Proliferation Treaty." Snyder, "A Coming Crisis on the Korean Peninsula?"

55. Jon Leverenz and Brett Gover, eds., *The World,* (New York: Rand McNally, 1996), 103-4.

56. United Press International, "UN Seeks More Aid for North Korea," UN World Food Programme (UNWFP), May 6, 1997, available online:
`http://biz.yahoo.com/upi/97/05/06/international_news/`
`norkorun_1.html`

57. "An alternative might be a multilateral effort to provide food credits (perhaps with continuing monitored deliveries by UNWFP) in proportion to North Korean progress toward economic transparency and fundamental agricultural reforms. By dealing multilaterally with the food problem as a core structural issue in North Korea's economy rather than as a political issue, South Korea, the United States, and Japan might be able to help North Korea while simultaneously inducing it to take initial steps toward reform and integration with the global economy." Snyder, "A Coming Crisis on the Korean Peninsula?"

58. Three articles contributed to the different perspectives concerning the future of North Korea: House, "Let North Korea Collapse"; Kevin Sullivan, "Survival Instinct: Don't Bet the Collective on North Korea's Imminent Collapse," *Washington Post,* March 9, 1997, sec. C, 1; and Steve Glain, "The Endgame in North Korea: Regime Could Go With a Bang, a Whimper—Or a Handshake," *Wall Street Journal,* February 27, 1997, sec. A, 12.

59. See House, "Let North Korea Collapse."

60. See Caspar Weinberger, *The Next War* (Washington, D.C.: Regnery Publishing, 1996).

61. Marcus Noland, "Why North Korea Will Muddle Through."

62. Thomas Ricks and Steve Glain, "U.S. Gears Up for North Korean Collapse," *Wall Street Journal,* June 26, 1997, sec. A, 14.

63. Ricks and Glain, "U.S. Gears Up for North Korean Collapse."

64. Motivated bias is one that distorts threat perception because individuals see what they wish to notice; unmotivated bias operates when they view what they expect to observe.

65. "When U.S. strategists began looking for the 'Iraqs of the future,' most eyes in Washington turned to Korea—the last remaining Stalinist regime in Asia and a longtime foe of the United States." Michael Klare, *Rogue States and Nuclear Outlaws* (New York: Hill and Wang, 1995), 136.

66. "The nation's 24 million people are living off an average 150 grams of food per day, or about 12 spoonfuls—one-fifth the intake experts say is needed for a healthful diet. Children and elderly are dying at an increasing rate . . ." "CNN Gets Rare Glimpse of North Korea," CNN Interactive, August 13, 1997. Available online:
`http://www.cnn.com/WORLD/9708/13/korea.gallery/index.html`

INDEX

preventive, 224-6, 230, 234,
  251
Weinberger, Caspar, 112
Wexford Brief, 51
Wilson, Edwin P., 150-2, 299
  Deputy Security Counsel for
    Counterinsurgency, 150

See also Libya
"window of opportunity," xii-xiii,
  66, 88, 208-9
  sanctions if leaders act from,
    35-6
World War I, 37, 225
World War II, 37, 234